T0350057

A Socio-Legal Study of Hacking

The relationship between hacking and the law has always been complex and conflict-ridden. This book examines the relations and interactions between hacking and the law with a view to understanding how hackers influence and are influenced by technology laws and policies. In our increasingly digital and connected world where hackers play a significant role in determining the structures, configurations and operations of the networked information society, this book delivers an interdisciplinary study of the practices, norms and values of hackers and how they conflict and correspond with the aims and aspirations of hacking-related laws. Describing and analyzing the legal and normative impact of hacking, as well as proposing new approaches to its regulation and governance, this book makes an essential contribution to understanding the socio-technical changes, and consequent legal challenges, faced by our contemporary connected society.

Michael Anthony C. Dizon is a Lecturer in Law at the University of Waikato, New Zealand. He previously worked as an information and communications technology lawyer and researcher for institutions and organizations in the Netherlands, the United Kingdom, and the Philippines.

Law, Science and Society

General editors

John Paterson
University of Aberdeen, UK

Julian Webb
University of Melbourne, Australia

For a full list of titles in this series, please visit www.routledge.com

Law's role has often been understood as one of implementing political decisions concerning the relationship between science and society. Increasingly, however, as our understanding of the complex dynamic between law, science and society deepens, this instrumental characterization is seen to be inadequate, but as yet we have only a limited conception of what might take its place. If progress is to be made in our legal and scientific understanding of the problems society faces, then there needs to be space for innovative and radical thinking about law and science. *Law, Science and Society* is intended to provide that space.

The overarching aim of the series is to support the publication of new and groundbreaking empirical or theoretical contributions that will advance understanding between the disciplines of law, and the social, pure and applied sciences. General topics relevant to the series include studies of:

- law and the international trade in science and technology;
- risk and the regulation of science and technology;
- law, science and the environment;
- the reception of scientific discourses by law and the legal process;
- law, chaos and complexity;
- law and the brain.

Titles in this series:

Law and the Management of Disasters
The Challenge of Resilience
Edited by Alexia Herwig and Marta Simonici

Gene Editing, Law, and the Environment
Life Beyond the Human
Edited by Irus Braverman

A Socio-Legal Study of Hacking
Breaking and Remaking Law and Technology
Michael Anthony C. Dizon

A Socio-Legal Study of Hacking

Breaking and Remaking Law and Technology

Michael Anthony C. Dizon

Routledge
Taylor & Francis Group
a GlassHouse Book

First published 2018
by Routledge
2 Park Square, Milton Park, Abingdon, Oxon OX14 4RN

and by Routledge
711 Third Avenue, New York, NY 10017

A GlassHouse book

Routledge is an imprint of the Taylor & Francis Group, an informa business

British Library Cataloguing-in-Publication Data
A catalogue record for this book is available from the British Library

Library of Congress Cataloging-in-Publication Data
Names: Dizon, Michael Anthony C., 1975– author.
Title: A socio-legal study of hacking: breaking and remaking law
   and technology/Michael Anthony C. Dizon.
Description: Abingdon, Oxon; New York, NY: Routledge, 2018. |
   Series: Law, science and society | Based on author's thesis
   (doctoral—Tilburg University, 2016) issued under title: Breaking
   and remaking law and technology: a socio-techno-legal study of
   hacking. | Includes bibliographical references and index.
Identifiers: LCCN 2017029594 | ISBN 9781138560826 (hbk)
Subjects: LCSH: Computers—Law and legislation. | Computer
   security—Law and legislation. | Hackers—Legal status, laws, etc. |
   Hacking—Social aspects.
Classification: LCC K564.C6. D59 2018 | DDC 345/.0268—dc23
LC record available at https://lccn.loc.gov/2017029594

ISBN: 978-1-138-56082-6 (hbk)
ISBN: 978-0-203-71136-1 (ebk)

Typeset in Galliard
by Apex CoVantage, LLC

Contents

Acknowledgments

Researching and writing this book, which is based on my PhD research, would not have been possible without the help of the following persons, groups and institutions. I would like to extend my gratitude to them for their contribution and assistance: my supervisors, Professor Ronald Leenes and Professor Bert-Jaap Koops, for their valuable guidance and feedback; Tilburg University for granting me the opportunity to carry out my research project; the faculty and staff of Tilburg Law School for their help and advice on academic and other matters; my former colleagues at the Tilburg Institute for Law, Technology, and Society (TILT) for their camaraderie and useful comments on my research, particularly Dr. Maurice Schellekens, Dr. Bryce Newell and Dr. Tjerk Timan for their detailed notes on specific chapters; the administrators and staff of the International Institute for the Sociology of Law for the grant to conduct research at their excellent library and documentation center; the organizers and students of Netherlands Graduate Research School of Science, Technology and Modern Culture (WTMC) Summer School 2014 for an informative week learning about science and technology studies; the faculty, staff and students of the Oxford Internet Institute's Summer Doctoral Programme 2015 for sharing their research and expertise with me; my wife, family and friends for their encouragement and support; and the Te Piringa – Faculty of Law, University of Waikato, for providing me with the time to complete this book. I would especially like to express my appreciation to the members of the Dutch hacker community for their openness and generosity in agreeing to interviews, chatting with me, listening and reacting to presentations about my research at hacker conferences, and allowing me to observe and participate at various hackerspaces and hacker events. I hope that I was able to capture the essence of hacker culture as much as possible and to see the world through your eyes.

Chapter 1

Hacking and law

Hackers and governance of the networked society

In today's digital, technical and connected world, technologists and technological groups (i.e., those primarily engaged in the creation, development, adoption, use, dissemination or control of information and communications technology) play an important role in the operations and governance of the "networked information society".[1] Increasingly, people's behaviors online and offline are influenced not only by states and governmental entities but also non-state actors and organizations. For instance, non-national and non-governmental entities and bodies that maintain the underlying protocols and technical architectures of computer networks such as the Internet Engineering Task Force (IETF) and the Internet Corporation for Assigned Names and Numbers (ICANN) influence what individuals and entities can or cannot do on the internet.[2] Similarly, innovators and technically proficient groups are able to help bring about or heighten profound changes in society. Free and open source software (FOSS) developer communities, for example, have served as models for greater openness and accessibility not just in software programming but also in the fields of education and content creation and distribution (e.g., Creative Commons and open access).[3] Activists have successfully used digital technologies to pursue political and social ends,[4] and the online groups Wikileaks and Anonymous have notoriously used their technical knowledge and skills to cause great disruption to political and technical systems to the embarrassment and dismay of governments and law enforcement bodies around the world.[5]

These technological actors and groups have a significant influence on technical, social and legal matters, due in part to the increasing technologization of society.[6] There is one particular technological group that has been very influential in advancing digital technologies and shaping culture since the late 1950s – hackers. From the early computer scientists and programmers at the Massachusetts Institute of Technology (MIT) who first used "hacker" as a self-referential term,[7] and through the succeeding generations of hackers – computer hobbyists, underground hackers, FOSS developers, hacktivists, and makers – hackers can and do shape law, technology and society in new and interesting ways.[8] Given that hacking has both technical and normative effects on society, understanding the relations and conflicts between hackers and the law is crucial to discerning how the networked information society is actually shaped, regulated and governed.

Of the many types of hackers, makers and hacktivists deserve particular attention. First, they have been receiving increasing public and media attention because of their innovative and disruptive technologies and activities. Second, they represent two ends of hacker culture – one is focused primarily on technological creation and the other on socio-political disruption. Finally, they both influence and are similarly affected by the two laws that are most pertinent to hacking, namely, computer crime and intellectual property laws. Through their technical projects and acts of hacktivism, makers and hacktivists are pushing not just technical but legal and social boundaries as well. Makers and hacktivists are similar in that they both engage in hacking activities in public. Makers are members of hackerspaces, which have open memberships and where hacking is done out in the open with most projects being documented and freely shared online. Similarly, hacking activities carried out by hacktivists are meant to raise public awareness and catalyze social action about important public interest issues. While their activities can be veiled in secrecy and anonymity, hacktivists ultimately seek to make a public impact.

Hack

The term "hacker" has been used to define and describe different individuals and groups. However, since there is not one but many types of hackers, it is difficult to come up with a single, universal definition that encompasses all of them. Even the meaning of a "hack" in relation to computers and technologies is contested and has been constantly evolving since it was first used in connection with the activities of the MIT computer hackers.[9] According to *The New Hacker's Dictionary*, a hack is characterized by "an appropriate application of ingenuity" to any field of activity.[10] For Levy, a hack "must be imbued with innovation, style, and technical virtuosity".[11] To Jordan, a "hack involves altering a pre-existing situation to produce something new; to hack is to produce differences".[12] Organizers of a hacker camp define hacking as "to use something in a creative way, not thought of when it was first invented".[13] Of the many descriptions of hacking, Turkle's characterization of the hack, which she first wrote in 1984, remains the most relevant, flexible and useful since, despite its high level of conceptualization, it is applicable to most types of hackers and hacking activities. She expounds on the meaning of hacking through the activities of the well-known hacker John Draper (Captain Crunch) who, using a whistle and his knowledge of the intricacies of the global telephone system, was able to make a free long-distance telephone call that "started in California, went through Tokyo, India, Greece, Pretoria, London, New York, and back to California".[14]

> Appreciating what made the call around the world a great hack is an exercise in hacker aesthetics. It has the quality of Howard's magician's gesture: a

surprising result produced with what hackers would describe as 'a ridiculously simple' means. Of equal importance to the aesthetic of the hack is that Crunch had not simply stumbled on a curiosity. The trick worked because Crunch had acquired an impressive amount of expertise of the telephone system. This is what made the trick a great hack, otherwise it would have been a minor one. Mastery is of the essence everywhere within hacker culture. Third, the expertise was acquired unofficially and at the expense of a big system. The hacker is a person outside the system who is never excluded by its rules.[15]

To paraphrase and refine the above quote from Turkle, whether as noun or verb, *a hack is about producing innovation through deceptively simple means, which belies the impressive mastery or expertise possessed by an actor who does not conform to the normal rules and expected uses of a technology or technical system.*[16] Hacking is basically the creative, innovative and unexpected use of technology. A hack, whether as product or process, is innovative because it is new, novel, different or surprising. A hack's deceptive simplicity tends to make it appear magical.[17] In my refined characterization of a hack, expertise can but does not have to be acquired unofficially or at the expense of a big system; the key is that a hack does not conform to the normal rules or expected uses of a technology. As Taylor states, " 'true' hacking is in the system but not of the system, and to remain true to itself it remains dependent upon, but not beholden, to that system".[18] Thus, the elements of a hack are (1) innovation, (2) simplicity, (3) mastery, (4) nonconformity and (5) technology.[19]

Despite the plurality of hackers and the various meanings attached to the word "hack", taken together, the multiplicity of actors, activities and meanings constitutes a loosely joined but distinct *hacker culture*. This culture is generally concerned with hacking technologies, particularly those pertaining to computing and communication, and espouses common yet contested norms and values such as, among others, openness, freedom of access, freedom of expression, autonomy, equality/meritocracy, transparency and privacy.[20] Because it originated from the early computer hackers at MIT, hacker culture is closely connected to different forms of computer culture and may be considered the latter's progenitor.[21] Hacking though is always at the forefront or the bleeding edge of technology creation and adoption. In the case of the MIT hackers, since computing was still a nascent field in the 1960s, the mere act of computer programming and finding ways to make computers do basic things like play music or display images was innovative.[22] However, by the time computer hardware and software were commercialized and commoditized in the 1980s, hackers were no longer interested in just writing software or designing personal computers, but in exploring, learning about and hacking even more interesting and challenging technologies and technical systems such as online Bulletin Board Systems (BBS) and computer and telecommunications networks.[23]

Computers are an important part of hacker culture, but hacking is not reducible to computers. Hacking involves pushing the limits of any technology and breaking the prescribed boundaries of all sorts of technical systems. The fact that hackers create and change technology is what separates them from individuals and groups who merely use or are enthusiastic about technology. Innovation, mastery and non-conformity are the elements that distinguish hacker culture from other technological cultures (e.g., gamer culture and cyberpunks).[24] Hackers are constantly innovating and pursuing new technical projects so that they can produce something new and surprise themselves and others.

Makers

Makers are a particular type of hacker who are interested in hacking all kinds of technologies (even IKEA furniture)[25] and they regularly hang out at communal workshops called "hackerspaces" to build, share and collaborate on projects.[26] Makers had their beginnings in Europe and the United States in the 1990s, but they only began to be recognized and referred to by that name by the mid to late 2000s.[27] Hackerspaces are "places in the community where local [hackers] can collectively meet, work, and share infrastructure".[28] The MakerBot 3D printer, the Pebble smart watch, the Square mobile payment system, and the user-sharing website Pinterest are some of the innovative products and services that were developed in hackerspaces.[29] Makers are at the forefront of exploring, developing and popularizing cutting-edge technologies such as 3D printers and autonomous drones that are expected to be legally, socially and economically disruptive. 3D printers are machines that can "print out" digital 3D objects or computer files as physical objects (normally made of plastic).[30] Once 3D printers are mass-produced and become a common household appliance, Anderson predicts that they will usher a "new industrial revolution" where ordinary people are able to create and produce almost anything in the comfort of their homes.[31] 3D printing could be as legally challenging for the manufacturing industry as the photocopier was to the publishing industry and online peer-to-peer (P2P) file sharing technology was to the music industry.[32]

Makers share an affinity with computer hobbyists in the United States in the 1970s that were part of so-called homebrew computer clubs, which is considered the birthplace of the personal computing revolution.[33] Computer hobbyists hacked in relative isolation in their own garages and went to club meetings, which were held in different locations, to show off their creations to others.[34] Unlike makers, club members did not have access to more or less permanent and open places containing tools and equipment where people could work side-by-side on projects or just stay and hang out – in other words, a combined laboratory and living room.

Hacktivists

In contrast to makers, hacktivists are those who hack for *overtly* socio-political purposes.[35] While all and even basic acts of hacking are political and socially relevant, overt intent is what distinguishes hacktivists from other types of hackers.[36] As Coleman explains, "In many other instances, geeks and hackers have no desire to act politically, even going as far as to disavow politics, but the technology they make and configure embodies values, and thus acts politically".[37] The use of the term "hacktivists" to refer to socially and politically motivated hackers came about as a result of the confluence of a number of factors – globalization and the awareness of its effects, greater and widespread use of computers and the internet by activists as well as the wider public, and hackers themselves becoming more politically aware and involved.[38] While the term "hacktivism" is a simple contraction of the words hack and activism, it is closely related to but distinct from broader forms of cyber-activism, cyber-protests and other types of technology-based activisms carried out by traditional activists.[39] What distinguishes hacktivism from general cyber-activism is that the former *is grounded in, draws from, or views itself as a part of hacker culture*, while the latter can but does not have to.[40] Furthermore, for hacktivists, the act of hacking itself constitutes both the form (expression and means) and the substance (content and message) of their activism – simultaneously a means and an end.[41] In this way, the oft-cited Zapatista movement of the 1990s, where an indigenous community and their supporters used the internet to publicize and further their socio-political objectives, can be categorized as cyber-activism rather than hacktivism, even though some elements of the cyber-protest involved acts of hacking by hacktivists who were part of the movement.[42]

Hacktivism can be carried out in different forms depending on the type of technology involved.[43] It can take the form of innocuous awareness campaigns and online self-organization, simple website defacement and site redirects, or more forceful and direct actions such as a distributed denial-of-service attack (DDoS) against the web servers of the target entity or breaking the security of the target's computer system.[44] A number of actions committed by hacktivists would be considered violations of different computer crime laws around the world. The controversy surrounding the whistleblower website Wikileaks and the many high-profile hacks and data breaches committed in its wake by online hacktivist groups such as Anonymous and LulzSec against governmental agencies and companies that they perceived to be oppressive and undemocratic have brought hacktivism into the public eye.[45] Concerns about cyber attacks have led to proposals for greater, stronger and stricter state and stronger regulation.[46] The conflicts between hacktivists and state actors are expected to continue to intensify.

Key themes and concepts

This book examines the relations and interactions between hackers and technology laws and policies with a view to proposing improved approaches to the regulation and governance of hacking as well as technology as a whole. An examination of the relationship between hacking and law involves and makes salient the following key themes and concepts.

Common acts of hacking

Hackers are multifaceted and they are part of and subject to equally complex and heterogeneous contexts and conditions. In order to get a handle on this multiplicity and complexity, one must first focus on the hack. Even though hackers come from diverse socio-economic backgrounds and have various motivations and beliefs, by focusing on what hackers actually do, it becomes possible to discern commonalities and connections among them.

As Taylor points out, the activity of hacking itself has not fundamentally changed; what has changed are the technological and social conditions within which hacking takes place.[47] Alleyne observes, for example, that the supposedly highly contentious ideological gap between free software developers and open source programmers recedes from view during the actual practice of hacking when both groups start creating "essentially the same object – source code, and [undertake the same] practice – code-sharing".[48] As Kelty explains, "for all the ideological distinctions at the level of discourse, [free software and open source] are *doing exactly the same thing* at the level of practice".[49] This does not mean that the substantial differences among the different types of hackers can be disregarded. Far from it, once a secure handhold is established by focusing initially on hacking activities, one is better able to grasp the complexity of hacker culture and the plural norms and values that are associated with it.

Because hacking is so semantically and culturally dense, using common everyday words to describe what a hack involves can help demystify it. Shorn of all its contested baggage,[50] hacking can be perceived as six common (in the sense of being both ordinary and shared) acts – *(1) explore, (2) break, (3) learn, (4) create, (5) share, and (6) secure.* These six common acts are derived and synthesized from some of the most well-known expressions of the components and characteristics of hacker culture as written by hackers themselves and by non-hackers interested in hacker culture.[51]

The six common acts are each connected to other related activities. The act to "explore" includes the activities of access, break in, disassemble and reverse engineer; while "break" is further comprised of the acts to disrupt, subvert, circumvent, damage and destroy. Other common acts also consist of various other activities – "learn" (know, master, control and understand), "create" (make, modify, improve and innovate), "share" (cooperate, collaborate and distribute), and "secure" (keep private, hide, encrypt and anonymize). These common acts are interconnected. For example, breaking can lead to learning but it can also produce sharing or creating (and the latter can lead back to learning). The value of perceiving hacking as being made up of six common yet interacting acts is that one can see how hacking actually operates and how it impacts law, technology and society.

Breaking and making

By focusing on the common hacking activities, one becomes cognizant of the paradoxical "creative-destructive" dynamic that is inherent in hacking. Hackers generally want to learn how things work, gain expertise and produce something innovative, new or surprising. However, to understand and master a particular technology, hackers need to be able to access or glimpse its inner workings. But since most technologies and systems are closed or sealed off (black boxes), hackers need to take them apart or break into them. *Breaking and making* is a pivotal theme that is present throughout the development and evolution of digital technologies vis-à-vis hacker culture. The history of computing and hacking is replete with seemingly contradictory conditions and outcomes that arise from the interactions between creation and destruction. No less than Alan Turing, who is considered one of the inventors of computers and computer science, was involved in the World War II computing and code-breaking efforts at Bletchley Park.[52] One of the first digital, stored-program computers, the Institute for Advanced Study (IAS) machine at Princeton, which was spearheaded by John von Neumann (who is credited with the eponymous computer architecture that is at the heart of many modern digital computers), was used to perform calculations necessary for building a hydrogen bomb.[53] The internet's precursor, the ARPANET, was built to enable academics and researchers to connect remotely to computers and other users and share computing resources and information.[54] However, since it was funded and built under the auspices of the US Department of Defense's Advanced Research Projects Agency (ARPA), it can be classified as military-related work produced by the military-industrial complex during the Cold War.[55] This may explain why the myth that the internet was made to survive a nuclear war still persists today.[56] Even hacker culture itself, which initially grew out of the activities of the early computer hackers at MIT, is suffused with the paradox of breaking and making – autonomy/control, anarchy/power, openness/secrecy and war/peace. As Levy points out, "ARPA money was the lifeblood of the hacking way of life" in the hacker utopia-dystopia on the ninth floor of Tech Square and "all the lab's activities, even the most zany or anarchistic manifestations of the Hacker Ethic, had been funded by the Department of Defense".[57]

Hacking is indeed a study in contradictions, and it is its magical ability to negotiate and bring together diametrically opposed forces and conditions that demonstrates its profound significance to law, technology and society. I argue that, like the natural philosophers, mathematicians, scientists, inventors and other innovators that preceded them, hackers occupy an extraordinary position since they are among the handful of social actors or groups that reside at the intersections of legal, social and technological domains.[58] Being both technical and epistemic communities,[59] hacker groups influence how the networked information society is configured and operates through their tools, norms and values. Studying hackers and hacking is crucial to understanding the techno-social changes and consequent legal challenges that society faces.

Norms and values

Social norms and values are two other significant concepts that are pertinent to understanding hacking's interactions with law. Social norms (or norms for short) are described as "generally accepted, sanctioned prescriptions for, or prohibitions against, others' behavior . . ., i.e. what others *ought* to do . . . *or else*".[60] Dohrenwend provides a very comprehensive conceptualization of a social norm, which he defines as "*a rule which, over a period of time, proves binding on the overt behavior of each individual in an aggregate of two or more individuals*".[61] To be a norm, its content must be "*known to at least one member of the social aggregate*".[62] Furthermore, the norm is considered binding because the member has either internalized it or "*external sanctions in support of the rule*" have been applied on him "*by the social aggregate*" or "*by an authority outside the social aggregate*".[63] A social norm thus involves "(1) a collective evaluation of behavior in terms of what it *ought* to be; (2) a collective expectation as to what behavior *will be*; and/ or (3) particular *reactions* to behavior, including attempts to apply sanctions or otherwise induce a particular kind of conduct".[64]

Values are closely connected to norms but remain a distinct concept. According to Kluckhohn's widely cited and influential definition, "*A value is a conception, explicit or implicit, distinctive of an individual or characteristic of a group, of the desirable which influences the selection from available modes, means, and ends of action*".[65] Rokeach similarly defines a value as "an enduring prescriptive or proscriptive belief that a specific mode of behavior or end-state of existence is preferred to an opposite or converse mode of behavior or end-state".[66] With regard to its characteristics, a value: is a "prescriptive or proscriptive belief"; is enduring yet subject to change; competes with other values (and is thus naturally subject to negotiation, balancing and prioritization); has "cognitive, affective and behavioral components"; and has conflict-resolution, decision-making and expressive functions.[67]

Despite their conceptual distinctions, norms and values are intimately interconnected to each other. Norms are frequently linked to and defined in relation to values.[68] For Giddens, norms are "[r]ules of behaviour that reflect or embody a culture's *values*, either prescribing a given type of behaviour, or forbidding it".[69] Gibbs likewise asserts that "[n]orms are based on cultural values".[70] The very notion of collective evaluations and expectations "implies the existence of shared values";[71] and values likewise concern normative propositions.[72] It is often the case that "[v]alue statements are . . . normative statements" as well.[73] The relationship between norms and values can thus be best described as symbiotic since "most norms are based upon established values" and "commonly held values often result in the formation of norms that insure the maintenance of [those] values".[74] Their inherent conceptual and empirical closeness may explain why they are commonly spoken of or referred to as simply "norms and values".[75]

Overview of chapters

To better understand the relations and interactions between hackers and the law and to improve the regulations that impact hacking, this book examines the social, technological and legal domains that affect hackers. Chapter 2 describes makers and hacktivists by situating them within the broader hacker culture and against the backdrop of the varied histories and typologies of hacking. The similarities as well as differences between makers and hacktivists and other types of hackers are highlighted particularly with regard to the technologies they used, their goals and motivations, the places and spaces they inhabited, and how they were treated by the law and public authorities. In Chapter 3, the focus is on social norms and values. The chapter discusses the prominent norms and values of makers and hacktivists. It also examines hacker manifestos as a source for understanding their social goals and rules of behavior. Chapter 4 examines the technology laws and policies that specifically affect hacking: computer crime, intellectual property and contract and anti-circumvention laws. The chapter analyzes these laws from the perspective of the norms and values of makers and hacktivists, discusses areas of conflict and congruence, and assesses whether such laws tend to restrict and/or support hacking. Chapter 5 delves into the perceptions and attitudes of makers and hacktivists toward law and public authorities. It explores hackers' different responses to law – from ignoring and avoiding the law to changing and resisting it, and to using or working within the legal system. The chapter includes detailed studies of high-profile cases in the Netherlands such as the hacking of the electronic voting machines and the Dutch national public transport card where hackers sought to change the law through hacking. Chapter 6 sets out and explains the normative conclusions of the book and possible areas of law reform that could be undertaken to improve technology laws and policies concerning hacking. The chapter proposes a change in the law's typical response to hacking. Rather than attempting to restrict or prosecute hacking, it would be better for public authorities to support and reach out to hackers through more collaborative and participatory approaches like the adoption and implementation of responsible disclosure rules for security testing and open data policies and initiatives to encourage creative and innovative uses of information and technology.

Notes

1 Julie Cohen, *Configuring the Networked Self* 3; see Manuel Castells, *The Internet Galaxy* 133 (who uses the term "network society").
2 See Andrew Murray, *The Regulation of Cyberspace* 74; see Kathy Bowrey, *Law and Internet Cultures* 47; see Jeanne Bonnici, *Self-Regulation in Cyberspace* 77.
3 See Christopher Kelty, *Two Bits* 3.
4 Andrew Chadwick, *Internet Politics* 114.
5 Peter Ludlow, "Wikileaks and hacktivist culture" 25; Noah Hampson, "Hacktivism" 512–513.
6 Patrice Flichy, *Understanding Technological Innovation* 17; Raul Pertierra, *The Anthropology of New Media in the Philippines* 16.
7 Paul Taylor, *Hackers* 13.
8 For more information on the different generations and types of hackers, see Steven Levy, *Hackers*; see Paul Taylor, "Editorial: Hacktivism"; see Kirsty Best, "The hacker's challenge" 266–267; see Gabriella Coleman and Alex Golub, "Hacker practice"; see Helen Nissenbaum, "Hackers and the contested ontology of

cyberspace"; Paul Taylor, "From hackers to hacktivists" 628–629 (who lists seven hacker generations).

9 "The meaning of 'hack'", in *The New Hacker's Dictionary*, Paul Taylor, *Hackers* 13.
10 "The meaning of 'hack'", in *The New Hacker's Dictionary*.
11 Steven Levy, *Hackers* 10.
12 Tim Jordan, *Hacking* 9; see also Tim Jordan, *Activism!* 120 (a hack is the "innovative" and "novel uses of technology").
13 OHM2013, "Call for participation".
14 Sherry Turkle, *The Second Self* 207.
15 Sherry Turkle, *The Second Self* 208.
16 Sherry Turkle, *The Second Self* 208.
17 Chris Anderson, *Makers* 82 (Arthur C. Clarke's famous quote: "any sufficiently advanced technology is indistinguishable from magic"); see also Lawrence Principe, "Renaissance natural magic" (the connection between magic and natural philosophy).
18 Paul Taylor, "From hackers to hacktivists" 633.
19 Sherry Turkle, *The Second Self* 208; see Paul Taylor, *Hackers* 14 (who sees the three main characteristics of a hack as simplicity, mastery and illicitness); see Paul Taylor, "From hackers to hacktivists" (for his three core elements of the hacking ethic).
20 Gabriella Coleman, "Hacker politics and publics" 513–514 (these common norms and values can even be contested, paradoxically, to the point of negation).
21 Steven Levy, *Hackers* x; Eric Raymond, "A brief history of hackerdom" 4.
22 Computer History Museum, "PDP-1 restoration project"; see also Pekka Himanen, "A brief history of computer hackerism" 186.
23 See Tim Jordan, *Hacking* 37.
24 See Paul Taylor, *Hackers* xv; Douglas Thomas, *Hacker Culture* xii; Bruce Sterling, *The Hacker Crackdown* 59.
25 IKEA hackers.
26 Hackerspaces.org; see Andrew Schrock, "What keeps hacker and maker spaces going?".
27 *Hackerspaces – The Beginning* 84.
28 John Borland, "'Hacker space' movement sought for US"; see also Hackerspace Open Day.
29 Artisan's Asylum, "Make a makerspace"; Steven Kurutz, "One big workbench".
30 Chris Anderson, *Makers* 82.
31 Chris Anderson, *Makers* 41.
32 See Simon Bradshaw, Adrian Bowyer and Patrick Haufe, "The intellectual property implications of low-cost 3D printing"; see Leanne Wiseman, "Beyond the photocopier"; see Sudip Bhattacharjee and others, "Impact of legal threats on online music sharing activity".
33 Steven Levy, *Hackers* 201 and 259; Robert Cringely, *Accidental Empires* 9.
34 Steven Levy, *Hackers* 212, 214 and 216.
35 See Paul Taylor, "Editorial: Hacktivism" 2 (who also uses the term overt); Paul Taylor, "From hackers to hacktivists" 626; see also Xiang Li, "Hacktivism and the first amendment" 302 and 305; see also Noah Hampson, "Hacktivism" 514.
36 Brian Alleyne, "We are all hackers now" 24 (who says "all hackers are political actors"); Tim Jordan, *Activism!* 135.
37 Gabriella Coleman, "Hacker politics and publics" 516.
38 Paul Taylor, "Editorial hacktivism" 5; Paul Taylor, "From hackers to hacktivists" 67; Tim Jordan, *Hacking* 71; Xiang Li, "Hacktivism and the first amendment" 303.
39 Stefania Milan and Arne Hintz, "Dynamics of cyberactivism" 2; Noah Hampson, "Hacktivism" 515; Brian Alleyne, "We are all hackers now" 11.

40 Brian Alleyne, "We are all hackers now" 11; Andrew Chadwick, *Internet Politics* 129–130.
41 Paul Taylor, "From hackers to hacktivists" 626; Noah Hampson, "Hacktivism" 531 (who argues that some forms of hacktivism are primarily expressive).
42 See Andrew Chadwick, *Internet Politics* 131–132; Paul Taylor, "From hackers to hacktivists" 634.
43 Noah Hampson, "Hacktivism" 517; David Gunkel, "Editorial: Introduction to hacking and hacktivism" 595.
44 See Noah Hampson, "Hacktivism" 1 (for a list of different forms of hacktivisms); see Andrew Chadwick, *Internet Politics* 130.
45 Xiang Li, "Hacktivism and the first amendment" 303; see also Parmy Olson, *We Are Anonymous*.
46 "Proposal for a directive of the European Parliament and of the Council on attacks against information systems and repealing Council Framework Decision 2005/222/JHA" 517.
47 Paul Taylor, "Editorial: Hacktivism" 2.
48 Brian Alleyne, "We are all hackers now" 20.
49 Christopher Kelty, *Two Bits* 14 (emphasis added).
50 See Derek Bambauer and Oliver Day, "The hacker's aegis" 44.
51 See Steven Levy, *Hackers* 28–31; see Chaos Computer Club, "Hacker ethics"; see Pekka Himanen, *The Hacker Ethic and the Spirit of the Information Age* 139–141; see Free Software Foundation, "What is free software"; see Christopher Kelty, *Two Bits* 14–15; see Mark Hatch, *The Maker Movement Manifesto* 1–2.
52 Douglas Thomas, *Hacker Culture* 13.
53 See George Dyson, *Turing's Cathedral*.
54 See Katie Hafner, *Where Wizards Stay Up Late* 41–42.
55 See Katie Hafner, *Where Wizards Stay Up Late* 41–42.
56 Internet Society, "Brief history of the Internet"; see John Naughton, *A Brief History of the Future* 96–98; but see Michael Belfiore, *The Department of Mad Scientists*.
57 Steven Levy, *Hackers* 125.
58 See Wiebe Bijker, Thomas Hughes and Trevor Pinch, *The Social Construction of Technological Systems*.
59 See Kasper Edwards, "Epistemic communities, situated learning and open source software development".
60 Richard Morris, "A typology of norms" 610.
61 Bruce Dohrenwend, "A conceptual analysis of Durkheim's types" 470.
62 Bruce Dohrenwend, "A conceptual analysis of Durkheim's types" 470.
63 Bruce Dohrenwend, "A conceptual analysis of Durkheim's types" 470.
64 Jack Gibbs, "Norms: The problem of definition and classification" 589 and 594.
65 Clyde Kluckhohn and others, "Values and value-orientations in the theory of action" 395; see also Milton Rokeach, *The Nature of Human Values* 9; see also Richard Morris, "A typology of norms" 610; see also Steven Hitlin and Jane Piliavin, "Values: Reviving a dormant concept" 362; see also James Spates, "The sociology of values" 30.
66 Milton Rokeach, *The Nature of Human Values* 5 and 25; see also Steven Hitlin and Jane Piliavin, "Values: Reviving a dormant concept" 362; but see Clyde Kluckhohn and others, "Values and value-orientations in the theory of action" 403 (who states that "the distinction between *ends* and *means* is somewhat transitory, depending upon time perspective"); see also Steven Hitlin and Jane Piliavin, "Values: Reviving a dormant concept" 366.
67 Milton Rokeach, *The Nature of Human Values* 6, 7, 12, 20 and 25; see also Clyde Kluckhohn and others, "Values and value-orientations in the theory of action" 395–396.

68 Gary Fine, "Enacting norms" 161; Christine Horne, "Sociological perspectives on the emergence of social norms" 4.; Michael Baurmann and others, *Norms and Values* 7 and 10.

69 Anthony Giddens, *Sociology* 1127 (emphasis added).

70 Jack Gibbs, "Norms: The problem of definition and classification" 586.

71 Jack Gibbs, "Norms: The problem of definition and classification" 589.

72 Clyde Kluckhohn and others, "Values and value-orientations in the theory of action" 390.

73 Clyde Kluckhohn and others, "Values and value-orientations in the theory of action" 398; see also Steven Hitlin and Jane Piliavin, "Values: Reviving a dormant concept" 379.

74 Richard Morris, "A typology of norms" 610; Amitai Etzioni, "Social norms: Internalization, persuasion, and history" 174.

75 Steven Hitlin and Jane Piliavin, "Values: Reviving a dormant concept" 359.

Chapter 2

Hacker culture

History and typology of hacking

As with any culture or subculture, hacker culture is constituted by manifold elements: norms and values, beliefs and ideologies, practices, rituals and ceremonies, language, symbols, technologies, status and roles, social organization, processes of meaning-making and ways of life.[1] Hacker culture is further complicated by the fact that it is made up of different types of hackers, who come from varied backgrounds, belong to wide-ranging demographics and possess traits that make them all distinct.[2] Because it is neither monolithic nor homogenous, hacker culture is very hard to pin down and its boundaries are difficult to precisely define. While it is not possible to speak of a pure hacker culture or an archetypical hacker group, there are certain core elements and characteristics that are held in common by these loosely joined individuals and groups who call themselves and each other hackers.[3] As Taylor says, "The connotations of hacking have changed significantly over time, even though the essential elements of the activity have remained relatively constant".[4]

This chapter does not intend nor aspire to provide a definitive account of hacker culture and history. It seeks, however, to construct a workable typology and narrative about different hacker types and periods in order to contextualize the emergence and development of makers and hacktivists.[5] Makers and hacktivists are separate and distinct types of hackers but they draw from and are part of hacker culture because they share a host of similar practices, experiences and beliefs with the wider community of hackers, including the common acts of hacking discussed in the previous chapter. To understand makers and hacktivists, it is essential to locate them first within the ever-changing historical and techno-social contexts of the broader hacker culture, and compare them with other types of hackers.

It is generally accepted that hacking's origins can be traced back to the computer scientists and programmers at the Massachusetts Institute of Technology (MIT) in the United States in the late 1950s.[6] They were the first to use the terms "hacker" and "hack" to describe themselves and their activities.[7] But how exactly hacker culture developed and evolved from these first computer hackers to the different hacker types that were dominant in the past and those that are salient today is subject of varying interpretations and explanations from hackers and those who write about them. For Alleyne, there are three hacker ideal types – open hackers, clandestine hackers and hacktivists.[8] Using an anthropological approach, Coleman and Golub classify hackers based on their ethical or moral practices:[9] hackers who adhere to "crypto-freedom and the politics of technology"[10] place strong emphasis on the value of security, privacy and secrecy; those who espouse the ideals of "free software and the politics of inversion"[11] tend to highlight the importance of freedom, openness, accessibility, sharing and creativity; and hackers who find affinity with "the underground and the politics of transgression"[12] are more concerned with matters relating to power, individual autonomy, evasion, subversion and defiance. From the perspective of computer crime law, hacking is said to have "four distinct focal periods": "the discovery of computer abuse (1946–76)";[13] "the criminalization of deviant computer use (1977–87)";[14] "the demonization of hackers (1988–1992)";[15] and "the censorship period (1993-[2001])".[16] The most comprehensive classification so far has been Taylor's seven hacker generations, which builds on Levy's account of early hackers – "true" hackers, hardware hackers and game hackers[17] – and appends hackers/crackers, microserfs, open source hackers, and hacktivists.[18] The typology of hackers that I adopt (which closely resembles Taylor's) consists of six types of hackers: computer scientists and programmers, computer hobbyists, underground hackers, free and open source software (FOSS) developers, hacktivists and makers. In my typology, each hacker type can be distinguished from each other based on what technology they hacked, why they hacked, where they hacked and how the law and authorities responded to them.

Of minicomputers and laboratories – computer scientists and programmers

The Hulking Giants

Based on Levy's journalistic account of the early history of hacking, the introduction and use in the late 1950s and 1960s of computers such as the TX-0 and the PDP-1 and their successors was vital to the genesis of hacker culture.[19] It is noteworthy that the birth and growth of hacking corresponded with greater freedom and access to increasingly more advanced, interactive and "hackable" computers.[20] Before the availability of these hacker-friendly machines, anyone interested in computing had to use large mainframe computers like the IBM 704, which hackers ominously and derisively called "the Hulking Giant".[21] Access to and use of these expensive mainframe computers were limited and complicated due to technical and social factors. These mainframe computers were located in highly controlled and well-protected laboratories that were administered and guarded by authorized computer operators, whom early hackers likened to a kind of priesthood.[22] As Levy explains, "The IBM 704 cost several million dollars, took up an entire room, needed constant attention from a cadre of professional machine operators, and required special air conditioning".[23] People outside of the priesthood could not directly use or program these mainframe computers (much less study or modify the hardware and software) as only the anointed computer operators had direct access to and could feed programs (as batch-processed punch cards) into the Hulking Giants.[24] It is therefore not surprising that hacker culture emerged and blossomed with the availability of more accessible and modifiable technologies.

The TX-0

The TX-0 (pronounced "Tix Oh" and short for "Transistorized eXperimental computer zero") was an experimental computer that used transistors rather than vacuum tubes, which made it smaller and easier to operate and maintain compared to the giant mainframe computers.[25] It had important technical innovations that made it more amenable to hacking: first, it had an actual computer monitor that made programming more interactive and immediate; second, programs could be fed into it using paper tapes that could be more conveniently produced using a typewriter-like Flexowriter rather than laborious punch cards; and, third, it was set up so that users could actually sit in front of the computer while programming and debugging their programs.[26] Levy explains the significance of these technical improvements of the TX-0 to the early hackers who were computer scientists and programmers in academic and research institutions in the late 1950s and the 1960s: "The user would first punch in a program onto a long, thin paper tape with a Flexowriter (there were a few extra Flexowriters in an adjoining room), then sit at the console, feed in the program by running the tape through a reader, and be able to sit there while the program ran".[27]

The social conditions surrounding the TX-0 also favored hacking. The early hackers, who were initially students and then became computer researchers at MIT, were invited to use the TX-0 by one of their former colleagues, and the technician in charge generally tolerated their use of the computer during off hours.[28] While they had access to the computer during regular office hours, computer hackers preferred to work at night and during the early hours of the morning when they had the computer all to themselves and they did not have to share computing time and power with other scientists at MIT's Research Laboratory of Electronics (RLE).[29]

With the TX-0, there were no priests or intermediaries that controlled or prevented access. While the TX-0 was located in the RLE, the early hackers treated it more as a place to hangout and create rather than a formal laboratory.[30] Instead of being suppressed or considered a cause for alarm by the university authorities and the US government (which provided major funding for early computer research), hacking was generally seen as a productive activity that should be encouraged or at least tolerated.[31] According to Raymond, government agencies "deliberately turned a blind eye to all the technically 'unauthorized' activity; [they] understood that the extra overhead was a small price to pay for attracting an entire generation of bright young people into the computing field".[32] As Sterling explains,

> Most of the basic techniques of computer intrusion: password cracking, trap-doors, backdoors, trojan horses – were created in college environments in the 1960s. . . . Outside of the tiny cult of computer enthusiasts, few people thought much about the implications of "breaking into" computers. This sort of activity had not yet been publicized, much less criminalized.[33]

The authorities' non-interference or support for early hacking activities could be explained by the fact that computer scientists were a relatively small and identifi-able group, there were not many computers at the time and they were all located in either university, research, military or corporate settings, and the impact or sphere of influence of these early hacking activities (including any actual or potential damage or harm) could only be felt within the four walls of the computer laboratory and were thus not a cause for concern or alarm.[34]

The PDP-1

With the subsequent introduction and use of the PDP-1 (or "Programmed Data Processor-1"), hacker culture truly flourished at MIT.[35] The PDP-1, which was created by Digital Equipment Corporation (DEC), was the first minicomputer and, like the TX-0 that inspired it, espoused the idea of "interactive comput-ing".[36] The PDP-1 had features that made it ideal for hacking: like the TX-0, the user could sit in front of the computer while programming; it was possible to attach different input and output (I/O) devices to it; and "it was the first commercial computer that focused on interaction with the user rather than the efficient use of computer cycles".[37] In addition to these technical advantages, the PDP-1 and the space where it was housed became the center of the hacker community at MIT because the early computer hackers had free access to them in both physical and technical senses. The PDP-1 was set up in a room in the RLE that hackers designated as the Kluge Room.[38] It was a place where hackers could devote all of their time programming and working on the computer with-out much interference from gatekeepers and outsiders.[39] With the PDP-1 and its successors, they had relatively unimpeded access to explore and learn about how the computer worked and close to full freedom to change and improve the computer's hardware and software. The ability and freedom to hack the PDP-1 produced important advances in computer science and engineering such as "early debugging, text editing, music and game programs, including the first computer video game, Spacewar".[40] They were able to produce these innovations through hacking: they *learned* about the inner workings of a computer and how, by giv-ing it the right instructions, they could *create* programs that made it perform various tasks; they had no qualms about *breaking* passwords, locks and other security devices in order to *explore* and gain access to computers and information; and they freely *shared* programs with each other by placing them in unlocked drawers. The early hackers were not concerned with keeping things *secure* since they saw this as a hindrance to the free access to and open use of knowledge and technology.

Even when the centers of hacking expanded, moved and proliferated to other areas at MIT (such as the hacker utopia on the ninth floor of Tech Square) and to more cities and research laboratories, the interactive and hackable computers remained the centerpiece of the creative, innovative and often chaotic spaces that hackers built around them.[41] Turkle writes, "Hackers don't live only with computers; they live in a culture that grows up around computers".[42] In fact, it can be argued that the computers themselves served as spaces within which hacking took place. As über-hacker Bill Gosper recounted to Levy, "In some sense, we lived inside the damn machine. It was part of our environment. There was a society in there".[43] For the early hackers, computers were simultaneously tools and spaces for making technology and changing their lives, and they were unconcerned about the authorities and the latter generally gave them free reign to do as they pleased.

Of microcomputers, garages and computer clubs – computer hobbyists

The Altair

If the TX-0 and the PDP-1 and their successors were the computers that epitomize the original computer hackers, it was the MITS Altair 8800 (Altair) and the Apple II that defined the computer hobbyists in the 1970s. From a technical standpoint, the Altair was not in the same league as the minicomputers that were used by the original hackers, which were at the time very advanced, powerful and expensive computing machines. Built by the company Micro Instrumentation and Telemetry Systems (MITS) in Albuquerque, New Mexico, and launched in the January 1975 issue of *Popular Electronics*, a magazine for electronics enthusiasts, the Altair was a barebones digital, programmable computer.[44] Aesthetically speaking, it was a squat, blue and gray metal box with red lights and silver switches on its black facade. Inside, it had five basic subsystems: a central processing unit (CPU) which "performs all the calculations, generates system timing, and makes all decisions";[45] the memory for storing information in the form of bits (binary 1s and 0s);[46] a front panel that contained switches and LED status indicators that served as the computer's main input and output interface;[47] a power supply;[48] and room for peripheral and memory expansion.[49] Compared to modern PCs, the Altair did not come out of the box with now standard I/O devices such as a keyboard, mouse or display (users could subsequently add some of these peripherals).[50] With regard to its operation, the Altair was not a paragon of interactive computing since instructions and programs had to be entered using its front switches and the results could only be displayed to the user in binary format.[51] Levy describes the Altair's lack of user-friendliness: it was

> a box of blinking lights with only 256 bytes of memory. You could put in a program only by flicking octal numbers into the computer by those tiny, finger-shredding switches, and you could see the answer to your problem only by interpreting the flickety-flock of the LED lights, which were also laid out in octal.[52]

Despite these limitations, the Altair had certain features and "affordances" that made it spark the computer revolution.[53] The fact that the Altair was not sold fully assembled but as a kit that users had to build themselves was not a shortcoming but a key feature. Having to put together the Altair themselves meant that computer hobbyists would not only be getting their own computers but they would also learn how computers worked. As Levy explains, "It was an education in itself, a course of digital logic and soldering skills and innovation".[54] Price was also a factor.[55] In contrast to the minicomputers and mainframe computers that cost hundreds of thousands, if not millions, of dollars, the Altair was available to the general public for under US$400.[56] At this price point, it was reasonably affordable, and a broader segment of society and not only well-funded researchers and laboratories could gain access to computing.[57] One reason why the Altair was relatively inexpensive was because it was made using off-the-shelf components and parts.[58] The use of off-the-shelf technologies meant that: parts were often readily available, commoditized and standardized; there was a greater likelihood that the components would be interchangeable and interoperable with those made by a wide range of other manufacturers; and, anyone (including other companies) could use the same or similar parts to build their own computers and peripherals.[59] The Altair's size and componentized design also made it possible to ship parts to hobbyists around the country for assembly in their own homes and garages, and, unlike the Hulking Giants, it could be built and used on a desk or work table, and it was portable enough to be brought and shown off at computer club meetings.[60]

Of course, what made the Altair truly remarkable was that it was open and hackable in many respects. Designed as a "general-purpose computer", it did not have a fixed purpose but it could be made to perform a multitude of functions and uses by simply running different software or incorporating other hardware and peripherals to it.[61] The Altair was built to run "thousands of possible applications" and infinitely expandable with "almost unlimited peripheral and memory expansion".[62] Some potential uses that were envisioned for the Altair included being a programmable scientific calculator, an intruder alarm system, a digital signal generator, a brain for a robot, an automatic drafting machine, a signal analyzer and a host of other devices.[63] As an electronics kit aimed at hobbyists, the Altair was so open that users could even request the company MITS to mail them the full assembly details (including etching and drilling guides, component-placement diagrams and other information).[64]

The Homebrew Computer Club

The hackable or "generative"[65] nature of the Altair was not confined to its technical aspects but it extended to the many techno-social fields that it engendered and fostered. The Altair is credited for spurring the formation of "personal computer conferences, clubs, stores, users' groups, software exchanges and company newsletters".[66] These social events, activities and gatherings that centered on computers were meant to encourage technical innovation, knowledge sharing and community building. Software exchanges, for instance, were events announced in computer magazines where hobbyists came together to meet other kindred spirits and share programs that they or other people had written.[67] Like the original MIT hackers, the free sharing of information, technical know-how and programs was part of the culture of computer hobbyists.[68]

Cooperation and sharing were the main thrusts of the most well-known computer club in the 1970s – the Bay Area Amateur Computer Users Group (better known as the Homebrew Computer Club).[69] Fred Moore, an activist, and Gordon French, an engineer, conceived the Homebrew Computer Club as a venue where people interested in computers could come together to teach and learn from each other.[70] As the flyer calling for the first meeting stated, the Homebrew Computer Club was "a gathering of people with like-minded interests. Exchange information, swap ideas, help work on a project, whatever".[71] It is interesting to note that the first meeting of the club on Wednesday, 5 March 1975, was held in a garage and the main item on the agenda was a working Altair that was on loan from MITS to the People's Computer Company, an organization that introduced children to computing and programming and hosted weekly Wednesday evening potlucks for computer aficionados.[72] Pursuant to an egalitarian, anti-establishment and countercultural ethos, the Homebrew Computer Club "had no membership requirements, asked no minimum dues . . ., and had no election of officers".[73] Its fortnightly meetings were subsequently held in various places including high-tech hubs like the Stanford Artificial Intelligence Lab (SAIL) and the auditorium of the Stanford Linear Accelerator (SLAC).

Hobbyist gatherings and garages were the main spaces and sites where hacking in the truest sense of the word took place: they *explored* and *learned* about computers by designing and *creating* one themselves; they had no qualms about *breaking* or being in breach of someone's copyright if this meant getting access to important knowledge and technology and *sharing* it with others; but, like the early MIT hackers, they were more concerned with making computers free and open rather than keeping them *secure*.[74] During club meetings, members would have a chance to tell the whole group what they were working on, people could also socialize and speak with others individually, and there were scheduled talks, demonstrations and new product announcements.[75] They were not

fond of secrecy and they openly disclosed rumors and secrets about new technological developments (including a chip containing Atari's soon to be launched
videogame *Pong*).[76] They unstintingly gave away tips and advice to others, and
showed off the computers, boards and devices that they created in their homes
and garages.[77] Part of the dynamic in these gatherings was the notion of building
on the work of others and sharing it back with the community.[78] The social norm
was that everyone helped each other for free.[79] According to Levy, some members
"used the club as a source of ideas and early orders, and for the beta-testing of
prototypes. Whenever a product was done you would bring it to the club and get
the most expert criticism available".[80] Like MITS's approach to the Altair, hobbyists were likewise expected to "distribute the technical specifications and the
schematics [of their creations] – if it involved software, you would disclose the
source. Everyone could learn from it, and improve on it if they care to and were
good enough".[81]

The free and open exchange of information was truly at the heart of these
gatherings; computer hobbyists believed that "[l]ike the unfettered flow of bits
in an elegantly designed computer, information should pass freely among the
participants in Homebrew".[82] For the Homebrew Computer Club, "the free
sharing of information was not just an aspect of it but the essential reason for its
existence".[83] It may be said that the great fascination with early microcomput-
ers is rooted in the fact that hobbyists perceived the general-purpose computer
as being both the manifestation of and the means to achieve their egalitarian,
democratic and countercultural ideals and aspirations of the late 1960s and early
1970s.[84] It was both a tool and a product of hacking. Levy explains the philosophy of computer hobbyists:

> They were hackers. They were curious about systems as the MIT hackers
> were, but, lacking daily access to the PDP-6s, they had to build their own
> systems. What would come out of these systems was not as important as the
> act of understanding, exploring, and changing the systems themselves – the
> act of creation, the benevolent exercise of power in the logical, unambiguous
> world of computers, where truth, openness, and democracy existed in a form
> purer than one could find anywhere else.[85]

The Apple II

In hindsight, it seems inevitable that the "most important computer in history"
would have its genesis in the Homebrew Computer Club's open, innovative and
collaborative milieu.[86] The Apple II, which was launched at the First Annual West
Coast Computer Faire in 1977, is considered the first commercially successful,
mass-market microcomputer.[87] Part of its success may be attributed to the fact that
it was a low-cost consumer product aimed at ordinary users rather than a kit targeted to hobbyists.[88] The Apple II had a number of features and innovations that
made it a world-changing product. First, it came in a simple yet sleek beige plastic

case that had a built-in keyboard so it resembled a typewriter.[89] There was clearly an attempt to make it look and feel like a consumer device that had a place in everyone's home or office.[90] Second, a television or monitor could be conveniently placed on top of the case and attached to serve as the display.[91] The Apple II could show texts and graphics on the screen in different resolutions and in color.[92] Third, the computer language BASIC was built into the computer's read-only memory (ROM), which meant that users could start up the Apple II and work right away and create programs without having to install or run additional software.[93] Fourth, aside from the keyboard and monitor, it had a number of I/O options.[94] Users could add a floppy disk drive or cassette tape device to store data and programs, connect a joystick or two paddles to play computer games, and produce sounds using the integrated speaker.[95] Fifth, it came with eight peripheral slots that made it possible to add and further expand the computer's capabilities.[96] The expansion slots were designed pursuant to an open architecture that allowed other manufacturers to build compatible peripherals and accessories for the Apple II.[97] Unlike the Altair, the Apple II was not only hackable, but user-friendly as well.

The Apple II, which finally brought computing to the masses, confirmed the widely held belief of many hackers that "most problems could be solved if only people could get together, communicate, and share solutions".[98] According to Levy,

> It was the fertile atmosphere of Homebrew that guided Steve Wozniak through the incubation of the Apple II. The exchange of information, the access to esoteric technical hints, the swirling creative energy, and the chance to blow everybody's mind with a well-hacked design or program[99]

made it possible to create a computer that fundamentally changed society. The club was an ideal place for hardware hackers like Wozniak because they could engage in creative experimenting with electronics as well as a bit of socializing with other technically minded people.[100] Wozniak, who attended the very first meeting of Homebrew in Moore's garage, joined the club primarily because he wanted to learn more about computers and to build his own.[101] The creative, free-spirited and communal environment suited Wozniak since his main purpose for building a computer was not for any commercial or profit-making purpose but simply to have fun and show it to his friends – a hobby.[102] Like the original MIT hackers, together with the joy of doing and making things, it was peer recognition and being considered a great hacker that motivated him the most.[103] Wozniak thrived within the "gift economy" or "gift culture" of Homebrew where everyone is expected to "[b]ring back more than you take".[104] As he received suggestions from other members on how to improve the computer he was developing, he freely shared the schematics of the board and monitor he created and gave away the source code of his programs.[105] As Sather explains,

> Wozniak was not a lone talent working in solitude at his cerebral pastime. He was a member of the Homebrew Computer Club, the club to end all clubs,

from whose membership rolls have come several microcomputer industry leaders. His friends were very interested in Steve's Apple and made substantial contributions to the Apple.[106]

Like other inventions, the Apple II was in truth not the creation of a single person (although Steve Wozniak's technical genius was an essential element) but it was a result of many people building on the work of others and various innovations coming together or developing on top of each other.[107] The Apple II was the product of Wozniak's inventiveness as well as the culture of openness, sharing and collaboration that was hardwired into the Homebrew Computer Club.

Blue boxes and paper tapes

In general, the interactions and dealings of computer hobbyists with the law in the 1970s were few and far between. Like the dominant technology companies at the time that made mainframe computers and calculators, the authorities considered the activities and creations of computer hobbyists as trivial or innocuous and not worth their serious attention.[108] However, there were two cases that would portend the escalating conflicts between hacking and law.

The first incident involved "phone phreaking", which is defined as the "art and science of cracking the phone network (so as, for example, to make free long-distance calls)".[109] The phone phreaker subculture was based on a simple but powerful hack. They discovered, among other things, that "the whistle that came in the Cap'n Crunch cereal box was tuned to the precise [2,600] frequency that enabled it to control the long-distance calling switches of the AT&T telephone network".[110] Phreakers could simply whistle into a telephone and then have the ability to make calls to anywhere in the world free of charge.[111] When the exploits of the phone phreakers, particularly Captain Crunch (who was John Draper, a member of the Homebrew Computer Club), gained public attention after an article about them appeared in *Esquire* magazine, Captain Crunch became the target of both hackers and law enforcement.[112] Hackers were interested in learning from him how phone phreaking worked, while the telephone companies wanted him stopped or apprehended. Steve Wozniak and Steve Jobs were able to find out who Captain Crunch was and he taught them "the art of building their own blue boxes, devices that were capable of gaining free – and illegal – access to the phone network".[113] Before they started the company Apple, Wozniak and Jobs "built their own [blue boxes], and not only used them to make free calls but at one point sold them door-to-door at the Berkeley dorms".[114] There was even an incident where the pair was caught red-handed with a blue box but they were able to convince the police that it was an electronic music synthesizer.[115] Captain Crunch was not so lucky. He was arrested, convicted and served time for phone fraud a number of times.[116] However, despite his arrest and conviction, he continued to share his knowledge of the secrets of phone phreaking because "he was unable to resist when people asked; the hacker in his blood just let the information flow".[117]

The case of phone phreaking is indicative of the deep-seated and uneasy tension between the need of hackers to explore, learn about technologies and make a change in the world and the desire of commercial interests and the authorities to keep their systems safe, protected and under their control. It is worth emphasizing that the motivation of most phone phreakers, including Captain Crunch, was to freely explore and learn how the worldwide telecommunications network worked rather than to make phone calls and not pay for them.[118] According to *The New Hacker's Dictionary*: "At one time phreaking was a semi-respectable activity among hackers; there was a gentleman's agreement that phreaking as an intellectual game and a form of exploration was OK, but serious theft of services was taboo".[119] Sterling recounts that "in the early days of phreaking, blue-boxing was scarcely perceived as 'theft', but rather as a fun (if sneaky) way to use excess phone capacity harmlessly".[120] Phone phreaking was about free as in freedom, not free calls.[121] Captain Crunch explains his fascination with phreaking:

> I do it for one reason and one reason only. I'm learning about a system. The phone company is a System. A computer is a System. . . . If I do what I do, it is only to explore a System. Computers. Systems. . . . The phone company is nothing but a computer.[122]

Levy similarly recounts how another member of Homebrew "would use the box [which Wozniak and Captain Crunch helped him make] only for connecting to the computer – a practice which in the hacker mind justifies lawbreaking – and not for personal gain in trivial matters like calling distant relatives".[123] When one considers that a significant number of the top phone phreakers in the 1970s were visually impaired, freedom to connect and access were their primary objectives and not to steal services or defraud phone companies.[124] For people who are highly dependent on telephones to keep in touch with and reach out to the outside world, long-distance phone charges were a significant barrier to accessibility.[125] Of course, phone phreaking was considered a form of telecommunications fraud under the law and phone companies lost revenues due to this activity.

The second incident concerned intellectual property rights and the "theft" of software. Like the MIT hackers who originally had their "paper tapes in a drawer, a collective program library where you'd have people use and improve your programs", many computer hobbyists freely shared the software they and others wrote.[126] The rationale was "computers belonged not to individuals but to the world of users".[127] The free sharing, copying, modification, access to and use of software were an integral part of the hobbyist culture. However, people like Bill Gates saw the potential of computers to create great economic and social value as part of a commercial enterprise.[128] After learning about the Altair, Bill Gates famously left Harvard to start with his friend Paul Allen a software company then called Micro-Soft in Albuquerque, New Mexico near the MITS factory.[129] Gates and Allen wrote a version of the BASIC computer language to run on the Altair (Altair BASIC), which was sold by MITS.[130] During an Altair traveling exhibition in a hotel in Palo Alto, California, some Homebrew Computer Club members spotted an Altair running an unreleased version of Altair BASIC (which was stored on paper tapes).[131] Someone decided to "borrow" a paper tape and asked another Homebrew member, Dan Sokol, to make copies.[132] At the next Homebrew meeting, Sokol brought over seventy copies and shared them for free with club members.[133] True to the collectivist spirit of hobbyists, "The only stipulation was that if you took a tape, you should make copies and come to the next meeting with *two* tapes. And give them away".[134] Hobbyists believed they were not stealing information as much as they were liberating it.[135] There were a number of reasons hobbyists used to justify their possession of "pirated" copies of Altair BASIC (MITS was greedy and the price of the software was too high, they had already pre-ordered and paid for the product from MITS anyway, etc.), but many agreed "it seemed *right* to copy".[136] In the mind of the computer hobbyists, "Why should there be a barrier of ownership standing between a hacker and a tool to explore, improve, and build systems?"[137]

When copies of Altair BASIC began to circulate in Homebrew and other computer clubs around the country, Gates and Allen were incensed since they only received royalties from MITS when a copy of the program was sold.[138] Gates wrote an "Open Letter to Hobbyists" which was published in a number of publications and newsletters including the Homebrew Computer Club's.[139] In his letter, Gates accused computer hobbyists of being thieves because most of them used software that they did not pay for or lawfully acquire ("As the majority of hobbyists must be aware, most of you steal your software" and "Most directly, the thing you do is theft").[140] He pointed out the incongruity of the fact that "Hardware must be paid for, but software is something to share. Who cares if the people who worked on it get paid?"[141] Interestingly, Gates argued against the ability of the cooperation and sharing model to produce useful innovation:

> One thing you do do is prevent good software from being written. Who can afford to do professional work for nothing? What hobbyist can put 3-man years into programming, finding all bugs, documenting his product and distribute for free?[142]

The law was never brought in to resolve the matter despite the fact that copyright protection over computer programs was recognized under the amendments to the US Copyright Act of 1976.[143] Gates's letter, however, produced ill feelings among computer hobbyists and, more importantly, this "software flap" and the success of the Apple II signaled a turning point in the culture and outlook of the community.[144]

Free and open versus proprietary and closed

As computer technologies and the computer market began to mature, hobbyists gradually realized that they could make real money from and exert ownership over their innovations.[145] Levy recounts how "the pioneers of Homebrew . . .

switched from building computers to *manufacturing* computers. . . . It retarded Homebrew's time-honored practice of sharing all techniques, of refusing to recognize secrets, and of keeping information going in an unencumbered flow".[146] Their focus had shifted from promoting freedoms that were essential for hacking to protecting (intellectual) property rights.

The split in the hobbyist community between hackers and entrepreneurs seems inevitable given the increasing commercial value of technologies and intellectual property and the widening distribution and impact of computers.[147] A similar shift occurred with the computer hackers at MIT where commercialism and the assertion of exclusive intellectual property rights over their hardware and software creations virtually exorcised the hacker spirit from its hallowed halls.[148] As the first hacker generations created their own companies and sought to develop and protect their proprietary technologies, barriers to sharing and collaboration were erected.[149] As Levy recounts:

> But even if people in the company were speaking to each other, they could not talk about what mattered most – the magic they had discovered and forged inside the computer systems. The magic was now a trade secret, not for examination by competing firms. By working for companies, the members of the purist hacker society had discarded the key element in the Hacker Ethic: the free flow of information.[150]

The initial openness and then gradual closure of technology seem to be an enigmatic property of the history of information and communications technology as well as hacking.[151] As illustrated above, a host of legal, technical and social factors and conditions contributed to or facilitated this vacillation between the opening and eventual closing of hacker communities and their technologies. This peculiar nature of innovation may be partly explained by Stewart Brand's famous observation about the innate and paradoxical tendency of information to move in two opposite directions:

> *Information wants to be free* because it has become so cheap to distribute, copy, and recombine – too cheap to meter. *It wants to be expensive* because it can be immeasurably valuable to the recipient. That tension will not go away. It leads to endless wrenching debate about price, copyright, 'intellectual property', the moral rightness of casual distribution, because each round of new devices makes the tension worse, not better.[152]

The same dynamic has played out between and among hackers. Dyed-in-the-wool, purist hackers like Wozniak aimed to make a difference with and through technology and shared their creations freely, whereas Gates and entrepreneurial hobbyists desired to change the world by commercializing their innovations, building companies and transforming entire industries.[153] This push-and-pull between the *free and open* versus the *proprietary and closed* philosophies to developing and distributing technologies split apart the early generations of hackers and continues to divide hacker culture today.[154] For better or worse, both open and closed models profoundly shaped the face of computing and helped diffuse the technologies, norms and values of hackers to the world at large through the next generations of hackers.

The PC revolution, which began in the late 1970s, brought computing out of laboratories and corporate computer rooms and into more people's hands, homes and workspaces.[155] It comes as no surprise that the widespread distribution and use of computers gave rise to two influential types of hackers in 1980s – underground hackers and free and open source software (FOSS) developers.

Of personal computers, modems and bedrooms – underground hackers

Bulletin Board Systems

A modern, general-purpose PC,[156] together with a modem and a telephone line, would open the doors for and become the tools of choice of a new generation of hackers. Underground hackers were not only keen on understanding the inner workings of their PCs but they used these technologies to connect with other people, computers and networks. In the United States, these mostly white, male teenagers and university students from middle-class backgrounds sought to establish their own unique identity and community and explore the vast electronic world of computer systems and telecommunications networks without interference from any authority or the expectations and rules of society.[157] Technological developments afforded them the ability to pursue these goals without having to physically leave the comfort of their homes and bedrooms.[158]

The electronic Bulletin Board System (BBS) was at the heart of the underground hacker community.[159] BBSes (or simply boards) were "the life-blood of the digital underground" and figured prominently in the many clashes between underground hackers and the law.[160] A BBS is defined in *The New Hacker's Dictionary* as "a message database where people can log in and leave broadcast messages for others grouped (typically) into topic groups".[161] Sterling explains how a BBS works:

> A "bulletin board system" can be formally defined as a computer which serves as an information and message-passing center for users dialing-up over the phone-lines through the use of modems. A "modem," or modulator-demodulator, is a device which translates the digital impulses of computers into audible analog telephone signals, and vice versa. Modems connect computers to phones and thus to each other.[162]

BBSes acted "as an electronic message center, and as a software library".[163] In essence, a BBS was a medium for sending and receiving messages and for storing and exchanging information, programs and other data between people and computers located in different parts of the country and even all over the world.[164] During the 1980s, there were three basic types of BBSes: private computer boards that were used internally by private entities; commercial boards run by companies that the general public could access for a fee; and free boards that did not charge for access and were run by systems operators (sysops) as a hobby out of their homes.[165] The BBS could be considered a forerunner of online discussion forums, chat rooms and social networking sites.[166]

Boards had particular attributes that made them appropriate domains of and instruments for the activities and communications of underground hackers, who, by and large, espoused libertarian and anti-establishment sentiments.[167] A BBS could be considered a prime example of "democratized technology"[168] since the barriers to entry were low and "anybody with a computer, modem, software and a phone-line can start a board".[169] A basic board was relatively simple and inexpensive to get up and running.[170] According to Beall, "The entire cost of the initial set-up can be as little as $2,000".[171] Furthermore, under US telecommunications law, BBSes were considered "enhanced services" and thus not subject to regulation or supervision by the US Federal Communications Commission (FCC) and other governmental bodies.[172] Despite their virtual character, another important feature of boards was the breadth and extent of their territorial influence.[173] BBSes could reach a national and even global audience since "[b]oards can be contacted from anywhere in the global telephone network, at NO COST to the person running the board – the caller pays the phone bills, and if the caller is local, the call is free".[174] BBSes were also extremely user-friendly. To access a board, users simply used their computers and modems to call the telephone number of a specific BBS and, once connected, log in using their usernames and passwords.[175]

BBSes were effectively a marketplace of ideas since the tens of thousands of boards that were created covered all conceivable topics and subject areas from pedestrian to fringe interests.[176] The free and open exchange of ideas and information was bolstered by the fact that boards "[offered] instant, multiple, interactive communications"[177] and supported anonymous and pseudonymous speech (users could employ made up usernames instead of their real names).[178] Of course, since sysops were themselves technically inclined, a majority of boards were about computers, phones, networks, hardware, software and services.[179]

The digital underground

The computer hackers and phone phreakers who made up the digital underground reveled in and thrived under the virtually limitless freedom and liberty offered by boards, especially the underground or hacker boards that they constructed for themselves.[180] They built communities and spread the hacker culture not just "in there" (in the computer) but, more importantly, "out there" in the growing networks of linked computers and telephone connections. What primarily distinguished underground boards from normal BBSes was the high degree of secrecy and pseudo-anonymity of and among users and their involvement with what the law and society would consider restricted, illicit or off limit topics, content and activities.[181] Underground hacker groups in the United States went by catchy, provoking or exaggerated names such as "Cult of the Dead Cow", "Phreaks and Hackers of America" and "Legion of Doom".[182] They also deliberately used intriguing pseudonyms (handles) and, tongue-in-cheek, portrayed themselves to the outside world as "punks, gangs, delinquents, mafias, pirates, bandits and racketeers".[183]

In and through boards, underground hackers "mainly and habitually communicated with each other in a disembodied, text-based environment about fast-changing technologies".[184] They communicated about topics that interested them the most – "hardware, software, sex, science fiction, current events, politics, movies, personal gossip".[185] Using the BBS's function as a software library, they created and shared what they considered exciting "forbidden knowledge" that needed to be openly accessed by everyone and distributed as widely as possible, such as copies of electronic underground magazines like *Phrack* and "philes", which were "pre-composed texts which teach the techniques and ethos of the underground" like "do-it-yourself manuals about computer intrusion".[186] Underground BBSes also contained software and computer games (whether legitimately owned or the pirated, cracked variety),[187] copies of manuals, books and other printed materials,[188] long-distance access codes and telephone credit card numbers,[189] and other kinds of computer intrusion information.[190] They engaged in various forms of hacking: they *explored* and *learned* about the intricacies of computer and telecommunications networks and did not hesitate to *break* any security measures that were in their way; they kept themselves *secure* by using techniques that concealed their identities and activities; and they discovered and *created* new technical hacks and exploits and *shared* them with others on BBSes. Underground hackers did not see their activities as "deviant behavior, but instead, the symbolic expression of their hostility to all large bureaucratic organizations that control informational or communications resources".[191]

Like the early computer hackers and computer hobbyists, underground hackers were generally not interested in stealing information or causing damage to technical systems.[192] According to sociological research, "hackers have diverse motivations" and they were generally "driven by more benign motivations such as curiosity, feelings of power, and the camaraderie of belonging to a community".[193] One of their primary motivations was to build a reputation for technological wizardry among peers and the wider underground community.[194] Because of this, "[t]he main reason that hackers do not intentionally damage networks or commit fraud is a type of communal boundary formation. Hackers do not see themselves as criminals and enforce a code of conduct that functions as a form of self-regulation".[195]

However, hackers are not irreproachable and some form of personal or pecuniary benefit can be derived from hacking. As Sterling points out,

> a big reputation in the digital underground did not coincide with one's willingness to commit "crimes". Instead reputation was based on cleverness and technical mastery. As a result, it often seemed that the HEAVIER the hackers were, the LESS likely they were to have committed any kind of common, easily prosecutable crime. *There were some hackers who could really steal. And there were hackers who could really hack. But the two groups didn't seem to overlap much, if at all.*
>
> *The best hackers, the most powerful and technically accomplished, were not professional fraudsters. They raided computers habitually, but wouldn't alter anything, or damage anything.*[196]

The principal aims of hacking were to freely explore and learn about computers and networks and to ensure that technologies remained free and open to all and independent from outside authority, control or interference.[197] It was not about financial gain but freedom of access.[198] For underground hackers, "computers and telephones [were] potent symbols of organized authority and the technocratic business elite".[199] They believed that "[s]ince access to information is power . . . control over the computer is yet another example of corporate and government oppression of the masses".[200] For example, the overriding reason why underground hackers dealt in long-distance phone codes was because dialing to a BBS outside of their local area would mean incurring very prohibitive long-distance charges on the part of teenage and twenty-something hackers.[201] By and large, underground hackers exhibited the key characteristics of: "[seeking] access to forbidden knowledge . . . fast turnover of members; small numbers but strongly interconnected communication; peer education; low-level and limited forms of formal organization; and a desire for exploration".[202] Furthermore, they were obsessive about and placed a high value on technology, secrecy, anonymity and confrontation with authority.[203]

Unlike their hands-off approach to the early hacker generations, the authorities did not turn a blind eye to the happenings in the digital underground.[204] Rather than tolerating the activities of underground hackers, beginning in the 1980s, governments around the world enacted computer crime laws that prohibited many forms of hacking and intensified law enforcement activities against these acts.[205] Some argue that the "timing of criminalization corresponds more closely to the public availability of personal computers and telephone modems than to the introduction of computerized data processing or abuse".[206] It also took time for government actors to become fully aware of the legal and social impact of hacking and other technical developments. Nissenbaum goes much further and believes that the "changes in the popular conception of hacking have as much to do with changes in specific background conditions, changes in the meaning and status of the new digital media, and the powerful interests vested in them, as with hacking itself".[207] While the pseudo-menacing posturing of underground hackers and their feelings of invisibility and invincibility from authorities may have contributed to the public's negative view of hacking,[208] it was the "confluence of media attention, law enforcement and legislative reactions to that attention, and computer security vendors' attempts to capitalize on" the fears, concerns and risks associated with hacking that ultimately resulted in hacking becoming a serious target of law, and underground hackers being depicted in and by the media as "a new villain, the 'malicious hacker'".[209] These factors and conditions helped solidify the association of hacking to crime and deviance in the public's mind.[210] Skibell explains that hackers being branded as criminals

> was not imposed by any single entity, but rather was formed by a network of actors including hacker themselves. They were complicit . . . in their own branding as criminals, and in many ways helped create the public personae that the industry thrived on and used to justify their own expertise.[211]

The first hacker generations were dismayed that "the word hacker had acquired a specific and negative connotation" and "quickly became synonymous with 'digital trespasser'".[212] Other types of hackers "deeply resent[ed] the attack on their values implicit in using the word 'hacker' as a synonym for computer-criminal".[213] Even if other hackers preferred to distance themselves from the activities of and the negative publicity surrounding underground hackers, these "kids" not only called themselves "hackers" but they also drew from and considered themselves a part of hacker culture.[214]

Of free and open source software, licenses and movements – FOSS developers

Free software

The enactment of computer crime laws and the stronger protection and enforcement of intellectual property rights from the 1980s onwards signaled the law's formal and definitive entry into the world of hacking and computers.[215] While computer crime laws were being used to prosecute members of the digital underground, commercial interests and the heightened concern for intellectual property rights were driving out the hacker ethic from the souls of computer hackers.[216] Even the hacker paradise at MIT was not spared. By the early 1980s, most of the original MIT hackers had either started or joined businesses or commercial enterprises whose primary objective was to exploit computer technologies and innovations for profit.[217]

Hoping to preserve the freedoms of users and the openness of computers, Richard Stallman, who had been a hacker at the MIT Artificial Intelligence Laboratory since 1971, decided that creating a completely free computer operating system that was faithful to hacker values would help rebuild the "software-sharing community" of hackers.[218] Developing a free operating system was essential because it is

> the basis for everything else that will happen in the machine. And creating one is the ultimate challenge. When you create an operating system, you're creating the world in which all the programs running the computer live – basically, you're making up the rules of what's acceptable and can be done and what can't be done. Every program does that, but the operating system is the most basic. It's like creating the constitution of the land that you're creating, and all the other programs running on the computer are just common laws.[219]

In creating an operating system, Stallman was animated by the belief that society could be changed for the better through the simple writing of software code.[220] For technical and practical reasons (e.g., flexibility, portability and ubiquity), Stallman chose to build an operating system that was compatible with Unix, an operating system that was developed by Dennis Ritchie and Ken Thompson at Bell Labs in 1969.[221] Unix was originally free for third parties to use and modify but it was closed and commercialized in the 1980s by the company that owned the intellectual property rights to the operating system.[222] Stallman called the project GNU, which "following a hacker tradition" was "a recursive acronym for 'GNU's Not Unix'".[223] As Stallman envisioned it, the GNU Project would produce a full operating system that included "command processors, assemblers, compilers, interpreters, debuggers, text editors, mailers and much more".[224] After announcing his plan for a "new UNIX implementation" on Usenet newsgroup in September 1983, Stallman resigned from MIT in January 1984 to devote himself to the development and advocacy of "free software".[225] In this way, the "last of the true hackers" had finally stepped out of "the ivory towers of academia [and] the blue-sky institutions of research"[226] and sought to bring hacker culture and values in the form of free software to the wider world of ordinary computer users.[227] Furthermore, unlike the early computer hackers and computer hobbyists, Stallman's approach to free software and hacking was markedly political and ideological.[228]

To be considered free software, users of a computer program must possess all of the "four essential freedoms":[229]

- The freedom to run the program, for any purpose (freedom 0).
- The freedom to study how the program works, and change it so it does your computing as you wish (freedom 1). Access to the source code is a precondition for this.
- The freedom to redistribute copies so you can help your neighbor (freedom 2).
- The freedom to distribute copies of your modified versions to others (freedom 3). By doing this you can give the whole community a chance to benefit from your changes. Access to the source code is a precondition for this.[230]

According to Stallman, the "free" in free software "is a matter of liberty, not price" and should be conceived of as "'free' as in 'free speech,' not as in 'free beer'".[231] Free software was the binary opposite of "proprietary software", which was "any program that carried private copyright or end-user license that restricted copying and modification".[232] The GNU Project was, therefore, both a means and an end to *free* software and to reestablish the values of community and cooperation among hackers.[233]

The idea and ideology of free software did not catch on right away.[234] Stallman encountered a number of technical, legal and resource-related difficulties during the early years of the GNU Project especially in the development of a GNU compiler and a GNU version of Emacs (GNU Emacs), a text editor.[235] These problems were expected given that Stallman faced a world where software development had undergone severe commercialization and legalization as manifested in proprietary software·and the legal regime that supported it.[236] At the time, the proprietary and closed mindset, which viewed computer programs as valuable assets protected under intellectual property laws and exploited and controlled commercially through restrictive software licenses, trade secrets and non-disclosure agreements, was decidedly dominant. It would take a truly great and inspired "hack" that brought to bear social, technical and legal knowledge and skills to transform the current state of affairs. Since hackers reside at the nexus of technology, society and, by the 1980s, law, they would be in a position to ignite and fan a revolution.

Copyleft

Stallman abhorred the idea of copyright or private ownership over software because it went against the culture of sharing and cooperation among hackers.[237] He considered this "a personal affront as well as a significant cultural threat" since he "fundamentally viewed the sharing of source code as the bedrock supporting the hacker practices of inquisitive tinkering and collaboration . . . the end of sharing amounted to the end of hacking".[238] Stallman particularly disliked copyright notices because it meant that, rather than working with and building on the work of others, a programmer was asserting his or her own individual authorship and sole authority over the program to the exclusion of others.[239] Williams explains that there were a number of arguments "that eventually softened Stallman's resistance to software copyright notices"[240] and copyright in general: first, copyright prevents computer programs from entering the public domain and thus precludes people from making derivatives of public domain works that are closed and proprietary;[241] second, a copyright notice may be seen as a form of attribution and recognition where, by publicly declaring that they are the authors, programmers expressly stake their reputation on their creations;[242] and, last and most importantly, a programmer can use the flexibility offered by the copyright bundle of rights and freedom of contract to creatively "give away certain rights in exchange for certain forms of behavior on the part of the user".[243]

In order to affirm and preserve important hacker norms and values as well as to preclude the mischief of GNU software becoming proprietary software,[244] Stallman, together with other free software developers who had formed the non-profit Free Software Foundation in 1985,[245] came up with a simple but paradigm-changing solution, which they called *copyleft*: "users would be free to modify [free software] just so long as they published their modifications. In addition, the resulting 'derivative' works would also have [to] carry the same [free software license]".[246] As Stallman explains,

> Copyleft uses copyright law, but flips it over to serve the opposite of its usual purpose. . . . The central idea of copyleft is that we give everyone permission to run the program, copy the program, modify the program, and distribute modified versions – but not permission to add restrictions of their own.[247]

GNU Emacs, the GNU Project's first software that was generally available to the public, was released in 1985 under the GNU Emacs General Public License, which contained copyleft license provisions.[248] The GNU Emacs software license explained:

> GNU Emacs is free . . . everyone is free to use it and free to redistribute it. . . . GNU Emacs is not in the public domain; it is copyrighted and there are restrictions on its distribution, but these restrictions are designed to permit everything that a good cooperating citizen would want to do.[249]

In parallel with their technical development work, Stallman and the Free Software Foundation continued to further develop and refine the concept of copyleft and the terms and conditions of free software licenses and, "by 1989, [they] had crafted a clear legal framework for free software" in the form of the GNU General Public License (the GPL).[250] The GPL was a more formal software license with its precise use of legal terminology and language, but, at its core, it still had the same radical copyleft licensing terms and provisions that guaranteed the four software freedoms.[251]

What makes the concept of copyleft and its implementation in the GPL so remarkable was that free software developers had to apply their combined knowledge and mastery of social norms, technical code and legal rules in an unusual and non-conformist way to produce an innovative and surprising result – that is, to make software free and open through the creative use of the very same rules of normally restrictive copyright law, and preserve vital rights and freedoms under legally binding and enforceable contracts.[252] Copyleft was a great "hack" since it deftly exhibited the key elements of innovation, simplicity, mastery and non-conformity. Whereas copyright would ordinarily declare "all rights reserved", copyleft went the opposite direction and, in a subversive yet playful way, made "all rights reversed".[253] In describing the GPL as a hack, Coleman states:

> Stallman approached the law much like a hacker treats technology: as a system that by virtue of being systematic and logical, is hackable . . . he relied

on the hacker technical tactic of clever reuse to imaginatively hack the law by creating the GNU GPL, a near inversion of copyright law.[254]

But the GPL is more than a software license since it has been "commonly referred to as the 'Constitution' of free software".[255] In a way, it also serves as a code of ethics and a manifesto for and about hacker culture since it expresses and enacts hacker norms and values.[256] As Coleman explains,

> Many hackers and developers learned about the ethical and legal message of free software early in its history, via the GPL or the 'GNU Manifesto,' both of which circulated on Usenet message boards and often accompanied pieces of free software.[257]

What is astounding about the GPL was that "Stallman had done more than close up the escape hatch that permitted proprietary offshoots. He had expressed the hacker ethic in a manner understandable to both lawyer and hacker alike".[258] Copyleft as expressed in the GPL was a profound socio-techno-legal hack:[259]

> As hacks go, the GPL stands as one of Stallman's best. It created a system of communal ownership within the normally proprietary confines of copyright law . . . instead of viewing copyright law with suspicion, hackers should view it as yet another system begging to be hacked.[260]

While Stallman and the Free Software Foundation made considerable advances in the 1980s in developing and advocating free software, it was the creation of the Linux operating system that would ultimately give rise to a world-changing, global movement.[261]

Linux

The goal of the GNU Project to create a free Unix-compatible operating system became a reality, when in the early 1990s, Linus Torvalds, then a student in Finland, created a "kernel"[262] and integrated existing GNU tools and components into it to produce Linux, an operating system that was licensed as free software under the GPL.[263] Since Linux was developed to work on ubiquitous PC architecture, ordinary users could run an elegant and powerful operating system on their desktop computers.[264]

In addition to being "a fully functional operating system composed entirely of free software",[265] what made Linux especially amazing was that it was developed and maintained by Torvalds and an online community of thousands of volunteer programmers located in various parts of the world.[266] According to Raymond, "the most important feature of Linux . . . was not technological but sociological".[267] Through the use of mailing lists, File Transfer Protocol (FTP) servers and other internet-based technologies, Linux and other free software developers could work collaboratively regardless of the physical and temporal distances between them.[268] These online developer communities "do not tend to rely on any single one of the three bases of authority theorized by Weber (tradition, law, or charisma)", and are often self-organized, have limited bureaucracies, and whose governance processes are based on consensus and meritocracy.[269] As normally physically isolated hackers found kindred spirits online, they established and spread hacker culture across the global network of networks. According to Coleman, on the internet,

> free software grew into a much larger technical and social movement in which geeks all over the world participated in the day-to-day development of free software. . . . This brought hackers' long-standing ideals and practices for collaborating to unforeseen heights, and accidentally shifted where and how hacking could occur".[270]

The online, collaborative and distributed development process and organizational model popularized by Linux "represent[ed] a relatively new approach to the development of complex software systems. Software development techniques used in [FOSS] projects are informal and self-managed with decisions generally made by meritocracy".[271] Linux was the "world's largest collaborative project"[272] and "demonstrated the feasibility of a large-scale, online collaboration effort where developers and users can be one and the same".[273] Linux was a clear refutation of Gates's claim in his letter to computer hobbyists that the free sharing of software prevented complex and quality software from being written.[274] In fact the "speed, reliability and efficiency" of the Linux development model equaled if not surpassed those of large software companies that made of closed and proprietary software.[275] Coleman explains the impact that "this new era of networked hacking" that free software and the open internet engendered:

> Linux initiated a global network of associations composed of hackers who, over time, came to not only identify and alter the principles of freedom first enshrined by Stallman but also shift the material practice of collaborative hacking. The pragmatic and ethical hallmarks of hacking – innovation, creativity, collaboration, a commitment to openness, and imaginative problem-solving – that Stallman established as a bulwark against proprietization became the basis of long-distance free software development.[276]

These online software development communities performed many acts of hacking: they *created* computer programs and distributed them under copyright licenses that ensured that anyone was free to *learn*, *explore*, modify and *share* the underlying source code; they intentionally *broke* and subverted the legal regime of intellectual property rights to preserve and protect the freedom and openness of their creations; and they believed that the free and open model to software development produced programs that were more robust and *secure*. Hackers were not only making free software available to everyone, but they were gaining supporters and adherents on a massive and global scale both online and offline.[277]

FOSS and other movements

Recognizing the revolutionary potential of the online, community-based model to software development,[278] Linux and other free software were rebranded as "open source" beginning in the late 1990s.[279] The shift of the nomenclature from "free" to "open source" was intended to distance Linux from the allegedly ideological undertones of "free software" and make it more appealing to enterprises and businesses.[280] Open source sought to emphasize Linux's technical (rather than moral or ethical) advantages over software developed using the hierarchical, top-down "Cathedral" method.[281] The aim was to make choosing open source a pragmatic as opposed to a political decision.[282] While there is a long-running debate about the difference between "free" versus "open source" software,[283] since scholars consider the schism a theoretical rather than practical matter,[284] I collectively refer to computer programs *produced and licensed* pursuant to the hacker ideals of free sharing and open collaboration as "free and open source software" (or FOSS for short).[285] Aside from Linux, Apache (web server), MySQL (database), Python (programming language), WebKit (browser rendering engine), Drupal (content management system), and Android (mobile operating system) are some of the many examples of FOSS that are extremely popular among developers and users alike.[286] There are likewise many developers and commercial companies whose activities and businesses are built on FOSS and the FOSS development model. Technology companies such as IBM, Oracle, Apple and Google contribute to FOSS projects.

The triumph of FOSS and its accompanying techno-social movement is all the more extraordinary when one considers that FOSS emerged during a period when the scope and degree of protection and enforcement of intellectual property rights were possibly at their most severe.[287] As Coleman explains, FOSS prospered remarkably "during an era of such unprecedented transformations in intellectual property law that critics have described it in ominous terms like 'information feudalism'. Never before has a single legal regime of copyrights and patents reigned supreme across the globe."[288] FOSS fundamentally changed the principles and practices of the software industry despite the adoption of treaties such as the Trade-Related Aspects of Intellectual Property Rights (TRIPS) and the WIPO Internet Treaties.[289] Part of the reason why FOSS was impervious and invisible to law was because, through the use of copyleft licenses, FOSS developers were working within the legal order and according to the letter of the law (although FOSS was ultimately subverting the system by playing on the latter's internal inconsistencies, gaps and conflicts).[290] Another reason why FOSS flew under the radar was because most everyone, including legislators, law enforcement and software companies were either oblivious to FOSS or considered it trivial and inconsequential.[291] Of course, in the 2000s after FOSS had made great headway to become a formidable force in the technology sphere, the SCO Group filed a number of unsuccessful cases against prominent companies that used and developed Linux,[292] and, in addition to spreading fear, uncertainty and doubt about FOSS, the software giant Microsoft started to demand licensing fees from companies using Linux on the ground that the latter were infringing some of its patents.[293] So, despite their keen appreciation and expertise in the vagaries of copyright and other intellectual property laws, FOSS developers were not fully immune to the influence of law.[294]

On a deeper level, FOSS and the FOSS movement are socially and culturally significant because they helped spread the hacker mentality and ideals beyond software and hacking. Their underlying "open anything"[295] philosophy has inspired similar movements, causes and campaigns across wide-ranging, non-technical domains – from academic publishing to education initiatives and to new modes of governance.[296] Open Access,[297] Creative Commons,[298] Access to Knowledge,[299] Open Science,[300] Open Government,[301] and Open Data[302] are some of the noteworthy causes and initiatives that draw from or have been sparked by FOSS.

Of the world wide web of computers and communities – hacktivists

Hacklabs, hackmeets and hacker cons

In the same way that the wider use and development of the internet and the World Wide Web (the Web) in the 1990s provided a technological base that allowed online FOSS developer communities to flourish, global computing and communications networks, coupled with the cross-cutting forces associated with globalization, profoundly affected hackers in two main ways: their greater socialization and politicization; and the broader dissemination and use of hacking technologies by hackers and non-hackers alike for socio-political purposes, causes and campaigns.[303] The development and expansion of socio-technical networks of people and technologies paved the way for the cross-fertilization between hackers (specifically their values and tools) and other groups and subcultures such as activists, anarchists and artists.[304] The global network of networks had a noticeable impact on radical groups and alternative movements: "The Internet amplifies, accelerates, and, in some ways, transforms communication within a group's internal organization, but it also changes the relationship between one group or movement's network and those of its potential competitors or collaborators".[305] The internet brought about internal and external changes in social groups and movements that made them both inwardly and outwardly focused.[306]

Technical networks made it possible for hackers to form social connections with other groups. According to Taylor, the "use of the world wide web [w]as an integral part of new social movements" as "electronic culture facilitate[d] the emergence of global groups of like-minded radicals".[307] Hacktivism thus came about due to the interfacing and interactions between hacker culture and other activist and alternative traditions.[308] It is worth pointing out that the Electronic Frontier Foundation (EFF), a prominent US digital rights organization, was started in 1990 as a direct result of the legal crackdowns against underground hackers and the perceived need to protect people's digital and civil freedoms.[309] As such, in contrast to early hacker generations, the activities of hacktivists do not remain solely within the technical realm but draw upon and bring to bear a combination of hacker, activist or artistic beliefs and praxis. The Critical Art Ensemble (CAE) and the Electronic Disturbance Theatre (EDT), which were formed in the mid-1990s, are well-known examples of hybrid associations and activities that hacktivists take part in.[310] The CAE is noteworthy for being the group that issued a formal call "for the development of electronic civil disobedience and the politicization of hackers".[311] Fusing hacking, media and art as a form of "culture jamming", the CAE "brought to fore issues of access frequency regulation, popular education, editorial policies and mass creativity, all of which pointed in the direction of lowering the barriers of participation for cultural and technological production".[312] The EDT, for its part, famously utilized a computer program called Tactical FloodNet to disrupt government websites in support of the Zapatista uprising in Mexico.[313]

In addition to these hybrid groups and campaigns, the merging of hacker and alternative cultures manifested itself as well in physical spaces and social gatherings – hacklabs and other hacker events. According to Yuill, hacklabs are

> voluntarily run spaces providing free public access to computers and the internet. They generally make use of reclaimed and recycled machines running GNU/Linux and . . . most hacklabs run workshops in a range of topics from basic computer use and installing GNU/Linux software, to programming, electronics, and independent (or pirate) radio broadcast.[314]

While hacklabs closely resemble makers' hackerspaces and they are often used synonymously, they differ in a number of ways.[315] For one, they are based on distinct histories and ideologies.[316] Unlike hackerspaces, which are located in leased premises, hacklabs were situated in squatted buildings or part of community centers and media labs.[317] While hackerspaces can trace their lineage to the Chaos Computer Club and its clubroom and eventual headquarters,[318] hacklabs were part of the anarchist squats and autonomist social centers.[319] They therefore drew from the broader anarchist and autonomous movements and "grew out of the needs and aspirations of squatters and media activists".[320] They also had close connections with alter-globalization and other radical, transnational causes.[321] As such, hacklabs were not just workshops but social centers that "would provide space for initiatives that sought to establish an alternative to official institutions".[322] Hacklabs were places to learn about or work on "free software development, security and anonymity, electronic art and media production".[323]

In addition to hacklabs, hacktivists gathered with other alternative groups in various conferences, camps and events.[324] The greater impetus and value placed on socialization led to more "networking, collective meetings and sharing experiences" by hackers.[325] The Chaos Computer Club and the hacker magazines *Phrack* and *2600* have organized regular hacker "cons" (short for conferences) in Europe and the United States that bring together different types of hackers and activists.[326] Organized by Italian hacktivists, hackmeetings or hackmeets are "temporary gathering of hackers and hacktivists in which skills, tools and knowledge are exchanged and projects developed".[327] Hackmeets involved "sharing collective information and knowledge about everything that concerns technology, from the computer to the radio, to video, to artistic experimentation".[328] Outdoor hacker camps were popularized by hacktivists in the Netherlands.[329] Hacker events evince how hacking is intimately a "networking practice".[330] In these physical and temporal spaces, hacktivists, activists and artists come together to work on, among other things, art projects, free software and recycled hardware.[331] In this way, "physical and virtual spaces [are] enmeshed due to the activists' use of electronic media communications" to connect with various socio-technical networks.[332]

Taking to the streets and the information superhighways

Hacktivists engage in *overtly* "politically motivated hacking" and draw "upon the resources of the hacker community and hacker culture".[333] The emergence of hacktivists should come as no surprise since hacking is inherently a political act.[334] From the very beginning, hacking "has often been combined with broad social and political goals".[335] The values and behaviors of the original hackers at MIT had a strong anti-establishment streak and countercultural dimension. These non-conformist attitudes and approaches toward technology, law and authorities are similarly shared and carried out by the succeeding generations of hackers.[336] Hacking has a highly politicized and subversive nature since the "distinguishing feature of hacking resides in its ingenious reinterpretation and re-engineering of the systems that it confronts".[337] However, unlike the MIT hackers, hacktivists do not view computers and other technologies as ends in themselves, but as critical means to achieve certain higher goals for the benefit of others and society.[338] While freedom of access and the openness of technologies continue to be important concerns, hacktivists have transcended the primary concerns of previous hacker generations and engage with issues that go beyond purely technical matters and require social commitment and political action in the physical world.[339] Taylor notes, "traditional political militancy allied to a new level of technology savvy has resolved the within/without dilemma that hackers generally avoided".[340] In this sense, hacktivists share an affinity with underground hackers who also engaged in techno-social hacking.[341] While members of the digital underground primarily used their technical knowledge and skills, the motivation of hacking for them was to produce socio-political change and have an impact on society.[342] As with underground hackers, hacktivists seek to "blend the social and the technical" and this requires bringing their cause and taking action in both real and virtual spaces.[343]

Unlike other hacker types who are generally content with making an impact on the world exclusively through technology, hacktivists want to directly engage with and change the technological society itself whether through technical or non-technical means and action. For hacktivists, "hacking and making social changes" occur "simultaneously, one in and of the other".[344] They desire to go beyond "hacking's over-identification with its tools" and use "techniques which can blend both technical methods and political aims".[345] As Jordan explains, "The rise of hacktivism has not superseded or destroyed hacker politics, but has reconfigured it within a broader political landscape"; that is, from " 'information politics', traditionally the centre of hacker politics, [to] a broadening out into non-virtual politics".[346]

This expansion and outward orientation means that hacktivists fight for their causes with their keyboards and their feet, on the so-called information super-highways and in the streets.[347] For example, during the activist mobilizations against the World Trade Organization (WTO) meeting in Seattle in 1999, "there were simultaneous online and offline protests. As demonstrators occupied the streets, hacktivists occupied websites".[348] The hacktivist group Anonymous simi-larly combined online hacking (e.g., conducting distributed denial-of-service (DDoS) attacks to impair access to the websites and online services of target gov-ernment agencies and companies) with traditional forms of activism like holding public street protests and mass demonstrations.[349] When hackers Jon Johansen and Dmitry Sklyarov were arrested and charged for violating the US Digital Mil-lennium Copyright Act when they published information on how to circumvent copy protection mechanisms on DVDs and ebooks, many hackers mobilized, took to the streets and the Web, protested in new and creative ways (e.g., trans-forming the controversial circumvention code into a poem so it would be pro-tected under freedom of speech), and were successful in getting charges against Sklyarov dropped.[350]

Hacktivism is considered a genuinely new form of socio-political mobilization because it "tactically combines the cyberspatial web and physical world".[351] It involves many forms of hacking: hacktivists *break* or interrupt the functioning of computer systems as a form of protest and civil disobedience; they design and *create* technologies that protect and keep *secure* the identity of activists and dissidents; and they are very public about their campaigns and causes and they openly *share* their technical know-how and creations so everyone is free to *explore* and build on their technologies and *learn* from their experiences. The merging of online and offline action is uniquely suited for transforming a world that is dependent on and governed by technology.[352] As Taylor states, due to "the ever-more closely imbricated nature of the technological and the social, [hacking] promises more radical results if successfully carried out. Each technical act of reversal promises to contain a more politically charged and symbolic payload".[353] Despite the two fronts that hacktivists engage in, it is important to note that the line between the real and the virtual is not always clear and hacks can impinge on both domains. As Jordan explains, "First, many real-world institutions are affected by cyberspace. Computer networks control all sorts of real-world facilities. . . . Second, violence is not always physical, and damage to emotions and selves can occur in virtual lands".[354] In this way, hacktivists can change and reshape both tangible and intangible realities.

Of open technologies, projects and spaces – makers

Open innovation

Makers share many things in common with previous hacker generations, especially computer hobbyists and FOSS developers. Makers primarily hack pursuant to the hacker tradition of freedom and openness.[355] However, makers are interested in all kinds of technologies and not only those relating to computing and communications.[356] They aspire for open innovation, i.e., to open everything and create anything.[357] Makers are involved in diverse projects such as "free software development, computer recycling, wireless mesh networking, microelectronics, open hardware, 3D printing, machine workshops and cooking".[358] They engage in various forms of hacking: they are not worried about voiding warranties and they freely *break* and take apart electronic devices in order to *explore* the insides of these black boxes, *learn* how they work and make them perform in new, surprising and *creative* ways; and they are very open about their activities and they make available and *share* information about their projects online. Even though their attention has expanded and gone beyond computers, they still adhere to the "hands-on imperative" espoused by the original MIT hackers that the best way to learn and create is through actual doing.[359] Like the computer hobbyists, they are community-oriented and they are adept at working on both hardware and software projects.[360] Continuing the work of FOSS developers, makers are trying to ensure that hardware is as accessible and generative as FOSS by developing appropriate licenses under which their creations can be freely distributed to and used by the public.[361] Despite the difficulty of exactly transposing copyleft to the physical realm of hardware,[362] this has not prevented makers from creating and building open technologies and platforms. For makers, "*open source* means open everything: electronics, software, physical design, documentation, even the logo".[363]

The worldwide maker community has produced and given rise to many products, services, communities and organizations that promote the idea of open innovation for commercial and non-commercial purposes. The RepRap project is a popular, low-cost and open source 3D printer that was created and developed by an online community of makers.[364] Drawing from the FOSS movement, "all of the designs produced by the project are released under a free software license, the GNU General Public License".[365] The electronics of the RepRap 3D printer are built on Arduino,[366] which is "an open-source physical computing platform based on a simple microcontroller board, and a development environment for writing software for the board".[367] A microcontroller is "a single chip that contains the processor (the CPU), non-volatile memory for the program (ROM or flash), volatile memory for input and output (RAM), a clock and an I/O control unit".[368] It is literally "a computer on a chip" and its basic architecture closely resembles the main components of PCs such as the Altair and the Apple II.[369] The Arduino hardware, software and documentation are made publicly available through creative commons and other FOSS licenses.[370] For example, "all of the original design files (Eagle CAD) for the Arduino hardware" are released "under a Creative Commons Attribution Share-Alike license, which allows for both personal and commercial derivative works, as long as they credit Arduino and release their designs under the same license".[371] Many makers use Arduino microcontroller boards to act as the brains of their projects,[372] and, like RepRap, a worldwide community of developers and users contribute to and support Arduino.[373]

Makers believe in the importance of free sharing and open collaboration so most projects are made available and worked on together online.[374] Like FOSS developers, makers have made full and extensive use of the internet to connect, communicate and collaborate on projects.[375] Reminiscent of computer hobbyists, makers "show off" their creations in both physical and virtual spaces for peer recognition and to get feedback from the community.[376] There are indeed significant parallels between makers and computer hobbyists. In the same way that the PC started as a hobbyist project in the Homebrew Computer Club, makers are developing low-cost 3D printers and other disruptive technologies in hackerspaces.[377] Makers and people writing about the maker movement are convinced that low-cost 3D printers have the potential to be as world-changing as the PC was, and they will lead to a digital manufacturing revolution.[378]

Hackerspaces

In addition to the open technologies and innovative projects that they are building, makers are especially distinct from other hacker types with regard to where they hack – hackerspaces. Hackerspaces have their origins in Europe and the United States in the 1990s.[379] However, they only became a global phenomenon and an international movement in the late 2000s as a result of the cross-fertilization between European and US hackers during events organized by the Chaos Computer Club in Germany in 2007 on how to develop and run "community-operated physical places, where people can meet and work on their projects".[380] The tangible, visible and public nature of hackerspaces has proven to be very beneficial to makers since it has led to "community involvement" both internally within their groups and externally with the local communities they inhabit.[381] Hackerspaces are physical sites where makers can "come and have meetings, do good works, and show the community what they're really about . . . show people that hackers aren't criminals, that they're creative types who have a way of making technology do things [that were not expected or] it wasn't originally intended for".[382] This is in stark contrast to the secrecy and mystery surrounding the underground hackers. In hackerspaces, makers "could be perfectly open about their work, organize officially, gain recognition from government and respect from the public by living and applying the [h]acker ethic in their efforts".[383]

Hackerspaces are typically communally organized and run.[384] They "tend to be loosely organized, governed by consensus, and infused with an almost utopian spirit of cooperation and sharing".[385] In general, hackerspaces are designed and built according to a catalog of basic "design patterns", which were presented at the Chaos Communication Congress in Germany in 2007.[386] The design patterns were based on and inspired by existing or best practices of the German hacker-spaces c-base and the Chaos Computer Club Cologne (C4), and are still consid-ered "the best guiding theory behind the global [h]ackerspace [m]ovement".[387] The templates offer guidance on or solutions to the wide range of issues which members of hackspaces face from establishment to day-to-day operation.[388] There are design patterns on sustainability, infrastructure, communications, inte-rior design, membership and fees, meetings, recruitment, decision-making, and members' rights and responsibilities.[389] Membership rights normally include get-ting a key to the hackerspace, use of common equipment and tools, and having a space to work on and store their projects.[390] Following the design patterns, "[m]ost members pay dues to cover rent and expenses and share the obligation of administration, publicity, documentation, and other duties essential to keeping a space open and flourishing".[391] A portion of the fees can go toward the purchase of equipment and tools.[392] Like the Homebrew Computer Club, there is a strong communitarian spirit within hackerspaces; "[m]ost of the space – and the tools – are shared by all members, with small spaces set aside for each member to store items and projects for their own use".[393] Aside from computers and communica-tions equipment, hackerspaces are full of diverse tools such as "laser cutters, 3-D printers, miter saws and other woodworking tools, esoteric electronics like spec-trophotometers and tiny single-chip computers known as microcontrollers".[394] Online group communications are carried out on or through mailing lists, wikis and Internet Relay Chat (IRC) channels.[395]

What is interesting about the communities and sites that form the hackerspace movement is that while they are steeped in their locality, they have a global ori-entation and outlook. Tweney explains, "Hacker spaces aren't just growing up in isolation: They're forming networks and linking up with one another in a decentralized, worldwide network" primarily through the website hackerspaces. org, which "collects information about current and emerging hackerspaces, and provides information about creating and managing new spaces".[396] In fact, becoming part of the global hackerspace community "is essentially a matter of self-declaration – an entry on the hackerspaces.org wiki is sufficient".[397] Through their engagement with their local communities, other hackerspaces and the world at large, makers are applying the hacker values of collaboration and sharing not just to their technical activities but to their social relations as well. Makers' openness to the outside world distinguishes them from previous generations of hackers who mainly lived out the hacker ethic exclusively within their groups.[398]

Among makers, there is an appreciation of the importance of being open "to the outside world" because it

> helps ensure our collective success and sustainability, helps show the world
> what hacking is all about and helps feed and cultivate projects and activities
> going on locally and globally. . . . we're not just in it for ourselves we're in it
> for our neighbors and our world.[399]

There is a pronounced "welcoming attitude" with makers and hackerspaces.[400] Mitch Altman, who founded the Noisebridge hackerspace in San Francisco and was part of the group of hackers who set the hackerspace movement in motion, says, "That welcoming attitude is proving powerfully attractive to many geeks. I can go to any hacker space anywhere in the world and be welcome there".[401]

Because of the mushrooming in the late 2000s of many places and sites with various names that offer the public access to tools and equipment to build things onsite, it can be quite confusing to distinguish a hackerspace from a "makerspace", a "hackspace", a "hacklab", a "fab lab", or a "techshop".[402] There is even an ongoing discussion as to whether it is better to append the word "hacker" or "maker" to the name of the spaces where makers hang out. Those who prefer makerspace claim that the terms "make" and "maker" are more "open and inclusive",[403] whereas "hack" and "hacker" tend to be limited and exclusionary.[404] This is reminiscent of reasoning behind the shift from "free" to "open source" software where it was similarly argued that the latter term, which seemed less risky and radical, was more palatable to a broader audience. As with the debate between the labels "free" versus "open source" software, I view the debate between hackerspace and makerspace as mainly an ideological rather than a practical matter. In fact, plenty of makers refer to themselves as hackers, and they do not make any distinction between a hackerspace and a makerspace and they use the terms synonymously.[405] There is also concern among the maker community that only those spaces that are connected to or have an agreement with the company Maker Media, which publishes MAKE magazine and organizes Maker Faire, can officially use the term makerspaces.[406] This goes against the free and open mentality of makers.

I prefer to use the term hackerspace since it highlights the fact that these sites draw from and belong to hacker culture. While Cavalcanti prefers the term makerspaces, his description of the characteristics of hackerspaces supports my view that the term hackerspace has a closer connection to the history and culture of hacking:

> In my mind, hackerspaces largely focused on repurposing hardware, working
> on electronic components, and programming . . . hackerspaces also became
> associated in my mind with tendencies towards collectivism, and radical
> democratic process as method for making decisions – an inheritance from
> European hackerspaces and early American hackerspaces.[407]

Whether a communal workshop occupied by makers and other hackers is offi-cially called a makerspace, hacklab,[408] hackspace,[409] or some other name, it will be *considered a hackerspace if it is grounded in, draws from or considers itself a part of hacker culture.*

Distinguishing a hackerspace from a fab lab or TechShop is a simpler affair. Unlike hackerspaces which "are set up by hackers for hackers with the principal mission of supporting hacking", the main goal of fab labs and TechShops is to "foster innovation".[410] A fab lab is short for "fabrication laboratory"[411] and it is part of a "global network of local labs, enabling invention by providing access to tools for digital fabrication".[412] Neil Gerschenfeld established the first fab lab at the Center for Bits and Atoms at MIT in 2005.[413] As conceived by Gerschenfeld, a fab lab is a place where specific tools and equipment are available for anyone to use so they can "make almost anything".[414] In contrast to hackerspaces, which are formed by a community of makers, fab labs are run by more formal organiza-tions, but "there is no formal procedure in how to become a Fab Lab, the process is monitored by MIT, and MIT maintains a list of all Fab Labs worldwide".[415] Interestingly, fab labs share the same principles of openness and collaboration of the FOSS movement and hackerspaces; its charter "stipulates open access, establishes peer learning as a core feature and requires that designs and processes developed in fab labs must remain available for individual use".[416] Despite the organizational differences between hackerspaces and fab labs, it should be noted though that makers and other hackers also frequent fab labs and many fab labs are active in the maker scene. TechShops are commercial spaces that started in 2006. People can have access to machinist equipment and design tools such as milling machines and laser cutters by paying a membership fee.[417] While TechShops are open to people within a local area, they are set up and run by a for-profit com-pany. It is important to bear in mind though that, even if hackerspaces are distinct from fab labs and TechShops, the social spheres of makers are not circumscribed exclusively to hackerspaces, and many makers and hackers do frequent other places and sites including fab labs.

Makerbot

With the increasing public attention and growing commercial interest in makers and their projects, it was inevitable that the maker movement, too, like the com-puter hobbyists, would have an "Apple II moment". To the consternation of the maker community that once wholeheartedly supported it, MakerBot is aiming, in more ways than one, to be the Apple of the 3D printing revolution.[418] When it was founded in 2009, the MakerBot company was an open hardware start-up that produced and sold an open source, desktop 3D printer kit.[419] MakerBot had its origins in the New York hackerspace NYC Resistor: its founders Bre Pet-tis, Zach Smith and Adam Mayer met there, and the first prototype of the 3D printer (then called the CupCake CNC) was made in the hackerspace.[420] The MakerBot 3D printer was based and built on open technologies like RepRap and

Arduino.[421] Like the Altair, the first MakerBot 3D printer was sold as a hobbyist kit and the specifications and designs were open to anyone.[422] MakerBot was popular among makers because "[t]he machine's modularity and its open plans make it attractive to tinkerers who are turned off by hacker-unfriendly 'black box' technologies".[423] Because the MakerBot hardware was open, "[a]s owners of previous batches build and use their machines, they make suggestions and improvements to the design of the machine. These improvements are implemented in future batches, and made available to current users as an upgrade".[424] Aside from hardware, the software and community surrounding MakerBot embraced free sharing and collaboration.[425] The MakerBot community used free software and open standards such as Skeinforge, ReplicatorG, Art of Illusion, and Blender (the latter two are 3D design and modeling programs).[426] The Thingiverse website, which Pettis started in 2008, helped community members communicate, share and collaborate online.[427] Like FOSS developers, users on the Thingiverse website could share their 3D designs and other source files, have other users modify and improve the files, and make everything available to the public.[428]

The creators and founders of MakerBot were stalwarts in the maker community and championed openness.[429] Pettis was part of the group that jumpstarted the hackerspace movement in the United States,[430] and Zach Smith was a founding member of RepRap and designed its motherboard.[431] The MakerBot company and its eponymous 3D printer were the darlings and poster children of the maker movement because, like Linux, they were concrete proof that a company could openly share and make public all of its technical know-how and innovations and produce a great product at a reasonable price, while still being a viable business.[432] MakerBot was at the forefront of democratizing 3D printing.[433] True to the hacker spirit, Pettis once empathically stated:

> At MakerBot, we take open source seriously. It's a way of life for us. We share our design files when we release a project because we know that it's important for our users to know that a MakerBot is not a black box.[434]

He also said,

> With MakerBot, you get not only the machine that makes things for you, but you also get an education into how the machine works and you can truly own it and have access to all the designs that went into it.[435]

It thus came as a great surprise to the maker community when MakerBot did not release as open source the hardware designs and software code of its "Replicator 2" desktop 3D printer in 2012.[436] MakerBot's reversal of its community outlook and commercial and legal strategy (including how it protected, licensed and exploited its intellectual property and technical know-how) seriously affected the maker community, and it caused a great degree of divisiveness, outrage, heated debate, and soul searching among makers.[437] Co-founder Zach Smith, who was at the time no longer part of the MakerBot company, severely criticized MakerBot's closure and called it "the ultimate betrayal".[438] Community members felt that MakerBot had "lost touch with the way that open source is supposed to work, and the core principles that the company was built upon".[439] As with the PC, business reasons and commercial interests were behind MakerBot's shift from free and open to proprietary and closed.[440] MakerBot had received US$10 million in outside venture capital funding,[441] and the Replicator 2 was the company's serious attempt to market a consumer-friendly 3D printer for the mass market with no assembly required (as the Apple II was for PCs).[442]

Rather than sharing everything and being completely open, MakerBot would only "share as much as possible" and be "as open as possible and still have a business at the end of the day".[443] As a result of the changed outlook, MakerBot would "not share the way the physical machine is designed or our GUI" as it had done with the previous generations of the 3D printer.[444] Echoing Steve Jobs's defense of the merits of Apple's centrally controlled and curated model to developing technologies (versus the open yet chaotic approach of rivals),[445] Pettis states,

> We've transitioned to a company that makes a tool, the MakerBot Replicator 2, that has set a new standard in desktop 3D printing because *it just works*. . . . It's a paradox because all this makes the hardware *less hacker friendly, but more user friendly.*[446]

Exposed to the pressures and demands of running a business, openness was no longer seen by MakerBot as a clear advantage but rather a weakness.[447] Pettis says, "I don't plan on letting the vulnerabilities of being open hardware destroy what we've created".[448] Reminiscent of Bill Gates's letter to computer hobbyists, Pettis wrote in a blog post, "If this is how the community treats a company that has shared a lot, it will be harder for other businesses and projects to choose open source as a way of sharing their work".[449] Many makers felt betrayed when MakerBot turned its back on open source and the maker community.[450] As Giseburt explains,

> Makers don't like black-box trinkets. They want something that, if they want to open it up and learn how it works, they can. They can also . . . scratch their own itch and solve whatever problem they are having, furthering the technology for the entire community.[451]

Financially speaking, like Apple, MakerBot's decision to become less open and more commercial appears to have paid off. In 2013, Stratasys, a major industrial 3D printer manufacturer, acquired MakerBot for US$403 million.[452]

Despite the controversies and debates surrounding MakerBot's closure and the impact of military funding of hackerspaces in the United States,[453] makers continue to build and work hard to ensure that the community and their projects remain free and open to all. Thanks in large part to the success and experience of hackers with the FOSS movement, the current situation is much better when compared to the state of computing and hacking in the early 1980s. Unlike the MIT hackers and computer hobbyists, makers today have a wide range of open technologies, platforms and standards that are available and accessible to them such as RepRap, Arduino and Linux. There are also many thriving technology companies like Adafruit, SparkFun, GitHub and Ubuntu that choose to open everything or "open source (almost) everything".[454] So even if companies like MakerBot decide to make their succeeding products and services proprietary and closed, it will not affect the many makers who prefer to work with and build on truly open projects. Further, since a number of these maker projects are released under copyleft licenses like the GPL, the freedom and openness of the underlying technologies are protected and guaranteed by the one-two punch of legal rules and social norms.[455]

Makers and hacktivists in context

Viewed from the panorama of hacker history, hacker culture and the different types of hackers clearly have a strong influence and impact on both makers and hacktivists. Like the other hacker types, makers and hacktivists are extremely passionate about technology, desire to gain expertise and mastery over it, and wish to use technology in new, innovate and unexpected ways. There is also a decidedly rebellious and non-conformist streak that runs through all types of hackers. Makers in particular continue the hacker tradition and practice of creatively using technology. But unlike the early computer scientists and programmers, makers are not only interested in hacking computer hardware, software and systems but all forms of technology. Nothing is off limits to hacking, not even biology or their own bodies.[456] With computer hobbyists, makers share the same curiosity and enthusiasm to learn more about, create and develop technologies like 3D printers. They do so not just for their own satisfaction but in order to benefit other makers and the public. Makers hope to ignite their own version of the PC revolution but this time with 3D printers and other digital manufacturing tools. Like the computer hobbyists, makers see the importance of meeting in person, sharing and working with others on their projects. But makers have gone beyond the casual club meetings of computer hobbyists and they have set up their own hackerspaces where they can hang out and hack with others. As with the computer hobbyists, they also greatly value free and open access to and use of information and technologies. Carrying on the praxis and goals of FOSS developers, makers similarly seek to keep their technologies and projects free for others to use and re-use by releasing them under FOSS licenses. Of course, as with the early computer scientists and computer hobbyists, they too face conflicts and tensions within their community when some of their members seek to assert and enforce intellectual property rights exclusively for personal profit or commercial gain.

Hacktivists, on the other hand, also possess the same anti-establishment attitude and countercultural goals of early computer scientists and computer hobbyists. But they do not consider technology to be an end in itself but as a powerful means for socio-political ends. Hacktivists have an affinity with underground hackers who similarly used information systems to build their communities and also to cause disruption and change in the wider world. In the same way that BBSes were at the center of the activities and interactions of underground hackers, hacktivists primarily use the internet for coordinating and carrying out their campaigns. But while underground hackers sometimes carried out acts of rebellion for its own sake or against what they perceived to be faceless authorities or monolithic bureaucracies, hacktivists undertake acts of hacktivism for more pressing or serious causes such as supporting oppressed groups or campaigning for human rights. While all hacker types are community oriented and possess some degree of social awareness, hacktivists are the most politicized and socially active among them. Because hacktivists push the boundaries the most in order to produce socio-political change, they are more likely to run afoul of the law and be the subject of legal prosecution than other hackers. While they also enjoy messing around with technology, hacktivists always have larger goals in mind and they seek to combine the technical and social domains with virtual and physical action. Hacktivists also believe in the ideals of FOSS developers and the technologies and systems they use are almost exclusively open source.

The preceding narrative about different hacker types and periods is not only valuable in how it properly situates makers and hacktivists within hacker culture, but it also reveals the recurring and dialectical conflicts that concern hacking. Aside from the perennial conflict between *free and open versus proprietary and closed*, another discernable tension is the contrasting policies that the law and public authorities take in relation to hacking: proscribing and prosecuting hacking activities as opposed to tolerating and encouraging them (*restrict versus support*). A further issue area is the distinct attitudes and responses that hackers have to law and public authorities – i.e., whether hackers choose to conform to the existing legal order or to avoid or creatively subvert it as FOSS developers have done (*conformity versus non-conformity*). With regard to their social orientation and involvement, there is a clear divergence between hackers who wish to remain isolated within and solely focused on their internal domains, and those who are socially and outwardly oriented and desire to engage with and change the wider world (*individual autonomy versus community and social responsibility*). Together with the *breaking and making* dynamic that pervades hacker culture, these themes continually arise throughout hacker history and so too with makers and hacktivists. The above conflicts come into sharper focus when viewed from the perspective of hacker norms and values, which are the subject of the next chapter.

Notes

1 See Gary Fine, "Enacting norms" 141; see Anthony Giddens, *Sociology* 1115.
2 See Bruce Sterling, *The Hacker Crackdown* 50.
3 See Helen Nissenbaum, "Hackers and the contested ontology of cyberspace" 204.
4 Paul Taylor, "From hackers to hacktivists" 627.
5 See Sheila Jasanoff, "Beyond epistemology" 411.

6 Steven Levy, *Hackers* x; Eric Raymond, "A brief history of hackerdom" 4; Bruce Sterling, *The Hacker Crackdown* 50; Douglas Thomas, *Hacker Culture* ix; OHM 2013, "Hack".

7 Sam Williams, *Free as in Freedom* 175–176; Steven Levy, *Hackers* 10; Eric Raymond, "A brief history of hackerdom" 4.

8 Brian Alleyne, "We are all hackers now" 17.

9 Gabriella Coleman and Alex Golub, "Hacker practice" 256.

10 Gabriella Coleman and Alex Golub, "Hacker practice" 259.

11 Gabriella Coleman and Alex Golub, "Hacker practice" 261.

12 Gabriella Coleman and Alex Golub, "Hacker practice" 263 and 266.

13 Richard Hollinger, "Computer crime" 76.

14 Richard Hollinger, "Computer crime" 78.

15 Richard Hollinger, "Computer crime" 78.

16 Richard Hollinger, "Computer crime" 79.

17 Steven Levy, *Hackers* v–vi.

18 Paul Taylor, "From hackers to hacktivists" 628–629.

19 Eric Raymond, *The Cathedral and the Bazaar* 4.

20 See Steven Levy, *Hackers* 41.

21 Steven Levy, *Hackers* 5.

22 Steven Levy, *Hackers* 5; Bruce Sterling, *The Hacker Crackdown* 60.

23 Steven Levy, *Hackers* 5.

24 Steven Levy, *Hackers* 5; Eric Raymond, "A brief history of hackerdom" 4; Pekka Himanen, "A brief history of computer hackerism" 186.

25 "TX-0 Computer".

26 "MIT TX-0 Computer 1953"; see Steven Levy, *Hackers* 14–16.

27 Steven Levy, *Hackers* 15; see also Pekka Himanen, "A brief history of computer hackerism" 186.

28 Steven Levy, *Hackers* 15–16 and 23.

29 Steven Levy, *Hackers* 15–16 and 23.

30 Steven Levy, *Hackers* 15–16 and 30.

31 Steven Levy, *Hackers* 90, 98, 115; Helen Nissenbaum, "Hackers and the contested ontology of cyberspace" 198.

32 Eric Raymond, "A brief history of hackerdom" 7.

33 Bruce Sterling, *The Hacker Crackdown* 60.

34 See Bruce Sterling, *The Hacker Crackdown* 60; Joseph Olivenbaum, "Rethinking federal computer crime legislation" 579; Gabriella Coleman, *Coding Freedom* 64–64.

35 Steven Levy, *Hackers* 41; Eric Raymond, "A brief history of hackerdom" 4; Computer History Museum, "PDP-1 restoration project".

36 Larry Press, "Before the altair" 28; Eric Raymond, "A brief history of hackerdom" 4.

37 Computer History Museum, "PDP-1 restoration project"; see also George Michael, "The PDP-1".

38 Steven Levy, *Hackers* 43.

39 Steven Levy, *Hackers* 43.

40 Computer History Museum, "PDP-1 restoration project"; see also Pekka Himanen, "A brief history of computer hackerism" 186.

41 Steven Levy, *Hackers* 65, 122, 123 and 133; Eric Raymond, "A brief history of hackerdom" 5; Stewart Brand, "SPACEWAR: Fanatic life and symbolic death among the computer bums".

42 Sherry Turkle, *The Second Self* 196; but see Paul Taylor, "From hackers to hacktivists" 631–632 (who discusses the negative effects of the early hackers' total immersion into computers).

43 Steven Levy, *Hackers* 78; see also Sherry Turkle, *The Second Self* 191 and 204.
44 Robert Cringely, *Accidental Empires* 61.
45 Edward Roberts and William Yates, "Altair 8800 minicomputer, Part I" 34.
46 Edward Roberts and William Yates, "Altair 8800 minicomputer, Part I" 36.
47 Edward Roberts and William Yates, "Altair 8800 minicomputer, Part I" 37.
48 Edward Roberts and William Yates, "Altair 8800 minicomputer, Part I" 38.
49 Edward Roberts and William Yates, "Altair 8800 minicomputer, Part I" 38.
50 Robert Cringely, *Accidental Empires* 53.
51 Robert Cringely, *Accidental Empires* 53.
52 Steven Levy, *Hackers* 195.
53 See Tim Jordan, *Hacking* 136; see Ian Hutchby, "Technologies, texts and affordances".
54 Steven Levy, *Hackers* 195.
55 Steven Levy, *Hackers* 196.
56 Edward Roberts and William Yates, "Altair 8800 minicomputer, Part I" 34.
57 See John Markoff, *What the Dormouse Said* 277.
58 Steven Levy, *Hackers* 188.
59 See Nathan Rosenberg, "Technological change in the machine tool industry"; Steven Levy, *Hackers* 207.
60 See Edward Roberts and William Yates, "Altair 8800 minicomputer, Part I" 34; see Steven Levy, *Hackers* 201.
61 Edward Roberts and William Yates, "Altair 8800 minicomputer, Part I" 34 and 38; see also Cory Doctorow, "Lockdown: The coming war on general-purpose computing".
62 Edward Roberts and William Yates, "Altair 8800 minicomputer, Part I" 38.
63 Edward Roberts and William Yates, "Altair 8800 minicomputer, Part I" 38.
64 Edward Roberts and William Yates, "Altair 8800 minicomputer, Part I" 38.
65 See Jonathan Zittrain, *The Future of the Internet* 2–3.
66 Forrest Mims III, "The tenth anniversary of the altair 8800" 60.
67 See Christina Lindsay, "From the shadows" 38.
68 Steven Levy, *Hackers* 118 and 232 (who called them "hardware hackers"); Pekka Himanen, "A brief history of computer hackerism" 187.
69 Steven Levy, *Hackers* 202–203; see Pekka Himanen, "A brief history of computer hackerism" 187.
70 Steven Levy, *Hackers* 197–199.
71 John Markoff, *What the Dormouse Said* 275–276; see also Steven Levy, *Hackers* 199.
72 Steven Levy, *Hackers* 165, 171 and 201; John Markoff, *What the Dormouse Said* 266; Larry Press, "Before the altair" 29.
73 Steven Levy, *Hackers* 203; see also John Markoff, *What the Dormouse Said* xiii and xv; see also Pekka Himanen, "A brief history of computer hackerism" 188; see also Bruce Sterling, *The Hacker Crackdown* 57.
74 See Robert Pool, "A history of the personal computer" 94.
75 Steven Levy, *Hackers* 216; John Markoff, *What the Dormouse Said* 277.
76 Steven Levy, *Hackers* 218–219.
77 Steven Levy, *Hackers* 212, 214 and 216.
78 Steven Levy, *Hackers* 219 and 220.
79 Steven Levy, *Hackers* 220.
80 Steven Levy, *Hackers* 221.
81 Steven Levy, *Hackers* 221.
82 Steven Levy, *Hackers* 214 and 216; see also John Markoff, *What the Dormouse Said* xx.
83 John Markoff, *What the Dormouse Said* 282.

84 John Markoff, *What the Dormouse Said* xii.
85 Steven Levy, *Hackers* 191
86 Steven Levy, *Hackers* 259.
87 Robert Cringely, *Accidental Empires* 62; Steven Levy, *Hackers* 272.
88 Robert Cringely, *Accidental Empires* 62; Steven Levy, *Hackers* 265; Steve Wozniak "Foreword".
89 James Fielding Sather, *Understanding the Apple II* 1–7; Steven Levy, *Hackers* 266 and 270.
90 Steven Levy, *Hackers* 266.
91 James Fielding Sather, *Understanding the Apple II* 1–5 and 1–10.
92 James Fielding Sather, *Understanding the Apple II* 1–5.
93 James Fielding Sather, *Understanding the Apple II* 1–1.
94 James Fielding Sather, *Understanding the Apple II* 1–8; Robert Cringely, *Accidental Empires* 62.
95 James Fielding Sather, *Understanding the Apple II* 1–8 and 1–10.
96 James Fielding Sather, *Understanding the Apple II* 1–4 and 1–9.
97 Steven Levy, *Hackers* 266.
98 Steven Levy, *Hackers* 197.
99 Steven Levy, *Hackers* 259.
100 Steven Levy, *Hackers* 252.
101 Steven Levy, *Hackers* 252; John Markoff, *What the Dormouse Said* 276.
102 Steven Levy, *Hackers* 256; Steve Wozniak "Foreword"; Pekka Himanen, "A brief history of computer hackerism" 188.
103 Steven Levy, *Hackers* 264; Eric Raymond, "A brief history of hackerdom" 204.
104 John Markoff, *What the Dormouse Said* 281; see also Eric Raymond, "A brief history of hackerdom" 204.
105 Steven Levy, *Hackers* 257–258; Robert Pool, " A history of the personal computer" 92; Pekka Himanen, "A brief history of computer hackerism" 188.
106 James Fielding Sather, *Understanding the Apple II* H-1; see also John Markoff, *What the Dormouse Said* 282.
107 Steven Levy, *Hackers* 259; but see Robert Cringely, *Accidental Empires* 62.
108 See Steven Levy, *Hackers* 188 and 259; Pekka Himanen, "A brief history of computer hackerism" 187.
109 "Phreaking", in *The New Hacker's Dictionary*.
110 John Markoff, *What the Dormouse Said* 271; see also Steven Levy, *Hackers* 253.
111 Sherry Turkle, *The Second Self* 207; John Soma and others, "Legal analysis of electronic bulletin board activities" 573.
112 John Markoff, *What the Dormouse Said* 272; Steven Levy, *Hackers* 255.
113 John Markoff, *What the Dormouse Said* 272; see also Bruce Sterling, *The Hacker Crackdown* 54; see also Ken Lindup, "The cyberpunk age" 638 (for other kinds of boxes that phreakers made).
114 Steven Levy, *Hackers* 251; see also Bruce Sterling, *The Hacker Crackdown* 54.
115 Phil Lapsely, "The definitive story of Steve Wozniak, Steve Jobs, and phone phreaking".
116 John Markoff, *What the Dormouse Said* 272.
117 Steven Levy, *Hackers* 255–256; see also Bruce Sterling, *The Hacker Crackdown* 62.
118 Ron Rosenbaum, "Secrets of the little blue box" 120; but see Steven Levy, *Hackers* 251 (Steve Wozniak and Steve Jobs built and sold blue boxes for profit)
119 "Phreaking"; see also Bruce Sterling, *The Hacker Crackdown* 52; see also Reid Skibell, "Cybercrimes & misdemeanors" 937.
120 Bruce Sterling, *The Hacker Crackdown* 54.

121 See Free Software Foundation, "The free software definition" (the free and open source software movement defines "free" in the sense of " 'free' as in 'free speech,' not as in 'free beer' ").

122 Ron Rosenbaum, "Secrets of the little blue box" 120; see also Steven Levy, *Hackers* 254; see also Sherry Turkle, *The Second Self* 208; see also Bruce Sterling, *The Hacker Crackdown* 53.

123 Steven Levy, *Hackers* 256.

124 Ron Rosenbaum, "Secrets of the little blue box" 120; Phil Lapsley, *Exploding the Phone*.

125 Phil Lapsley, *Exploding the Phone*.

126 Steven Levy, *Hackers* 118.

127 Steven Levy, *Hackers* 118.

128 Steven Levy, *Hackers* 228.

129 John Markoff, *What the Dormouse Said* 284; Robert Cringely, *Accidental Empires* 54–55.

130 Steven Levy, *Hackers* 229.

131 Steven Levy, *Hackers* 231.

132 Steven Levy, *Hackers* 231; John Markoff, *What the Dormouse Said* 284.

133 Steven Levy, *Hackers* 232; John Markoff, *What the Dormouse Said* 284–285.

134 Steven Levy, *Hackers* 232.

135 Steven Levy, *Hackers* 230–232.

136 Steven Levy, *Hackers* 232; see also John Markoff, *What the Dormouse Said* 285.

137 Steven Levy, *Hackers* 232.

138 Steven Levy, *Hackers* 232; John Markoff, *What the Dormouse Said* 285.

139 Steven Levy, *Hackers* 232–233.

140 Bill Gates, "Open letter to hobbyists"; see also Robert Cringely, *Accidental Empires* 55; see also Forrest Mims III, "The tenth anniversary of the altair 8800" 81 ("Without intending to, MITS made software piracy a widespread phenomenon").

141 Bill Gates, "Open letter to hobbyists".

142 Bill Gates, "Open letter to hobbyists".

143 See Gabriella Coleman, *Coding Freedom* 67; Sam Williams, *Free as in Freedom* 106.

144 Steven Levy, *Hackers* 233 and 265; see also Sam Williams, *Free as in Freedom* 89.

145 Steven Levy, *Hackers* 264; Paul Taylor, "From hackers to hacktivists" 629.

146 Steven Levy, *Hackers* 276.

147 Robert Cringely, *Accidental Empires* 55; John Markoff, *What the Dormouse Said* 286.

148 Steven Levy, *Hackers* 441–442.

149 Steven Levy, *Hackers* 442; E. Gabriella Coleman, *Coding Freedom* 68.

150 Steven Levy, *Hackers* 277 and 442–447 (for an account of the LISP machine conflict); see Sam Williams, *Free as in Freedom* 83–87 (who provides details on how the LISP machine conflict that divided the hackers at the MIT Artificial Intelligence Lab developed)

151 See Tim Wu, *The Master Switch*.

152 See Stewart Brand, *The Media Lab* 202 (emphasis added).

153 Steven Levy, *Hackers* 264.

154 John Markoff, *What the Dormouse Said* 287; see Rob Giseburt "Is one of our open source heroes going closed source?".

155 See Reid Skibell, "The myth of the computer hacker" 340.

156 The term "PC" is used as a generic term and is not limited to IBM PCs and computers based on the "Wintel" architecture that gained market dominance in

the late 1980s and 1990s. Notable PCs that came after the Apple II include the TRS-80, Atari 400 and 800, Commodore PET and 64, BBC Micro, Sinclair ZX Spectrum, and, most importantly, the IBM PC and the Apple Macintosh.

157 See Bruce Sterling, *The Hacker Crackdown* 63–65 and 90; Douglas Thomas, *Hacker Culture* xiii; John Soma and others, "Legal analysis of electronic bulletin board activities" 574; Debora Halbert, "Discourses of danger and the computer hacker" 363; Reid Skibell, "The myth of the computer hacker" 340; Richard Hollinger, "Hackers: Computer heroes or electronic highwaymen?" 12; Ken Lindup, "The cyberpunk age" 638.

158 Bruce Sterling, *The Hacker Crackdown* 54 and 81; Damian Gordon, "Forty years of movie hacking" 25.

159 Tim Jordan, *Hacking* 37.

160 Bruce Sterling, *The Hacker Crackdown* 69; see also Tatiana Bazzichelli, *Networking: The Net as Artwork* 136.

161 "BBS", *The New Hacker's Dictionary*.

162 Bruce Sterling, *The Hacker Crackdown* 69; see also John Soma and others, "Legal analysis of electronic bulletin board activities" 572.

163 Charles Cangialosi, "The electronic underground: Computer piracy and electronic bulletin boards" 267.

164 Robert Beall, "Developing a coherent approach to the regulation of computer bulletin boards" 499 and 501; Bruce Sterling, *The Hacker Crackdown* 70; Eric Jensen, "Computer bulletin boards and the first amendment" 217; Charles Cangialosi, "The electronic underground: Computer piracy and electronic bulletin boards" 283.

165 Robert Beall, "Developing a coherent approach to the regulation of computer bulletin boards" 500–501; Bruce Sterling, *The Hacker Crackdown* 69; Eric Jensen, "Computer bulletin boards and the first amendment" 221.

166 See Robert Beall, "Developing a coherent approach to the regulation of computer bulletin boards" 499.

167 Bruce Sterling, *The Hacker Crackdown* 64 and 73; Tim Jordan, *Hacking* 38; John Raulerson, "Cyberpunk politics: Hacking and bricolage" 122.

168 See Andrew Feenberg, "Democratizing technology: Interest, codes, rights" 192–193; see Eric von Hippel, *Democratizing Innovation* 1; Chris Anderson, *Makers* 63.

169 Bruce Sterling, *The Hacker Crackdown* 70.

170 Robert Beall, "Developing a coherent approach to the regulation of computer bulletin boards" 501; see Bruce Sterling, *The Hacker Crackdown* 70.

171 Robert Beall, "Developing a coherent approach to the regulation of computer bulletin boards" 501; Eric Jensen, "Computer bulletin boards and the first amendment" 220.

172 Bruce Sterling, *The Hacker Crackdown* 70; see also Eric Jensen, "Computer bulletin boards and the first amendment" 219–220.

173 Eric Jensen, "Computer bulletin boards and the first amendment" 222.

174 Bruce Sterling, *The Hacker Crackdown* 70.

175 See Robert Beall, "Developing a coherent approach to the regulation of computer bulletin boards" 499–500; see Bruce Sterling, *The Hacker Crackdown* 71; Eric Jensen, "Computer bulletin boards and the first amendment" 218.

176 Robert Beall, "Developing a coherent approach to the regulation of computer bulletin boards" 501; Eric Jensen, "Computer bulletin boards and the first amendment" 222; Bruce Sterling, *The Hacker Crackdown* 73.

177 Eric Jensen, "Computer bulletin boards and the first amendment" 223.

178 Bruce Sterling, *The Hacker Crackdown* 70–71 and 76; Eric Jensen, "Computer bulletin boards and the first amendment" 223–224; Charles Cangialosi, "The electronic underground: Computer piracy and electronic bulletin boards" 276.

179 Robert Beall, "Developing a coherent approach to the regulation of computer bulletin boards" 501; Eric Jensen, "Computer bulletin boards and the first amendment" 222; Bruce Sterling, *The Hacker Crackdown* 73.

180 Bruce Sterling, *The Hacker Crackdown* 73; John Soma and others, "Legal analysis of electronic bulletin board activities".

181 Robert Beall, "Developing a coherent approach to the regulation of computer bulletin boards" 502; Paul Taylor, *Hackers* 28; Tim Jordan, *Hacking* 33–34.

182 Bruce Sterling, *The Hacker Crackdown* 74–75.

183 Bruce Sterling, *The Hacker Crackdown* 75 and 78; see also Tim Jordan, *Hacking* 33–34.

184 Tim Jordan, *Hacking* 29.

185 Bruce Sterling, *The Hacker Crackdown* 77.

186 Bruce Sterling, *The Hacker Crackdown* 77–79, 85 and 87; see also Robert Beall, "Developing a coherent approach to the regulation of computer bulletin boards" 502.

187 Robert Beall, "Developing a coherent approach to the regulation of computer bulletin boards" 502; Bruce Sterling, *The Hacker Crackdown* 80.

188 Bruce Sterling, *The Hacker Crackdown* 80.

189 Robert Beall, "Developing a coherent approach to the regulation of computer bulletin boards" 502; Eric Jensen, "Computer bulletin boards and the first amendment"225.

190 Eric Jensen, "Computer bulletin boards and the first amendment" 225; John Soma and others, "Legal analysis of electronic bulletin board activities" 574.

191 Richard Hollinger, "Hackers: Computer heroes or electronic highwaymen?" 9.

192 John Soma and others, "Legal analysis of electronic bulletin board activities" 574; David Wall, *Cybercrime* 55; Joseph Olivenbaum, "Rethinking federal computer crime legislation" 581; Reid Skibell, "Cybercrimes & misdemeanors" 936–937.

193 Reid Skibell, "Cybercrimes & misdemeanors" 937; see also Paul Taylor, *Hackers*; see also Tim Jordan and Paul Taylor, "A sociology of hackers".

194 Bruce Sterling, *The Hacker Crackdown* 90; Reid Skibell, "The myth of the computer hacker" 341.

195 Reid Skibell, "Cybercrimes & misdemeanors" 937; see also Tim Jordan, *Hacking*; see also Paul Taylor, *Hackers*; see also Michelle Slatalla and Joshua Quittner, *Masters of Deception*.

196 Bruce Sterling, *The Hacker Crackdown* 90 (emphasis added).

197 Bruce Sterling, *The Hacker Crackdown* 82; Wayne Rumbles, "Reflections of hackers in legal and popular discourse" 75; Richard Hollinger, "Hackers: Computer heroes or electronic highwaymen?" 11–12.

198 Reid Skibell, "Cybercrimes & misdemeanors" 919 and 937.

199 Bruce Sterling, *The Hacker Crackdown* 54.

200 Richard Hollinger, "Hackers: Computer heroes or electronic highwaymen?" 9.

201 Bruce Sterling, *The Hacker Crackdown* 80–81; Richard Hollinger, "Hackers: Computer heroes or electronic highwaymen?" 9; Ken Lindup, "The cyberpunk age" 639.

202 Tim Jordan, *Hacking* 28–30.

203 Tim Jordan, *Hacking* 28–29; Ken Lindup, "The cyberpunk age" 639.

204 Helen Nissenbaum, "Hackers and the contested ontology of cyberspace" 199–200.

205 Joseph Olivenbaum, "Rethinking federal computer crime legislation" 581–582; Ian Lloyd, *Information Technology Law* 215; Tim Jordan, *Hacking* 39; Helen Nissenbaum, "Hackers and the contested ontology of cyberspace" 196; Debora Halbert, "Discourses of danger and the computer hacker" 364; Reid Skibell, "The myth of the computer hacker" 349.

206 Richard Hollinger and Lonn Lanza-Kaduce, "The process of criminalization: The case of computer crime laws" 116.

207 Helen Nissenbaum, "Hackers and the contested ontology of cyberspace" 200; see also David Wall, *Cybercrime* 9–10.

208 Helen Nissenbaum, "Hackers and the contested ontology of cyberspace" 198; Bruce Sterling, *The Hacker Crackdown* 59, 62, 64, 91 and 96 ("Hackers weren't 'invisible'. They THOUGHT they were invisible; but the truth was, they had just been tolerated too long"); Reid Skibell, "The myth of the computer hacker" 346; Tim Jordan, *Hacking* 19 and 39; Derek Bambauer and Oliver Day, "The hacker's aegis" 45.

209 Jay BloomBecker, "Computer crime update" 628 and 637; see also Debora Halbert, "Discourses of danger and the computer hacker"; see also Reid Skibell, "The myth of the computer hacker"; see also Paul Taylor, *Hackers* 1; see also Richard Hollinger and Lonn Lanza-Kaduce, "The process of criminalization: The case of computer crime laws" 114–115.

210 Jay BloomBecker, "Computer crime update" 649; Ulrich Wuermeling, "Hacking for the KGB" 21; "A short history of the CCC" 86.

211 Reid Skibell, "The myth of the computer hacker" 346; see also Paul Taylor, *Hackers* xiii and 5; see also Reid Skibell, "Cybercrimes & misdemeanors" 943.

212 Steven Levy, *Hackers* 456; David Wall, *Cybercrime* 54; Derek Bambauer and Oliver Day, "The hacker's aegis" 44 and 45.

213 Bruce Sterling, *The Hacker Crackdown* 59; see also Reid Skibell, "Cybercrimes & misdemeanors" 937.

214 Steven Levy, *Hackers* 456; Bruce Sterling, *The Hacker Crackdown* 59; see David Wall, *Cybercrime* 68.

215 See Joseph Olivenbaum, "Rethinking federal computer crime legislation" 584.

216 Gabriella Coleman, *Coding Freedom* 61.

217 Steven Levy, *Hackers* 440 and 447; Richard Stallman, "The GNU project" 17–18; Sam Williams, *Free as in Freedom* 81.

218 Richard Stallman, "The GNU project" 17, 19 and 21; see also Sam Williams, *Free as In Freedom* 81.

219 Linus Torvalds and David Diamond, *Just for Fun* 75.

220 Tim Jordan, *Hacking* 43–44; see Linus Torvalds and David Diamond, *Just for Fun* 238.

221 Eric Raymond, *The Cathedral and the Bazaar* 8; E. Gabriella Coleman, *Coding Freedom* 76; Linus Torvalds and David Diamond, *Just for Fun* 56; Bruce Sterling, *The Hacker Crackdown* 107.

222 Richard Stallman, "The GNU project" 19, 24 and 25; Sam Williams, *Free as in Freedom* 79, 93 and 112; Eric Raymond, *The Cathedral and the Bazaar* 12–14; Tim Jordan, *Hacking* 53; Bruce Sterling, *The Hacker Crackdown* 111–112.

223 Richard Stallman, "The GNU project" 19; see also Linus Torvalds and David Diamond, *Just for Fun* 58.

224 Richard Stallman, "The GNU project" 19 and 24; see also Sam Williams, *Free as in Freedom* 115.

225 Richard Stallman, "Initial announcement"; see also Sam Williams, *Free as In Freedom* 79–80; see also Richard Stallman, "The GNU project" 20; see also Eric Raymond, *The Cathedral and the Bazaar* 11.

226 Richard Stallman, "The GNU project" 21 (It should be noted though that while Richard Stallman severed formal ties with MIT as an employee, he remained physically present at MIT and continued to use the facilities of the MIT AI Lab upon the invitation of the Lab's head even after he resigned); Sam Williams, *Free as in Freedom* 90; Paul Taylor, "From hackers to hacktivists" 629.
227 Steven Levy, *Hackers* 170, 437, 461 and 465.
228 Sam Williams, *Free as in Freedom* 92; E. Gabriella Coleman, *Coding Freedom* 88.
229 Free Software Foundation, "The free software definition".
230 Free Software Foundation, "The free software definition".
231 Free Software Foundation, "The free software definition"; see also Richard Stallman, "The GNU project" 20.
232 Sam Williams, *Free as in Freedom* 89.
233 Richard Stallman, "The GNU project" 19; E. Gabriella Coleman, *Coding Freedom* 70.
234 Sam Williams, *Free as in Freedom* 90–91; E. Gabriella Coleman, *Coding Freedom* 70–71.
235 Sam Williams, *Free as in Freedom* 91–92; Richard Stallman, "The GNU project" 21; Gabriella Coleman, *Coding Freedom* 69–70.
236 See Gabriella Coleman, *Coding Freedom* 88.
237 Steven Levy, *Hackers* 441.
238 Gabriella Coleman, *Coding Freedom* 68.
239 Steven Levy, *Hackers* 441; Sam Williams, *Free as in Freedom* 106.
240 Sam Williams, *Free as in Freedom* 107.
241 People can do anything with works in the public domain, including making derivatives of these works that are no longer freely accessible to the public; see Free Software Foundation, "What is Copyleft?"; Sam Williams, *Free as in Freedom* 108.
242 Sam Williams, *Free as in Freedom* 107.
243 Sam Williams, *Free as in Freedom* 107; see also Michael Dizon, "The symbiotic relationship between global contracts and the international IP regime" 562.
244 Richard Stallman, "The GNU project" 22; Sam Williams, *Free as in Freedom* 108.
245 Sam Williams, *Free as in Freedom* 93; Richard Stallman, "The GNU project" 23; Gabriella Coleman, *Coding Freedom* 68.
246 Sam Williams, *Free as in Freedom* 107–108 and 111; see also Richard Stallman, "The GNU project" 22.
247 Richard Stallman, "The GNU project" 22.
248 Sam Williams, *Free as in Freedom* 93 and 108.
249 GNU Emacs General Public License.
250 Gabriella Coleman, *Coding Freedom* 69; see also Sam Williams, *Free as in Freedom* 109.
251 GNU General Public License version 1; Gabriella Coleman, *Coding Freedom* 70; Gabriella Coleman, "Code is speech" 424.
252 See Gabriella Coleman, *Coding Freedom* 70 and 88.
253 Richard Stallman, "The GNU project" 23; see also E. Gabriella Coleman, *Coding Freedom* 70.
254 Gabriella Coleman, *Coding Freedom* 69–70.
255 Gabriella Coleman, *Coding Freedom* 76.
256 Sam Williams, *Free as in Freedom* 108 and 110; Tim Jordan, *Hacking* 63.
257 Gabriella Coleman, *Coding Freedom* 70.
258 Sam Williams, *Free as in Freedom* 109.
259 See Michael Dizon, "Rules of a networked society" 95; see Christopher Kelty, "Culture's open sources" 502.

260 Sam Williams, *Free asiIn Freedom* 110.
261 Sam Williams, *Free as in Freedom* 116 and 118; Richard Stallman, "The GNU project" 28; Gabriella Coleman, *Coding Freedom* 76; Tim Jordan, *Hacking* 64–65.
262 See Computer Desktop Encyclopedia, "Kernel".
263 Sam Williams, *Free as in Freedom* 120–121; Richard Stallman, "The GNU project" 28; Gabriella Coleman, *Coding Freedom* 74; Eric Raymond, *The Cathedral and the Bazaar* 15; Linus Torvalds and David Diamond, *Just for Fun* 59, 84, 96 and 163.
264 Eric Raymond, *The Cathedral and the Bazaar* 15; Sam Williams, *Free as in Freedom* 121; Linus Torvalds and David Diamond, *Just for Fun* 54–56 (who explain the elegance and power of Unix); Bruce Sterling, *The Hacker Crackdown* 107.
265 Sam Williams, *Free asiIn Freedom* 121.
266 Gabriella Coleman, *Coding Freedom* 75; Eric Raymond, *The Cathedral and the Bazaar* 16 and 21; Tim Jordan, *Hacking* 43; Margaret Elliot and Walt Scacchi, "Mobilization of software developers" 20.
267 Eric Raymond, *The Cathedral and the Bazaar* 16.
268 Gabriella Coleman, *Coding Freedom* 75–76; Eric Raymond, *The Cathedral and the Bazaar* 21; Tim Jordan, *Hacking* 49; Margaret Elliot and Walt Scacchi, "Mobilization of software developers" 17.
269 Siobhan O'Mahony and Fabrizio Ferraro, "The emergence of governance in an open source community" 8, 11, 22 and 25.
270 Gabriella Coleman, *Coding Freedom* 88.
271 Margaret Elliot and Walt Scacchi, "Mobilization of software developers" 15.
272 Linus Torvalds and David Diamond, *Just for Fun* 122.
273 Gwendolyn Lee and Robert Cole, "The case of the Linux Kernel development" 636.
274 See Bill Gates, "Open letter to hobbyists"; Tim Jordan, *Hacking* 43–44; Linus Torvalds and David Diamond, *Just for Fun* 227.
275 Gwendolyn Lee and Robert Cole, "The case of the Linux Kernel development" 636; see also Eric Raymond, *The Cathedral and the Bazaar* 21 and 33; see also Gabriella Coleman, *Coding Freedom* 76–77.
276 Gabriella Coleman, *Coding Freedom* 75,
277 Linus Torvalds and David Diamond, *Just for Fun* 122.
278 Gwendolyn Lee and Robert Cole, "The case of the Linux Kernel development" 642.
279 Eric Raymond, *The Cathedral and the Bazaar* 175.
280 Eric Raymond, *The Cathedral and the Bazaar* 175–176; Linus Torvalds and David Diamond, *Just for Fun* 164 and 166–167.
281 Eric Raymond, *The Cathedral and the Bazaar* 21 and 175–177; see also Josh Lerner and Jean Tirole, "The economies of technology sharing".
282 Eric Raymond, *The Cathedral and the Bazaar* 175.
283 Richard Stallman, "Why Open Source misses the point of free software"; David Berry, "The contestation of code".
284 Brian Alleyne, "We are all hackers now" 20; Christopher Kelty, *Two Bits* 14.
285 See "The free software definition"; see Open Source Initiative, "The open source definition" (for precise definitions of what are considered FOSS).
286 See Michael Dizon, "Rules of a networked society" 94–95.
287 Gabriella Coleman, *Coding Freedom* 62 and 72.
288 Gabriella Coleman, *Coding Freedom* 62.
289 Gabriella Coleman, *Coding Freedom* 72.
290 Gabriella Coleman, *Coding Freedom* 73; see Andrew Feenberg, "Escaping the iron cage, or, subversive rationalization and democratic theory".

291 Gabriella Coleman, *Coding Freedom* 69–70; Sam Williams, *Free as in Freedom* 91.
292 See *SCO Group v. International Business Machines, Inc.*
293 Margaret Elliot and Walt Scacchi, "Mobilization of software developers" 22–23; Linus Torvalds and David Diamond, *Just for Fun* 167.
294 See Gabriella Coleman, "Code is speech".
295 Linus Torvalds and David Diamond, *Just for Fun* 232 and 234.
296 Lawrence Lessig, *Code: Version 2* 199.
297 UK Open Access Implementation Group, "The case for open access".
298 Creative Commons; see Lawrence Lessig, *Code: version 2* 199; but see Niva Elkin-Koren, "Exploring creative commons".
299 Access to Knowledge.
300 The OpenScience Project.
301 Open Government Initiative.
302 Open Data Commons.
303 Tim Jordan, *Activism!* 14; Paul Taylor, "From hackers to hacktivists" 637; Maxigas, "Hacklabs and hackerspaces" 2; see Lauren Langman, "A critical theory of Internetworked social movements" 51 (for the consequences of globalization).
304 Paul Taylor, "From hackers to hacktivists" 637; Tim Jordan, *Activism!* 19, 23 and 127.
305 Andrew Chadwick, *Internet Politics* 118; Lauren Langman, "A critical theory of Internetworked social movements" 58–60.
306 Andrew Chadwick, *Internet Politics* 118; Paul Taylor, "From hackers to hacktivists" 630; Maxigas, "Hacklabs and hackerspaces" 2; Stefania Milan and Arne Hintz, "Dynamics of cyberactivism" 1.
307 Paul Taylor, "From hackers to hacktivists" 637–638.
308 See Stefania Milan and Arne Hintz, "Dynamics of cyberactivism"; see Martina Gillen, "Is there still a future for online protest in the Anonymous world?" 5.
309 Bruce Sterling, *The Hacker Crackdown* 12; Maxigas, "Hacklabs and hacker-spaces" 5.
310 Tim Jordan, *Activism!* 120–121; Maxigas, "Hacklabs and hackerspaces" 2–3; Jordan, *Hacking* 71–72.
311 Critical Art Ensemble, *Electronic Civil Disobedience* 7; see also Tim Jordan, *Activism!* 120; see also Andrew Chadwick, "Internet politics" 132; see also Tatiana Bazzichelli, *Networking: The Net as Artwork* 173; see also Paul Taylor, "Editorial: Hacktivism" 5; see also Giovanni Ziccardi, *Resistance, Liberation Technology and Human Rights in the Digital Age* 6.
312 Maxigas, "Hacklabs and hackerspaces" 3.
313 Tim Jordan, *Activism!* 121; Andrew Chadwick, "Internet politics" 131–132; Tatiana Bazzichelli, *Networking: The Net as Artwork* 173 (the Tactical Flood-Net code, like other hacktivist tools, is released under a FOSS licence); Simon Yiull, "All problems of notation will be solved by the masses"; Lauren Langman, "A critical theory of Internetworked social movements" 71.
314 Simon Yiull, "All problems of notation will be solved by the masses".
315 Maxigas, "Hacklabs and hackerspaces" 1.
316 Maxigas, "Hacklabs and hackerspaces" 1.
317 Simon Yiull, "All problems of notation will be solved by the masses"; Maxigas, "Hacklabs and hackerspaces" 1–2.
318 Maxigas, "Hacklabs and hackerspaces 4; *Hackerspaces – The Beginning* 6–7.
319 Simon Yiull, "All problems of notation will be solved by the masses"; Maxigas, "Hacklabs and hackerspaces" 1; Johannes Grenzfurthner and Frank Apunkt Schneider, "Rewriting hacking the spaces".
320 Maxigas, "Hacklabs and hackerspaces" 1–3; see also Johannes Grenzfurthner and Frank Apunkt Schneider, "Rewriting hacking the spaces".

321 Maxigas, "Hacklabs and hackerspaces" 4.
322 Maxigas, "Hacklabs and hackerspaces" 2; see also Johannes Grenzfurthner and Frank Apunkt Schneider, "Rewriting hacking the spaces"; see also Tatiana Bazzichelli, *Networking: The Net as Artwork* 166.
323 Maxigas, "Hacklabs and hackerspaces" 4.
324 Maxigas, "Hacklabs and hackerspaces" 5; Peter Ludlow, "Wikileaks and hacktivist culture" 25–26.
325 Tatiana Bazzichelli, *Networking: The Net as Artwork* 141.
326 *Hackerspaces – The Beginning* 7; Maxigas, "Hacklabs and hackerspaces" 5; Shmeck, "25 years of summercon"; see Gabriella Coleman, "The hacker conference" 49.
327 Simon Yiull, "All problems of notation will be solved by the masses"; see also Maxigas, "Hacklabs and hackerspaces" 3; see also Tatiana Bazzichelli, *Networking: The Net as Artwork* 163–164.
328 Tatiana Bazzichelli, *Networking: The Net as Artwork* 164.
329 Maxigas, "Hacklabs and hackerspaces" 5; Tatiana Bazzichelli, *Networking: The Net as Artwork* 143.
330 Tatiana Bazzichelli, *Networking: The Net as Artwork* 139.
331 Maxigas, "Hacklabs and hackerspaces" 4; Simon Yiull, "All problems of notation will be solved by the masses".
332 Maxigas, "Hacklabs and hackerspaces" 3.
333 Andrew Chandwick, "Internet politics" 129–131; see also Tim Jordan, *Activism!* 119; see also Paul Taylor, "From hackers to hacktivists" 629; see alson Tim Jordan, *Hacking* 96.
334 Gabriella Coleman, "Hacker politics and publics" 516; Brian Alleyne, "We are all hackers now" 24; Paul Taylor, "From hackers to hacktivists" 629.
335 Andrew Chadwick, *Internet Politics* 131; see also Lauren Langman, "A critical theory of Internetworked social movements" 63.
336 Paul Taylor, "From hackers to hacktivists" 644.
337 Paul Taylor, "From hackers to hacktivists" 633.
338 Paul Taylor, "From hackers to hacktivists" 630; Peter Ludlow, "Wikileaks and hacktivist culture" 26.
339 Tim Jordan, *Activism!* 121; Paul Taylor, "From hackers to hacktivists" 630.
340 Paul Taylor, "From hackers to hacktivists" 637.
341 Tatiana Bazzichelli, *Networking: The Net as Artwork* 139; Andrew Chandwick, "Internet politics" 133 (US underground hackers Cult of the Dead Cow also took part in hacktivism); Tim Jordan, *Activism!* 127–128 (who explains Cult of the Dead Cow's hacktivism).
342 Tatiana Bazzichelli, *Networking: The Net as Artwork* 140.
343 Paul Taylor, "From hackers to hacktivists" 636.
344 Jordan, *Hacking* 97.
345 Paul Taylor, "From hackers to hacktivists" 634 and 641.
346 Tim Jordan, *Activism!* 121.
347 Tim Jordan, *Activism!* 126; Paul Taylor, "Editorial: Hacktivism" 7; Reid Skibell, "Cybercrimes & misdemeanors" 938.
348 Tim Jordan, *Activism!* 122; see also Lauren Langman, "A critical theory of Internetworked social movements" 68.
349 Gabriella Coleman, "Anonymous: From the Lulz to collective action"; Martina Gillen, "Is there still a future for online protest in the Anonymous world?" 5; Stefania Milan and Arne Hintz, "Dynamics of cyberactivism" 9.
350 Gabriella Coleman, "Code is speech" 435, 437, 441,444, 446 and 447.
351 Paul Taylor, "From hackers to hacktivists" 640 and 644; see also Andrew Chadwick, *Internet Politics* 115.

352 Lauren Langman, "A critical theory of Internetworked social movements" 53–54; Noah Hampson, "Hacktivism" 517 and 536.
353 Paul Taylor, "From hackers to hacktivists" 644.
354 Tim Jordan, *Activism!* 126.
355 Travis Good, "What is 'making'?".
356 IKEA hackers; Andrew Schrok, "What keeps hacker and maker spaces going?"; Peter Troxler, "Libraries of the peer production era".
357 Chris Anderson, *Makers* 94; Bre Pettis, "Open Source ethics and dead end derivatives".
358 Maxigas, "Hacklabs and hackerspaces" 5.
359 Steven Levy, *Hackers* 28; see also Andrew Schrok, "What keeps hacker and maker spaces going?".
360 Dylan Tweney, "DIY freaks flock to 'hacker spaces' worldwide".
361 Open Source Hardware Association, "Open Source Hardware (OSHW) Statement of Principles 1.0"; Chris Anderson, *Makers* 19.
362 Andrew Katz, "Towards a functional licence for open hardware"; Walter, "The Makerbot/Thingiverse move to the dark side".
363 Chris Anderson, *Makers* 94.
364 RepRap Project; Chris Anderson, *Makers* 20.
365 RepRap Project.
366 RepRap Project.
367 Arduino, "What is arduino?".
368 Computer Desktop Encyclopedia, "Microcontroller".
369 Computer Desktop Encyclopedia, "Microcontroller".
370 Arduino, "What is arduino?"; Arduino, "Frequently asked questions".
371 Arduino, "Frequently asked questions".
372 Instructables, "Arduino projects"; Thingiverse, "Things tagged with 'arduino'"; Maxigas, "Hacklabs and hackerspaces 6.
373 Arduino,; but see Massimo Banzi, "Fighting for arduino" (about the falling out between Arduino's core developers over intellectual property and commercial issues).
374 Chris Anderson, *Makers* 21; see Instructables, accessed 12 June 2017; see Thingiverse.
375 Travis Good, "What is 'making'?"; Ken Denmead, "Why the maker movement is here to stay".
376 Ken Denmead, "Why the maker movement is here to stay"; Peter Troxler, "Libraries of the peer production era".
377 Chris Anderson, "The new makerbot replicator might just change your world"; Chris Anderson, *Makers* 22–23.
378 Chris Anderson, "The new makerbot replicator might just change your world"; Chris Anderson, *Makers* 102.
379 Gus Cavalcanti, "Is it a hackerspace, makerspace, techshop or fablab?"; Nick Farr, "Respect the past, examine the present, build the future".
380 Hackerspaces.org (for a definition of hackerspaces); see also Gus Cavalcanti, "Is it a hackerspace, makerspace, techshop or fablab?"; see also *Hackerspaces – The Beginning*; see also John Borland, "'Hacker space' movement sought for US"; see also Dylan Tweney, "DIY freaks flock to 'hacker spaces' worldwide"; see also Jens Ohlig and Lars Weiler, "Building a hacker space"; see also Andrew Schrok, "What keeps hacker and maker spaces going?"; see also Chris Anderson, *Makers* 18; see also Maxigas, "Hacklabs and hackerspaces" 5.
381 John Borland, "'Hacker space' movement sought for US"; see also Dylan Tweney, "DIY freaks flock to 'hacker spaces' worldwide"; see also Steven Kurutz, "One big workbench".

382 John Borland, "'Hacker space' movement sought for US".

383 Nick Farr, "Respect the past, examine the present, build the future"; see also Peter Troxler, "Libraries of the peer production era".

384 Dylan Tweney, "DIY freaks flock to 'hacker spaces' worldwide"; Steven Kurutz, "One big workbench".

385 Dylan Tweney, "DIY freaks flock to 'hacker spaces' worldwide"; see also Steven Kurutz, "One big workbench"; see also Maxigas, "Hacklabs and hackerspaces" 6.

386 Jens Ohlig and Lars Weiler, "Building a hacker space"; Dylan Tweney, "DIY freaks flock to 'hacker spaces' worldwide".

387 Nick Farr, "The rights and obligations of hackerspace members"; see also Jens Ohlig and Lars Weiler, "Building a hacker space"; see also Nick Farr, "The rights and obligations of hackerspace members"; see also Maxigas, "Hacklabs and hackerspaces 5; see also *Hackerspaces – The Beginning* 11.

388 Jens Ohlig and Lars Weiler, "Building a hacker space".

389 Jens Ohlig and Lars Weiler, "Building a hacker space".

390 Nick Farr, "The rights and obligations of hackerspace members"; see also Maxigas, "Hacklabs and hackerspaces 6.

391 Nick Farr, "The rights and obligations of hackerspace members"; see also Steven Kurutz, "One big workbench".

392 Steven Kurutz, "One big workbench"; Peter Troxler, "Libraries of the peer production era".

393 Dylan Tweney, "DIY freaks flock to 'hacker spaces' worldwide"; see also Peter Troxler, "Libraries of the peer production era"; see also Ken Denmead, "Why the maker movement is here to stay".

394 Steven Kurutz, "One big workbench".

395 Jens Ohlig and Lars Weiler, "Building a hacker space"; Maxigas, "Hacklabs and hackerspaces" 6.

396 Dylan Tweney, "DIY freaks flock to 'hacker spaces' worldwide".

397 Peter Troxler, "Libraries of the peer production era"; see also Dylan Tweney, "DIY freaks flock to 'hacker spaces' worldwide".

398 Maxigas, "Hacklabs and hackerspaces 8.

399 Nick Farr, "The rights and obligations of hackerspace members"; see also Andrew Schrok, "What keeps hacker and maker spaces going?".

400 Dylan Tweney, "DIY freaks flock to 'hacker spaces' worldwide".

401 Dylan Tweney, "DIY freaks flock to 'hacker spaces' worldwide".

402 Gus Cavalcanti, "Is it a hackerspace, makerspace, techshop or fablab?"; Maxigas, "Hacklabs and hackerspaces" 1.

403 Dale Dougherty, "From hackers to makers"; see also Artisan's Asylum, "Make a makerspace".

404 Gus Cavalcanti, "Is it a hackerspace, makerspace, techshop or fablab?".

405 Gus Cavalcanti, "Is it a hackerspace, makerspace, techshop or fablab?"; see OHM2013 (where the words hacker and maker are used together and often interchangeably).

406 Gus Cavalcanti, "Is it a hackerspace, makerspace, techshop or fablab?".

407 Gus Cavalcanti, "Is it a hackerspace, makerspace, techshop or fablab?".

408 See Maxigas, "Hacklabs and hackerspaces – tracing two genealogies" (while there are important distinctions between hackerspaces and hacklabs, I would ultimately include hacklabs under the general category of hackerspaces since they both draw from hacker culture).

409 Gus Cavalcanti, "Is it a hackerspace, makerspace, techshop or fablab?" (in the United Kingdom, it appears that the convention is to call hackerspaces as hackspaces).

410 Maxigas, "Hacklabs and hackerspaces" 4.
411 Peter Troxler, "Libraries of the peer production era".
412 "The fab charter".
413 Gus Cavalcanti, "Is it a hackerspace, makerspace, techshop or fablab?"; Chris Anderson, *Makers* 46.
414 Neil Gerschenfeld, "How to make almost anything"; see also Chris Anderson, *Makers* 46.
415 Peter Troxler, "Libraries of the peer production era"; see also Maxigas, "Hacklabs and hackerspaces" 4.
416 Peter Troxler, "Libraries of the peer production era"; see also Chris Anderson, *Makers* 46.
417 Gus Cavalcanti, "Is it a hackerspace, makerspace, techshop or fablab?"; Peter Troxler, "Libraries of the peer production era".
418 Rob Giseburt, "MakerBot's mixed messages about open source, Their Future"; Chris Anderson, "The new makerbot replicator might just change your world"; Chris Anderson, *Makers* 20.
419 Ken Denmead, "Makerbot origins".
420 Ken Denmead, "Makerbot origins"; Walter, "The makerbot/thingiverse move to the dark side"; Rob Giseburt, "Is one of our open source heroes going closed source?".
421 Ken Denmead, "Makerbot origins"; Rob Giseburt, "Is one of our open source heroes going closed source?"; Chris Anderson, *Makers* 107.
422 Ken Denmead, "Makerbot origins".
423 Ken Denmead, "Makerbot origins".
424 Ken Denmead, "Makerbot origins"; see also Rob Giseburt, "Is one of our open source heroes going closed source?".
425 Rob Giseburt, "Is one of our open source heroes going closed source?".
426 Ken Denmead, "Makerbot origins".
427 Ken Denmead, "Makerbot origins".
428 Ken Denmead, "Makerbot origins"; Chris Anderson, *Makers* 72–74.
429 Bre Pettis, "Open source ethics and dead end derivatives".
430 Dylan Tweney, "DIY freaks flock to 'hacker spaces' worldwide".
431 Rob Giseburt, "Is one of our open source heroes going closed source?"; Ken Denmead, "Makerbot origins"; *Hackerspaces – The Beginning* 99.
432 See Ashlee Vance, "Bre pettis: 3D printing's first celebrity"; Ken Denmead, "Makerbot origins"; Phillip Torrone, "Life, $10M in funding, and beyond"; Chris Anderson, *Makers* 108.
433 Rob Giseburt, "Is one of our open source heroes going closed source?".
434 Bre Pettis, "Open Source ethics and dead end derivatives"; see also Phillip Torrone, "Life, $10M in funding, and beyond".
435 Bre Pettis, "Open source ethics and dead end derivatives"; see also Phillip Torrone, "Life, $10M in funding, and beyond".
436 Rob Giseburt, "MakerBot's mixed messages about open source, Their Future"; Bre Pettis, "Let's try that again"; Walter, "The makerbot/thingiverse move to the dark side".
437 Rob Giseburt, "MakerBot's mixed messages about open source, Their Future"; Josef Prusa, "Occupy thingiverse test cube", Thingiverse; Bre Pettis, "Fixing misinformation with information"; Bre Pettis, "Let's try that again"; Walter, "The makerbot/thingiverse move to the dark side"; Bre Pettis, "Thingiverse updates Terms of Use and License options"; Richard McCarthy, "Our lawyer explains the thingiverse terms of service"; John Baichtal, "Brazilian 3D printer company weighs in on the makerbot controversy"; Tigoe, "In defense of open source innovation and polite disagreement".

438 Rob Giseburt, "Makerbot's mixed messages about open source, their future".

439 Rob Giseburt, "Makerbot's mixed messages about open source, their future"; see also Walter, "The makerbot/thingiverse move to the dark side".

440 Rob Giseburt, "Makerbot's mixed messages about open source, their future"; Bre Pettis, "Fixing misinformation with information"; Bre Pettis, "Let's try that again"; Rob Giseburt, "Is one of our open source heroes going closed source?".

441 Rob Giseburt, "Makerbot's mixed messages about open source, their future"; Bre Pettis, "Let's try that again"; Walter, "The makerbot/thingiverse move to the dark side"; Phillip Torrone, "Life, $10M in funding, and beyond"; Chris Anderson, *Makers* 95.

442 Bre Pettis, "Fixing misinformation with information"; Bre Pettis, "Let's try that again".

443 Bre Pettis, "Fixing misinformation with information"; see also Walter, "The makerbot/thingiverse move to the dark side".

444 Bre Pettis, "Let's try that again"; see also Computer Desktop Encyclopedia "GUI".

445 Tim Wu, "Does a company like Apple need a genius like Steve Jobs".

446 Bre Pettis, "Let's try that again" (emphasis added).

447 Bre Pettis, "Fixing misinformation with information".

448 Bre Pettis, "Fixing misinformation with information".

449 Bre Pettis, "Let's try that again".

450 Rob Giseburt, "MakerBot's mixed messages about open source, their future".

451 Rob Giseburt, "Is one of our open source heroes going closed source?".

452 Stratasys, "Stratasys to acquire makerbot, merging two global 3D printing industry leaders"; D.C. Denison, "Reactions to the makerbot-stratasys deal".

453 Mitch Altman, "Hacking at the crossroad: US military funding of hackerspaces" (which is eerily similar to the US government's funding of the early MIT computer hackers).

454 Tom Preston-Werner, "Open source (almost) everything"; see also Peter Troxler, "Libraries of the peer production era"; see also Chris Anderson, *Makers* 19 and 107.

455 See Phillip Torrone, "The {unspoken} rules of open source hardware"; Bre Pettis, "Open source ethics and dead end derivatives".

456 See Sara Tocchetti, "DIYbiologists as 'makers' of personal biologies"; Denisa Kera, "Hackerspaces and DIYbio in Asia".

Chapter 3

Hacker norms and values

While the previously chapter delved into what hackers did, where they hacked, and how the law and authorities viewed and responded to them, this chapter explains the *why* of hacking by examining hackers' norms and values. Norms and values are extremely relevant and crucial in determining how makers and hacktivists interact with the law and public authorities. In justifying the importance of social norms to law, Etzioni states, "the study of social norms is of considerable importance for the full study of law" since "social norms affect behavior in general and the law specifically".[1] Posner is similarly unequivocal: "A full understanding of law requires consideration of norms".[2] Studying their norms and values can help elucidate hackers' actions, beliefs and attitudes, especially in relation to technology law and policy.[3]

Norms and values of makers and hacktivists

Based on my research on hackers in the Netherlands, I was able to observe the following 19 hacker values: anonymity, community development, consensus, creativity and innovation, curiosity, efficiency, equality and meritocracy, freedom of access, freedom of expression, freedom of information, fun and play, decentralization and self-governance, individual autonomy and liberty, openness, personal growth, privacy, security, social development, and transparency. However, some values stood out more than others. The five that were prioritized and considered most important by hackers were: *creativity and innovation, curiosity, individual autonomy and liberty, community development,* and *social development.*

While there is a general commonality in what hackers value most, there is some variance among the different types of hackers. For makers, aside from creativity and innovation and individual autonomy and liberty, they also prize the values of openness and transparency. In comparison, hacktivists, in addition to individual autonomy and liberty and community and social development, consider curiosity and equality and meritocracy to be very significant. I also spoke to a few ethical hackers and for them, besides creativity and innovation, curiosity, and community and social development, they also place great store in the value of security.

Creativity and innovation

It comes as no surprise that creativity and innovation is considered one of the most significant values for hackers. This is expected given that innovation is an essential element of a hack and "hacking in itself is just creatively using technology".[4] The makers, hacktivists and other hackers I spoke to generally define themselves and their activities in relation to technological creativity and innovation. As Maker K explains, "I am a hacker because I'm creative. I like to know how to change [things]. I really like to know how things work".[5] Maker F says, "I'm a maker in a sense that I'm a creative person. So I'm always creating things. I'm making things".[6] Some consider "[m]aking [or] creating something" as "a valuable experience in its own right".[7] Hacktivist D sees "hackers as people who reuse technology in ways not imagined by the people who [developed] the thing, program or technology".[8] Whether for makers or hacktivists, hacking is about having a "creative [and] critical approach to technology".[9]

Creativity and innovation is prized more by makers than hacktivists. Makers are especially passionate about building or doing new things with technology, whereas hacktivists are more inclined to use technology as means for achieving socio-political goals. For makers, the great appeal of hacking is that "you can take something and reorganize or reshuffle it to make something completely different".[10] According to Maker C, "This inner thing, that maker spirit, this whole idea of just doing stuff, that's how we learn".[11] Some describe it as a "mentality and attitude . . . [of] finding where you can stretch a system to do new things".[12] Maker A even believes "it's in my blood" to build and create things.[13]

The value of creativity and innovation though does not simply remain a personal or individual goal but is shared and pursued by the entire group or community. In hackerspaces, for instance, "everybody is searching for smart solutions, original combinations, and cheap solutions"[14] and "the typical project that we [do] are for fun and to learn and to do cool stuff".[15] Makers subscribe to the do-it-yourself mentality and would rather build something than buy it. People who can build their own 3D printers, CNC machines, laser cutters and laser light projectors from scratch are held in high esteem in the community, especially if they were able make them better and cheaper than commercially available models. But for makers, it is not enough to have produced these machines. They consider it essential to share what they learned with others. There is a clear understanding among makers that the ability to *create* is intimately connected to each person's propensity to *share* and *learn* from each other, which are both common acts of hacking. As Maker I states, "having discovered that there is this dynamic where people build on top of each other, and you really want to also be part of that, and you want more people to become part of that".[16] Part of the allure of working together in a hackerspace is that "we build very cool equipment . . . that we are proud [of], and everybody can join".[17] The value of creativity and innovation has a distinct social dimension and purpose, which is why, for Maker C, "I want to let anyone make anything [and] do whatever I can . . . to bring that about".[18] In fact, the motto of one hackerspace is "to creatively use technology to improve the world".[19]

This imperative to create and be creative with technology seems to be hard-wired to the very constitution of hackers. As Hacktivist C exclaims, "There's no in-between. Either I go forward or stop and start doing something else".[20] There is an unmistakable impetus to innovate. As Maker K reflects, "Yeah, I suppose that's really what motivates me. I just think, can we do that, how better can we do it".[21] The need to be creative and innovative can also be quite an obsession for some. As recounted by Ethical Hacker A,[22] "For me it's really difficult to do the same trick over and over again. I don't like that . . . What I do like is things that are different each and every time".[23] The comparison between hackers, artists and other creative types is unavoidable since they can all be described as "creative people with a lot of passion [and] doing a lot of good work".[24] It is worth noting that there are a number of artists and designers who are part of or have close ties to the hacker community and art installations figure prominently at hacker camps and events.[25]

Curiosity

Creativity and innovation are intimately related to another value – curiosity. These values seem to naturally go hand-in-hand and statements made by hackers about curiosity generally relate to creativity and innovation, and vice versa. The close connection between curiosity and creativity and innovation is evident as well to the hackers who took part in my research. Ethical Hacker B says, "if I look at creativity and innovation, I think that also covers curiosity".[26] Another hacker concurs, "curiosity is similar [to] creativity and innovation".[27] What differentiates curiosity from creativity and innovation is that the former is an instrumental value for hackers to explore and learn how things work, while the latter is concerned with a terminal goal of producing something new or different.

Even though hackers seem to prioritize creativity and innovation slightly more than curiosity, the latter remains an essential value that is commonly shared among makers, hacktivists and other hackers. What makes curiosity so significant to hackers is that it "necessarily precedes" and is "a necessary condition" for hacking.[28] For many makers and hacktivists, curiosity is one of the main reasons or motivations why they pursued or engaged in hacker projects and activities.[29] According to Hacktivist E, "[my] curiosity is fulfilled throughout all of these activities".[30] Maker A says that curiosity "usually starts my thinking process",[31] and, for Maker E, "it's always curiosity that drives the next thing".[32] Hacking is propelled by a natural curiosity to understand how technology works and how to make it better.[33] "I'm curious about how it works, how I can make something work better, how I can make it smaller [or] bigger", explains Maker A.[34] Maker K describes the thinking and creative process, "I just like seeing the what if. That's I suppose what really motivates me. What if, could we do that? Then I go off and . . . try it".[35] Curiosity thus leads to various paths to *explore* and *learn* about technology, which are common acts of hacking. "I really like to experiment with a lot of stuff", says Maker A.[36] This desire to experiment is also carried over in hacker camps where hackers "expect some interesting new discoveries and observations about the technology we see around us in our everyday lives".[37]

One interesting aspect of curiosity is that it includes a sense of play and a bit of innocent mischief. Hackers explain the reason why they hold outdoor hacker camps, "Because we can. And fun, definitely [for] fun".[38] Being curious about technology normally involves "playing, having fun, and discovering stuff that wasn't there before".[39] According to Maker F, "I always like things I don't know and which tickle" my interest.[40] For hackers, it seems curiosity is an imperative that must be acted on. As Hacktivist E explains, "I was simply too curious and the outcomes of my online adventures were simply too rewarding".[41] When posed with the challenge of "Can you do this? Can you [3D] print this?", Maker K's recounts, "I go, ok I don't know, let's find out".[42] Following one's curiosity admittedly involves not just creative but also destructive activities. While working on a project, it is sometimes necessary to *break* things. As Ethical Hacker B recounts, "we don't really know how it works . . . so maybe [one] could . . . look to see if you can try to mangle with it".[43] Most hackers will "try to find a hole [and] break it open as far as possible so they can get in".[44] However, it is important to point out that, as Ethical Hacker B states, "I never really wanted to abuse it . . . [I] just [wanted] to know how the system works".[45] There is no malicious intent to cause damage. Of course, there is the possibility that hackers may accidentally cause damage to systems. In these cases, they will endeavor to minimize or fix the accidental or incidental damage they caused. Furthermore, while curiosity naturally involves playfulness, it is also a serious matter. As Hacktivist B explains, curiosity is "a mindset [where] we relate to the rest of the world without accepting the usual understanding of it".[46] It provides "a wider view [of] the meaning of the technologies that we live with".[47] Makers and hacktivists seek to "apply their critical curiosity and creativity to bring about methods to cope with the upcoming changes" in society.[48]

Individual autonomy and liberty

For makers and hacktivists, being creative, innovative or curious would not be possible in the absence of the requisite value of individual autonomy and liberty. Both makers and hacktivists regard this value as extremely important because it is similarly a means to achieve other values as well as a goal in its own right. Liberty of choice and action is deemed essential to hacking since it would be impossible to engage in any or all of the common acts of hacking (*explore, break, learn, create, share* and *secure*) in the absence of this value. According to Maker E, "For us, it has a lot of advantages that we dictate our own path. We have nobody to answer to".[49] Maker L exhorts, "Give people more freedom because with all those [requirements] that's not possible. You have to do [this], you have to do that. You sometimes feel constrained in doing things. You're less free".[50] Maker F explains the relationship between individual autonomy and liberty to creativity and innovation: "Because only if you don't have boundaries and it feels like you could do whatever you want, you could be on a higher level".[51] As Maker B succinctly puts it, "hackers are the most autonomous and creative . . . people in the IT sector",[52] and, as such, it is commonly believed that having greater autonomy leads to more creativity.

An interesting revelation though that came up during my interviews and conversations with hackers is that despite being so technically minded and focused, they see the importance of freedom and autonomy not just with but also from technology. They are very much aware of "the danger of getting too dependent on systems and on centralized information dominance", and that "we need to always be able to have our individual responsibility and freedom to choose".[53] They caution that "blind faith in ICT in particular leads to erosion of democratic principles and human rights".[54] For Hacktivist E, "individuals should not be unreasonably forced [to use] systems, especially when those systems contradict the interests of individuals".[55] Some hackers would like "to take the technical expertise of the hacking scene out of its isolation [and] place it within the broader perspective of the societal structures it shapes and is part of".[56] As Maker I reflects, "I think the beauty of hacking is that it balances out a little bit the concentration or asymmetry of power", whether it be political, technological or legal.[57] Many hackers believe that they can change the world and make it better through their hacking projects and activities.

Whether as individuals or as groups, hackers are undoubtedly very autonomous, independent and self-directed.[58] At hacker camps, people would typically spend long periods transfixed and hacking away at their own computers seemingly oblivious to everyone beside or near them. The phenomenon of being "alone together" is common too among hackers.[59] According to Maker D, most people "like to do their own projects".[60] Even in the communal setting of a hackerspace, "most projects are done by one person", although "people hope that other people will help [out] or do something similar".[61] Maker D explains why individual liberty and autonomy is highly prized among them, "If you build software on your own, you can decide how to do it yourself. That's a good thing".[62] For Hacktivist E,

> autonomy also includes deciding how the equipment you buy works. The freedom to tinker allows the pursuit of hacker values [such as], for instance, to improve its features, to disable limitations that prevent sharing and fair use, or to make it more secure and less privacy-invasive.[63]

Of course, for some hacktivists, too much autonomy can also be an issue since "we run up into the fact that we are all sort of quite anarcho-communist people that do not listen to each other".[64]

Community development

Despite the strong emphasis on individual autonomy and liberty, makers and hacktivists alike see the importance of building and being active in their communities. Hackers in the Netherlands even formed an umbrella group of hackerspaces and hacker organizations in the belief that "Together we are stronger than alone".[65] Dutch hackerspaces are on friendly terms with one another and they try to assist each other by giving "tips and tricks or experiences in setting up and keeping alive a hackerspace or event".[66] They also use the regular hacker camps and events to meet, catch up, share knowledge and ideas, and collaborate on projects. Many hackers at these hacker camps initially appeared shy and introverted, but they were actually quite friendly and sociable with and among other hackers. They all knew each other. In the evenings, hacker camps had a party club vibe where people would hang out in small groups, chat, drink beer and Club-Mate, tell stories, joke around and have fun. The atmosphere was lively and upbeat but never rowdy. While it is true that hackers like their independence, hacker camps and other community events are important shared experiences for them.[67] Many hackers were excited about upcoming hacker camps and waxed lyrical about previous hacker camps to which they had been. Some people wore t-shirts from past hacker camps they attended. There was a strong spirit of community and volunteerism at these camps. "[E]very visitor is both participant and volunteer" and everyone is expected to pitch in and actively take part.[68] The entire camp was community-driven and organized and run by volunteers. Everyone was counted on to lend a hand: lay down power and internet cables across the camp grounds, build walkways, put up tents, move and set up equipment, man the entrance, drive the shuttle vans, cook food, pick up refuse, fix clogged toilets and showers, and give talks and workshops to others.[69] Camp wristbands and t-shirts prominently bear the word "crew" to remind everyone to help out since this is their camp.

This community spirit is quite useful as well when it comes to hackers' technical projects and activities. To *learn* how things work or to *create* something new are integral aspects and goals of hacking. But for makers and hacktivists, these are not enough. For them it is important as well to work together and *share* what they learned or created with others. At camps, for example, people taught each other how to mine for bitcoins, splice fiber optic cables and run a Tor server. They understand that sharing is essential to promoting not only creativity and innovation but also community development. There is a palpable communitarian ethos within the hacker community especially among makers. Building and having a sense of community is crucial, for instance, when setting up a hackerspace. As Maker B explains, hackerspaces are "a common place to connect [with] each other" and, like hacker camps and conferences, they act like a "kind of the physical touchdown" for the hacker community.[70] For Maker E, a hackerspace is "a community project so the word community obviously . . . reverberates through everything we do".[71] Makers have varied reasons or motivations for going to hackerspaces, but many of them join "for the community mostly".[72] They can quite easily work on their projects alone at home but makers who frequent hackerspaces "want to share and collaborate".[73] They view hackerspaces as "just a big place where everybody can come together and work and hang out, drink a cup of coffee, but also find cutting edge technology".[74] While makers obviously go to hackerspaces to work on technical projects, ultimately, "it's about the people".[75] For them a hackerspace is "not about the machines. It's about the facility. It's about the place where people come together."[76] Because of this, "at the same time as we are trying to facilitate a group or a community feel, we also want to empower everybody individually and make them grow", relates Maker E. Maker D further elaborates, "we want to [help develop] these people so they can become better hackers [and] technologists, and build something [in] the space".[77]

Like the computer hobbyists who started the PC revolution, collaborating with others makes perfect sense for makers and hacktivists alike. For them, it is a very logical and practical decision since working together is more effective and produces better results. According to Hacktivist C, in order to have a greater impact, "you always have . . . to talk to others and put yourself [in] a team".[78] When dealing with technical or social issues, people at hackerspaces or hacker events have the "urge to meet with other people and talk about it and . . . address certain topics".[79] According to Maker B, "it's inherent in the set up of an open space where everyone is welcome and [everybody is] thinking and working on these issues".[80] The advantage of sharing is that people can "brainstorm about what they're thinking about or just to chat. In [this] way, you can . . . make a really nice community that helps each other".[81] It is common practice for makers to show "what you do, what's available. [You learn from] people and hope other people can use your ideas. So [your project is] not only for you but everybody can use it".[82]

Sharing and collaboration also produce a virtuous cycle where people are so "enthusiastic, so into what they are creating, what they are making. And they want to share it".[83] It is a common experience among makers that "people are willing to share their ideas with us because we also share with them. . . . We start by sharing with them".[84] The projects they work on do not remain individual technical pursuits, because, according to Maker I, "helping each other out [is] also a part of it".[85] Like the FOSS developers who champion the benefits of technologies and systems that are free and open, Maker A believes that "if we just share everything we do . . . we [can have] a whole lot more positive world than we [have] in now".[86] Makers understand that "technology is a really powerful thing and by sharing those improvements you build on top of each other. You are lowering barriers".[87] According to Maker I, "I really like the fact that we've done a few things together that many . . . people started believing in, taking up and contributing to".[88] Maker L agrees, "I think that is one of the most important things [with] hacking. Because if you are open, people can learn from you [and] you can learn from other people".[89] Community development is thus a necessary corollary to individual autonomy and liberty because "it's very difficult to do this by yourself. If everybody [did] it by [themselves], everyone [would] fail".[90]

Social development

Intimately related to and following closely from community development is the value of social development. The hackers are not simply content with building their communities and learning how the world works. As with their approach to any technology, makers and most especially hacktivists also want to change and improve the world. They genuinely want to understand "how we can change things and how can we make things better".[91] Hacktivist D explains the relationship between community development, social development and individual autonomy and liberty: "Having a healthy community and social development depends on people having enough individual autonomy and liberty to inform themselves and to be . . . a member of society or a member of the community".[92] Which is why when hackers organized workshops targeted to the general public to teach people how to use computers and other technologies more safely and securely, "we very explicitly don't want people to come over, hand over their laptops, and we install stuff for [them] and give [the laptops] back."[93] According to a hacker, they "want to help and teach people, but not do [everything] for them".[94] For instance, hackers freely and voluntarily offered their knowledge and skills and took an active role in helping local councils develop a digital fabrication lab or convert a bus into a mobile hacking space to service their local communities. Dutch hackerspaces also hold an annual "Hackerspace Open Day" where they give the public a behind-the-scenes tour of their spaces and offer workshops and hands-on training on soldering, laser cutting and building devices with Arduino.[95]

There is a notable dynamic among makers and hacktivists. While they value their personal liberty and autonomy from external controls and restraints, at the same time, they are equally aware that they are part of a wider community and they are keen on using their freedoms for the benefit of others and society as a whole. They understand that it is necessary to "balance individual liberties with . . . broader social needs [and within] broader social systems".[96] As Maker I relays, we "really feel like we're part of the bigger community" than just the hacker community.[97] Hackers may place great importance on the individual and their individuality, but because of their social goals and beliefs, they are far from being self-centered or individualistic.

Makers and hacktivists are cognizant of their social responsibility. They have "a feeling of responsibility for educating and protecting society".[98] As Maker D relates, "It's good to do stuff for [yourself] but we [often] forget . . . that there's also a lot of work to do in improving this society".[99] They see the imperative "to steer those developments into directions that have a collective good".[100] For makers, 3D printing is about technical and social change. Maker C explains, "I see [that] the skill set of making and . . . 3D printing can . . . [help people] make anything they want and improve their lives".[101] Maker C continues, "That's why I'm so fascinated with 3D printing. The idea [that] these machines can help . . . with a bunch of other technologies. For me these things are important".[102] Maker I agrees, "I think we can really change things and allow other people to also create change" with 3D printers.[103] Maker I reflects on the role of technology in producing social change: "In a way, we're not creating the major change but we're creating a platform for change. . . . I like creating infrastructure because that can create a bigger effect".[104]

Hacking is often thought of as being a completely technical pursuit. But for makers and hacktivists, they recognize the social dimensions and obligations of hacking. This is especially true since "society is more . . . dependent on technology".[105] As Hacktivist B states, "any interaction with technology at some point does affect society in a way that goes far beyond the manufacturing of an object or artifact".[106] Maker I concurs, "There's so much technology changing society. If . . . we start thinking about this technology in a different way and by hacking" there can be a "macro effect".[107] For Maker D as well, "I [am always] aware that I do it for people and [I] try to [help] people . . . become better in what they do".[108] Maker D continues, "Sharing information, building a platform for people to improve society. . . . We want to become great people. That's more important than building one great product".[109] Makers and hacktivists believe that they have an important social role to play and having a "network of hackers is important because it's a kind of a backbone for society" that is becoming increasingly technological and ever more connected.[110] They maintain that "society increasingly depends on hackers to act as its conscience on these matters".[111]

Other prominent norms and values

Aside from the preceding five values that makers and hacktivists consider to be the most significant, there were other values that were particularly notable, namely: openness, freedom of access, transparency, security, and privacy. These values were especially prominent during discussions about controversial topics such as the high profile hacking of electronic voting machines and the Dutch national public transport card (the OV-chipcard).

Openness and freedom of access

Openness has always been a central value for hackers.[112] As discussed at length in Chapter 2, openness was a motive principle for previous hacker generations like computer hobbyists and FOSS developers, and the same is true for makers and hacktivists. Openness is a requisite to perform any and all of the common acts of hacking: *explore, break, learn, create, share* and *secure*. Makers especially value openness. "I think being open to the world with the things you do is very important", explains Maker L, "What for me is important in hacking is [that the technology is] open [and] everybody can use it".[113] The ethos of openness extends not just to their technologies and technical activities, but also to their social relations and how they deal with others. "Being open" is fundamental "so everybody can get connected to each other".[114] Maker F recounts, "because we are so open, I think most people we work with [see it as] a common thing to do".[115] Maker E similarly reflects, "it is amazing . . . that if you are so open and you share everything, then other people start doing that too".[116] Openness thus plays a crucial role in community building. This is especially true in hackerspaces where, according to Maker E, "we try to be as open as possible. We don't want to set boundaries".[117] Echoing a common sentiment in other hackerspaces, in relation to what happens within and to the hackerspace, "we throw everything out in the open. Too much maybe but we have absolutely no secrets. . . . Everything is out in the open and we try to spread that, and people automatically accept that".[118] The proclivity for openness and inclusiveness is evident as well at hacker camps where people strive to have a welcoming and festive atmosphere. At camps, save for the police and other public authorities, "[i]t is not acceptable to make others feel unwelcome because they are" different, and "[d]iscrimination, sexism, harassment and dismissive, demeaning and/or offending language are unacceptable".[119]

For most hackers, being open means embracing, developing and using technologies that are free and open source. At hacker camps, having a black ThinkPad running Linux was de rigueur. FOSS is definitely one of the principal embodiments of the value of openness. Most of the technologies that makers and hacktivists create and use are released under a FOSS license or are in the public domain.[120] Software is often made available on open repositories like GitHub. As Maker A relates, "A lot of [our] stuff is open source. A lot of people who do open source are really open about it".[121] Maker L explains the appeal of free and open source: "If a project I'm working [on is a free and] open source project . . . [and] not a closed source project, people who want to participate are able to [do so]. . . . It's not a closed group".[122] The fondness for technologies that are free and open is the reason why the decision of MakerBot to abandon openness and become a closed and proprietary company was exceptionally upsetting for makers. "Yeah, they went from a very open company to a very, very closed company", states Maker K.[123] According to Maker C, "There is always a tension especially because of MakerBot. They came out saying we're open hardware, [let's] change the world, and they ended up selling out to a company and being closed source".[124] There is a general feeling of disappointment and even betrayal among makers. Maker I explains, "You don't just say you're open source, but you actually have to do it. If you don't, a lot of people will really start disliking you".[125]

Openness also makes a lot of sense from a technical and practical perspective. There is a common belief among hackers that free and open is not merely necessary but also inevitable. According to Maker J, "It just doesn't work to say that you can keep things a secret. [With] technology, that's not going to work".[126] For many hackers, openness is the most sensible approach to technology. As Hacktivist D puts it, "Having technology [that is] more open, allowing people to hack it and make it . . . fit . . . their lifestyle or their personality, is a much more democratic and more natural approach to technology".[127] The epitome of this approach is the FOSS development model that many hackers subscribe to (see Chapter 2).

Openness directly relates to and supports another important hacker value – freedom of access. According to Maker H, "the hacker ethos is about making technology accessible to all people from all walks of life".[128] Similarly, for Hacktivist B, hacking represents "an opening to [have] a more free relationship [with] technology" and "freedom of access was one of the core values of [the hackerspace] from the beginning".[129] Emphasizing the social dimensions of hacking, Maker D narrates how "I like the project because it gives all citizens access to participating with IT".[130] Developing and using open source technologies and projects are integral to ensuring and promoting freedom of access. Maker D explains makers' experiences with and affection for open source software and hardware, "Everything is available and [people] don't feel limited. They feel that they can do [anything] they want".[131] Maker D further explains,

> Open source is very mature. . . . People can download everything they want and . . . use it for their own hobby. For software, they are not . . . limited. . . . For electronics, they can do everything they can because . . . open source hardware is always available.[132]

Transparency

Closely related to openness and freedom of access is the value of transparency. While these values are interconnected and overlap, transparency relates more to the actual state of technical and non-technical systems and structures. So, while openness and freedom of access generally pertain to the rights and capabilities in relation to technology, transparency concerns the character or condition of the technology or system itself. The goal of transparency is strongest among makers and ethical hackers possibly because of their need to *learn* about the inner workings of technical systems. Maker I explains the rationale for transparency in hacker projects: "usually all of their designs and code, everything is already on Github so you know what you're getting into".[133] Hacktivist C sums up the ideal of transparency whether for technologies, institutions or governments: "maximum transparency, minimum overhead, and maximum flow".[134]

In the same way makers and hacktivists insist on openness and freedom of access in their technologies and communities, they also expect and desire greater transparency from government and social institutions. As Maker L explains, "openness [and] open data . . . [are] very important" but "transparency is also" very necessary "especially for government".[135] Many makers and hacktivists perceive the government as a monolithic black box and there is palpable animosity and distrust particularly after the Edward Snowden revelations. Some hackers believe that secrecy breeds wrongdoing. They point to the incongruence and even hypocrisy of the situation: "the government wants to know much more about you, but wants to give out less information about itself".[136] While the Dutch government has formally tried to reach out and engage with the hacker community, many hackers share Hacktivist F's feeling that "it cannot be a true reaching out because there's no transparency. There's no true transparency. We don't really know what they're doing".[137] Hacktivists F continues, "The level of knowledge exchange will always be asymmetrical. So [we] think that there's very little to win for our communities to engage in that way".[138] Maker L agrees, "[governments] do all those kinds of things [like mass surveillance] but want the things they do to be kept secret".[139]

Hackers and people associated with the hacker community have used freedom of information laws as part of their hacking campaigns and projects. Availing of freedom of information requests, they seek to gain access to critical information and data about and from public authorities. According to one hacker, "If you look at it, it's a very short law but the implications are very big".[140] A hacker points out, "using freedom of information, I can use it against the government to reveal things".[141] For a number of hackers, freedom of information requests can be used to provide more transparency in government and greater freedom of access to public sector information. A few members of the hacker community view freedom of access as close to an absolute right: "Go to the military and police and say we're paying [for] your system. Open your data and see what you have. They will have to say, 'No, no, no'. You keep asking 'Why, why, why?' And in the end, they'll say state interest, and you go, which state, what's left of that state?"[142] However, many hackers have a less radical outlook and see the benefits of following the necessary procedures since "it's better to engage in a legal [or] policy way with those types of institutions through . . . freedom of information requests".[143]

Hackers find out about freedom of information laws either by actually "submitting FOIA requests, attending FOIA events, and sharing FOIA-related news on social media".[144] They also learn from journalists and people "with semi-legal background or at least with experience with freedom of information [laws]".[145] "Most of those guys became street-wise for sending the wrong [requests]. [They now know] how you should ask the question that [the government] cannot say no [to]", explains a hacker.[146] Hackers may use a freedom of information procedure "to force [government officials] to [put] what they stated on the phone on paper".[147]

However, resorting to freedom of information laws is neither straightforward nor without difficulties. It is worth noting that freedom of information requests were made in the voting computers campaign but "attempts to retrieve the source code of the machines via the Freedom of Information Act failed, because the source code is intellectual property of the producer" (see Chapter 5).[148] Similar requests were made in relation to the OV-chipcard hacks but they ultimately proved unproductive (see Chapter 5). A hacker explains the problems they face:

> We have freedom of information. We have official rules, but all the time governments [and] municipalities everywhere find it an annoyance and try

to blockade the openness of [the] information as much as possible. So people have to go to court. It takes a lot of time. Yeah, I find that it [could] be better.[149]

"They like to fight freedom of information requests", recounts a hacker, "Postpone them as much as they can . . . yeah, you see that a lot".[150] Furthermore, even if public authorities do respond, the information they provide is often not very useful because "all the interesting questions were not answered, because of . . . it's important to the country not to reveal it . . . national security".[151]

Makers and hacktivists would really like to see greater transparency in government. For Maker L, transparency is critical for democracy and fairness: "If a government wants to know a lot about me, I sure want to know everything from my government".[152] While there are some hackers who subscribe to a radical form of government transparency, there are those like Maker J who "don't really subscribe to the whole freedom of information philosophy. I think there is some information that doesn't have to be free necessarily".[153] However, Maker J clarifies, "but I do believe that for the most important things, [public authorities] need to be transparent about how they work, how they operate".[154] Ethical Hacker B agrees that even just "a bit of transparency would be nice, and even that can be achieved with technology . . . in that sense there's a lot possible but I don't know if everyone wants it".[155] It is interesting to note that the Dutch national and local governments have supported a number of open data initiatives and projects but the greatest hurdle to achieving a more transparent government is political or cultural rather than technical.[156] Based on personal experience, Maker B explains that the primary impediments to greater government transparency and open data are "cultural because technical[ly] it can be solved".[157]

Security

Hackers are very security conscious. They make it a point to make their computers and network connections safe and secure by, among others things, modifying and hardening their laptops, running more security-focused operating systems or software, using strong passwords, employing encryption, locking their computers when they are away, preferring to connect to the internet via wired rather than wireless connections, and accessing the Web using virtual private networks. Hacker camps are considered technology and security conferences and many of the presentations and hands-on workshops are about information security.[158]

Maker and hacktivists wholeheartedly agree that security is extremely important because of its intrinsic connection with other hacker values. Hacktivist D explains, "with individual autonomy and liberty, you only can achieve [this] if . . . privacy, security and anonymity are already there".[159] For Ethical Hacker B, "There are these . . . terms which are often placed closed to [each other] like privacy [and] anonymity, but . . . I guess they are covered by the term security".[160] Ethical hackers and hacktivists place great store on security because, for the former, they primarily engage in testing and securing systems and, for the latter, the security of their persons and computers is a main concern when they undertake socio-political campaigns. Ethical hackers in particular understand that in order to properly *secure* a technology or system, they first have to *explore* and *learn* how it works and this requires breaking or knowing how to *break* it. According to Ethical Hacker A, "The first step in attacking a system is knowing how it works [and] being able to work with it".[161] Securing systems and technologies is all the more difficult because, as Maker G says, "Systems are really complex. And if you want to defend, you have to find all the bugs . . . if you want to attack, you have to find one".[162]

While not all hackers are security professionals, they are all concerned about security and they see the importance of people using secure and robust technologies and fixing those that have security vulnerabilities. Maker H relates, "Hacking doesn't necessarily have to do with IT security, but there is a growing influence on at least the IT security aspect".[163] Despite or possibly because of their technical adeptness, most hackers view technology with a critical eye and have a healthy distrust of it. Ethical Hacker A explains the problem with security and technology:

> Something that makes it really interesting for me is that we don't . . . trust technology only. Or if you [trust] technology, in my opinion, you should open the technology and allow everyone to look at it and have a fair discussion about possible weaknesses in it. . . . So I think, hacking or security testing is a very interesting tool to prove that things are not OK.[164]

This skepticism is appropriate given that, as Maker J notes, "I was sort of surprised and appalled by the state of security in infrastructures that we have currently".[165]

Security is therefore seen as both a technical and a social imperative. Hacktivist E unequivocally states, "If vulnerabilities exist, they must be found and fixed".[166] For Maker B, the role of the hacker community is to act as "a kind of public watchdog for IT quality".[167] "As hackers, it's important for us to let policymakers, let lawmakers, the Parliament, know what those risks are", explains Maker L.[168] Maker J concurs, "I also feel that my knowledge helps me . . . improve the situation for security".[169] While hacking for the purposes of security testing has yet to gain widespread public acceptance, hackers unanimously agree that "bringing vulnerabilities to light is positive and constructive".[170] Hackers believe that they do not actually break systems but merely identify weaknesses in them since the systems were already broken in the first place because of existing vulnerabilities. As Ethical Hacker B argues, "It's not that someone here actually makes something broken, but [he or she] just identifies a weakness".[171]

Privacy

Last but far from being least, the value of privacy remains crucial for makers and hacktivists. As privacy is a complex subject and conceptually difficult to qualify and quantify, there is no unanimity among hacker as to what privacy definitely means. For some, privacy is about one's private life being free from the scrutiny or interference of others especially the government and commercial companies. Maker L feels that his privacy is infringed by extensive government surveillance: "Sometimes you . . . have the feeling, am I free to move around this country . . . without being tracked by the government?"[172] For other hackers, privacy is about independence or autonomy over one's personal life or private information. As Hacktivist D explains, "I think it's also a very one-dimensional idea of what privacy is. Privacy is not about keeping your data to yourself. Privacy for me is much more about having control and agency in which aspects . . . are known about you".[173] Hacktivist E agrees, "privacy is a problem of autonomy".[174]

What makes the matter of privacy all the more complicated is that it is inherently interconnected with other values. "You cannot have freedom of expression without privacy", claims Hacktivist F. According to Hacktivist E, "We're in a continuous split as well when it comes, for instance, [to] privacy and security".[175] But hackers like Maker L argue that "people put it that [with] privacy and security . . . you have to pick one over the other. I don't agree with that".[176] Maker L believes, "You can be open but have your privacy".[177] Hacktivist D supports this position by explaining, "There are many different moments in my life where I decided to give up some of my privacy to share [and talk] to a lot of people".[178] But Hacktivist D clarifies, "But it's much more about being in charge. That I am the one deciding that these . . . people are going to hear it and nobody else but them".[179]

While hackers may not completely see eye-to-eye on the exact meaning of privacy and how best to achieve it, they are in full agreement that it is an important value that must be preserved and protected. At hacker camps, taking photographs or videos of people is strictly frowned upon since "many participants are not keen on being in pictures, movies or audio recordings without their consent".[180] Hackers' concerns about privacy became extremely heightened in the aftermath of the Snowden revelations. Maker D recounts, "Privacy became the highest priority . . . when Snowden got out and warned us all".[181] The Snowden leaks confirmed what a number of hackers had suspected all along. Whether through the actions of governments and commercial companies or the technologies and systems they use, "I see a very big threat to privacy in the way . . . society is [currently] developing", says Maker J.[182] For Maker L, "I see in this country [and] all over the world, [we are] losing more and more [our] privacy".[183] There is a high degree of distrust and animosity among hackers toward governments, companies and even their own technologies. Hacktivist D relates, "I don't trust my own machine. You know, I have a laptop at home, which I generally don't trust. I also have my telephone. I have a sticker over my camera".[184] Hacktivist D continues, "People think privacy is important but they have . . . machines around them that they don't understand. They feel the machines are threatening their privacy".[185]

Post-Snowden, there has been a discernible increase in the number of hacker projects that directly deal with the matter of privacy and security. According to

Maker G, in the Dutch hacker scene, "yeah I guess there's some extra enthusiasm to getting more projects to defend against this".[186] Projects that make privacy and security tools more accessible and usable are on the rise and hackers like Maker J agree that, "I think that's a very good development".[187] For example, members of the hacker community have organized public workshops that are "basically about inviting people over for a 3-hour workshop with their laptops. And then we have . . . a menu of different tools you can install and we try to empower people to feel more in control of their machines".[188] While there is still heightened tension and anxiety and sometimes even paranoia among the hackers, on the whole, they have chosen a very self-reliant and do-it-yourself attitude and response to the problem of government surveillance and other threats to their privacy. Ethical Hacker B explains the constructive and pragmatic approach that many hackers have adopted concerning privacy and technology, "In general, if you really think something is violating [your] privacy then I'd rather . . . [try] to expose it or fix it even, [rather] than just dig myself [in] some hole saying I don't want to use it".[189] Maker L concurs, "It's hard to keep your privacy. Sometimes you can't, so . . . you make the best choice you can. But if possible I make the choice to keep my privacy".[190]

Hacker manifestos

Hacker norms and values can also be discerned from their written statements and other writings about their culture. Of the many texts and documents that have been written by or on behalf of hackers, the manifesto has proven to be a popular genre to express and enact their norms and values. Hacker manifestos are therefore valuable sources and materials for understanding hackers' conceptions and evaluations of and responses to what they consider acceptable conduct and desirable goals. According to Yanoshevsky, "The term manifesto, strictly speaking, applies to (often short) texts published in a brochure, in a journal or a review, in the name of a political, philosophical, literary or artistic movement".[191] It is traditionally "written collaboratively by a [fringe or marginalized] group and always on behalf of [that] group" who speaks of "We" versus "They".[192] It is generally written in short, urgent prose,[193] and often contains numbered theses or bulleted lists of the movement's key principles, statements and ideals.[194] Manifestos are normally written during times of social crises and upheaval,[195] and they carry out this struggle through programs or instructions for radical change.[196] While manifestos articulate and affirm certain norms and values,[197] they similarly transgress and transform other rules and standards of the acceptable and desirable both within and outside the manifesto writer's social world.[198] These manifestos are indisputably normative and aspirational.[199]

The nature and characteristics of manifestos help explain why there has been a long tradition of manifesto making among hackers. For individuals and groups who are used to harnessing technical codes and instructions to transform their environment, the idea of "chang[ing] reality with words" is both logical and appealing.[200] Hackers have always been viewed by mainstream society as subcultures or fringe groups. And, as seen in Chapter 2, all the different hacker types experienced periods of crisis and change where it was critical for them to affirm to themselves or assert to others their group identity and culture.[201] The five hacker manifestos examined below reveal important norms, values, beliefs and concerns of different types of hackers.

The hacker ethic

Among hackers, Levy's "The Hacker Ethic" is widely considered to be one of the founding declarations of some of the core elements and principles of hacker culture. "The Hacker Ethic" is particularly relevant because it is the first formal codification of the principles and philosophy of the first hacker generations. Prior to this, hacker culture and statements about its norms and values were not explicitly written down and were simply accepted and implicitly conformed to by hackers.[202] It is also worth noting that Levy wrote "The Hacker Ethic" during a period of crisis and change for hackers. As explained in Chapter 2, by the early 1980s, the originally free and open culture of hacking was giving way to the increasing commercialization, proprietization and closure of computing. This was also a time when hackers were beginning to be vilified in and by the media, and prosecuted by authorities.[203] It may be said that Levy was not just writing about, but also for and on behalf of the first generations of hackers. While this reveals an apparent partiality or bias that Levy has in favor of hackers, it is clear that he meant "The Hacker Ethic" and his entire book to be a wake-up call and an exhortation for people to recognize the important role that hackers play in society and to preserve the freedom, openness and dynamism of computer innovation.[204] At time he wrote his book, Levy was not very optimistic about the original hacker culture's chances of survival since he referred to Richard Stallman, who would become the founder of the free software movement, as "the last of the true hackers".[205]

Many hackers and of all types, including the famous German hacker collective, the Chaos Computer Club, refer to and use "The Hacker Ethic" as their founding principles and guides for action.[206] Despite being written by a person outside of their community, many hackers claim to subscribe to "The Hacker Ethic". As Jordan and Taylor explain,

> Rather than hackers themselves learning the tenets of the hacker ethic, as seminally defined by Steven Levy, they negotiate a common understanding of the meaning of hacking of which the hacker ethic provides a ready articulation. Many see the hacker ethic as a foundation of the hacker community.[207]

True to the manifesto genre, "The Hacker Ethic" is comprised of six tenets that are written in a hortatory and exaggerated style, tone and language: "Access to computers . . . should be unlimited and total. Always yield to the Hands-On

Imperative!", "All information should be free", "Mistrust Authority – Promote Decentralization", "Hackers should be judged by their hacking, not bogus criteria such as degrees, age, race, or position", "You can create art and beauty on a computer", and "Computers can change your life for the better".[208]

These tenets are clearly normative in character and are statements about what hackers value. For instance, the first tenet (total and unlimited access to computers) involves values concerning openness, freedom of information, freedom of access and personal growth. The second tenet (all information should be free) similarly affirms the importance of openness, freedom of information, freedom of access and transparency to hackers. The values of individual autonomy and liberty and decentralization and self-governance are supported by the third tenet (mistrust authority). The fourth tenet (judgment based on actions and ability) clearly relates to equality and meritocracy and creativity and innovation. With regard to the fifth tenet (creation of art and beauty), the values of freedom of expression and creativity and innovation are specifically implicated. Finally, the sixth tenet (life improvement) clearly supports the value of personal growth.

The conscience of a hacker

The Mentor's "The Conscience of a Hacker" is another manifesto that has been highly influential in the hacker community.[209] The piece was written by the Mentor in January 1986 after his arrest, and first appeared in the online hacker magazine *Phrack* later that year.[210] He was a member of the prominent American underground hacker group, Legion of Doom, and ran his own underground Bulletin Board System (BBS).[211] Aside from being a hacker, he was also a writer and became managing editor at Steve Jackson Games, a role-playing and strategy game company that was raided by the authorities as part of the crackdown on underground hackers.[212]

"The Conscience of a Hacker" has the hallmarks of a manifesto. It is made up of short paragraphs but the writing is very literary and poetic with its use of repetition and refrains (e.g., "Damn kid", "They're all alike", "you call us criminals"). It has a polemical and combative tone and uses aggressive and defiant language. To illustrate, the Mentor writes:

> We make use of a service already existing without paying for what could be dirt-cheap if it wasn't run by profiteering gluttons, and you call us criminals. We explore . . . and you call us criminals. We seek after knowledge . . . and you call us criminals.[213]

The words "we" and "us" (as opposed to the "you" or "they" of parents and authority figures) are used to refer to the community of underground hackers. The Mentor is decrying his and other hackers' recent arrests and adamantly affirms the identity, norms and values of underground hackers, which he believes are diametrically opposed to the status quo, including the legal order. In this highly provocative and evocatively written piece, the Mentor makes normative and value-laden statements about what hackers consider important: curiosity ("My crime is that of curiosity"), equality and meritocracy ("We exist without skin color, without nationality, without religious bias"), freedom of access ("We make use of a service already existing without paying for what could be dirt-cheap if it wasn't run by profiteering gluttons"), freedom of information ("We seek after knowledge"), individual autonomy and liberty ("We explore. . . . This is our world now"), creativity and innovation ("I found a computer. Wait a second, this is cool. It does what I want it to"), fun and play ("All he does is play games") and personal growth ("a door opened to a world").[214] He ends with the forceful and resolute lines, which signal the manifesto's moment of action: "I am a hacker, and this is my manifesto. You may stop the individual, but you can't stop us all . . . after all, we're all alike".[215] "The Conscience of a Hacker" is both a call for solidarity and a call to action among the underground hackers during a time when their group identity and personal security were being threatened by increasing criminal prosecution by law enforcement.

The GNU manifesto

"The GNU Manifesto" was written and subsequently reworked by Richard Stallman during the early years of the GNU Project.[216] The document does not merely explain the objectives and underlying philosophy of the GNU Project but, as a manifesto, it has the further aim of seeking out and inspiring kindred spirits to join the cause of free software and take immediate action.[217] Like "The Hacker Ethic", it was written during a time of great crisis when the commercialization and the steadfast focus of treating software as exclusive property were undermining the original tenets of the hacker community. Stallman explains the problems that he and other hackers faced at the time:

> the Golden Rule requires that if I like a program I must share it with other people who like it. Software sellers want to divide the users and conquer them, making each user agree not to share with others. I refuse to break solidarity with other users in this way.[218]

This hortatory and oppositional style and tone is present throughout the text. Stallman for example speaks of how the GNU Project will allow him to "to continue to use computers without dishonor".[219] While the manifesto is written in the first person, Stallman is actually writing to and speaking on behalf of the "We" of hackers and computer programmers who place great importance on sharing, collaboration and community building.[220]

The manifesto's main objective was to challenge the closed and proprietary approach to software development that was becoming ever more dominant, and to reinvigorate the culture of sharing and openness among hackers. As Stallman writes:

> Many programmers are unhappy about the commercialization of system software. It may enable them to make more money, but it requires them to feel in conflict with other programmers in general rather than feel as comrades. The fundamental act of friendship among programmers is the sharing of programs[221]

However, unlike "The Hacker Ethic" and "The Conscience of a Hacker", "The GNU Manifesto" has clear and definite program for radical action and social change. A major part of the plan involved building a "complete Unix-compatible software system" and "give it away free to everyone who can use it".[222] But instead of making the GNU Project a purely technical pursuit, "The GNU Manifesto" sought to promote an alternative and subversive approach to software development that ensured that the GNU Project remained free and open to all. The manifesto contains the beginning formulation of the idea of copyleft:

> GNU is not in the public domain. Everyone will be permitted to modify and redistribute GNU, but no distributor will be allowed to restrict its further redistribution. That is to say, proprietary modifications will not be allowed. I want to make sure that all versions of GNU remain free.[223]

The manifesto proposed a radical and powerful way to create and share computer code while remaining true to the values of the hacker community. "The GNU Manifesto" actualized the manifesto's moment of action by asking other programmers to join the movement and produce free software.[224]

"The GNU Manifesto" is suffused with statements about vital hacker norms and values. The values of openness, freedom of information and freedom of access are supported by the norm of sharing ("copying all or parts of a program is as natural to a programmer as breathing, and as productive. It ought to be as free").[225] For Stallman, the free sharing of computer code is logical and desirable because it promotes the values of efficiency ("It means that much wasteful duplication of system programming effort will be avoided. This effort can go instead into advancing the state of art"), social development ("restricting their use of [a program] is destructive because the restrictions reduce the amount and the ways the program can be used. This reduces the amount of wealth that humanity derives from the program"), and individual autonomy and liberty ("Complete system sources will be available to everyone. As a result, a user who needs changes in the system will always be free to make them himself").[226] The manifesto also upholds the importance of creativity and innovation ("If anything deserves a reward, it is social contribution. Creativity can be a social contribution, but only in so far as society is free to use the results").[227] In his defense of the free software development model, Stallman mentions how hackers prize the values of personal growth and fun and play ("[Programmers] got many kinds of nonmonetary rewards: fame and appreciation, for example. And creativity is also fun, a reward in itself").[228]

An anonymous manifesto

Hacktivist manifestos are closely related to and mainly build on the earlier writings of underground hackers like the Mentor. While no hacktivist manifesto has yet been as popular, influential or canonical as the three discussed above, "An Anonymous Manifesto" is a typical example of hacktivists' writings about their goals and concerns.[229] This document was written by members of the hacktivist group Anonymous, which is composed of technical and non-technical persons.[230] Anonymous claims to have "no leaders, no hierarchical structure, nor any geographical epicenter",[231] and, typical of hacker groups, has fluid membership and a high turnover rate.

"An Anonymous Manifesto" was written in early 2011 when the group was engaging in bold acts of hacktivism, including carrying out distributed denial-of-service (DDoS) attacks, against companies and governments around the world that they believe were acting unfairly and unjustly.[232] Since Anonymous was being equally praised and vilified in the media for their actions, this manifesto was an attempt by a few members of the group to formally set down in writing their aims and philosophy for their own as well as others' edification. As they say at the beginning of the manifesto: "Recently there has been some confusion as to our identities and our motives. Some of us would like to try and clear a few things up".[233]

"An Anonymous Manifesto" is what people normally expect a manifesto to be. First, the title declares that it is so. Second, it is a brief text that contains numbered theses of the group's principles. Third, its language and tone are hortatory and defiant. Additionally, the text is publicly asserted and signed by a collective "We". The manifesto is meant to be a critical discursive attack on dominant and powerful institutions and organizations and aims to stand up to them. The manifesto moment takes places when the reader is enjoined: "Becoming Anonymous is simple. Just take action".[234] Like "The Conscience of a Hacker", it similarly ends in an ominous way:

> We are Anonymous.
> We are Legion.
> We do not Forget.
> We do not Forgive.
> Expect Us.[235]

As a formal declaration of their goals and beliefs, the manifesto contains explicit and unequivocal statements about their norms and values. Members of Anonymous clearly value anonymity ("Anonymous is everyone. Anonymous is no one.

Anonymous exists only as an idea. You also can be Anonymous."),[236] but they also want to expressly "promote an open, fair, transparent, accountable and just global society".[237] In many statements in the text, the following values are plainly manifest: openness ("promote an open . . . global society"), freedom of information and freedom of access ("a society must be allowed to share information unrestricted and uncensored"), individual autonomy and liberty ("uphold the rights and liberties of its citizens"), privacy ("No citizen should be denied protection against any undue interference to his/her privacy"), transparency ("maintain an open and transparent society"), creativity and innovation ("to maintain cultural and technological evolution"), and decentralization and self-governance ("Citizens must be allowed to organize their own institutions without being harassed by existing institutions privileged by greater resources, influence and power").[238]

This is the maker manifesto

It is interesting to note that the interest in the manifesto genre has not waned among makers. "This is the Maker Manifesto" is typical of the manifestos written by makers.[239] Maker manifestos normally consist of a single page containing a numbered list of the key principles and statement of and about a group that has been graphically designed and laid out to look visually interesting or eye-catching. This is unlike the manifestos of previous hacker generations that were merely printed or laid out using simple texts without any thought about design. In addition, maker manifestos are generally less radical and aggressive in both their outlook and proposed actions. They are written primarily for the members of their community and deal with internal matters and concerns.

"This is the Maker Manifesto" was written on the occasion of a Maker Faire in Africa. Compared to the "An Anonymous Manifesto", the words used are not polemical, but they remain hortatory and aspirational because the aim is to produce personal and social development through direct and immediate action ("If you want something you've never had, then you've got to do something you've never done").[240] It is written for and by the "We", makers in Africa ("We will remake Africa with our own hands").[241]

The manifesto plainly seeks to achieve or promote values relating to: freedom of access ("We will share what we make"), creativity and innovation ("We will see challenges as opportunities to invent"), individual autonomy and liberty ("We will be responsible for acting on our own ideas"), and community development ("We will share what we make, and help each other make what we share").[242] Like "The Hacker Ethic", it champions the "Hands-On Imperative" ("We will remake Africa with our own hands" and "We will be obsessed with improving things, whether just a little or a lot").[243] The document further underscores the important activities of sharing and working together ("We will forge collaborations").[244] It powerfully hammers home these values through repetition by starting all declarations with the phrase "We will".[245] The manifesto's moment of action takes place when the forward-looking and repeated phrase "We will" is set in motion by the title "This is the Maker Manifesto",[246] which declares that the time to act is now.

All in all, hacker manifestos exhibit the norms and values of different types of hackers and hacker culture as a whole. As expressions of their beliefs and aspirations, manifestos are a rich source for examining their norms and values. Furthermore, for hackers themselves, manifestos symbolize and are touchstones of their identity and culture. These writings play a key role in the community formation and socialization of hackers. Manifestos like "The Hacker Ethic" and "The GNU Manifesto" are texts that hackers actually live by and they serve as constant calls to action.

Norms and values in conflict

With respect to their norms and values, makers and hacktivists share many things in common. The values of creativity and innovation, curiosity, and individual autonomy and liberty rank highest for both of them. Makers and hacktivists also place great importance on having free and open access to and use of information and technology. But there are differences between them as well. While they both highly prize community development and social development, makers place greater emphasis on the former whereas hacktivists have the end goal of social development when undertaking their hacking projects and activities. Their stronger concern for community development may be explained by the fact that makers regularly interact and spend more time with other makers in their hackerspaces. In contrast, hacktivists have fewer opportunities to socialize with one another and their interactions are often focused more on furthering their campaigns and causes. Makers also place added emphasis on openness and transparency because they need to have full access to technologies and systems in order to use them in new and interesting ways. On their part, hacktivists consider privacy and security to be of utmost importance. Compared to makers, hacktivists spend considerable attention and resources making sure that their and other people's technologies, systems and communications are private and secure due in no small part to the more serious and heavier nature of their activities.

Based on my research and in contrast to how hackers are generally depicted in popular and mass media, makers and hacktivists are not malicious, antisocial outlaws who are out to steal information and damage computers. In light of their norms and values, makers and hacktivists prize and strive to produce technical creativity and innovation for their own and other people's benefit. While their activities may be disruptive, they are not motivated by malice but are simply curious about learning how something works. Even though they cherish their individual autonomy and liberty, makers and hacktivists are very much socially conscious and community focused in their orientation and actions. Furthermore, they endeavor and aspire to achieve personal and social goals such as greater openness and freedom of access to technology, more transparency in government, better security of information systems, and stronger privacy protection.

It bears stressing though, that hacker norms and values are never stable or at rest, and neither do they exist peacefully in separate domains. They are in fact inherently and constantly interacting with each other. For instance, makers and hacktivists espouse openness and freedom of access to information and technology, but they are equally concerned with ensuring the privacy and security of computer systems and data. Based on my observations, makers and hacktivists are able to partly resolve this apparent incongruity by creating and using technologies and undertaking activities that are specific to some but not all of their values. For example, in relation to open source 3D printers, privacy and security are not major concerns and the primary focus of this technology is openness, creativity and innovation, and freedom of access. Privacy and security though are essential when hacktivists produce or use anonymization tools, encryption software and other security- and privacy-enhancing technologies. By compartmentalizing or tying their norms and values to the specific purposes and functions of different technologies, they are able to avoid some of these issues and contradictions. However, hackers' modular approach to technology vis-à-vis their norms and values cannot resolve all the conflicts that may arise. For instance, while penetration testing software and tools are designed for testing and improving the security of computer systems, they have also been used to comprise computers and breach the privacy of users. This means that makers and hacktivists cannot depend solely on technical design decisions to address these inconsistencies. Consider the values of individual autonomy and liberty and social development. While hackers seem to be able to strike a balance whereby they use their individual freedoms to achieve communal and social goals, there is no true equilibrium and things are never completely settled. There is a constant push and pull between varying and competing priorities and interpretations of these and other values. There are some hackers who believe in complete transparency and would not hesitate in disclosing any information that they discover, even it includes the personal data of ordinary users. There are a few makers who would pursue curiosity and creativity and innovation above all despite the potential risks to themselves and others. But what aids makers and hacktivists better deal with these conflicts, is that they do not hack in isolation, they socialize with other hackers, and they imagine themselves as belonging to the hacker community and the wider society. Being socially consciousness and active helps them go beyond their personal preferences and reconcile the tensions between their individual freedoms and their social responsibility.

Much attention, space and time have been devoted in this and the preceding chapter to describing and explicating the characteristics and nuances of hacker culture, norms and values, especially with regard to makers and hacktivists. Taking such a deep and prolonged dive into makers' and hacktivists' social worlds and their ways of meaning-making is crucial because it is a necessary and foundational step to more fully understanding the explicit and implicit reasons, intentions and motivations for their actions, beliefs and technological creations. As this chapter has shown, hackers are not value-free individuals and groups, and neither do they exist in a normative vacuum. Far from being "lawless" people or existing in a state of anomie, makers and hacktivists possess and perform multiple norms and values, and the social fields and spaces they inhabit and the technologies they produce are "normatively full"[247] and thickly value-laden.

The ways makers and hacktivists interpret and defend their varied norms and values (especially in times of crisis and change) can reveal a lot about why they act the way they do within their communities, and, equally important, how they react to external influences, threats and interferences particularly those arising from law and public authorities. The essentiality of studying the interactions and conflicts between norms and values becomes readily apparent when one recognizes that laws themselves express and enact expectations, evaluations, and prescriptions of the appropriate and the desirable, and these invariably come into conflict with hacker norms and values.

Notes

1 Amitai Etzioni, "Social norms: Internalization, persuasion, and history" 160 and 162.
2 Richard Posner, "Social norms and the law: An economic approach" 365.
3 Jack Gibbs, *Norms, Deviance, and Social Control* 2 and 16.
4 Interview with Maker J.
5 Interview with Maker K.
6 Interview with Maker F.
7 OHM2013, "Make".
8 Interview with Hacktivist D.
9 Interview with Hacktivist B.
10 Interview with Maker K.
11 Interview with Maker C.
12 Interview with Hacktivist A.
13 Interview with Maker A.
14 Interview with Maker B.
15 Interview with Maker D.
16 Interview with Maker I.
17 Interview with Maker D.
18 Interview with Maker C.
19 Interview.
20 Interview with Hacktivist C.
21 Interview with Maker K.
22 See Cassandra Kirsch, "The grey hat hacker" 386 (an ethical hacker, also known as a white hat hacker, is a person who breaks into a computer or information system to "find security flaws" and improve its security); see also Ronald Raether Jr., "Data security and ethical hacking" 55.
23 Interview with Ethical Hacker A.
24 Interview with Maker B; see also Paul Graham, *Hackers & Painters*.
25 See OHM2013, "Program"; see OHM2013, "Call for participation".
26 Interview with Ethical Hacker B.
27 Interview with Ethical Hacker A.
28 Interview with Hacktivist E.
29 Interview with Maker J; Interview with Hacktivist B.
30 Interview with Hacktivist E.

31 Interview with Maker A.
32 Interview with Maker E.
33 Interview with Hacktivist B.
34 Interview with Maker A.
35 Interview with Maker K.
36 Interview with Maker A.
37 OHM2013, "Press release".
38 OHM2013, "FAQ".
39 Interview with Hacktivist D.
40 Interview with Maker F.
41 Interview with Hacktivist E.
42 Interview with Maker K.
43 Interview with Ethical Hacker B.
44 Interview with Maker A.
45 Interview with Ethical Hacker B
46 Interview with Hacktivist B.
47 Interview with Hacktivist B.
48 OHM2013, "Call for participation".
49 Interview with Maker E.
50 Interview with Maker L.
51 Interview with Maker F.
52 Interview with Maker B.
53 Interview with Maker B.
54 OHM2013, "Call for participation".
55 Interview with Hacktivist E.
56 Interference, "Calling for papers".
57 Interview with Maker I.
58 Interview with Maker I.
59 See Sherry Turkle, *Alone Together*.
60 Interview with Maker D.
61 Interview with Maker G.
62 Interview with Maker D.
63 Interview with Hacktivist E.
64 Interview with Hacktivist C.
65 Hackerspaces.nl; see also Hackerspace Open Day.
66 Hackerspaces.nl.
67 See Gabriella Coleman, "The hacker conference: A ritual condensation and celebration of a lifeworld" 65.
68 OHM2013, "Press release".
69 See OHM2013, "FAQ"; see OHM2013, "Press release".
70 Interview with Maker B.
71 Interview with Maker E.
72 Interview with Maker G.
73 Interview with Maker B.
74 Interview with Maker E.
75 Interview with Maker E.
76 Interview with Maker E.
77 Interview with Maker D.
78 Interview with Hacktivist C.
79 Interview with Maker B.
80 Interview with Maker B.
81 Interview with Maker A.

82 Interview with Maker L.
83 Interview with Maker A.
84 Interview with Maker I.
85 Interview with Maker I.
86 Interview with Maker A.
87 Interview with Maker I.
88 Interview with Maker I.
89 Interview with Maker L.
90 Interview with Maker D.
91 OHM2013, "Observe".
92 Interview with Hacktivist D.
93 Interview.
94 Interview.
95 Hackerspace Open Day.
96 Interview with Hacktivist A.
97 Interview with Maker I.
98 OHM2013, "Hack".
99 Interview with Maker D.
100 Interview with Hacktivist B.
101 Interview with Maker C.
102 Interview with Maker C.
103 Interview with Maker I.
104 Interview with Maker I.
105 OHM2013, "Call for participation".
106 Interview with Hacktivist B.
107 Interview with Maker I.
108 Interview with Maker D.
109 Interview with Maker D.
110 Interview with Maker B.
111 OHM2013, "Call for participation".
112 Interview with Hacktivist B.
113 Interview with Maker L.
114 Interview with Maker D.
115 Interview with Maker F.
116 Interview with Maker E.
117 Interview with Maker E.
118 Interview with Maker E.
119 OHM2013, "Guidelines".
120 See OHM2013, "FAQ".
121 Interview with Maker A.
122 Interview with Maker L.
123 Interview with Maker K.
124 Interview with Maker C.
125 Interview with Maker I.
126 Interview with Maker J.
127 Interview with Hacktivist D.
128 Interview with Maker H.
129 Interview with Hacktivist B.
130 Interview with Maker D.
131 Interview with Maker D.
132 Interview with Maker D.
133 Interview with Maker I.

134 Interview with Hacktivist C.
135 Interview with Maker L.
136 Interview with Maker L.
137 Interview with Hacktivist F.
138 Interview with Hacktivist F.
139 Interview with Maker L.
140 Interview.
141 Interview.
142 Interview.
143 Interview.
144 Interview.
145 Interview.
146 Interview.
147 Interview.
148 Bart Jacobs and Wolter Pieters, "Electronic voting in the Netherlands" 11.
149 Interview.
150 Interview.
151 Interview.
152 Interview with Maker L.
153 Interview with Maker J.
154 Interview with Maker J.
155 Interview with Ethical Hacker B.
156 Noor Huijboom and Tijs Van den Broek, "Open data: An international comparison of strategies" 9; see Anneke Zuiderwijk and others, "Socio-technical impediments of open data".
157 Interview with Maker B.
158 See OHM2013, "Call for participation".
159 Interview with Hacktivist D.
160 Interview with Ethjcal Hacker B.
161 Interview with Ethical Hacker A.
162 Interview with Maker G.
163 Interview with Maker H.
164 Interview with Ethical Hacker A.
165 Interview with Maker J.
166 Interview with Hacktivist E.
167 Interview with Maker B.
168 Interview with Maker L.
169 Interview with Maker J.
170 Interview with Maker H.
171 Interview with Ethical Hacker B.
172 Interview with Maker L.
173 Interview with Hacktivist D.
174 Interview with Hacktivist E.
175 Interview with Hacktivist B.
176 Interview with Maker J.
177 Interview with Maker L.
178 Interview with Hacktivist D.
179 Interview with Hacktivist D.
180 OHM2013, "FAQ".
181 Interview with Maker D.
182 Interview with Maker J.
183 Interview with Maker L.

184 Interview with Hacktivist D.
185 Interview with Hacktivist D.
186 Interview with Maker G.
187 Interview with Maker J.
188 Interview.
189 Interview with Ethical Hacker B.
190 Interview with Maker L.
191 Galia Yanoshevsky, "Three decades of writing on manifesto" 261 (citing Abastado); Brian Fauteux, "Manifestos and the shape of punk to come" 466.
192 Martin Puchner, "Manifesto = theatre" 455; see also Mary Ann Caws, *Manifesto* xx and xxiii; see also Galia Yanoshevsky, "The decades of writing on manifesto" 279 and 282.
193 Mary Ann Caws, *Manifesto* xxi, xxiii and xxvii; Martin Puchner, "Manifesto = theatre" 451 and 464; Galia Yanoshevsky, "The decades of writing on manifesto" 264.
194 Mary Ann Caws, *Manifesto* xxvi; Martin Puchner, "Manifesto = theatre" 451; Natalie Alvarez and Jenn Stephenson, "A manifesto for manifestos" 4.
195 Galia Yanoshevsky, "The decades of writing on manifesto" 263; Mary Ann Caws, *Manifesto* xxiii (who says that manifestos can also define a moment of crisis).
196 Brian Fauteux, "Manifestos and the shape of punk to come" 467; Galia Yanoshevsky, "The decades of writing on manifesto" 268; Teresa Ebert, "Manifesto as theory" 553.
197 Galia Yanoshevsky, "The decades of writing on manifesto" 268.
198 Teresa Ebert, "Manifesto as theory" 556.
199 Teresa Ebert, "Manifesto as theory" 556; Martin Puchner, "Manifesto = theatre" 452.
200 Galia Yanoshevsky, "The decades of writing on manifesto" 264.
201 See Goran Therborn, "Back to norms!" 869.
202 Steven Levy, *Hackers* x and 27.
203 Steven Levy, *Hackers* ix; see Debora Halbert, "Discourses of danger and the computer hacker".
204 Steven Levy, *Hackers* x and 464.
205 Steven Levy, *Hackers* 437.
206 Chaos Computer Club, "Hacker ethics".
207 Tim Jordan and Paul Taylor, "A sociology of hackers" 774–775.
208 Steven Levy, *Hackers* 28–34.
209 David Wall, *Cybercrime* 55.
210 The Mentor, "The conscience of a hacker".
211 Bruce Sterling, *The Hacker Crackdown* 89 (see Chapter 2 for more information about hackers and BBSes).
212 Bruce Sterling, *The Hacker Crackdown* 246 and 274; see "GURPS Cyberpunk".
213 The Mentor, "The conscience of a hacker".
214 The Mentor, "The conscience of a hacker".
215 The Mentor, "The conscience of a hacker".
216 Richard Stallman, "The GNU manifesto"; see Chapter 2 for history and context.
217 Richard Stallman, "The GNU manifesto".
218 Richard Stallman, "The GNU manifesto".
219 Richard Stallman, "The GNU manifesto".
220 Richard Stallman, "The GNU manifesto".
221 Richard Stallman, "The GNU manifesto".
222 Richard Stallman, "The GNU manifesto".
223 Richard Stallman, "The GNU manifesto".

224 Richard Stallman, "The GNU manifesto".
225 Richard Stallman, "The GNU manifesto".
226 Richard Stallman, "The GNU manifesto".
227 Richard Stallman, "The GNU manifesto".
228 Richard Stallman, "The GNU manifesto".
229 Anonymous, "An anonymous manifesto".
230 Gabriella Coleman, "Anonymous: From the Lulz to collective action"; see Parmy Olson, *We Are Anonymous*.
231 Gabriella Coleman, "Anonymous: From the Lulz to collective action".
232 Gabriella Coleman, "Anonymous: From the Lulz to collective action".
233 Anonymous, "An anonymous manifesto".
234 Anonymous, "An anonymous manifesto".
235 Anonymous, "An anonymous manifesto".
236 Anonymous, "An anonymous manifesto".
237 Anonymous, "An anonymous manifesto".
238 Anonymous, "An anonymous manifesto".
239 Maker Faire Africa, "This is the maker manifesto".
240 Maker Faire Africa, "This is the maker manifesto".
241 Maker Faire Africa, "This is the maker manifesto".
242 Maker Faire Africa, "This is the maker manifesto".
243 Maker Faire Africa, "This is the maker manifesto".
244 Maker Faire Africa, "This is the maker manifesto".
245 Maker Faire Africa, "This is the maker manifesto".
246 Maker Faire Africa, "This is the maker manifesto".
247 John Griffiths, "What is legal pluralism?" 34.

Chapter 4

Laws on hacking

Of the laws that are material to hacking, computer crime laws and intellectual property laws are without doubt the most significant and consequential to hackers. This is not surprising given that computer crime legislations specifically target activities concerning illegal or unauthorized access and use of computer systems and data, and intellectual property laws are chiefly concerned with the exclusive rights of control over access to and use of information, content and know-how.[1] While much of the discussion centers on these two fields, other areas of law are also tackled.

Computer crime laws

Brief history and development

As touched on in Chapter 2, a number of factors and conditions led to the outlawing and criminalization of hacking.[2] Beginning in the 1980s, governments around the world enacted computer crime laws and intensified prosecutions and enforcement activities against hacking-related activities.[3] In the United States, for example, "[t]he first federal computer-crime legislation was proposed in 1979" but it was not formally adopted until 1984.[4] This federal law was subsequently revised to "set up a more comprehensive legal framework for the prosecution of computer crimes",[5] and became the US Computer Fraud and Abuse Act (US CFAA).[6] The US CFAA like other computer crime laws concerns the prohibition of "a variety of acts involving the use of computers" and "the prosecution of certain crimes accomplished by means of a computer".[7] It bears noting that the first computer crime laws in the United States were enacted by state legislators in Florida and Arizona as early as 1978,[8] but, until 1984, less than 200 cases were prosecuted and fewer still went to trial under these and other subsequent state computer crime laws.[9] Most of these cases involved insiders (i.e., disgruntled employees or disloyal agents) who exceeded their authority instead of outside hackers who had no authority at all to access the relevant computers.[10] A number of European countries similarly passed their own computer crime statutes in the 1980s and early 1990s.[11] It is notable that Germany, the Netherlands, Italy and Finland adopted computer crime laws notwithstanding or possibly because of the existence of prominent and distinctly recognizable hacker traditions and cultures within their respective jurisdictions.[12] As with the US CFAA, European computer crime laws prohibit and penalize various acts and conduct, most specifically "unauthorized access", "trespass" and "causing damage" to computers and data.[13]

With the greater availability and use of computers and their interconnection with wider and ultimately global information and communications networks from the 1980s onwards, computer crime has become a growing national, regional and international concern and many state actors have sought to address or find solutions to it.[14] For instance, the Organisation for Economic Co-operation and Development (OECD) has published reports, guidelines, recommendations and implementation plans on computer-related crime and information security since the mid-1980s.[15] The OECD's proposed policies on computer crime were addressed to international and regional bodies, state agencies, private entities and even individual computer users.[16] However, the establishment of a formal and harmonized international legal regime on computer crime would only take place after the start of the millennium through the adoption of the Council of Europe's Convention on Cybercrime (the Convention on Cybercrime).[17] The Convention was released for ratification in 2001 and was the outcome of years of discussions and consultations among governments and other interested parties.[18] The Convention entered into force in 2004 and, at the time of writing, has been ratified or acceded to by 48 states and counting, including quite a number of countries outside of Europe like the United States, Australia and Japan.[19] All EU Member States have signed the Convention and most have formally ratified it.[20]

The Convention on Cybercrime is widely "regarded as the most complete international standard to date, since it provides a comprehensive and coherent framework embracing the various aspects relating to cybercrime".[21] As "the leading international instrument" on computer crime, many of the Convention's principles and provisions have been replicated or translated into regional and national laws.[22] The European Union for its part adopted Council Framework Decision 2005/222/JHA on attacks against information systems (the Framework Decision) in 2005 and, like the Convention on Cybercrime, it "requires that Member States criminalise the acts of attempting or obtaining illegal access to or perpetrating illegal interference with, information systems, together with acts intended to instigate, aid, or abet the practice".[23] In 2013, the Framework Decision was replaced by Directive 2013/40/EU on attacks against information systems (the Cybercrime Directive).[24] The aim of the Directive is to build on the Framework Decision and the Convention of Cybercrime and "amend and expand" the legal rules and processes in light of current practices and technologies used in cybercrime particularly the creation and use of "botnets" to carry out large-scale attacks.[25] The primary objective of the Directive is "to approximate the criminal laws of the Member States in the area of attacks against information systems by establishing minimum rules concerning the definition of criminal offences and the relevant sanctions".[26] It seeks to accomplish this by having a "common approach" across the European Union with regard "to the constituent elements of criminal offences by introducing common offences".[27] The Convention on Cybercrime and the Directive criminalize "offences against the confidentiality, integrity and availability of computer data and systems".[28] These acts fall under the general category of "computer security crimes".[29]

Computer crime and hacking

Criminalization may be deemed to be the most forceful response of the law and public authorities to hacking activities and technologies.[30] Computer crime laws prohibit certain forms of hacking by declaring them to be illegal and imposing criminal liability and penalties like imprisonment and fines on those who engage in such acts or conduct. Equating hacking to criminality and deviance has profound consequences for hackers.[31] By broadly outlawing and prosecuting hacking-related activities, computer crime laws tend to restrict and hinder the capability of makers, hacktivists and other types of hackers to creatively and constructively access and use information and technology.

In contrast to the more complex and dense meaning of hacking propounded in this book, under the Convention on Cybercrime and related or analogous regional and national computer crime laws and policies, hacking is used as a generic term to describe "the basic offence of dangerous threats to and attacks against the security (i.e., the confidentiality, integrity and availability) of computer systems and data".[32] While hacking *per se* is not formally and specifically defined and criminalized under the Convention or the Cybercrime Directive, the term is repeatedly used by public authorities and the media as a shorthand for activities that impair the security and integrity of computers.[33] Computer crime laws are sometimes called "anti-hacking statutes".[34] It may not have been the law's intention, but hacking has nonetheless been associated and lumped together with computer crime.[35] As a result, many projects and activities of makers and hacktivists end up being viewed as *prima facie* illegal and potentially in violation of the five kinds of computer security crimes: illegal access, illegal interception, data interference, system interference, and misuse of devices.[36]

Illegal access

Access or entry without right

Illegal or unauthorized access is generally considered to be the essence or crux of computer security crime.[37] Under the Convention on Cybercrime, illegal access is committed by intentionally accessing "the whole or any part of a computer without right".[38] In technical terms, access involves entering any part or aspect of a computer or information system including "hardware, components, stored data of the system installed, directories, traffic and content-related data".[39] The phrase "without right" may be understood as referring to "conduct undertaken without authority (whether legislative, executive, administrative, judicial, contractual or consensual) or conduct that is otherwise not covered by established legal defences, excuses, justifications or relevant principles under domestic law".[40] The Cybercrime Directive specifically defines "without right" as that "which is not authorised by the owner or by another right holder of the system or of part of it, or not permitted under national law".[41] It must be "understood in a broad sense and including persons who are not entitled to act as they did either in their own right or by authority of those who had a right".[42] Therefore, both outsiders (who have no authority to access a computer system) and insiders (who have exceeded their authority) can commit this offense.[43]

Under computer crime laws, mere entry, intrusion or access to a computer without right or sans the permission of the owner is already a punishable offense.[44] In crafting the provision on illegal access in this way, the drafters opted for a broad application of and a restrictive approach to criminalization.[45] While it is true that the Convention grants state parties the option to include "additional qualifying circumstances" for the commission of the crime,[46] such as "infringing security measures, special intent to obtain computer data, other dishonest intent that justifies criminal culpability, or the special requirement that the offence is committed in relation to a computer system that is connected remotely to another computer system",[47] the United States and most European countries chose the default position and did not incorporate any of these qualifications into their national laws.[48] A handful of countries opted to include either infringing security measures or special or dishonest intent as an element of illegal access.[49] The Netherlands, which originally required infringing a security measure as a requisite for committing illegal access, removed this condition when the relevant Dutch law was amended in 2006.[50]

In a curious development though, the requirement of infringing of a security measure has been made mandatory under the updated Cybercrime Directive.[51] European policy makers have not proffered an explicit reason why this new requirement has been included.[52] It is worth noting that "infringing security measures" was part of the original wording of the crime of unauthorized access that was proposed by the Select Committee of Experts on Computer-related Crime, which was originally tasked by the Council of Europe's European Committee on Crime Problems to study the issue of computer-related crime in the mid to late 1980s.[53] Further, European lawmakers appear to impliedly agree with a proposal made by the legal scholar, Orin Kerr, that illegal or unauthorized access should be limited to "*access that circumvents restrictions by code*".[54] Kerr explains the rationale for limiting illegal access to cases where there is an infringement of a security measure:

> my proposal to limit the scope of unauthorized access to the circumvention of code-based restrictions draws a more balanced line between openness and privacy. . . . The proposal would allow Internet users to use the Internet . . .

without the chilling effect of possible criminal sanctions arising from the breach of . . . contractual terms.[55]

Kerr's position is seemingly confirmed in one of the recitals of the Cybercrime Directive, which states that

> contractual obligations or agreements to restrict access to information sys-tems by way of a user policy or terms of service, as well as labour disputes as regards the access to and use of information systems of an employer for private purposes, should not incur criminal liability.[56]

According to Freitas and Goncalves, the legal and policy implication of the new requirement is that infringing a security measure is "now considered a minimum legal standard that national States can further develop or not" and/or "the mini-mum rules concerning illegal access that were established by the European Union in Article 2 (1), of the Framework Decision 2005/222/JHA go beyond what is required in the current state of affairs".[57] The inclusion of infringing a security measure as an additional element of the crime of illegal access is a notable devel-opment in computer crime laws in Europe.

Objectives and justifications

The Convention on Cybercrime's restrictive approach to computer security crimes can be further explained and justified in relation to the norms and values that the drafters sought to uphold or realize. The express statements and rules about the acceptable and the desirable contained in the Convention, particu-larly its Preamble, cluster around three main concerns: (1) deterrence, prosecu-tion or correction of inappropriate or undesirable behavior; (2) promotion of innovation and technology use and development; and (3) protection of public safety and order. Of the three, the first is the principal focus of the Conven-tion as evidenced by such declarations as the necessity to: "deter action directed against . . . computer systems, networks and computer data as well as [their] mis-use", "effectively combating such criminal offences, by facilitating their detec-tion, investigation and prosecution", and "make criminal investigations and proceedings concerning criminal offences related to computer systems and data more effective and to enable the collection of evidence in electronic form of a criminal offence".[58]

In relation to the value of promoting innovation, the Convention asserts the need "to protect legitimate interests in the use and development of information technologies" and "to seek common responses to the development of the new information technologies based on the standards and values of the Council of Europe".[59] When they speak about preventing "damage to legitimate interests", the drafters of the Convention for the most part refer to the individuals and organizations that own, control or commercially develop computer systems and data.[60] It is worth quoting at length the reasoning behind criminalizing mere access:

> The need for protection reflects the interests of organisations and individuals to manage, operate and control their systems in an undisturbed and uninhibited manner. The mere unauthorised intrusion, i.e. "hacking", "cracking" or "computer trespass" should in principle be illegal in itself. It may lead to impediments to legitimate users of systems and data and may cause alteration or destruction with high costs for reconstruction. Such intrusions may give access to confidential data (including passwords, information about the targeted system) and secrets, to the use of the system without payment or even encourage hackers to commit more dangerous forms of computer-related offences, like computerrelated fraud or forgery.[61]

Illegal access is therefore also viewed as a "basic offense" that can potentially lead to the carrying out of other, more serious cyber attacks or crimes.[62]

The third value of public safety and order is stated succinctly as "the protection of society against cybercrime".[63] While the drafters of the Convention believed that "the introduction and development of effective security measures" was the "most effective means of preventing unauthorised access", they still made the latter a crime on the ground that

> a comprehensive response has to include also the threat and use of criminal law measures. A criminal prohibition of unauthorised access is able to give additional protection to the system and the data as such and at an early stage.[64]

The underlying rationale for criminalizing offenses against the security and integrity of computers was that "[t]echnical measures to protect computer systems need to be implemented concomitantly with legal measures to prevent and deter criminal behaviour".[65] In the Netherlands, the inclusion of the (later abolished) requirement of infringing a security measure for illegal access "was considered relevant as an incentive to encourage people and companies to protect their computers".[66]

Conflicts with acts, norms and values of hacking

While the Convention's stated and implied standards and goals represent vital social concerns and public interests and are worthy of promotion and protection as such, they also conflict with and have significant ramifications on both other and others' norms and values, especially those of hackers who are inevitably affected by computer crime laws. There is no question that the criminalization and prosecution of malicious activities and destructive cyber attacks on computer systems and data are proper under the law. However, due to the vagueness and excessive breadth of the law, the crime of illegal access strikes at the heart of hacking since it broadly prohibits access to and use of computer systems and data and it does not provide adequate exemptions or qualifications for creative and benign forms of hacking.[67] As previously mentioned, free and open access to information and technology and being able to use them in new, innovative and unexpected ways are conditions and goals of hacking.[68] But, since hackers can, legally speaking, only enter or access a computer or system that they own or have authority or permission to use (otherwise they may be subject to criminal prosecution), their present and future practices, activities and projects are severely inhibited.[69] The far-reaching impact of the crime of illegal access on makers and hacktivists is all the more apparent when viewed in light of the six common acts of hacking. Under computer crime laws, hackers are generally forbidden by default to *explore* or *break* a computer system without permission even if the aim is to *learn* how it works. As a consequence, they cannot *create* new technologies or produce innovations that they can *share* with others. Furthermore, and here's the rub, by not being able to hack and test a computer system, hackers cannot make it more *secure*, which ironically is one of the prime objectives of computer crime laws.[70] Expecting or requiring hackers to seek or obtain prior permission from system owners before they can creatively explore a system is unrealistic given that it is not in their character to ask for permission first before accessing or using technology. In addition, hackers consider requesting *ex ante* permission to be a futile exercise because they believe system owners would refuse their request outright since the latter are generally averse to the discovery of vulnerabilities and weaknesses in their information systems. It must be remembered that it was computer system owners and other private interests who were instrumental in getting computer crime laws passed in the first place.[71] But it should be noted that the attitude of computer owners towards hacking is changing and they are becoming more open to hackers exploring and testing their information systems (see Chapter 6 on responsible disclosure rules and bug bounty programs).

Illegal access can also have a detrimental effect on hacker norms and values. Criminal prosecution, whether threatened or actual, for unauthorized access directly clashes with the norms and values of openness, freedom of access, and freedom of information since computers and knowledge about them are closed off to hackers by default. Further, makers and hacktivists cannot pursue other goals such as curiosity, fun and play, creativity and innovation, transparency, and security since illegal access makes computers black boxes that they cannot freely take apart and explore. It bears repeating that makers and hacktivists generally undertake hacking projects and activities with no malice or intent to cause damage and they do so for the benefit of their community and society as a whole. They are far from being vandals who just want to have fun at someone else's expense. The lack of freedom to access computers has negative effects on hackers' individual autonomy and liberty to follow and develop their own interests, their ability to improve themselves (personal growth), and their positive role and contribution to their communities (community development) and the world at large (social development). As explained in the previous chapters, hackers are socially conscious and have a communitarian ethos, which means that they do not seek personal growth for its own sake but always in relation to how they can contribute to their community and the wider society.

It is interesting to note that the drafters of the Convention on Cybercrime were quite cognizant that criminalizing mere entry to a computer system would have negative consequences. They acknowledge in the Exploratory Report to the Convention that reservations about or opposition to making access to a computer a crime "stems from situations where no dangers were created by the mere intrusion or where even acts of hacking have led to the detection of loopholes and weaknesses of the security of systems".[72] The Select Committee of Experts on Computer-related Crime that was originally tasked by the Council of Europe's European Committee on Crime Problems to study the issue of computer-related crime in the mid to late 1980s had reasonably good knowledge about hacking. In its Recommendation No. R (89) 9 on computer-related crime (Recommendation No. (89) 9), the Committee describes hacker culture in quite a nuanced way:

> Hackers explore the capabilities of computers and communications, causing them to perform to their limits. . . . Pure unauthorised access to computer systems is mainly committed by young hackers, who have a variety of motives. They may intend to improve data protection; they may want to overcome the challenge of a company's security system; they may enjoy infiltrating data banks, or they may want to boast among friends or to the press. When some cases become public, these acts of hacking can be useful for the detection of loopholes in computer systems.[73]

However, despite having a fair understanding of hackers, the Committee still recommended the criminalization of unauthorized access because in its words:

> the committee considers them as dangerous because system errors, failures, blockades or even crashes may be caused; data may be destroyed by negligence, or security deficiencies, found by acts committed as a challenge, may subsequently be used for financial fraud or for the modification of stored data. . . . The activity of hacking may give access to confidential data which the hacker may use to his own advantage. . . . In addition, hackers often avoid payments, for example with the aid of so-called 'blue boxes'.[74]

Rather than leaving space for the creative albeit disruptive aspects of hacking, the Committee quite understandably decided on a simpler and more conservative approach. Following the lead and echoing the attitude of the Committee, the drafters of the Convention opted for the broad approach to criminalizing illegal access.[75]

Problem of excessive breadth and vagueness

Because of the widespread adherence to this broad application and interpretation of the crime of illegal access, it comes as no surprise that, according to legal scholars, the foremost criticisms against the law are that it suffers from excessive breadth, vagueness and over-criminalization.[76] Since the 1980s, the legitimacy, soundness and effectiveness of computer crime laws have been perennially questioned based on these grounds.[77] The primary reason why computer crime laws, especially the provisions on illegal access, are considered overly broad and vague and that they over-criminalize hacking is because they do not include "subjective criteria" for establishing the *mens rea* of the proscribed offenses, and thus result in a unreasonably low "threshold for culpability".[78]

A number of early computer crime laws distinguished innocent acts of computer exploration done by well-intentioned hackers from those harmful activities committed by computer criminals that threatened or caused damage to computer systems and data.[79] For example, an early California law "criminalized unauthorized access to a computer file made under false pretenses, but excluded actions that were not 'malicious' in nature".[80] As borne out by the legislative histories of these early US computer crime laws, they were "intended to apply only to crime of computer misuse and not to crimes incidentally involving the use of a computer".[81] A similar light-touch approach to illegal access was initially considered in other countries. For example, the Scottish Law Commission in the late 1980s recommended the criminalization of illegal access but subject to the condition that the perpetrator had the intention "of procuring an advantage for himself or another person; or of damaging another person's interest".[82] Following this formulation, either a motive of personal gain or an intention to cause damage was a necessary element for the commission of the crime. Thus, for illegal access to be committed, the proposed law would require an ulterior motive or "unauthorised access plus an intent to cause harm to the interests of the computer owner".[83] The rationale for this higher or stricter *mens rea* standard was to avoid over-criminalization and to ensure that a hacker who gains "access to a system 'with no intent of abusing its contents and who causes no damage'" would not be held criminally liable.[84]

However, due to the growing interest and demand by various parties to strengthen and broaden the scope computer crime laws, the subjective criteria of malice or criminal intent was in time either removed from or not incorporated into most computer crime laws,[85] although some countries such as Austria, Lithuania, Estonia, Hungary, Mexico, Portugal, Romania and Slovakia did include infringing security measures or special or dishonest intent as an additional requirement.[86] In the United States, a number of states amended their laws to remove the requirement of malicious intent.[87] Similarly, legislators in the United Kingdom ultimately decided that "the act of obtaining unauthorised access should be made unlawful regardless of whether the perpetrator possessed any ulterior motive" or intended to cause damage.[88] As a result, certain hacking-related activities "would be declared criminal even where hackers acted out of a sense of curiosity or from the desire to test their computing skills by overcoming security devices intended to prevent unauthorised persons from obtaining access to a computer system".[89] Thus, the all-important "legal distinction between benign trespass and harmful cracking has been virtually written out" of the law.[90]

Unintended consequences and negative effects

Additionally, the overly broad and vague application and interpretation of the crime of illegal access by public prosecutors, the courts and other authorities have produced further negative knock-on effects in the areas of security, competition and innovation, and the everyday use of technology.[91] These "deleterious effects" and unintended consequences of computer crime laws do not only concern or impact the purported targets of computer crime laws (i.e., computer criminals and malicious attackers), but they also affect security researchers, market competitors, ordinary users and other actors.[92]

Although counterintuitive, one of the ironic outcomes of criminalizing illegal access is that it ultimately results in making computer systems and data less secure.[93] In the computer security industry, it is axiomatic that properly securing a system is a difficult and complex matter, and it requires the active involvement of a group of people with deep knowledge of and masterful skills in specific technologies or systems who can rigorously and ingeniously scan, test and attempt to penetrate them – in other words, hackers.[94] The trouble with illegal access is that it makes it risky for hackers to test the security of systems because of the low threshold for committing the offense (i.e., mere access).[95] The law problematically "doesn't make any distinction between bona fide research and criminal activity".[96] There have been a number of notable cases and instances where hackers and security researchers have been either threatened with prosecution or actually charged for violating computer crime laws for conducting security research and testing and disclosing information about their findings.[97] Computer crime laws tend to produce a "chilling effect" whereby hackers and "independent researchers around the world working to improve security have faced legal threats under existing laws, despite the fact they have no malicious intentions and are performing work that ultimately serves the public".[98] Society as a whole can benefit from hacking for the purposes of security testing because "there can be very important democratic interests in having access to systems to test for security vulnerabilities even when 'authorization' to do so is refused".[99]

Security researchers are not the only ones who are adversely affected by computer crime laws. Companies and commercial enterprises have been threatened or sued for violating the illegal access provision by their market rivals.[100] The use of criminal prosecution and the threat of criminal liability as proxies or alternatives to market competition was never the goal or intention of computer crime laws.

Companies, particularly those providing internet-based services, have used illegal access as a means to impede or "stifle competition" and use the law's "imprecise language to stymie competitors who create new tools that would spur the economic market and give consumers more choice".[101] In most of these cases, the acts sought to be suppressed do not infringe or have anything to do with the security of a company's system.[102] The law is merely utilized as an instrument to protect and preserve a perceived competitive advantage, whether it be business, technical or information related.[103] While a person or business has the right resort to any action or remedy that is available to them to seek relief within the bounds of law, what is troubling with these cases is that they are backed by the threat of criminal liability and sanctions, including imprisonment. It is problematic when computer crime laws are not used to protect the security of computer systems and data, but rather to preserve ways of doing business, which should be generally open to free and robust competition. This misapplication of computer crime laws has a detrimental effect on competition and innovation, which is, again, ironically another primary goal of these laws.[104]

Ordinary users are also not spared from the negative effects of the legal prohibition against illegal access. Because illegal access is open to expansive interpretation and application by law enforcement bodies and the courts, even the common, everyday practices of ordinary users and their normal uses of technology can be construed as being in violation of the law when coupled with restrictive contracts and terms of service.[105]

Exploitable gaps, loopholes and contradictions

Despite the broad application of the crime of illegal access, it is still possible for hackers to engage in hacking activities by taking advantage of a few, small but quite exploitable gaps, loopholes and internal contradictions within the law, whether for tactical purposes or as points of subversion or transformation. Under computer crime laws, it is generally accepted and understood that no criminal liability should attach "for accessing a computer system that permits free and open access by the public, as such as is 'with right' ".[106] This means that (subject of course to the important assumption or qualification that a mere violation of contractual terms of use is not covered by computer crime laws) there is a general albeit implied permission granted to the public at large to freely access and use publicly available or public-facing computers or systems.[107] As such (and assuming there are no inordinately restrictive terms of service), hackers have much more leeway to use information and technological products and services that are offered or targeted to the general public such as Facebook, YouTube and Amazon, as well as e-government websites and services since they have been granted authority or permission to use them (in contrast to completely private computer systems). In their roles as users and consumers, hackers are afforded certain basic yet quite serviceable rights and protections to engage in hacking projects and activities. Specifically in relation to public websites, internet users (including hackers) have an implicit yet clear right to access and use such websites. As explained by the drafters of the Convention,

> the maintenance of a public web site implies consent by the web site-owner that it can be accessed by any other web-user. The application of standard tools provided for in the commonly applied communication protocols and programs, is not in itself 'without right', in particular when the rightholder of the accessed system can be considered to have accepted its application.[108]

This means that the use of web browsers, "bots", "crawlers" and other standard or common internet tools, techniques and practices are within the ambit of lawful access, subject of course to technical or contractual stipulations to the contrary (e.g., a prohibition against crawling contained in a robot.txt file).[109]

The overriding policy reason and consideration for the preceding gaps and qualifications is that "*legitimate and common activities inherent in the design of networks, or legitimate and common operating or commercial practices* should not be criminalised".[110] For instance, the drafters of the Convention were very clear that "the mere sending of an e-mail message or a file to that system" did not amount to illegal access.[111] This restrained approach makes perfect sense because, if one recalls, the essence of computer security crimes like illegal access is to protect against acts that infringe the integrity of computers and data. The drafters of the Convention were quite clear that computer security crimes "are intended to protect the confidentiality, integrity and availability of computer systems or data and not to criminalise legitimate and common activities inherent in the design of networks, or legitimate and common operating or commercial practices".[112]

Illegal interception

Capture data transmissions and emissions

Illegal interception is the second species of computer security crime. It is perpetrated through the intentional interception "without right, made by technical means, of non-public transmissions of computer data to, from or within a computer system, including electromagnetic emissions from a computer system carrying such computer data".[113] Interception involves "listening to, monitoring or surveillance of the content" of both inter- and intra-computer communications.[114] It can accomplished either "directly, through access and use of the information systems, or indirectly through the use of electronic eavesdropping or tapping devices by technical means".[115] The phrase "transmissions of computer data" covers "all forms of electronic data transfers, whether by telephone, fax, e-mail or file transfer".[116] Under the law, interception through "technical means" may be done through the use of a computer system, "electronic eavesdropping or tapping devices . . . technical devices fixed to transmission lines as well as devices to collect and record wireless communications. They may include the use of software, passwords and codes" including "spyware and surveillance software".[117]

The crime of illegal interception prohibits the tapping, eavesdropping or recording of both electronic data transmissions and emissions.[118] It also applies to the unauthorized capturing of "data between computer and keyboard or of residual radiation from a computer screen".[119] The interception of electromagnetic emissions, "radiation and electronic fields surrounding the computer (terminal), for example for display on the eavesdropper's screen",[120] is popularly known as "van Eck phreaking". This process is named after a Dutch researcher who published a paper on the possibility of monitoring information displayed on a video terminal (even from as far away as 1 kilometer) by "picking up and decoding the electromagnetic interferences" and emissions that it produced and reconstructing the data on a normal TV receiver.[121] Aside from computers, other parts and components of an information system that emit or leak electromagnetic emissions as part of their normal operations include power cables, computer and network cables, power lines, cable TV, wireless access points, and even metal desks and metal ducts and pipes.[122] It is worth pointing out that van Eck phreaking (alternatively called a TEMPEST attack) was utilized during the successful hacking of electronic voting machines in the Netherlands in 2006, which resulted in the latter's withdrawal from use in Dutch elections.[123]

There are various ways to intercept electronic communications and transmissions. Two popular means are keystroke logging and man-in-the-middle attacks. Keystroke logging is accomplished when an attacker installs on target computers a "keylogger" program that monitors and captures users' keystrokes without their knowledge, and then storing or sending the information back to the attacker for reconstruction and analysis.[124] There is a natural connection between illegal access and illegal interception since gaining physical or electronic access to a target computer is normally a prerequisite for the installation of a keylogger, and the intercepted data is often used to access other computers and systems.[125] Interception can also be done through a man-in-the-middle attack.[126] Attackers can insinuate themselves or their devices between two communicating computers and then capture data being sent between the two without the communicating parties noticing.[127] This is often done by hijacking or impersonating an intermediate communications device (e.g., a WiFi router or a cellular access point) or a computer server or network used by the target parties.

Legal and social justification

In addition to the three main objectives of computer security crime (i.e., deterrence, technology development and security), the criminalization of illegal interception is also meant to extend the protection of the right to privacy of communications and correspondence to digital communications.[128] Infringing the secrecy and confidentiality of communications is therefore the gist of the offense.[129] As the drafters of the Convention explain, the term "'non-public' qualifies the nature of the transmission (communication) process and not the nature of the data transmitted. . . . The term 'non public' does not *per se* exclude communications via public networks".[130]

Compared to illegal access, illegal interception is not as highly problematic for hackers. For one, the act of illegal interception is more narrowly and clearly delimited. For example, "the use of common commercial practices, such as employing 'cookies', is not intended to be criminalised as such, as not being an interception 'without right' ".[131] Likewise, as explicitly stated by the drafters of the Convention, even though radio connections are technically covered, it is not a crime to intercept "any radio transmission which, even though 'non public', takes place in a relatively open and easily accessible manner and therefore can be intercepted, for example by radio amateurs".[132] In order to further delimit the scope of illegal access, the drafters of the Convention also included the requirement of "technical means" as "a restrictive qualification to avoid over-criminalisation".[133]

It bears pointing out that, unless interception is absolutely necessary to gain access to or use of a system or to test its security (which is seldom the case), hackers generally do not need nor want to intercept electronic communications. As shown in Chapter 3, makers and hacktivists place great value on their and others people's privacy, particularly the confidentially and secrecy of communications and correspondence.[134] Despite a number of high profile data privacy breaches committed by some hackers,[135] makers and hacktivists on the whole consider privacy to be a paramount norm and value that needs to be vigorously upheld and protected, mainly through the development, distribution and use of privacy-enhancing technologies.[136]

Data interference and system interference

Damage or hinder computer data and systems

The third and fourth kinds of computer security crime are data interference and system interference. Data interference involves the intentional "damaging, deletion, deterioration, alteration or suppression of computer data without right".[137] In the Cybercrime Directive, the phrase "or by rendering such data inaccessible" has been incorporated in the definition of the offense. It is worth pointing out that, because of the many possible reasons or motivations for a person to damage computer data (e.g., for profit or personal gain, revenge, political or ideological reasons, or public attention), the Select Committee of Experts on Computer-related Crime thought it best that the offense of data interference should pertain specifically to computer data and programs rather than the entire information system. Their rationale for this was that

> referring to the act and its immediate effect on the software or the stored data rather than to remote consequences for the whole system is preferable

in order to effectively protect such software and the data concerned from mischievous damage and interference.[138]

As further explained by the Committee

The specific character of damage done to data means that . . . it is not a matter of injuring the substance of the object and thus impairing its utilisation but rather a matter of altering the quality of the information in stored data and programs, which may obviously reduce their potential use.[139]

Physical damage to the information system is not required.[140] It should be noted that the prohibited act of data interference affects both the quantitative and qualitative aspects of a computer program or data.[141] In addition, "[d]ata and programs are protected in different stages, regardless of whether they are stored, processed or transferred by means of computer-automated equipment".[142] For its part, system interference is intentionally causing "the serious hindering without right of the functioning of a computer system by inputting, transmitting, damaging, deleting, deteriorating, altering or suppressing computer data".[143] The Cybercrime Directive also adds the requisites of "seriously hindering *or interrupting*".[144] The offence of system interference is also called "computer sabotage".[145]

Under the Convention on Cybercrime, the terms "damaging" and "deterioration" concern the "negative alteration of the integrity or of information content of data and programmes".[146] The act of "deletion" involves destroying data and making it unrecognizable.[147] "Alteration" is about the change or "modification of existing data" in such a way that "it changes the informational quality of the data or programs, usually to the disadvantage of the person concerned".[148] Alteration also covers the "[t]he input of malicious codes, such as viruses and Trojan horses . . . as is the resulting modification of the data".[149] Under Dutch law, "adding data" is expressly included in the list of prohibited acts because, while the act "does not interfere with existing data as such, it does interfere with the integrity of documents or folders, so that it can be seen as a more abstract form of data interference".[150] "Suppression" pertains to "any action that prevents or terminates the availability of the data to the person who has access to the computer or the data carrier on which it was stored".[151] Technically, a person can be held liable for the crime of data interference for any unauthorized change of data. Under Dutch law, "[t]here is no threshold – even unlawfully changing a single bit is an offense".[152] While the interference must be done intentionally, under Dutch law, a person can also be held liable for data interference through negligence "if serious damage is caused".[153]

In relation to system interference, hindering "refers to actions that interfere with the proper functioning of a computer system. Such hindering must take place by inputting, transmitting, damaging, deleting, altering or suppressing computer data".[154] According to the drafters of the Convention, "functioning" should be understood in a technologically neutral way, and thus covers and protects "all kinds of functions" of "all kinds" of computers and telecommunications systems.[155] A further requisite of the offense of system interference is that the hindering must be "serious".[156] The requirement of seriousness is meant to prevent over-criminalization.[157] While the prerogative and responsibility of defining what serious means falls on state parties, the drafters of the Convention consider this to be an example of serious interference: "the sending of data to a particular system in such a form, size or frequency that it has a significant detrimental effect on the ability of the owner or operator to use the system, or to communicate with other systems".[158] Under Dutch law, for example, there is serious damage when a computer system is not "available for several hours".[159] As with data interference, in Dutch law, system interference can also be committed through negligent acts.[160]

The main legal interest sought to be protected by the criminalization of data and system interference is "the integrity and proper functioning or use of stored computer data or computer programs".[161] On its face, the law appears to be solely concerned with the rights and interests of the owners, operators or users of computer data and systems.[162] But, as Recommendation No. (89) 9 states, "the protection of the functioning of the systems is of great interest not only to the owners/users of them, but in many cases also to the public".[163] In addition to the substantial economic value of information systems and the considerable loss that would be incurred in cases of harm or damage to them, data and system interference "may not only have great economic consequences, but may also lead to disastrous human consequences".[164] As such, the "proper functioning of companies and organisations as well as of social processes is particularly at stake here".[165] In line with this, the law seeks to promote other social goals or values like "combating organised crime, increasing the resilience of computer networks, protecting critical information infrastructure and data protection".[166]

Cyber attacks as a form of system interference

One of the primary objectives of the Cybercrime Directive is to combat the growing number and intensity of "large-scale cyber attacks" that cause serious data and system interference.[167] Specifically, the Directive aims to introduce and impose "criminal penalties for the creation of botnets".[168] A botnet is "a network of computers that have been infected by malicious software (computer virus)".[169]

> Such network of compromised computers ('zombies') may be activated to perform specific actions such as attacks against information systems (cyber-attacks). These 'zombies' can be controlled – often without the knowledge of the users of the compromised computers – by another computer. This 'controlling' computer is also known as the 'command-and-control centre'. The persons who control this centre are among the offenders, as they use the compromised computers to launch attacks against information systems. It is very difficult to trace the perpetrators, as the computers that make up

the botnet and carry out the attack, might be located elsewhere than the offender himself.[170]

Botnets are often used to carry out denial-of-service (DoS) attacks, which is an

> assault on a network that floods it with so many requests that regular traffic is either slowed or completely interrupted. Unlike a virus or worm, which can cause severe damage to databases, a DoS attack interrupts network service for some period.[171]

A distribute denial-of-service (DDoS) attack is one that employs a "big botnet" of hundreds or thousands of zombie computers that can "cause considerable damage, e.g. in terms of disrupted system services, financial cost, loss of personal data, etc."[172] While there are various ways and different motivations for conducting DDoS attacks, overall they are "largely characterized by massive participation, disruption of communications and reliance on the net's structural vulnerabilities".[173]

The Directive is also particularly concerned with protecting "critical infrastructure" related to computer and telecommunications systems, which is

> an asset, system or part thereof located in Member States which is essential for the maintenance of vital societal functions, health, safety, security, economic or social well-being of people . . ., and the disruption or destruction of which would have a significant impact.[174]

According to the European Commission, these large-scale cyber attacks "pose a serious risk to public interests" because they can cause "serious damage".[175] While the Directive allows Member States to "determine what constitutes serious damage", illustrative examples include "disrupting system services of significant public importance, or causing major financial cost or loss of personal data or sensitive information".[176]

Aside from DDoS attacks, other common activities or technologies that may be used to damage computer data or seriously hinder the functioning of information systems include spam attacks[177] and malware[178] such as computer viruses,[179] worms,[180] trojans,[181] back doors,[182] and logic bombs.[183]

Lawful versus unlawful interference

The offenses of data and system interference are generally not pertinent or applicable to makers. Makers generally do not need to change or interfere with other people's computer data or systems in order to build or work on their projects. They legitimately own, buy, possess or create the information or technologies that they hack and thus have the rights to access and use them. The most disruptive activity they may engage in is reverse engineering, which is a legally permitted under certain conditions.[184] In contrast, hacktivists find themselves squarely in the crosshairs of the law because they tend to engage in more radical and disruptive acts of cyber protests and electronic civil disobedience to advance their sociopolitical causes and campaigns.[185]

Hacktivist groups like Anonymous typically resort to DDoS attacks,[186] website defacements,[187] site redirects,[188] ping storms,[189] and breaking into systems to obtain data and then making the data public.[190] Pursuant to computer crime laws, engaging in these types of activities exposes the attackers to criminal liability for data and system interference whether they are cybercriminals doing it for fraudulent purposes or personal gain, or hacktivists endeavoring to achieve a higher goal or social value.[191] There is, however, a debate as to whether aggressive and transgressive acts of hacktivism should be recognized and protected under the law as legitimate forms of cyber protests or electronic civil disobedience.[192] Although nothing further came out of it, Anonymous even filed a formal public petition on the US whitehouse.gov website asking that DDoS attacks carried out by hacktivists be recognized as lawful protests and not subject to criminal prosecution.[193] There is some basis for conceiving of hacktivism as the digital equivalent of street protests. As Li explains, hacktivists and traditional protesters have similar motivations, desire to bring as much publicity and attention to their campaigns and protest actions, and, as they engage in mass actions, they need to mobilize and mass their presence and numbers at a specific place and time to get as much impact and attention from the target of the protest, as well as the general or relevant public.[194] Hacktivism and traditional protests are alike in that they both aim "to effect political or social change, often in response to a particular political or social event".[195] Hacktivists, for instance, have undertaken DDoS attacks against repressive foreign governments, site redirects against racist groups and website defacements that parody government officials.[196]

But attempts to equate cyber protests with traditional mass actions (and the applicability of consequent legal protections afforded to the latter) have been disputed on a number of grounds.[197] First of all, the rights to assemble and protests are not absolute whether in the physical or virtual world, and they are subject to reasonable regulation. Further, under US law, it is believed that "[h]acktivism that causes damage (for example, information theft) or involves the manipulation of hijacked private property (for example, DDoS attacks using involuntary botnets) therefore is not likely to be considered expression at all".[198] Across the pond, Hampson holds a similar view: "It would not be surprising if British courts refused to recognize a free speech exception to the CMA [Computer Misuse Act] for hacktivism, even under the HRA [Human Rights Act]".[199] One of the strongest arguments against granting legitimacy to certain forms of hacktivism like DDoS attacks is that the latter are "censorial in nature" and, thus, not worthy of legal much less constitutional protection.[200] The reasoning behind this is that if "the information posted on a website constitutes speech by another party", then attacking or interrupting the target websites results in the muzzling or censorship of others.[201] Furthermore, since a website is someone else's private property, "a hacktivist has no . . . right to exercise speech 'on' another's website",[202] and "the law . . . does not protect speech on private property against the wishes of the owner".[203] Jordan similarly opines that a DDoS attack "is the restraint of information, the jamming and prevention of someone contributing to or receiving information, by preventing their website or Internet connections from working".[204] There is even disagreement among hacktivists about the propriety of DDoS attacks.[205] Oxblood Ruffin of the hacker group Cult of the Dead Cow is emphatic about his disapproval:

> Denial of Service attacks are a violation of the First Amendment, and of the freedoms of expression and assembly. No rationale . . . makes them anything other than what they are – illegal, unethical, and uncivil. One does not make a better point in a public forum by shouting down one's opponent.[206]

It may also be said that the level and extent of disruption caused by DDoS attacks are highly disproportionate because it is one of "the most destructive of all available means of getting a message across online".[207] There is sufficient legal basis then to conclude that DDoS attacks "against privately created websites are unlikely to qualify for constitutional protection"[208] since they "are mere conduct, devoid of expression because a downed website does not communicate the content of any intended message".[209] Moreover, as with website defacements, site redirects and ping storms, "it is unlikely that information theft or virtual sabotage qualify as symbolic speech" that would benefit from legal protection.[210] Based on the law as it currently stands, there seems to be a legal consensus and social agreement that certain extreme forms of cyber protests such as DDoS attacks are not constitutionally protected speech or activities, and are punishable under computer crime laws.[211]

In addition, hacktivism has been accused of suffering from certain democratic deficiencies.[212] First of all, the voluntary nature of cyber protests has been called into question, especially in cases where computers of ordinary users were co-opted to form part of a botnet without their knowledge or consent.[213] Second, the argument that cyber protests are lawful mass and direct actions of citizens is severely weakened because the use of increasingly effective and sophisticated technologies often means that less people are required to carry them out.[214] The paradoxical results of making technology a central and considerable part of protest actions is that it "cuts in two separate ways: (1) technology lowers the barriers to participation, and (2) fewer active participants are required to execute an effective cyberattack (as compared with a traditional protest)".[215] Because there is less engagement of and by the public, it is harder to justify cyber protests as the will of the people as opposed to being the actions of a minority. Finally, there have been some misgivings about the level of commitment and actual participation of some hacktivists.[216] As Li points out,

> when compared with traditional protests, cyberattacks are less costly to execute in terms of actual resources as well as physical effort and public

presence . . . while traditional protests are accomplished through picketing, marches, or public sit-ins, hacktivism is accomplished through a variety of digital tools, often from behind a computer screen.[217]

Since many forms of hacktivism are conducted anonymously and in relative isolation, there is in certain cases "low personal cost assumed by the participants".[218] Because of the low barrier for participation and the presumed lower risks involved, it may be said that an act of hacktivism, "which does not incur any significant personal cost for the participants, takes away the element of a public act, normally met in acts of civil disobedience".[219] Unlike street protests, hacktivists also find it much harder to feel or build a sense of solidarity to their cause.[220]

Despite the above legal and social criticisms of hacktivism, it should be borne in mind that not all acts of hacktivism and the consequent data and system interference that they produce are negative or destructive. In fact, hacktivism can produce positive effects and can be quite constructive. Hacktivists have played a significant role in many socio-political protests, movements and even revolutions around the world.[221] While their participation is mostly confined to the technical matters, hacktivists have made valuable contributions to diverse actions and causes.[222] For instance, Anonymous provided protesters in Tunisia with technical assistance, instructions and tools to circumvent government surveillance and internet blockages during the Arab Spring.[223] Hacktivists also produce and use computer programs and devices for themselves and others to bypass firewalls and other technical restrictions to the free flow of information and route around government censorship and filtering.[224] They may also hack information systems to bring attention to security weaknesses and not to exploit the discovered vulnerabilities.[225] After Edward Snowden's revelations in 2013 of the US government's global electronic surveillance operations, hacktivists and other types of hackers have been mustering and concentrating their efforts and resources toward developing better encryption, anonymizing and other security and privacy-enhancing technologies that everyone (especially ordinary citizens and users) can freely access and use to protect their privacy and security both online and offline.[226] It is interesting to note that most if not all of the software that hacktivists create (e.g., the Low Orbit Ion Cannon (LOIC for short) that members of Anonymous used in high-profile DDoS attacks in support of WikiLeaks) are either licensed as free and open source software (FOSS) or released as public domain works online, and are thus publicly available to and freely modifiable by anyone who has internet access.[227]

Some hacktivists even intentionally choose to be less dependent and reliant on the power and efficiencies offered by technology in order not to cause damage or permanent disruption.[228] For example, they opt for a quite low-tech approach to disrupting a target's website that simply requires participants to manually and repeatedly press the "reload" button on their web browsers when accessing the site.[229] They only wish to slow down the website and not take it completely offline.[230] Although less efficient, this approach produces similar effects to an automated DoS attack, but is arguably more legally defensible because it requires the genuine and actual involvement of a mass of people, and visiting a website and pressing the reload button is *prima facie* a legitimate and common online activity.[231] The benefit and rationale for hacktivists is they "choose a technically inefficient means to serve politically efficient ends".[232]

It is important to remember that hacktivists interfere with information systems not for its own sake or as an end in itself, but to promote a political cause or social value that they agree with or believe in.[233] More often than not, these social goals and values concern or relate to the "rights of free speech and access to information".[234] Hacktivism like traditional activism is ultimately about gaining and raising public awareness, support and engagement for their own or others' socio-political causes and campaigns.[235] Their actions are less concerned with damaging or hindering computer data or system *per se*, but are meant to support social movements and promote cultural change. While their activities center on or are directly aimed at technology, their fundamental aim is social action. Hacktivism closely resembles civil disobedience in that they both are "public, non-violent and conscientious act[s] contrary to law . . . with the intent to bring about a change in the policies or law of the government".[236] Hacktivists "aim to enroll people, to draw them into discussion, reflection and action".[237] Enlisting or gaining the support of the general or relevant public is crucial because it does not only improve the chances of success of their campaigns, but, equally important, it provides democratic legitimacy to their actions. As Jordan clarifies,

> A mass of people is key, because then the protest is not about one person's technical abilities, but about the choice of many people to protest. This provides the same legitimation for a protest as thousands of people in the street might. It makes the protest a popular protest.[238]

As shown above, hacktivism is an exceedingly complex socio-technical phenomenon, and any attempt to label it as an illegal act of data and system interference as opposed to a legitimate form of protest is a difficult exercise. While it is true that "most current forms of hacktivism are rightly regulated or prohibited outright", there are strong legal and public policy reasons to support the position that "a narrow subset of hacktivism should be protected on the grounds that it is primarily expressive, does not involve the hijacking of computers or networks, and causes no significant damage".[239] Hampson correctly argues that

> forms of hacktivism that are primarily expressive, that do not involve obtaining or exploiting illegal access to computers or networks for commercial advantage or financial gain, and that cause little or no permanent damage, should receive at least some protection as a legitimate form of protest.[240]

Thus, a "categorical prohibition on all forms of hacktivism" should be avoided because it "may sweep up socially productive uses of cyberattacks as a form of protest".[241] It must be remembered that political protests and social movements manifest and embody changing norms and values within a community or society.[242] Social movements are a prime "source of authoritative ethical visions" and normative expectations of individuals and groups.[243] As such, the interpretation and application of the law (including the important concept of "without right") should be flexible and mutable in order to adjust to people's changing evaluations and understandings of the appropriate and the desirable, rather than repressing or excising them at the outset.

Misuse of devices

The last species of computer security crime is called misuse of devices. For this offense to apply, the perpetrator must intentionally and without right produce, distribute or make available "a device, including a computer program, designed or adapted primarily for the purpose of committing" other computer security crimes,[244] or possess "a computer password, access code, or similar data", both of which must be carried out with intent to use the device and password to commit such crimes.[245] These illicit or prohibited tools include devices, computer programs, computer passwords, access codes and similar data such as stolen credit card numbers and user credentials. Under the Convention, "distribution" requires "the active act of forwarding data to others", while "making available" involves "placing online devices for the use of others".[246] The rationale for the criminalization of misuse of devices is two-fold. First, authorities want to discourage the acquisition of "hacker tools" for "criminal purposes".[247] This is so because the crime of misuse of devices seems naturally connected to the commission of other computer security crimes discussed above. For instance, the creation or possession of a computer virus is normally a preliminary step to the actual use of the virus to conduct data or system interference.[248] Second, criminalizing misuse of devices is meant to serve as a disincentive or deterrence to the creation of a "black market of cybercrime tools".[249] The drafters of the Convention were of the view that "[t]o combat such dangers more effectively, the criminal law should prohibit specific potentially dangerous acts at the source".[250]

With respect to its scope of application, the crime of misuse of devices is on the whole carefully circumscribed. As explained by the drafters of the Convention,

> In order to avoid the danger of overcriminalisation where devices are produced and put on the market for legitimate purposes, e.g. to counterattacks against computer systems, further elements are added to restrict the offence. Apart from the general intent requirement, there must be the specific (i.e. direct) intent that the device is used for the purpose of committing any of the offences established in Articles 25 of the Convention.[251]

This means that for the offense of misuse of devices to be committed, the general intent to make available or possess the illicit tool or access code must be coupled with a specific or direct intent that such tool or code is to be used for the purpose of breaching the security of a computer system or data. The Convention explicitly states that there should be no criminal liability if the tool or code "is not for the purpose of committing" a computer security crime "such as for the authorised testing or protection of a computer system".[252] As further explained by the Convention drafters,

> tools created for the authorised testing or the protection of a computer system are not covered by the provision. This concept is already contained in the expression "without right". For example, testdevices ("crackingdevices") and network analysis devices designed by industry to control the reliability of their information technology products or to test system security are produced for legitimate purposes, and would be considered to be "with right".[253]

The offense of misuse of devices is therefore restricted "to cases where the devices are objectively designed, or adapted, primarily for the purpose of committing an offence. This alone usually excludes dualuse devices".[254] This policy position is adopted as well in the Cybercrime Directive.[255]

The crime of misuse of devices does not appear to be too troublesome for makers and hacktivists.[256] The hacking tools, information and instructions that they produce, distribute, make available or possess do not fall within the purview of misuse of devices because they are more often than not publicly released or explicitly marketed for legitimate purposes such as security testing, privacy enhancement, reverse engineering, interoperability, technical improvements, replacement or repair, academic research, education and public awareness, and for other public interests.[257] Even LOIC, a popular tool among hacktivists to perform DoS attacks, is promoted as dual-use technology that is a "network stress testing and denial-of-service attack application".[258] While there is nothing in the law that can prevent an overzealous or overreaching public prosecutor from filing a case, the law is quite clear that unless there is also a specific intent that the devices and codes are to be used to commit criminal acts then no liability should attach to their mere production, possession or distribution.[259] Hackers can thus avoid prosecution through the simple expedient of expressly highlighting or publicly making known the fact that their devices, programs and codes are primarily intended for legitimate purposes. Of course, any claim of legitimate purpose and use will only stand if the producers, distributors, users and possessors of these tools and codes do not perform acts or engage in other activities that belie their asserted benign purposes.

Intellectual property laws

Fraught history of intellectual property and socio-technical innovation

While their effects on hacking may not be as direct, immediate and pronounced as those associated with computer crime laws, intellectual property laws similarly have a deep and far-reaching impact on the freedom and ability of hackers to engage in their personal and social projects and pursuits. The uneasy relationship between hacking and intellectual property is quite understandable given that technological innovations in general have an intimate yet conflict-ridden history with intellectual property laws.[260] The first intellectual property law, the Statute of Anne (a copyright legislation enacted in 1710),[261] was a reaction to the invention, widespread use and disruptive changes brought about by the movable-type printing press.[262] Since then, additions, modifications, revisions and expansions to intellectual property laws have occurred virtually in lockstep with the emergence and adoption of techno-social advances and changes.[263] For instance, the major treaty revisions to the Berne Convention were done "to find responses to new technological developments (such as sound recording technology, photography, radio, cinematography and television)".[264] As Lessig recounts, the invention of sound recording machines resulted in the creation of new recording rights at the turn of the twentieth century, the advent of radio produced performance rights, and the popularity of cable television led to the statutory grant of rebroadcast rights.[265] But the relations between technology and intellectual property are far from being one-way or asymmetric. As was evident with the first generations of hackers, the assertion, exploitation and enforcement of intellectual property rights can both adversely and positively affect the practices and culture of a technical and epistemic community, as well as the production and dissemination of technology as a whole. The propensity of intellectual property and technological innovations to be at odds with each other has much to do with the goals, norms and values sought and embedded in intellectual property laws, and the delicate balancing of multiple, complex and competing interests that are at the heart of the laws and policies on technology, information and innovation.[266] These clashes between technical innovation and intellectual property are quite evident in the case of makers and hacktivists where the norms and value of hacking often come into conflict with the aims of intellectual property laws.

Intellectual property balance

The term "intellectual property" broadly refers to "the legal rights which result from intellectual activity in the industrial, scientific, literary and artistic fields".[267] There are many kinds of intellectual property rights and they apply to various forms of intellectual creations or "creations of the mind".[268] Basically, copyright covers "literary and artistic works" or expressions of ideas (such as computer code and programs, printed manuals, written instructions, and technical drawings, plans and specifications);[269] patents[270] are granted for novel and nonobvious inventions that are capable of industrial application (e.g., 3D printing technologies, computer hardware, and certain computer-implemented inventions with a "further technical effect"[271]); trademarks are distinctive signs used to identify good and services (e.g., marks or logos of FOSS projects like Linux, Firefox and Android);[272] industrial designs "protect the original ornamental and non-functional features of an industrial article or product that result from design activity" (like the design of and ornamentations on devices);[273] databases are granted *sui generis* protection in Europe in light the "investment of considerable human, technical and financial resources" for their arrangement, storage and access (i.e., information and data stored on computer systems and servers);[274] and the *sui generis* protection of topographies of integrated circuits covers the layout-designs of electronic circuits and semiconductor chips (which are an integral part of those all-important microprocessors, memory chips, microcontrollers and printed circuit boards that lie at the heart of computer systems and information technologies).[275]

Despite the various types of intellectual property, it may be said that intellectual property laws are ultimately about balancing the rights of control and access to creative information, knowledge and know-how,[276] which is why it is extremely relevant to hacking. The main purposes and rationale of intellectual property laws are two-fold:

> One is to give statutory expression to the moral and economic rights of creators in their creations and the rights of the public in access to those creations. The second is to promote . . . creativity and the dissemination and application of its results and to . . . contribute to economic and social development.[277]

Intellectual property rights are legislative creations, i.e., statutorily granted exclusive rights on specific uses of intangible property.[278] According to Lessig, "Intellectual property rights are a monopoly that the state gives to producers of intellectual property in exchange for their production of it. After a limited time, the product of their work becomes the public's to use as it wants".[279] There is strong support for intellectual property rights from a legal and public policy perspective because they are believed to play a key role in "economic, social and cultural growth".[280] Intellectual property laws are geared towards the incentivization, promotion and protection of cultural and technical creativity, invention and innovation for the benefit of both creators and society as a whole.[281] There is, thus, inextricably bound in the kernel of intellectual property laws and policies, a legal and social imperative to strike a balance between the grant of exclusive rights to creators and the right of the public to gain access to and use such intellectual creations.[282] This so-called "intellectual property balance" is an integral part of intellectual property laws and rights. As stated in Article 7 of the TRIPS Agreement:

> The protection and enforcement of intellectual property rights should contribute to the promotion of technological innovation and to the transfer and dissemination of technology, to the mutual advantage of producers and users of technological knowledge and in a manner conducive to social and economic welfare, and to a balance of rights and obligations.[283]

Intellectual property laws are ultimately meant to "to achieve the optimal balance between the grant of incentives to create and the right of the public to use such creations".[284] As Lessig explains,

> The balance that intellectual property law traditionally strikes is between the protections granted the author and the public use or access granted everyone else. . . . Built into the law of intellectual property are limits on the power of the author to control use of the ideas she has created.[285]

The ability of persons and the wider public to access and make use of others' intellectual creations is thus an indispensable component and consideration of the intellectual property balance.

It should be pointed out, though, that it is the "law [that] strikes this balance. It is not a balance that would exist in nature".[286] As affirmed by the WIPO Standing Committee on Copyright and Related Rights, "[s]triking this balance is left as a matter for national legislation. Value judgments will need to be made, and these will clearly vary according to the society and culture concerned".[287] While it is true that the law and public authorities traditionally bear the onus of "balancing incentives to create and accessibility of information",[288] it is important not to downplay the vital role that public and socio-cultural practices play in locating and adjusting this balance. Determining, establishing and preserving such a delicate or optimal equilibrium between the competing requirements of incentives/control vis-à-vis access and use is critical because it must "reflect the balance between the need to induce creation and the need to guarantee public access to information", as well as the ability of members of the public to reasonably use such works and inventions.[289]

In actuality, however, achieving the right balance between control versus access (whether through legislative enactments, policy directives, enforcement actions or everyday practices) is neither straightforward nor unproblematic.[290] In fact, together with the growth and popularity of computing, digital technologies and information networks since the 1970s, there has been an ineluctable march towards an ever-increasing expansion, protection and strict enforcement of intellectual property rights at the expense of the public's right to access and use information and technology.[291] These changes in intellectual property laws were precipitated by "new technological developments" such as, among others, "reprography, videotechnology, compact cassette systems facilitating 'home taping,' satellite broadcasting, cable television, the increase of the importance of computer programs, computer-generated works and electronic databases".[292] The succeeding decades saw the formal and express acknowledgement of copyright protection over software,[293] as well as the legal recognition of patents over software (in the United States) and computer-implemented inventions (in Europe and other parts of the world).[294] The expansion and ratcheting up of intellectual property rights continued through the 1990s and early 2000s on both an international and national level with the adoption of the TRIPS Agreement, the

WIPO Internet Treaties, bilateral agreements and national anti-circumvention laws,[295] the recognition of the applicability and enforceability of copyright in the digital environment,[296] and the corresponding case law and jurisprudence based on these treaties and statutes. Whether individually or in aggregate, these laws and policies on intellectual property have had a long-standing impact on the production and dissemination of innovation and other techno-social practices (including hacking).

Broad exclusive rights yet narrow limitations and exceptions

Quite a number of legal and scholarly writings have been published decrying the current state of affairs of intellectual property rights.[297] These scholars believe that, with regard to the intellectual property balance, "the pendulum has swung too far" in favor of incentivizing creators to the detriment of public access to and use of intellectual creations.[298] Under the current legal regime of intellectual property, the exclusive rights granted to creators are expansive and interpreted broadly, whereas the limitations and exceptions to these rights are very specific and narrowly applied.[299]

Of the many kinds of intellectual property rights, copyright and patents are the most material to hackers. Copyright consists of a bundle of exclusive rights to authorize the reproduction, translation, adaptation, alteration, making derivatives, distribution, public performance, communication to the public, making available to the public, rent and use of literary and artistic works.[300] Patents grant inventors or owners the exclusive rights to prevent third parties from "making, using, offering for sale, selling, or importing" the patented products without their consent.[301] With regard to patented processes, inventors have exclusive rights to stop other persons and entities from "using the process", as well as to bar the use, offer for sale, sale, or import of products "obtained directly by that process".[302] These exclusive rights on their face seem to be relatively fair and reasonable. However, due to the confluence of socio-technical trends such as the growing digitization of information and the centrality of technology in the networked society, coupled with the ever-expanding and deepening scope of intellectual property rights, the impact and applicability of copyright and patents on hacking and technology development as a whole have never been as great or as far reaching as it currently exists, and will continue to be so.[303] The intensifying digitization and technologization of social life means many aspects of people's behaviors and activities whether online and offline are subject to intellectual property laws and rights.[304] Lessig remarks that "in the digital world, life is subject to copyright law. Every single act triggers the law of copyright. Every single access or use is either subject to a license or illegal, unless" it is subject to a statutory limitation or exception such as the right to make quotations.[305] As many aspects of people's lives are mediated by and through various computing and information technologies,[306] copyright and patent laws and rights pervade and influence people's actions and what they are able to do with their own and others' information and technologies.[307] This also means that, "[b]ecause of the changes in digital technology, it is now possible for the law to regulate every single use of creative work in a digital environment".[308]

Despite the current state of affairs, it should be remembered that limitations and exceptions to intellectual property rights were central policy issues and areas of debate even during the negotiations of the Berne Convention in the 1880s and other subsequent international treaties because of their essential role in maintaining the intellectual property balance.[309] As explained by WIPO Standing Committee on Copyright and Related Rights, "[i]t has long been recognized that restrictions or limitations upon authors, and related rights may be justified in particular cases" and "limits to absolute protection are rightly set by the public interest".[310] For instance, limitations and exceptions to copyright have been justified based on the following purposes and grounds: informatory, educational, public access, convenience, archival preservation, new industry, state power, *de minimis*, necessity and public interest.[311] It should be noted that these and other limitations and exceptions to intellectual property rights are based on economic as well as "non-economic 'public policy' considerations".[312] While intellectual property laws *prima facie* seem to place greater emphasis on creators and their exclusive economic and moral rights, it bears stressing that these laws are also "underpinned by some kind of non-author centered and non-economic normative consideration" whether it be freedom of information, participatory democracy, public debate and discourse, education, or information and knowledge distribution.[313]

As things currently stand, the restrictive application and uses of intellectually property laws tend to restrain the ability of hackers to engage in the common acts of hacking – to *explore, break, learn, create, share* and *secure* information and technologies. Furthermore, the statutory limitations and exceptions are narrowly circumscribed and only some of them are relevant or directly apply to hacking.[314] Notwithstanding the legal obstacles and constraints that are firmly in place, the few limitations and exceptions to intellectual property rights do provide some albeit limited space and freedom for hackers to carry out their hacking projects and campaigns.[315] Quite interestingly though, despite or perhaps because of these restrictions, hackers tend to reside and even thrive in the gaps, contradictions and margins of the law (see Chapter 5).

The following limitations and exceptions under international, European and Dutch copyright and patent laws afford makers and hacktivists (as well as other hackers and ordinary users) some agency and play to creatively and constructively access and use information and technology.

Reverse engineering, decompilation and use of software

Directive 2009/24/EC on the legal protection of computer programs (the Software Directive) contains two exceptions to the exclusive rights of copyright that are indispensable to hacking – reverse engineering and decompiling of software.[316] Reverse engineering is a highly technical process whereby "a person other than the original program developer is able to determine the ideas and principles that underlie the functional elements of the software by examining its external inputs and outputs".[317] Also called "black box" analysis, this form of reverse engineering does not require direct access to the computer program's source code and other hidden or internal specifications.[318] The Software Directive expressly provides that a person "shall be entitled, without the authorization of the right-holder, to observe, study or test the functioning of the program in order to determine the ideas and principles which underlie any element of the program".[319] The ability to reverse engineer though is subject to the conditions that such person has "a right to use a copy of a computer program" and it must be done "while performing any of the acts of loading, displaying, running, and transmitting or storing the program which he is entitled to do so".[320] Unlike decompilation, reverse engineering does not have to be limited to achieving interoperability and can be undertaken for such bread-and-butter hacker activities as observing, studying or testing how a program works.[321]

Decompilation, for its part, entails accessing and studying the actual code and internal workings of the computer program.[322] It should be noted that decompilation is more strictly regulated compared to black box analysis since the former can only be undertaken when it is "indispensable to obtain the information necessary to achieve the interoperability of an independently created computer program with other programs".[323] Furthermore, it is subject to a number of conditions: first, the decompilation must be "performed by the licensee or by another person having a right to use a copy of a program"; second, "the information necessary to achieve interoperability has not previously been readily available to the person"; and, third, it is "confined to the parts of the original program which are necessary in order to achieve interoperability".[324] There are also additional caveats on what a person can do with the information obtained through decompilation. Such decompiled data can only be used to "achieve interoperability" with an "independently created program", it cannot "be given to others, except when necessary for the interoperability of the independently created computer program", and it must not "be used for the development, production or marketing of a computer program substantially similar in its expression, or for any other act which infringes copyright".[325] If these restrictions were not enough, the Software Directive also has a general "safeguard clause", which states that the decompilation provisions should be narrowly interpreted and must not be applied "in a manner which unreasonably prejudices the rightholder's legitimate interests or conflicts with a normal exploitation of the computer program".[326] In any event, as with reverse engineering, the right to decompile software cannot be waived, bargained away or contravened by contract and stipulations to the contrary are null and void.[327] The Court of Justice of the European Union explained the rationale for the law's prohibition against such contractual stipulations in the landmark case of *SAS Institute v World Programming*: "Article 5(3) of Directive 91/250 seeks to ensure that the ideas and principles which underlie any element of a computer program are not protected by the owner of the copyright by means of a licensing agreement".[328] In the United States though, there have been conflicting court decisions on the validity or enforceability of license clauses that prevent the licensee or user from reverse engineering or decompiling a computer program because there is no express statutory prohibition under US law.[329]

Interestingly, in addition to reverse engineering and decompilation, the Software Directive recognizes a limited but valuable exception to the exclusive rights granted to the original software developer – the right to use. Under the law, users who lawfully acquired a program have a general and quite obvious right to use it, and such use "shall not require authorisation by the rightholder where they are necessary for the use of the computer program by the lawful acquirer in accordance with its intended purpose, including for error correction".[330] A US court has similarly ruled that "[c]onsumers who purchase a product containing a copy of embedded software have the inherent legal right to use that copy of the software. What the law authorizes, [the company] cannot revoke".[331] While this general right to use may be modified or suppressed through contractual stipulations, there are specific rights of use such as "making a back-up copy" and the "act of correction of its errors" cannot be prohibited or avoided by contract.[332]

It is quite apparent that the drafters of the Software Directive sought to balance the exclusive rights of the original program developers with the right of users to make reasonable and even innovative (in case of reverse engineering or decompilation) uses of computer programs.[333] While it is possible to argue whether they did not go far enough or they went too far,[334] the drafters seem to be well aware of a fundamental and incontrovertible principle about software and technology as a whole – they are meant to be used. As stated in Software Directive, "The function of a computer program is to communicate and work together with other components of a computer system and with users".[335] While this statement primarily concerns the value of interoperability in and of computer systems and data,[336] it likewise speaks to the desirability of ensuring, as a matter of public policy, that people (including hackers) are able to actually use software and understand how it works.[337] The rights to reverse engineering, decompile and use software are indeed pertinent to makers and other types of hackers because they directly involve the common acts of hacking (*explore*, *break*, *learn* and *create*), and the information or knowledge gained from these activities may be utilized to perform or pursue other common acts (*share* and *secure*). In addition, reverse engineering and decompilation are clearly connected to and may be used to advance the hacker norms and values of openness, freedom of access, transparency and curiosity.

Temporary acts of reproduction

Closely related to the above exceptions for reverse engineering, decompilation and use of software is the limitation for temporary acts of reproduction.[338] Under

Directive 2001/29/EC on the harmonization of certain aspects of copyright and related rights in the information society (the Copyright Directive) and its implementation into Dutch law, temporary acts of reproduction that "are transient or incidental [and] an integral and essential part of a technological process" do not require the authorization of the copyright owner.[339] This exemption is subject to the condition that the "sole purpose" of the reproduction is "to enable" a "lawful use" or "a transmission in a network between third parties by an intermediary".[340] Furthermore, such temporary reproduction should have "no independent economic significance".[341] A use is deemed lawful "where it is authorised by the rightholder or not restricted by law".[342]

According to the drafters of the Copyright Directive, the policy rationale for this limitation is due to the fact that

> its transient and incidental character may point to the lack of any real economic conflict with the normal exploitation of protected works, while the fact that it is an integral and necessary part of a larger process leading to a communication of a work may indicate that this is not something that the author/right-holder needs to control.[343]

Examples of normal or everyday uses of information technologies that produce such exempted temporary copies include "reproductions on Internet routers, reproductions created during web browsing or copies created in Random Access Memory (RAM) of a computer, copies stored on local caches of computer systems or copies created in proxy servers".[344] This limitation on the reproduction right is sensible given that, in order to properly access and use any software or digital content, it is necessary for parts or the entire work to be reproduced as part of the normal functions and operations of a computer or information system.[345] The exemption for temporary acts of reproduction is clearly analogous to the right to use of software under the Software Directive although the former applies more broadly to any copyrighted work, especially those in digital form. And like the right to use software, the exception for making transient and incidental copies ensures that hackers can safely engage in some common acts of hacking, especially *explore*, *learn* and *create*.

Private and non-commercial copying and use

Copyright and patent laws contain an important exception for private and non-commercial uses of protected works. While it is true that "private copying is not a right but a statutory exception" and it is not found in the Berne Convention,[346] "[t]he principle of freedom to make private copies appears in almost all regimes, but in very different forms or stated in very different ways".[347] The Copyright Directive provides for a private copying exception whereby "reproductions on any medium made by a natural person for private use and for ends that are neither directly nor indirectly commercial" do not require the right holder's authorization.[348] Similarly, under the Dutch Copyright Act, a copy or reproduction that is "carried out without any direct or indirect commercial motivation and is intended exclusively for personal exercise, study or use by the natural person who made the reproduction" is an excepted use.[349] According to a WIPO study, "private" should be understood as being "distinct from 'professional' or 'commercial' uses".[350] It should be noted that only individual persons can avail of the private use exception and such use or copying must be done for non-commercial purposes. "Non-commercial" has been interpreted as meaning "such uses do not conflict with the normal exploitation of the work . . . and that this is a non-economic normative factor that is to be weighed against the author's economic interests".[351] This exception of course is subject to the requirements that "rightholders receive fair compensation", the procedure for which is provided for under national law.[352] It should be noted as well that the private copying exception does not apply to software under the Dutch Copyright Act and the Software Directive.[353]

Patent laws contain a similar exception to the exclusive rights of patent holders for private and non-commercial uses and purposes.[354] According to a WIPO study, "[i]t is common not to extend the exclusive patent rights to third parties' activities that are performed in the private sphere or for non-commercial purposes only".[355] As long as a patented product or process is used for personal and non-commercial purposes, then it is covered by an explicit exception under most jurisdictions.[356] The Dutch Patent Act contains a similar exception for non-business uses.[357]

The private use and copying exception benefits hackers. This means that they have some freedom to hack, access and use any copyrighted works or patented technologies that they lawfully possess as long as they do so in private and for personal, non-commercial uses, which most hackers are inclined to do anyway at the outset. Pursuant to this exception, hackers have the ability to *explore*, *break*, *learn*, *create* and *secure* information and technologies. The one major caveat though is that because the exception is limited to private and non-commercial uses, they cannot distribute or *share* their innovations with others, especially the wider public, without potentially running afoul of the exclusive rights of copyright or patent holders. This prohibition on sharing is at odds with hacker norms and values of openness, freedom of access, freedom of information, community development and social development.

Scientific research and teaching

Another important exception to copyright and patents laws is the ability to copy or use intellectual creations for purposes of teaching or scientific research. Under the Copyright Directive, the authorization of the copyright holder is not required in cases of

> use for the sole purpose of illustration for teaching or scientific research, as long as the source, including the author's name, is indicated, unless this

turns out to be impossible and to the extent justified by the non-commercial purpose to be achieved.[358]

The act of teaching covers "elementary as well as advanced teaching and works intended for self- instruction".[359] The drafters of the Copyright Directive elucidate the scope and limitations of this exception in relation to educational institutions:

> When applying the exception or limitation for non-commercial educational and scientific research purposes, including distance learning, the non-commercial nature of the activity in question should be determined by that activity as such. The organisational structure and the means of funding of the establishment concerned are not the decisive factors in this respect.[360]

The exception thus also covers any copying or use of protected works done by for-profit education institutions as long as it is undertaken for education or scientific research purposes.[361] This exception may be useful for hackers or security researchers who work in or in association with universities or other educational institutions.

While copyright laws generally require that the copying and use exception for teaching purposes must be done as part of or within the confines of formal education, the exception for scientific research is much broader. It can be done outside of an educational setting, it applies to any person undertaking what is broadly understood as scientific research and not just scientists, and it is done in private.[362] Like the teaching exception, it is the nature and purpose of the activity (i.e., non-commercial and for scientific purposes) that determines the applicability of the exception for scientific research. Since many hacking projects and activities have as their initial goals to *explore* and *learn* how things work (which may be deemed scientific pursuits), makers, hacktivists and other hackers can claim protection under the research exception.

Patent laws also have a similar exception for scientific research and experimental purposes.[363] Under Dutch law, there is an exception for acts done solely for research on the patented invention.[364] The exemption for scientific research and experiments "enables researchers to examine the stated effects of patented inventions and improve such patented inventions without having to fear infringing the patent".[365] As explained by the WIPO Standing Committee on the Law of Patents, the policy rationale for this exception is the importance of creating a "positive environment for research activities" that can "add to the development of technologies, which is precisely one of the objectives of the patent system".[366] The WTO Dispute Settlement Panel similarly confirmed in the *Canada – Patent Protection of Pharmaceutical Products* case that "both society and the scientist have a 'legitimate interest' in using the patent disclosure to support the advance of science and technology".[367] The exemption though is not absolute. While "the research exemption applies to research *on* or *into* a patented invention, for example, working on the patented invention in order to explore unknown effects or further develop the invention", it does not normally cover "research made *with* the patented invention".[368] The scientific research exemption therefore permits experiments on the patented invention but not the use of the invention in contexts outside of such experiments. In any event, the scientific research exemption is a boon to hackers as they are able to openly examine, experiment on and even improve patented technologies. They can perform all of the common acts of hacking on a patented technology – *explore, break, learn, create, share* and *secure*. In contrast to the private copying and use exception where sharing is impeded, hackers as researchers have a greater ability to *share* and communicate what they have learned about a patented invention since the grant of a patent is predicated on the public disclosure and transparency about how the invention works.[369] The scientific research exemption thus advances a number of hacker norms and values such as openness, freedom of access, transparency, curiosity, creativity and innovation, efficiency, community development and social development.

Repair of equipment

The Copyright Directive contains an exception to reproduce or use a copyrighted work "in connection with the demonstration or repair of equipment".[370] This exception is akin to the right to use software under the Software Directive, where a lawful user or possessor can perform acts necessary to use a protected work, including correcting errors or repairing technical issues. In the United States, a right to repair whether involving copyright or patents has been recognized by courts.[371] This right to repair protects hackers and ordinary users "especially those who engage in this activity for noncommercial purposes".[372] This exception is especially pertinent to makers because they prefer to use and work with technologies and equipment that are reparable.[373]

Fair use and the three-step test

Fair use is possibly one of the most useful and powerful limitations and exceptions to copyright.[374] However, this legal doctrine is only adopted and followed in the United States and a few other jurisdictions such as Israel, Korea, Liberia, the Philippines, Sri Lanka, Taiwan and Uganda.[375] It is generally not adhered to in Europe.[376] While some European countries have the concepts of "fair dealing" or "fair practice", these should not be confused with fair use as they only apply in specific cases and they are not as flexible and robust in adapting to techno-social changes as the latter.[377] For instance, a country in Europe would have to amend its national laws to recognize the lawfulness of the widely accepted practice of users ripping music CDs to play music on their portable devices.[378]

Fair use represents the first of two differing approaches to establishing limitations and exceptions to copyright. They can either be "(i) open-ended, formulaic provisions, and (ii) 'closed lists'".[379] The fair use doctrine is a prime example of the open-ended approach. Under US law, specifically section 107 of the US

Copyright Act 1976, four factors are considered in determining whether a reproduction or use of a copyrighted work is an excepted fair use:

(1) the purpose and character of the use, including whether such use is of a commercial nature or is for nonprofit educational purposes;
(2) the nature of the copyrighted work;
(3) the amount and substantiality of the portion used in relation to the copyrighted work as a whole; and
(4) the effect of the use upon the potential market for or value of the copyrighted work.[380]

The open-ended formulation of the fair use doctrine means that it has to be applied on a case-by-case basis. What this approach sacrifices with regard to legal certainty and consistency,[381] it makes up for with its "obvious advantage of flexibility" and responsiveness to socio-technical advances, which "enables new kinds of uses to be considered as they arise, without having to anticipate them legislatively".[382] This flexibility permits courts to adjust or adapt "the scope of limitations" of intellectual property rights "to new circumstances and challenges, such as the digital environment. Leaving this discretion to the courts reduces the need for constant amendments to legislation that may have difficulty in keeping pace with the speed of technological development".[383] As Ginsburg notes, "The fair use exception permits a variety of unauthorized reproductions or derivative works, sometimes even for commercial purposes".[384] The application of the fair use doctrine in the United States has bolstered many groundbreaking and disruptive technical innovations and cultural practices such as videocassette recorders and the time-shifting of television watching, digital music players and the place-shifting of music listening, internet search engines and the indexing of the Web, and book scanning and indexing by libraries.[385]

The open-ended style of fair use in the United States sharply contrasts with the closed list approach to copyright limitations and exceptions in Europe as expressed in Article 5 of the Copyright Directive.[386] The Copyright Directive contains an exclusive and exhaustive list of limitations and exceptions to the rights of authors and copyright holders.[387] While this approach offers greater clarity and legal certainty about the rights and obligations of parties to a protected work,[388] it lacks the flexibility and dynamism of fair use. Under the closed list approach, if a new technology is developed and new cultural practices emerge (or vice versa), their lawfulness is judged based on whether they fall within the existing statutory limitations and exceptions, which as seen above are not plentiful and are strictly and narrowly applied. This is one of the underlying reasons why intellectual property rights and socio-technical innovations have such a fraught history: the former relies on the solidity and consistency of law whereas the latter flourishes with technical disruption and social change. The open-ended style of fair use appears better suited than the closed list approach to adapt to rapid and ever increasing techno-social change that is a distinctive feature of living in the networked society.

While the concept of fair use may not exist in European copyright laws, it can be argued that the Copyright Directive already contains a key principle in intellectual property laws that is as robust as the fair use doctrine and may potentially be applied in a similarly flexible manner. At the end of the enumerated list of limitations and exceptions in the Copyright Directive, there is an important proviso that states: "The exceptions and limitations provided . . . shall only be applied in certain special cases which do not conflict with a normal exploitation of the work or other subject-matter and do not unreasonably prejudice the legitimate interests of the rightholder".[389] This proviso reproduces the so-called "three-step test" originally found in the Berne Convention.[390] The three-step test requires that a statutorily granted limitation or exception must: (1) apply only "in certain special cases"; (2) "does not conflict with a normal exploitation of the work"; and (3) "does not unreasonably prejudice the legitimate interests of the author".[391] The three-step test is a "general formula" used to assess whether an existing or proposed statutory limitation or exception to the reproduction right is in accordance with the policies and objectives of intellectual property laws.[392] It generally "operates as an overriding requirement" in assessing the validity of any limitation or exception.[393] In order to comply with the test, national legislators must "provide reasonably narrow exceptions (a quantitative component), with a well-defined public interest justification (the normative/qualitative component)".[394] The three-step test was "intended to serve as a flexible balancing tool offering national policy makers sufficient breathing space to satisfy economic, social, and cultural needs".[395]

While it is not a specific limitation or exception to copyright *per se*,[396] I agree with other scholars that the three-step test as stated in the Berne Convention and other international laws could be treated as being akin to the fair use doctrine and may likewise be applied as an open-ended standard to determine whether a specific or actual use of a protected work is legitimate or permissible.[397] What is interesting about the three-step test is that, unlike the fair use doctrine, it applies not just to copyright but also to other intellectual property rights such as patent, database and design rights.[398] According to the WIPO, "Originally a test of limited application under Berne, it has now been adopted as a general template for limitations and exceptions under the TRIPS Agreement, the WCT and the WPPT".[399] The test is "emerging as an unavoidable norm in copyright law but also in other areas of intellectual property".[400] Being such an encompassing and influential principle,[401] it may be contended that the three-step test can serve as a standard not only for evaluating the validity of existing or proposed statutory limitations and exceptions, but also the legitimacy of all manner of possible uses of protected works and inventions.[402] Applying the three-step test in this way offers tremendous benefits to hackers since their inherently innovative technologies and practices can be weighed and assessed from a more practical and policy-oriented perspective rather than the strict application of rigid and closed limitations and exceptions to exclusive intellectual property rights. This proposal is explored and expanded some more in Chapter 6.

Contract and anti-circumvention laws

Despite some of the liberty and autonomy offered by the limitations and exceptions to copyright and patents laws and the exploitable gaps and loopholes in computer crime laws discussed above, the ability of hackers to engage in hacking projects and activities are often further suppressed by and through contracts and anti-circumvention mechanisms. Working in conjunction with computer crime, intellectual property and anti-circumvention laws, these private contractual arrangements and technological protection measures act as a hybrid regime of techno-legal rules that are wont to impede various forms and acts of hacking. The use of restrictive contractual provisions and technological constraints can expand and magnify the rights and control of owners and creators over their information systems or intellectual creations because, under computer crime and intellectual property laws, the lawfulness or legitimacy of most forms of access or use fundamentally hinges on the presence or absence of authorization or permission from the owner or creator. Owners and creators therefore possess and wield much discretion and power in determining who can access and use their information and technologies, in what manner such access and use is carried out, and, most critically, what laws apply (including whether or when the law has been breached). As explained below, this state of affairs has a palpably negative effect on hacking.

Contracts

Contractual terms and conditions

Contracts are essentially private yet legally binding agreements that are consented or entered into by and between parties that set out their rights and obligations with regard to a specific subject matter.[403] Pursuant to the principles of freedom of contract and party autonomy, the contracting parties have the ability to decide for themselves the terms and conditions of their agreement.[404] Contracts represent the private law between the parties,[405] and the law and legal institutions will generally recognize, uphold and enforce such contractual stipulations and arrangements, unless there is a specific or exceptional ground under the law to rescind, annul or declare the entire contract or a contractual provision unlawful, unenforceable or void.[406] This ability or freedom to contract enables parties to enter into and perform all sorts, forms and manner of private arrangements and stipulations, which, in turn, shapes and pervades all aspects of social and economic life.[407] Specifically in relation to intellectual property, De Werra explains that:

> Contract law has always played an essential role in the system of copyright law because contracts have been the usual vehicle by which copyrighted works have been put to use. . . . In all the specialized markets . . . the basic rule has always been freedom of contract.[408]

Technology and intellectual property contracts can take the form of standard boilerplate contracts and licensing agreements such as end-user license agreements (EULAs), non-disclosure agreements (NDAs), website terms of service, "shrink-wrap licences, click-through or click-wrap agreements, access contracts" and other terms of use.[409] In the context of the networked information society, it is virtually impossible to imagine a situation where contracts and contract law do not apply. It is no wonder then that contracts are considered "the principal instrument for legal innovation and legal standardization", as well as the foremost means by which the terms and conditions for accessing and using information and technologies are set.[410]

Freedom and restraints of contract

It should be noted though that there is a crucial condition that undergirds freedom of contract. Freedom of contract is based on the assumption that the parties freely negotiated and consented to the terms of the contract because they had more or less equal bargaining positions or stood on a relatively level playing field.[411] But this is not normally the case when it comes to matters relating to access and use of information, technology and intellectual property where the bargaining power of the contracting parties is most often asymmetric and lopsided. As seen in relation to intellectual property rights, it is the owners or creators who usually have a dominant bargaining position and can set the terms and conditions that are most advantageous to them. In most cases, users, consumers and hackers alike have to agree to contracts of adhesion (with their long list of provisions and impenetrable language), which are drafted by and for the benefit the owners and creators and much be accepted on a "take it or leave it" basis.[412] It is true that, in theory, users (including makers and hacktivists) still have the option of not using a particular information system or protected work. However, the pervasiveness, embeddedness and essentiality of certain information technology and intellectual property in daily life and the lack of viable alternatives render such a choice moot.[413] Whether its listening to music, reading an ebook, joining a social networking site, reading news online, downloading an app, conducting a web search or even using a smartphone or computer, many common activities and most popular or dominant information and technology products and services (e.g., iTunes, the Kindle Store, Facebook, the Apple App Store, Google, Android or Windows) require people to assent to more or less restrictive licenses or terms of use. How reasonable or feasible would it be for someone who wants to genuinely participate and be involved in the information society to refuse to use those products and services and reject their contractual terms or licenses?

In addition to hackers' and ordinary users' lack of genuine bargaining power and ability to negotiate, what is especially egregious about the technology and intellectual property contracts commonly used today (with the exception of free and open licenses) is that they are a means through which people waive or bargain away through contract even the few existing rights, opportunities and freedoms that they have under the law.[414] This is legally possible and permissible because, aside from a few instances, there is no explicit prohibition under the law that bars parties from contracting away their legal rights and privileges.[415] Under intellectual property laws,

> Subject to discrete exceptions and qualifications . . ., the general rule is that the initial endowment of rights and obligations . . . may be subsequently modified, transferred, limited, suppressed, waived, disposed of, or bargained away by contracts or through voluntary agreements between parties following the principle of freedom of contract.[416]

Save for the specific cases of reverse engineering, decompilation and making backup copies, the other limitations and exceptions to intellectual property rights that apply to hackers can be waived or diminished through contracts.[417] Contracts have the ability "to rewrite the balance that copyright law creates".[418] For instance, "copyright owners have . . . used contractual restrictions to augment copyright limits on user modifications to their copies of protected works".[419] Private contractual arrangements can also be used to "control and delimit all possible ways by which a user may use the licensed software by imposing a multitude of obligations and restrictions that exceed those set under the applicable IP laws".[420] The combination of exclusive intellectual property rights with overly restrictive contracts produces what is tantamount to "'privately legislated intellectual property rights' that override public policy and default rules on IP as contained in international and national IP laws".[421]

While it is true that the FOSS movement, through the use of copyleft licenses, defensive patent publications and other creative-subversive techno-legal tactics, has acted as a valuable counterbalance to the maximalist approach and restrictive application of contractual provisions in relation intellectual property,[422] the misapplication or abuse of freedom of contract remains the standard practice among many corporate and commercial owners and creators of information systems and intellectual property, and the private legal arrangements they impose serve as barriers to hacking since these generally tend to impede rather than promote free and open access to and creative uses of information and technology, which lies at the core of hacking projects and activities. Unlike computer crime laws (which generally concern what technologies and systems can be the targets of hacking), contract law affects what means or tools hackers can use for hacking.

Contracts and computer crime

A similarly troublesome situation exists when restrictive contracts and computer crime laws are applied together. The owners and creators of computer systems and data can contractually stipulate what users can or cannot do. While it is well within their rights to exert as much control over their technologies based on their general right of ownership, contractual restrictions when pushed to the extreme and enforced together with computer crime laws become highly problematic and of questionable legitimacy because they threaten "to put the immense coercive power of criminal law in the hands of those who draft contracts".[423] As argued by the Electronic Frontier Foundation, "violating a private agreement or duty should not carry the grim shadow of criminal liability", but the reverse seems to be the general tendency or outcome when restrictive contractual agreements work hand in hand with computer crime laws.[424] It is worth recalling that *access or use without right or authority* is a common element in the first four computer security crimes. Since a user's right or authority to use or access most technologies or intellectual property rights is founded or predicated on an existing contractual agreement or license, then a breach of contract can also result in a violation of criminal law.[425]

In a growing number of cases especially in the United States, public prosecutors and some courts have taken the view that the crime of illegal access can apply to breaches of contractual terms and conditions and employment agreements.[426] The rationale behind this interpretation is that once a user or an employee breaches the agreed terms of use, their access to the relevant information system has become without or in excess of their authority.[427] In the United States, for instance, public prosecutors have filed criminal charges against ordinary users and employees for using a computer system in excess of their authority.[428] Their expansive construction of the law "threaten[s] to criminalize any breach of contract or employee disloyalty involving computers".[429] Most courts have disagreed with this overzealous interpretation of the law and have refused to hold ordinary users criminally liable for simply breaching standard terms of use or service.[430] In the cases where the courts found employees guilty of the crime of illegal access, there was evidence of actual or intent to cause harm or damage.[431] While it is true that courts have on the whole interpreted and applied the illegal access provision reasonably and judiciously and public prosecutors may be given the benefit of the doubt to not abuse their discretion[432] in prosecuting minor cases or trivial activities,[433] these are not acceptable reasons or "justification[s] for ignoring fundamental flaws in the statute" such as the problematic definition of illegal access and its misapplication in relation to contract law.[434] As a US Court of Appeals ruled in the case of *US v Valle*, where an employee was criminally prosecuted under the US Computer Fraud and Abuse Act for violating the employer's computer use policy:

> While the Government might promise that it would not prosecute an individual for checking Facebook at work, we are not at liberty to take prosecutors at their word in such matters. A court should not uphold a highly problematic interpretation of a statute merely because the Government promises to use it responsibly.[435]

Applied in conjunction with restrictive contracts, the illegal access provision hangs as a veritable sword of Damocles over the heads of all users and consumers of technological products or services where certain uses are not expressly permitted in the relevant contract, agreement or license by the owners, producers or providers.[436] Even if it is argued that the threat is mainly theoretical, there is something particularly egregious about the idea that "private parties, rather than lawmakers, would be in a position to determine what conduct is criminal – simply by prohibiting it in an agreement".[437] It is a basic principle of law that a breach of contract is subject to civil not criminal liability.[438] While it is true that "without right" is an element of many other crimes, the unique nature and characteristics of information, computer data and digital technologies make the commission of a crime like illegal access and the triggering of criminal liability for a breach of contract far too easy or trivial to commit.

Criminalizing terms of service violations is all the more troubling given that these terms are contained in contracts of adhesion, which are non-negotiable and "often vague, lopsided and subject to change without notice".[439] Since almost all information and technology products, services and systems nowadays are subject to contractual licenses and conditions, hackers as well as users who creatively use or access any of these technologies or content can be subjected to criminal prosecution for simply violating a private agreement. The problem with vague laws is that they are "dangerous precisely because they give prosecutors and courts too much discretion to arbitrarily penalize normal, everyday behavior".[440]

It is good to note though that EU legislators hold the position that the mere violation of contractual terms and conditions should not trigger the application of computer crime laws. The Cybercrime Directive expressly states that:

> contractual obligations or agreements to restrict access to information systems by way of a user policy or terms of service, as well as labour disputes as regards access to and use of information systems of an employee for private purposes, should not incur criminal liability where the access under such circumstances would be deemed unauthorised and thus would constitute the sole basis for criminal proceedings.[441]

While this statement is contained in a recital, "the preamble . . . serves as a guideline for the interpretation of the operative part of the text"[442] and has a controlling effect on the enforcement of the Directive. Moreover, even though the preamble is not a source of rights and obligations *per se*, it may serve as a legal basis or reason for courts and other public authorities in interpreting or deciding on the applicability of the Directive's provisions.

Anti-circumvention rules

Technological protection measures

Apart from contracts, the rights and obligations under intellectual property and computer crime laws (most notably the power of owners and creators to control access to and use of their information and technologies) can be greatly modified and expanded through technical means such as copy protection mechanisms, digital rights management (DRM), rights management information and other technological measures. Rights holders, for instance, can use DRM "to restrict a user's access to and control of digital content".[443] The legal regime that protects and prohibits the circumvention of these technological protection measures is founded on the anti-circumvention provisions of the WIPO Copyright Treaty and the WIPO Performances and Phonograms Treaty, otherwise known as the WIPO Internet Treaties.[444]

Under the WIPO Internet Treaties, contracting state parties are obliged to provide "adequate legal protection and effective legal remedies against the circumvention of effective technological measures that are used by authors in connection with the exercise of their" copyright and related rights.[445] Technological measures can take the form of "devices that prevent access to a work except on certain conditions, or copy-protection or other devices that restrict or prevent various infringing uses".[446] In addition, states are required to "provide adequate and effective legal remedies against" certain acts that may "induce, enable, facilitate or conceal an infringement" of the exclusive rights of authors and creators.[447] The prohibited acts are: removing or altering "any electronic rights management information without authority"; and distributing, importing for distribution, broadcasting or communicating "to the public, without authority, works or copies of works knowing that electronic rights management information has been removed or altered without authority".[448] Rights management information is defined under the treaties as any "information which identifies the work, the author of the work, the owner of any right in the work, or information about the terms and conditions of use of the work, and any numbers or codes that represent such information" that "is attached to a copy of a work or appears in connection with the communication of a work to the public".[449]

The Copyright Directive, which incorporates the anti-circumvention provisions of the WIPO Internet Treaties into EU law, makes the act of circumventing technological measures illegal, but subject to the qualification that the "person concerned carries out in the knowledge, or with reasonable grounds to know, that he or she is pursuing that objective".[450] Furthermore, the acts related to distribution and public communication must be carried out for "commercial purposes".[451] A circumvention technology, information or activity falls within the prohibition if it is either: (a) "promoted, advertised or marketed for the purpose of circumvention", (b) of "only a limited commercially significant purpose or use other than to circumvent", or (c) "primarily designed, produced, adapted or performed for the purpose of enabling or facilitating the circumvention" of any "effective technological measure".[452] Under the Directive, a "technological measure" is defined as "any technology, device or component that, in the normal course of its operation, is designed to prevent or restrict acts, in respect of works or other subject-matter" that is "not authorized by the rightholder" or under law, and it is considered "effective" if, "through application of an access control or protection process, such as encryption, scrambling or other transformation of the work or other subject-matter", the protection objective is achieved.[453] The Copyright Directive also makes it illegal for any person to remove or alter any electronic rights-management information, or to distribute or make available to the public protected works and subject-matter whose "electronic rights-management information has been removed or altered without authority".[454] This legal prohibition is subject to the proviso that "such person knows, or has reasonable grounds to know, that by so doing he is inducing, enabling, facilitating or concealing an infringement of any copyright or any rights related to copyright".[455] In the Netherlands, the anti-circumvention provisions are contained in the Dutch Copyright Act and they hew closely to the Copyright Directive.[456]

Whether pursuant to the WIPO Internet Treaties or their different regional or national law implementations, the anti-circumvention provisions essentially outlaw three activities: (1) breaking or defeating technological measures that protect and set the terms and limits of access and use of information and technology placed by the owners or creators; (2) distributing or communicating to the public technologies or information about circumvention; and (3) distributing or making available to the public protected works whose technological measures or rights management information have been removed.[457] It should be noted though that with respect to technological measures concerning computer programs it is the specific provisions of the Software Directive and not the Copyright Directive that apply.[458] This means that in Europe anti-circumvention rules do not apply to acts of reverse engineering or decompilation software.[459] Furthermore, it appears that circumventing technological protection measures for the purpose of reverse engineering or decompiling a computer program is considered lawful and cannot be waived or defeated by contract.[460] This is tremendously beneficial to hackers since two of the primary reasons why they break the DRM on a computer program are either to enable them to understand how it works or to make the program interoperable with other software, content or data.[461] It should be noted though that outside of Europe, the anti-circumvention laws of some countries restrict or "outlaw most reverse engineering ('circumvention') of technically protected copyrighted works and the making or offering of tools to enable such reverse engineering".[462]

The adoption of anti-circumvention laws was admittedly well intentioned. According to WIPO, the WIPO Internet Treaties and their anti-circumvention provisions were meant to "address the challenges posed by today's digital technologies, in particular the dissemination of protected material over digital networks such as the Internet".[463] As with other amendments and revisions to intellectual property laws, the anti-circumvention rules were primarily a response to "developments in technology and in the marketplace".[464] There was a fear that "digital technology" would "undermine the basic principles of copyright and related rights" and lead to the "disruption of traditional markets for the sales of copies of computer programs, music, art, books and movies".[465] The drafters of the WIPO Internet Treaties believed that, in the digital networked environment, intellectual property rights could not be "applied efficiently without the support of technological measures of protection and rights management information necessary to license and monitor uses".[466] While "[t]here was agreement that the application of such measures and information should be left to the interested rights owners", the drafters still deemed it necessary that "appropriate legal provisions were needed to protect the use of such measures and information".[467] In relation to preserving the intellectual property balance, the underlying rationale was that, by giving authors and creators greater legal protection and control over their works, they would be incentivized to make their works publicly and widely available in digital format and on information networks.[468] The expressed policy reasons behind anti-circumvention laws were both economic and social.[469] While the law was meant to "sustain the national copyright industries, attract investment, and protect local creativity",[470] there was also recognition that "it was necessary to maintain a balance between these rights and the 'larger public interest,' particularly education, research and access to information".[471] However, as explained below, anti-circumvention rules have proven to be ineffective against digital piracy and they have produced technical and legal barriers that inhibit legitimate users (including hackers) from reasonably accessing and using information and technologies.

Techno-legal barriers

Despite their laudable objectives, anti-circumvention laws have proven to be extremely contentious and problematic.[472] One of the primary aims of anti-circumvention laws is to prevent digital copyright infringement. But, in practice, it is hackers rather than intellectual property infringers and pirates who are inhibited by the law. Samuelson explains that hackers or tinkerers

> who plan to make non-infringing uses of technically protected works are, oddly enough, more likely to be deterred by the anti-circumvention laws than those who tinker to infringe. After all, the payoff of infringement may be large, and it is often easy for destructive tinkerers to hide in the darknet.[473]

Further, while the WIPO claims that the WIPO Internet Treaties "reflect a broad international agreement as to how copyright and related rights should be handled . . . in the context of digital technologies", and "[t]he ultimate result has been widely acknowledged as balanced and fair", this appears to be true only for those commercial authors, creators and others with vested interests who stand to directly benefit from these laws.[474] In fact, the legitimacy and acceptance of anti-circumvention laws and technologies have been criticized and objected to "even at the time of the adoption of the WIPO Internet Treaties".[475] Contrary to what the WIPO asserts, anti-circumvention rules are neither reasonable nor balanced from the viewpoint of hackers and ordinary users,[476] and they do not "help minimize the gap between the digital haves and have-nots".[477] The truth is, the combination of technological measures with legal prohibitions against circumvention has resulted in a hybrid regime of techno-legal rules that on two levels grants owners and creators more control over their information and technology that is beyond what is formally envisioned and expressly provided for under the law.[478] This techno-legal regime of anti-circumvention "permits a much more fine-grained control over access to and use of protected material than the law permits, and it can do so without the aid of the law".[479] Furthermore, even though the WIPO Internet Treaties and the Copyright Directive recognize the importance of establishing limitations and exceptions to anti-circumvention rules (e.g., for cryptography research),[480] most countries have not made full use of this authority, and the few limitations and exceptions that exist are of strict and limited application.[481] To make matters worse, under the law, even these limitations and exceptions can be waived or suppressed through contracts and technological measures.[482]

It comes as no surprise then that these anti-circumvention rules have produced negative effects and unintended consequences.[483] There have been a number of documented cases of anti-circumvention laws and technologies adversely affecting "freedom of expression, privacy, competition law, academic research and consumer protection".[484] There is also a well-grounded fear that anti-circumvention rules could "allow any copyright owner, through a combination of contractual terms and technological measures, to repeal the fair use doctrine with respect to an individual copyrighted work".[485] Technological measures have indeed been utilized to "curb fair use, limit access to materials that has passed out of copyright and into the public domain, work in consumer-unfriendly ways, and require disclosure of personal information that could raise privacy concerns".[486] While it is true that owners and creators have the right to adopt any technical, contractual, legal and other means at their disposal to protect their property,[487] a balance must be struck and maintained by and in the law that equally recognizes and takes account of the legitimate interests of users and other social goals and values.

The charges of illegitimacy and excessive breadth that hound anti-circumvention rules is quite evident from the fact that some of their problematic uses do not even directly concern or relate to the prevention of intellectual property right infringement, which is the main purpose and stated objective of the law.[488] Instances where anti-circumvention laws and rules have been applied and enforced even though they have nothing to do with copyright piracy include: a telephone company preventing users and others parties from unlocking mobile phones,[489] a game developer company suing another company that produced a program that made playing a massively multiplayer online role-playing game (MMORPG) less tedious,[490] companies attempting to stave off the creation and introduction of more innovative or competing products and services in the market,[491] technology companies threatening or barring security researchers from disclosing security vulnerabilities,[492] movie companies preventing users who lawfully purchased DVDs from format shifting,[493] and car and tractor companies dissuading people from tinkering with or fixing their vehicles.[494] Clearly, the above cases "pose virtually no risk of enabling infringement of commercially exploited copyrighted works . . . TPMs [technological protection measures] are being used to thwart competition in certain industry sectors, with the anti-circumvention rules as reinforcements".[495]

Anti-circumvention rules, whether of the technical, legal or hybrid variety, are the very antithesis of hacking because they produce a kind of "de facto access rights that do not only prohibit unauthorised copying of digital works but also create techno-legal barriers that restrict wider access to and dissemination of knowledge".[496] The main issue that hackers have with technological measures like DRM is that the law itself prevents them from "exercising their own right to respond to these techno-legal restrictions" because "the act of circumvention per se is rendered unlawful under international and state laws, regardless of whether the circumvention is carried out for a lawful use" such as for private and non-commercial copying.[497] There is an imbalance and lack of fairness in the law because "copyright owners may, with some exceptions, protect the technological measures they employ to prevent access and copying, while users are not similarly free to defeat those measures".[498] The law as it currently stands gives too much control to owners and creators of information and technology to decide how the latter can be accessed or used. As Lessig and Cohen argue, hackers as well as ordinary users should have "a right to resist, or 'hack' trusted systems to the extent that they infringe on traditional fair use" or other limitations and exceptions to intellectual property rights.[499]

The frustration that hackers have with anti-circumvention rules is further exacerbated by the fact that in actuality these technological measures are never foolproof or completely "effective", and it is quite trivial for hackers to get around or break them.[500] Despite the ease by which these measures can be defeated, hackers are dissuaded from hacking these measures because the law itself makes such circumvention illegal, regardless of the absence of malicious intent or purpose. In truth, based on my discussions with hackers, it is the very possibility or threat of prosecution rather than the actual filing of court cases that creates a chilling effect.[501] For instance, hackers recount how people they know stopped offering proxies to get around the block of The Pirate Bay in the Netherlands or providing Tor[502] services after receiving formal cease and desist letters from private companies or informal telephone calls and communications from public authorities. As a result, through the use of techno-legal controls, anti-circumvention rules doubly restrict what hackers can do with information and technology and nullify their ability to perform all six common acts of hacking – *explore, break, learn, create, share* and *secure*. Furthermore, when access to and use of technology and intellectual property are so thoroughly locked down in this manner, a long list of hacker norms and values are stifled: openness, freedom of information, freedom of access, freedom of expression, individual autonomy and liberty, transparency, curiosity, creative and innovation, community development and social development.[503]

Conflicts and correspondences
between hacking and law

Based on the foregoing analysis, existing technology laws and policies tend to restrict rather than support hackers. In general, computer crime laws are very broad and restrictive and over-criminalize hacking. Because of the vague and low legal thresholds for committing computer security crimes, many hacking activities, including those that are creative or innocuous, are subject to criminal prosecution. While intellectual property laws are meant to promote the creation and dissemination of creative works and inventions, there is an evident imbalance in these laws because they provide greater protection to the rights of creators and inventors at the expense of the rights of the public to reasonably use these creations. So while creators and inventors are granted extensive and exclusive rights of control over their creations, the corollary limitations and exceptions to these rights that could benefit hackers and ordinary users and preserve the intellectual property balance are few and far between. As discussed above, the situation is made even worse for hackers because contracts and technological protection measures have been used to expand and ratchet up the application of computer crime and intellectual property laws.

The above examination reveals the numerous conflicts and incongruities as well as some fundamental correspondences and similarities between the goals and values of hacking and those of hacking-related laws. It is curious to see how hacking and the law share and seek to protect and promote essentially the same social values, interests and goals, yet in practice each has different and often opposing normative views and approaches as to which specific values to prioritize and how to achieve them. Computer crime laws have a laudable goal of safeguarding the integrity and security of information systems, but their restrictive approach (particularly the offense of illegal access) severely curtails what activities and projects hackers can reasonably and legally undertake. With regard to intellectual property laws, hackers are prodigious creators and users of information and technology but their ability to innovate is constrained by the quite limited exceptions to the free and open use or re-use of copyrighted works and patented inventions. On top of this, the controls and prohibitions under computer crime and intellectual property laws are further amplified and enlarged by the use of ever more restrictive contracts and anti-circumvention technologies and rules that tend to both legally and technically preclude potentially creative and unexpected uses of protected information and technologies.

What is ironic though is that, despite all these, the above laws essentially share some of the same values of hacking. Like intellectual property laws, the main goal of hacking is to produce creative works and innovative technologies and disseminate them as widely as possible. Protecting the security of computer systems and data, which is the primary objective of computer crime laws, is considered an important value as well among hackers. This means that, while they may have serious differences, hacking and law are connected on a fundamental level and, through these areas of connection and intersection, it may be possible to resolve the tensions between them.

Based on the above, it comes as no surprise then that hackers and the law are constantly interacting with one another, and they seem determined to question and challenge each other's position. The clashes as well as congruence between hackers and the law are thrown into greater relief in the next chapter, which examines how hackers actually view, respond to and interact with law and public authorities. Zeroing in on these plural and complex interactions is pivotal since they serve as the crucial means or mechanisms by and through which technology laws and policies concerning hacking are developed, contested, negotiated and remade.

Notes

1 See Recommendation No. R (89) 9 on computer-related crime 54; see Lawrence Lessig, *Code: Version 2.0* 171.
2 See Jay BloomBecker, "Computer crime update" 628 and 637.
3 Joseph Olivenbaum, "Rethinking federal computer crime legislation" 581–582; Ian Lloyd, *Information Technology Law* 215; Tim Jordan, *Hacking* 39.
4 Joseph Olivenbaum, "Rethinking federal computer crime legislation" 582; see also Orin Kerr, "Interpreting 'access' and 'authorization' in computer misuse statutes" 1615.
5 Joseph Olivenbaum, "Rethinking federal computer crime legislation" 582; see also Orin Kerr, "Interpreting 'access' and 'authorization' in computer misuse statutes" 1615; see also Ian Lloyd and Moira Simpson, "Computer crime" 242.
6 Richard Hollinger, "Computer crime" 78; Joseph Olivenbaum, "Rethinking federal computer crime legislation" 584; Cyrus Chung, "The computer fraud and abuse act" 236; Reid Skibell, "Cybercrimes & misdemeanors" 912.
7 Joseph Olivenbaum, "Rethinking federal computer crime legislation" 584–585.
8 Richard Hollinger and Lonn Lanza-Kaduce, "The process of criminalization: The case of computer crime laws" 101; Orin Kerr, "Interpreting 'access' and 'authorization' in computer misuse statutes" 1615.
9 Jay BloomBecker, "Computer crime update" 645; Richard Hollinger, "Computer crime" 78; Cyrus Chung, "The computer fraud and abuse act" 239; Ian Lloyd and Moira Simpson, "Computer crime" 245; Orin Kerr, "Interpreting 'access' and 'authorization' in computer misuse statutes" 1630; Reid Skibell, "Cybercrimes & misdemeanors" 939.
10 Richard Hollinger, "Computer crime" 78; Cyrus Chung, "The computer fraud and abuse act" 239; Jay BloomBecker, "Computer crime update" 645; Ian Lloyd and Moira Simpson, "Computer crime" 245; Orin Kerr, "Interpreting 'access' and 'authorization' in computer misuse statutes" 1630; Reid Skibell, "Cybercrimes & misdemeanors" 939.
11 Ian Lloyd and Moira Simpson, "Computer crime" 242.
12 Ian Lloyd and Moira Simpson, "Computer crime" 242.
13 Joseph Olivenbaum, "Rethinking federal computer crime legislation" 585; Cyrus Chung, "The computer fraud and abuse act" 237; Charles Doyle "Cybercrime"; Ian Lloyd, *Information Technology Law* 209; Ian Lloyd and Moira Simpson, "Computer crime" 262.
14 Ian Lloyd and Moira Simpson, "Computer crime" 242.

15 Ian Lloyd, *Information Technology Law* 217–218; Ian Lloyd and Moira Simpson, "Computer crime" 242.

16 Ian Lloyd, *Information Technology Law* 217–218.

17 Ian Lloyd, *Information Technology Law* 216–217; Convention on Cybercrime.

18 Lorenzo Picotti and Ivan Salvadori, "National legislation implementing the convention on cybercrime" 4; Ian Lloyd, *Information Technology Law* 216–217; Convention on Cybercrime.

19 Convention on Cybercrime; Lorenzo Picotti and Ivan Salvadori, "National legislation implementing the convention on cybercrime" 4.

20 Convention on Cybercrime; see European Commission, "Proposal for a directive on attacks against information systems" COM(2010) 517, 2.

21 European Commission, "Proposal for a Directive of the European Parliament and of the Council on attacks against information systems and repealing Council Framework Decision 2005/222/JHA" COM(2010) 517, 2; see also Lorenzo Picotti and Ivan Salvadori, "National legislation implementing the convention on cybercrime" 4.

22 Ian Lloyd, *Information Technology Law* 221; see also Council Directive 2013/40/EU on attacks against information systems, recital 15.

23 Council Framework Decision 2005/222/JHA of 24 February 2005 on attacks against information systems [2005] OJ L069; Ian Lloyd, *Information Technology Law* 218–219.

24 Council Directive 2013/40/EU of 12 August 2013 on attacks against information systems and replacing Council Framework Decision 2005/222/JHA [2013] OJ L218/8.

25 Council Directive 2013/40/EU on attacks against information systems, recitals 5, 15 and 34; see European Commission, "Proposal for a Directive on attacks against information systems" COM(2010) 517, 3.

26 Council Directive 2013/40/EU on attacks against information systems, recital 1.

27 Council Directive 2013/40/EU on attacks against information systems, recital 8.

28 Convention on Cybercrime, Title I; see also Lorenzo Picotti and Ivan Salvadori, "National legislation implementing the convention on cybercrime" 13.

29 See David Wall, *Cybercrime* 10, 49 and 53 (who prefers to use the term "computer integrity crimes").

30 See Reid Skibell, "Cybercrimes & misdemeanors" 943.

31 Helen Nissenbaum, "Hackers and the contested ontology of cyberspace" 196; Debora Halbert, "Discourses of danger and the computer hacker" 364; Reid Skibell, "The myth of the computer hacker" 349.

32 Explanatory Report to the convention on cybercrime, paras 35, 44 and 49.

33 David Wall, *Cybercrime* 10, 49 and 53; Explanatory Report to the Convention on Cybercrime, paras 44 and 71; see Juerd Waalboer and others, "Open letter to public prosecutor: Hacking"; see Pedro Freitas and Nuno Goncalves, "Illegal access to information systems and the Directive 2013/40/EU" 55; see Debora Halbert, "Discourses of danger and the computer hacker".

34 See Marcia Hofmann and Rainey Reitman, "Rebooting computer crime law Part 1"; see Michael Dizon, "Rules of a networked society" 92.

35 David Wall, *Cybercrime* 10, 49 and 53; see also Explanatory Report to the Convention on Cybercrime, para 44.

36 Explanatory Report to the Convention on Cybercrime, para 43; see David Wall, *Cybercrime* 10, 49 and 53.

37 See Joseph Olivenbaum, "Rethinking federal computer crime legislation" 585 and 622; see Cyrus Chung, "The computer fraud and abuse act" 236; see Orin

Kerr, "Interpreting 'access' and 'authorization' in computer misuse statutes" 1597, 1615 and 1616; see Ian Lloyd, *Information Technology Law* 222.

38 Convention on Cybercrime, art 2.

39 Explanatory Report to the Convention on Cybercrime, para 46; see also Lorenzo Picotti and Ivan Salvadori, "National legislation implementing the convention on cybercrime" 14.

40 Explanatory Report to the Convention on Cybercrime, para 38.

41 Council Directive 2013/40/EU on attacks against information systems, art 2 (d); see also Lorenzo Picotti and Ivan Salvadori, "National legislation implementing the convention on cybercrime" 13.

42 Recommendation No. R (89) 9 on computer-related crime 46.

43 See Orin Kerr, "Interpreting 'access' and 'authorization' in computer misuse statutes" 1630; see Recommendation No. R (89) 9 on computer-related crime 52; see Ken Lindup, "The cyberpunk age" 645; see Joseph Olivenbaum, "Rethinking federal computer crime legislation" 590 (on a US court ruling that an authorized computer user can be held liable for unauthorized access when he enters parts of the system that he has no authority to access); see Richard Hollinger and Lonn Lanza-Kaduce, "The process of criminalization: The case of computer crime laws" 102.

44 Explanatory Report to the Convention on Cybercrime, para 44; see also Lorenzo Picotti and Ivan Salvadori, "National legislation implementing the convention on cybercrime" 14 and 17.

45 Explanatory Report to the Convention on Cybercrime, para 40 and 49.

46 Convention on Cybercrime, arts 2, 3, 7 and 8; Explanatory Report to the Convention on Cybercrime, para 59.

47 Convention on Cybercrime, art 2; Explanatory Report to the Convention on Cybercrime, para 49 and 50.

48 European Commission, "Report based on Article 12 of the Council Framework Decision of 24 February 2005 on attacks against information system" COM(2008) 444, 14 July 2008, 4; see also Lorenzo Picotti and Ivan Salvadori, "National legislation implementing the convention on cybercrime" 15.

49 Lorenzo Picotti and Ivan Salvadori, "National legislation implementing the convention on cybercrime" 14.

50 Bert-Jaap Koops, "Cybercrime legislation in the Netherlands" 7.

51 Council Directive 2013/40/EU on attacks against information systems, art 3.

52 Pedro Freitas and Nuno Goncalves, "Illegal access to information systems and the Directive 2013/40/EU" 59–60.

53 Recommendation No. R (89) 9 on computer-related crime 51.

54 Orin Kerr, "Interpreting 'access' and 'authorization' in computer misuse statutes" 1649.

55 Orin Kerr, "Interpreting 'access' and 'authorization' in computer misuse statutes" 1651.

56 Council Directive 2013/40/EU on attacks against information systems, recital 17.

57 Pedro Freitas and Nuno Goncalves, "Illegal access to information systems and the Directive 2013/40/EU" 59.

58 Convention on Cybercrime, Preamble; see also Richard Hollinger and Lonn Lanza-Kaduce, "The process of criminalization: The case of computer crime laws" 114 and 115; see also Orin Kerr, "Interpreting 'access' and 'authorization' in computer misuse statutes" 1656; see also Reid Skibell, "Cybercrimes & misdemeanors" 934.

59 Convention on Cybercrime, Preamble.

60 Explanatory Report to the Convention on Cybercrime, para 9.

61 Explanatory Report to the Convention on Cybercrime, para 44.
62 Lorenzo Picotti and Ivan Salvadori, "National legislation implementing the convention on cybercrime" 13 and 17.
63 Convention on Cybercrime, Preamble.
64 Explanatory Report to the Convention on Cybercrime, para 45.
65 Explanatory Report to the Convention on Cybercrime, para 5.
66 Bert-Jaap Koops, "Cybercrime legislation in the Netherlands" 7.
67 Explanatory Report to the Convention on Cybercrime, para 44.
68 See Richard Hollinger, "Hackers: Computer heroes or electronic highwaymen?" 9.
69 See Council Directive 2013/40/EU on attacks against information systems, art 2 (d); see Electronic Frontier Foundation, "Submission to the European Parliament on the draft directive on attacks against computer systems" 5.
70 See Tom Brewster, "US cybercrime law being used to target security researchers".
71 See Helen Nissenbaum, "Hackers and the contested ontology of cyberspace" 202 and 206; see Wayne Rumbles, "Reflections of hackers in legal and popular discourse" 73; see Reid Skibell, "The myth of the computer hacker" 344.
72 Explanatory Report to the Convention on Cybercrime, para 49.
73 Recommendation No. R (89) 9 on computer-related crime 50; see also Ian Lloyd and Moira Simpson, "Computer crime" 263.
74 Recommendation No. R (89) 9 on computer-related crime 50–51.
75 Explanatory Report to the Convention on Cybercrime, paras 44 and 49; see also Recommendation No. R (89) 9 on computer-related crime 51.
76 Joseph Olivenbaum, "Rethinking federal computer crime legislation" 604; Orin Kerr, "Interpreting 'access' and 'authorization' in computer misuse statutes" 1600; Cyrus Chung, "The computer fraud and abuse act" 242; Reid Skibell, "Cybercrimes & misdemeanors" 912, 915 and 917; Christine Galbraith, "Access denied" 358; Cassandra Kirsch, "The grey hat hacker" 394.
77 See Reid Skibell, "Cybercrimes & misdemeanors" 910, 912 and 945; see Samantha Jensen, "Why broad interpretations of the CFAA fail" 98 and 119.
78 Recommendation No. R (89) 9 on computer-related crime 53; Reid Skibell, "Cybercrimes & misdemeanors" 916 and 940.
79 Reid Skibell, "Cybercrimes & misdemeanors" 911 and 912; see Richard Hollinger and Lonn Lanza-Kaduce, "The process of criminalization: The case of computer crime laws" 104.
80 Richard Hollinger and Lonn Lanza-Kaduce, "The process of criminalization: The case of computer crime laws" 104.
81 Cyrus Chung, "The computer fraud and abuse act" 238.
82 Ian Lloyd and Moira Simpson, "Computer crime" 261; see also Recommendation No. R (89) 9 on computer-related crime 51.
83 Ian Lloyd and Moira Simpson, "Computer crime" 266.
84 Ian Lloyd and Moira Simpson, "Computer crime" 267.
85 Reid Skibell, "Cybercrimes & misdemeanors" 911; Richard Hollinger and Lonn Lanza-Kaduce, "The process of criminalization: The case of computer crime laws" 115; see also Recommendation No. R (89) 9 on computer-related crime 49–50.
86 Lorenzo Picotti and Ivan Salvadori, "National legislation implementing the convention on cybercrime" 14.
87 Richard Hollinger and Lonn Lanza-Kaduce, "The process of criminalization: The case of computer crime laws" 115.
88 Ian Lloyd and Moira Simpson, "Computer crime" 261.
89 Ian Lloyd and Moira Simpson, "Computer crime" 261.
90 Reid Skibell, "Cybercrimes & misdemeanors" 921; see also Tom Brewster, "US cybercrime law being used to target security researchers".

91 Electronic Frontier Foundation, "Let's fix draconian computer crime law"; see also Marcia Hofman and Rainey Reitman, "Rebooting computer crime law Part 1"; see also Electronic Frontier Foundation, "Submission to the European Parliament on the draft directive on attacks against computer systems" 5; see also Zoe Lofgren and Ron Wyden, "Introducing Aaron's law".

92 Electronic Frontier Foundation, "Submission to the European Parliament on the draft directive on attacks against computer systems" 5; see also Cassandra Kirsch, "The grey hat hacker: Reconciling cyberspace reality and the law" 393–394; see also Samantha Jensen, "Abusing the computer fraud and abuse act" 116 and 120; see also Christine Galbraith, "Improper use of the computer fraud and abuse act to control information on publicly accessible Internet Websites" 318, 319, 330, 342 and 343; see also Cindy Cohn and Marcia Hoffman, "Rebooting computer crime law Part 2"; see also Adrian Cho, "University hackers test the right to expose security concerns"; see also Hanni Fakhoury, "The US crackdown on hackers is our new war on drugs".

93 Reid Skibell, "Cybercrimes & misdemeanors" 938–939; Electronic Frontier Foundation, "Submission to the European Parliament on the draft directive on attacks against computer systems" 5 and 8.

94 Cassandra Kirsch, "The grey hat hacker" 396; Electronic Frontier Foundation, "Submission to the European Parliament on the draft directive on attacks against computer systems" 7; Cindy Cohn and Marcia Hoffman, "Rebooting computer crime law Part 2".

95 Tom Brewster, "US cybercrime law being used to target security researchers"; Cassandra Kirsch, "The grey hat hacker" 392.

96 Tom Brewster, "US cybercrime law being used to target security researchers".

97 Lisa O'Carroll, "Scientist banned from revealing codes used to start luxury cars"; see also Adrian Cho, "University hackers test the right to expose security concerns"; see also Tom Brewster, "US cybercrime law being used to target security researchers"; see also Electronic Frontier Foundation, "Submission to the European Parliament on the draft directive on attacks against computer systems" 5, 6 and 8.

98 Electronic Frontier Foundation, "Submission to the European Parliament on the draft directive on attacks against computer systems" 5 and 8; see also Derek Bambauer and Oliver Day, "The hacker's aegis" 2, 34 and 51; see also Tom Brewster, "US cybercrime law being used to target security researchers"; see also Adrian Cho, "University hackers test the right to expose security concerns".

99 Electronic Frontier Foundation, "Submission to the European Parliament on the draft directive on attacks against computer systems" 8; see also Joseph Olivenbaum, "Rethinking federal computer crime legislation" 605.

100 Christine Galbraith, "Access denied" 318, 319, 330, 333, 342 and 343; see also Electronic Frontier Foundation, "Submission to the European Parliament on the draft directive on attacks against computer systems" 3–4.

101 Electronic Frontier Foundation, "Submission to the European Parliament on the draft directive on attacks against computer systems" 4; see also Cindy Cohn and Marcia Hoffman, "Rebooting computer crime law Part 2".

102 Parker Higgins, "Critical fixes for the computer fraud and abuse act".

103 Parker Higgins, "Critical fixes for the computer fraud and abuse act".

104 Convention on Cybercrime, Preamble; Council Directive 2013/40/EU on attacks against information systems, recital 2; see also Cindy Cohn and Marcia Hoffman, "Rebooting computer crime law Part 2"; see also Electronic Frontier Foundation, "Submission to the European Parliament on the draft directive on attacks against computer systems" 2.

105 Orin Kerr, "Vagueness challenges to the computer fraud and abuse act" 1562, 1578, 1579; see also Cyrus Chung, "The computer fraud and abuse act" 233–234; see also Marcia Hofman and Rainey Reitman, "Rebooting computer crime law Part 1"; see also Electronic Frontier Foundation, "Submission to the European Parliament on the draft directive on attacks against computer systems" 5; see also Cassandra Kirsch, "The grey hat hacker" 393.
106 Explanatory Report to the Convention on Cybercrime, para 47.
107 Christine Galbraith, "Access denied" 323 and 362; Lorenzo Picotti and Ivan Salvadori, "National legislation implementing the convention on cybercrime" 13.
108 Explanatory Report to the Convention on Cybercrime, para 48.
109 Explanatory Report to the Convention on Cybercrime, paras 48 and 58; see also Google, "Crawling & indexing"; see also M.H.M. Schellekens, "Robot.txt: Balancing interests of content producers and content users"; see also Christine Galbraith, "Access denied" 349–350.
110 Explanatory Report to the Convention on Cybercrime, para 38 (emphasis added).
111 Explanatory Report to the Convention on Cybercrime, para 46; but see Bert-Jaap Koops, "Cybercrime legislation in the Netherlands" 10 (it is subject to specific anti-spam laws); see also European Commission, "Questions and answers: Directive on attacks against information systems" MEMO/13/661, 4 July 2013, 6.
112 Explanatory Report to the Convention on Cybercrime, para 43.
113 Convention on Cybercrime, art 3; see also Council Directive 2013/40/EU on attacks against information systems, art 6; see also Recommendation No. R (89) 9 on computer-related crime 54 and 55.
114 Explanatory Report to the Convention on Cybercrime, para 53; see also Council Directive 2013/40/EU on attacks against information systems, recital 9 (for a more detailed definition).
115 Council Directive 2013/40/EU on attacks against information systems, recital 9; see also Recommendation No. R (89) 9 on computer-related crime 54.
116 Explanatory Report to the Convention on Cybercrime, para 52.
117 Explanatory Report to the Convention on Cybercrime, para 53; David Wall, *Cybercrime* 59 and 60; see also European Commission, "Questions and answers: Directive on attacks against information systems" MEMO/13/661, 4 July 2013, 6 (spyware is "software that is installed on a user's computer without his knowledge. Such software transmits information on the user and his habits once connected to the Internet. The information gathered this way is usually intended for use by advertisers").
118 Recommendation No. R (89) 9 on computer-related crime 53.
119 Bert-Jaap Koops, "Cybercrime legislation in the Netherlands" 8.
120 Recommendation No. R (89) 9 on computer-related crime 53.
121 Wim van Eck, "Electromagnetic radiation from video display units" 269 and 276; see also Robert Gehling, Ryan Ashley and Thomas Griffin, "Electronic emissions security" 306 (for more information on emissions security).
122 Robert Gehling, Ryan Ashley and Thomas Griffin, "Electronic emissions security" 306, 307 and 308.
123 Bart Jacobs and Wolter Pieters, "Electronic voting in the Netherlands: From early adoption to early abolishment" 11; see Robert Gehling, Ryan Ashley and Thomas Griffin, "Electronic emissions security" 307–308 (for a discussion of TEMPEST)
124 David Wall, *Cybercrime* 60.
125 See Explanatory Report to the Convention on Cybercrime, para 59.

126 See Ryan Iwahashi, "How to circumvent technology protection measures without violating the DMCA" 508–509.

127 See Jeffrey Bardzell, "Virtual worlds and fraud" 746.

128 Explanatory Report to the Convention on Cybercrime, para 51; Recommendation No. R (89) 9 on computer-related crime 53.

129 Recommendation No. R (89) 9 on computer-related crime 54.

130 Explanatory Report to the Convention on Cybercrime, para 54.

131 Explanatory Report to the Convention on Cybercrime, para 58.

132 Explanatory Report to the Convention on Cybercrime, para 56.

133 Explanatory Report to the Convention on Cybercrime, para 53; Recommendation No. R (89) 9 on computer-related crime 54.

134 Chaos Computer Club, "Hackerethics"; see Eric Hughes, "A cypherpunk's manifesto"; see Julian Assange and others, *Cypherpunks*.

135 See Verizon, "2012 Data Breach Investigations Report" 4, 6, 15, 19 and 20; Ingrid Lunden, "Hacktivists to blame for 58 percent of stolen data In 2011, Says Verizon Study"; Gabriella Coleman, "Anonymous: From the Lulz to collective action".

136 See Tim Jordan, *Activism!* 127; see Julian Assange and others, *Cypherpunks*; see Bits of Freedom, "Internet-freedom toolbox"; see Open Technology Fund, "Projects"; see Tactical Technology Collective, "Security in-a-box"; see Riseup; see Electronic Frontier Foundation, "Surveillance self-defense".

137 Convention on Cybercrime, art 4 para 1; see also Recommendation No. R (89) 9 on computer-related crime 44.

138 Recommendation No. R (89) 9 on computer-related crime 43; see also Explanatory Report to the Convention on Cybercrime, para 65.

139 Recommendation No. R (89) 9 on computer-related crime 44.

140 Xiang Li, "Hacktivism and the first amendment" 311; see Explanatory Report to the Convention on Cybercrime, para 60; see Recommendation No. R (89) 9 on computer-related crime 45.

141 Recommendation No. R (89) 9 on computer-related crime 44; see also Lorenzo Picotti and Ivan Salvadori, "National legislation implementing the convention on cybercrime" 19.

142 Recommendation No. R (89) 9 on computer-related crime 45.

143 Convention on Cybercrime, art 5; see also Lorenzo Picotti and Ivan Salvadori, "National legislation implementing the convention on cybercrime" 22.

144 Council Directive 2013/40/EU on attacks against information systems, art 4 (emphasis added).

145 Explanatory Report to the Convention on Cybercrime, para 65; see Recommendation No. R (89) 9 on computer-related crime 46.

146 Explanatory Report to the Convention on Cybercrime, para 61; see also Recommendation No. R (89) 9 on computer-related crime 45.

147 Explanatory Report to the Convention on Cybercrime, para 61; Recommendation No. R (89) 9 on computer-related crime 45.

148 Explanatory Report to the Convention on Cybercrime, para 61; Recommendation No. R (89) 9 on computer-related crime 61.

149 Explanatory Report to the Convention on Cybercrime, para 61; Recommendation No. R (89) 9 on computer-related crime 60–61.

150 Bert-Jaap Koops, "Cybercrime legislation in the Netherlands" 8.

151 Explanatory Report to the Convention on Cybercrime, para 61; see also Recommendation No. R (89) 9 on computer-related crime 45.

152 Bert-Jaap Koops, "Cybercrime legislation in the Netherlands" 8 (but this is subject to the prosecutorial discretion of the public prosecutor).

153 Bert-Jaap Koops, "Cybercrime legislation in the Netherlands" 8; see also Explanatory Report to the Convention on Cybercrime, para 63.

154 Explanatory Report to the Convention on Cybercrime, para 66; Recommendation No. R (89) 9 on computer-related crime 49; see also Lorenzo Picotti and Ivan Salvadori, "National legislation implementing the convention on cybercrime" 20.

155 Explanatory Report to the Convention on Cybercrime, para 65; Recommendation No. R (89) 9 on computer-related crime 48 and 49.

156 Explanatory Report to the Convention on Cybercrime, para 67; Lorenzo Picotti and Ivan Salvadori, "National legislation implementing the Convention on Cybercrime" 23.

157 Lorenzo Picotti and Ivan Salvadori, "National legislation implementing the convention on cybercrime" 23.

158 Explanatory Report to the Convention on Cybercrime, para 67; see also Lorenzo Picotti and Ivan Salvadori, "National legislation implementing the convention on cybercrime" 20.

159 Bert-Jaap Koops, "Cybercrime legislation in the Netherlands" 8.

160 Bert-Jaap Koops, "Cybercrime legislation in the Netherlands" 9.

161 Explanatory Report to the Convention on Cybercrime, paras 60 and 65; see also Recommendation No. R (89) 9 on computer-related crime 44.

162 Recommendation No. R (89) 9 on computer-related crime 47; see also Explanatory Report to the Convention on Cybercrime, para 65.

163 Recommendation No. R (89) 9 on computer-related crime 46.

164 Recommendation No. R (89) 9 on computer-related crime 43 and 46.

165 Recommendation No. R (89) 9 on computer-related crime 43.

166 European Commission, "Proposal for a Directive on attacks against information systems" COM(2010) 517, 4.

167 Council Directive 2013/40/EU on attacks against information systems, recitals 5, 6, 13 and 26; see also European Commission, "Proposal for a Directive on attacks against information systems" COM(2010) 517, 3.

168 Council Directive 2013/40/EU on attacks against information systems, recital 5.

169 European Commission, "Questions and answers: Directive on attacks against information systems" MEMO/13/661, 4 July 2013, 1 and 5.

170 European Commission, "Questions and answers: Directive on attacks against information systems" MEMO/13/661, 4 July 2013, 5.

171 Computer Desktop Encyclopedia; see also European Commission, "Questions and answers: Directive on attacks against information systems" MEMO/13/661, 4 July 2013, 5; see also Andrew Chadwick, *Internet Politics* 130; see also Xiang Li, "Hacktivism and the first amendment" 306–307; Tim Jordan, *Activism!* 124; Argyro Karanasiou, "The changing face of protests in the digital age" 100.

172 European Commission, "Questions and answers: Directive on attacks against information systems" MEMO/13/661, 4 July 2013, 5; see also Xiang Li, "Hacktivism and the first amendment" 307; see also Argyro Karanasiou, "The changing face of protests in the digital age" 100.

173 Argyro Karanasiou, "The changing face of protests in the digital age" 100; see also Noah Hampson, "Hacktivism" 532.

174 Council Directive 2013/40/EU on attacks against information systems, recital 4.

175 Council Directive 2013/40/EU on attacks against information systems, recital 5.

176 Council Directive 2013/40/EU on attacks against information systems, recital 5.

177 Andrew Chadwick, *Internet Politics* 130 (also called "email bombing", this type of attack utilizes "automation software to inundate an email mailbox . . . with the aim of crippling an organization's email capabilities"); see also Lorenzo

Picotti and Ivan Salvadori, "National legislation implementing the convention on cybercrime" 23.

178 European Commission, "Questions and answers: Directive on attacks against information systems" MEMO/13/661, 4 July 2013, 5 (a contraction of malicious software, malware is "computer software designed to infiltrate or damage or computer system without the owner's consent. It is distributed through a variety of means (emails, computer viruses, and botnets)"); see also Andrew Chadwick, *Internet Politics* 130.

179 Computer Desktop Encyclopedia, "Virus"; see also Recommendation No. R (89) 9 on computer-related crime 43.

180 Computer Desktop Encyclopedia, "Worm".

181 Computer Desktop Encyclopedia, "Trojan".

182 Computer Desktop Encyclopedia, "Back door".

183 Computer Desktop Encyclopedia, "Logic bomb"; see also European Commission, "Questions and answers: Directive on attacks against information systems" MEMO/13/661, 4 July 2013, 5; see also Explanatory Report to the Convention on Cybercrime, para 67 and 68; see also Bert-Jaap Koops, "Cybercrime legislation in the Netherlands" 8–9; see also Recommendation No. R (89) 9 on computer-related crime 43; see also Xiang Li, "Hacktivism and the first amendment" 311; Argyro Karanasiou, "The changing face of protests in the digital age" 101 (citing Samuel).

184 See Directive 2009/24/EC on the legal protection of computer programs.

185 Andrew Chadwick, *Internet Politics* 130; Xiang Li, "Hacktivism and the first amendment" 310–311; Noah Hampson, "Hacktivism" 514 and 520.

186 Gabriella Coleman, "Anonymous: From the Lulz to collective action".

187 Andrew Chadwick, *Internet Politics* 130 (considered the "the most common form of hacktivism", it is carried out by "breaking into and altering the content of a website to change its content"); see also Xiang Li, "Hacktivism and the first amendment" 307; Noah Hampson, "Hacktivism" 519.

188 Xiang Li, "Hacktivism and the first amendment" 307 ("hacking into the web server and altering the address settings to redirect visitors to a different website"); see also Andrew Chadwick, *Internet Politics* 130 (the act of "intercepting web traffic destined for a particular site and redirecting it elsewhere").

189 Andrew Chadwick, *Internet Politics* 130 ("uses the Internet 'ping' program (used to test the presence of a computer on a network) to overload a server by flooding it with 'ping' requests").

190 Xiang Li, "Hacktivism and the first amendment" 308 ("hacking into a private network and stealing information or data. Publication or release of the stolen data sometimes follows the attack.").

191 Argyro Karanasiou, "The changing face of protests in the digital age" 99 and 100.

192 See Mathias Klang, "Civil disobedience online"; see Xiang Li, "Hacktivism and the first amendment" 304; Tim Jordan, *Activism!* 127 ("a new class of civil disobedience"); see Argyro Karanasiou, "The changing face of protests in the digital age" 99, 101 and 107.

193 Xiang Li, "Hacktivism and the first amendment" 304 (but the petition did not progress because "it failed to meet the signature threshold" that was "required to guarantee a White house response"); see also Argyro Karanasiou, "The changing face of protests in the digital age" 99.

194 Xiang Li, "Hacktivism and the first amendment" 308, 309 and 324; Tim Jordan, *Activism!* 124; Argyro Karanasiou, "The changing face of protests in the digital age" 104.

195 Xiang Li, "Hacktivism and the first amendment" 308; see also Mathias Klang, "Civil disobedience online" 7–8; see also Argyro Karanasiou, "The changing face of protests in the digital age" 103.
196 Paul Taylor, "Editorial: Hacktivism"; Andrew Chadwick, *Internet Politics* 131–132; Seth Kreimer, "Technologies of protest: Insurgent social movements and the first amendment in the era of the Internet" 156–157; Peter Ludlow, "WikiLeaks and hacktivist culture" 26.
197 See Joshua McLaurin, "Making cyberspace safe for democracy".
198 Noah Hampson, "Hacktivism: A new bread of protest in a networked world" 533; see also Joshua McLaurin, "Making cyberspace safe for democracy" 236.
199 Noah Hampson, "Hacktivism: A new bread of protest in a networked world" 535.
200 Xiang Li, "Hacktivism and the first amendment" 322; see also Tim Jordan, *Activism!* 126; see also Jennifer Chandler, "Security in cyberspace: Combatting distributed denial of service attacks" 240; see also Argyro Karanasiou, "The changing face of protests in the digital age" 108.
201 Xiang Li, "Hacktivism and the first amendment" 321 and 322; see also Jennifer Chandler, "Security in cyberspace: Combatting distributed denial of service attacks" 240.
202 Xiang Li, "Hacktivism and the first amendment" 323; see also Argyro Karanasiou, "The changing face of protests in the digital age" 105 and 107.
203 Xiang Li, "Hacktivism and the first amendment" 313; see also Mathias Klang, "Civil disobedience online" 8.
204 Tim Jordan, *Activism!* 133–134; Xiang Li, "Hacktivism and the first amendment" 321.
205 Kirsty Best, "Visceral hacking or packet wanking? The ethics of digital code" 229.
206 Oxblood Ruffin, "Hacktivismo".
207 Argyro Karanasiou, "The changing face of protests in the digital age" 105, 106 and 109.
208 Xiang Li, "Hacktivism and the first amendment" 316 and 318; see also Joshua McLaurin, "Making cyberspace safe for democracy" 246.
209 Xiang Li, "Hacktivism and the first amendment" 321.
210 Xiang Li, "Hacktivism and the first amendment" 320 and 321; see also Tim Jordan, *Activism!* 127; see also Noah Hampson, "Hacktivism" 537; see also Argyro Karanasiou, "The changing face of protests in the digital age" 105.
211 See Joshua McLaurin, "Making cyberspace safe for democracy" 2456; see Noah Hampson, "Hacktivism: A new bread of protest in a networked world" 537; see Argyro Karanasiou, "The changing face of protests in the digital age" 107; see Kenneth Einar Himma, "Hacking as politically motivated digital civil disobedience: Is hacktivism morally justified?" 22; see Mathias Klang, "Civil disobedience online" 4 and 7; see Xiang Li, "Hacktivism and the first amendment"; see Seth Kreimer, "Technologies of protest: Insurgent social movements and the first amendment in the era of the internet" 158.
212 Xiang Li, "Hacktivism and the first amendment" 309.
213 Xiang Li, "Hacktivism and the first amendment" 309.
214 Xiang Li, "Hacktivism and the first amendment" 309; Oxblood Ruffin, "Hacktivismo".
215 Xiang Li, "Hacktivism and the first amendment" 309; see also Oxblood Ruffin, "Hacktivismo".
216 Joshua McLaurin, "Making cyberspace safe for democracy" 245; see also Oxblood Ruffin, "Hacktivismo".
217 Xiang Li, "Hacktivism and the first amendment" 309.

218 Argyro Karanasiou, "The changing face of protests in the digital age" 101; see also Noah Hampson, "Hacktivism" 541.
219 Argyro Karanasiou, "The changing face of protests in the digital age" 101 and 102.
220 Tim Jordan, *Activism!* 125.
221 Tim Jordan, *Activism!* 122–123; Paul Taylor, "Editorial: Hacktivism"; Andrew Chadwick, *Internet Politics* 131–132; E. Gabriella Coleman, "Anonymous: From the Lulz to collective action".
222 Paul Taylor, "Editorial: Hacktivism"; Andrew Chadwick, *Internet Politics* 131–132; Peter Ludlow, "WikiLeaks and hacktivist culture" 26.
223 Gabriella Coleman, "Anonymous: From the Lulz to collective action".
224 Tim Jordan, *Activism!* 128–129; Electronic Frontier Foundation, "Submission to the European Parliament on the draft directive on attacks against computer systems" 9.
225 Tim Jordan, *Activism!* 130–131.
226 See Bits of Freedom, "Internet-freedom toolbox"; see Open Technology Fund, "Projects"; see Tactical Technology Collective, "Security in-a-box"; see Riseup; see Electronic Frontier Foundation, "Surveillance self-defense".
227 Tim Jordan, *Activism!* 130; see Praetox Technologies, "LOIC".
228 See Tim Jordan, *Activism!* 123.
229 Tim Jordan, *Activism!* 123; see also Paul Taylor, "From hackers to hacktivists" 635.
230 Tim Jordan, *Activism!* 123.
231 See Tim Jordan, *Activism!* 123.
232 Tim Jordan, *Activism!* 125.
233 Xiang Li, "Hacktivism and the first amendment" 304; Argyro Karanasiou, "The changing face of protests in the digital age" 103.
234 Argyro Karanasiou, "The changing face of protests in the digital age" 103.
235 See Tim Jordan, *Activism!* 125; see also Xiang Li, "Hacktivism and the first amendment" 324–326.
236 Argyro Karanasiou, "The changing face of protests in the digital age" 101 (citing Rawls).
237 Tim Jordan, *Activism!* 125.
238 Tim Jordan, *Activism!* 125.
239 Noah Hampson, "Hacktivism" 542; see also Xiang Li, "Hacktivism and the first amendment" 304 and 329; see also Argyro Karanasiou, "The changing face of protests in the digital age" 109.
240 Noah Hampson, "Hacktivism" 531–532.
241 Xiang Li, "Hacktivism and the first amendment" 304.
242 Tim Jordan, *Activism!* 23.
243 Tim Jordan, *Activism!* 10.
244 Convention on Cybercrime, art 6 1(a)i; see also Explanatory Report to the Convention on Cybercrime, para 71; see also Bert-Jaap Koops, "Cybercrime legislation in the Netherlands" 10.
245 Convention on Cybercrime, art 6 1(a)ii and 6 1(b); see also Council Directive 2013/40/EU on attacks against information systems, art 7; see also Explanatory Report to the Convention on Cybercrime, paras 71 and 76; see also Bert-Jaap Koops, "Cybercrime legislation in the Netherlands" 10.
246 Explanatory Report to the Convention on Cybercrime, para 72.
247 Explanatory Report to the Convention on Cybercrime, para 71.
248 Explanatory Report to the Convention on Cybercrime, para 72.
249 Bert-Jaap Koops, "Cybercrime legislation in the Netherlands" 10; see also Explanatory Report to the Convention on Cybercrime, para 71.

250 Explanatory Report to the Convention on Cybercrime, para 71.
251 Explanatory Report to the Convention on Cybercrime, para 76.
252 Convention on Cybercrime, art 6 2.
253 Explanatory Report to the Convention on Cybercrime, para 77.
254 Explanatory Report to the Convention on Cybercrime, para 73; see also Electronic Frontier Foundation, "Submission to the European Parliament on the draft directive on attacks against computer systems" 10.
255 Council Directive 2013/40/EU on attacks against information systems, recital 16.
256 See Explanatory Report to the Convention on Cybercrime, para 73; but see Electronic Frontier Foundation, "Submission to the European Parliament on the draft directive on attacks against computer systems" 10;.
257 See Electronic Frontier Foundation, "Submission to the European Parliament on the draft directive on attacks against computer systems" 8.
258 Praetox Technologies, "LOIC"; see also Argyro Karanasiou, "The changing face of protests in the digital age" 102.
259 See Electronic Frontier Foundation, "Submission to the European Parliament on the draft directive on attacks against computer systems" 9.
260 See Jane Ginsburg, "Copyright and control over new technologies of dissemination" 1617, 1619 and 1620; see Michael Dizon, "Does technology trump intellectual property?" 125.
261 Jessica Litman, *Digital Copyright* 15.
262 Lawrence Lessig, *Code: version 2.0* 172; Nicola Lucchi, "The supremacy of techno-governance" 200; see also James Boyle, *The Public Domain* 8.
263 Lawrence Lessig, *Code: version 2.0* 172.
264 WIPO International Bureau, "The WIPO Copyright Treaty (WCT) and the WIPO Performances and Phonograms Treaty (WPPT)" 2; see also Michael Dizon, "Does technology trump intellectual property?" 130–131.
265 Lawrence Lessig, *Code: version 2.0* 172; see also Jessica Litman, *Digital Copyright* 18; see also Jane Ginsburg, "Copyright and control over new technologies of dissemination" 1616 and 1627.
266 See Lawrence Lessig, *Code: version 2.0* 192.
267 WIPO, *WIPO Intellectual Property Handbook* 3; see also Berne Convention for the Protection of Literary and Artistic Works, art 2(1).
268 WIPO, *WIPO Intellectual Property Handbook* 422; see Agreement on Trade-Related Aspects of Intellectual Property Rights, art 1(2) and (3).
269 Berne Convention for the Protection of Literary and Artistic Works, art 2(1); see also Agreement on Trade-Related Aspects of Intellectual Property Rights, art 9(2) and 10; see also Dutch Copyright Act, arts 1 and 10; see also Case C-406/10 *SAS Institute Inc. v World Programming Ltd* [2012], paras 32 and 46.
270 Paris Convention for the Protection of Industrial Property; Agreement on Trade-Related Aspects of Intellectual Property Rights, art 27 (1); see also WIPO Standing Committee on the Law of Patents, "Exclusions from patentable subject matter and exceptions and limitations to the rights" 2 and 19.
271 See Convention on the Grant of European Patents (European Patent Convention); see European Patent Office, "Patents for software? European law and practice" 13–14; see Andres Guadamuz, "The software patent debate"; see Robin Widdison, "Software patents pending?".
272 Agreement on Trade-Related Aspects of Intellectual Property Rights, art 15.
273 WIPO, *WIPO Intellectual Property Handbook* 112; see also Agreement on Trade-Related Aspects of Intellectual Property Rights, art 25(1).
274 Directive 96/9/EC on the legal protection of databases, recitals 7 and 13.
275 Agreement on Trade-Related Aspects of Intellectual Property Rights, art 35 and 36; see also Treaty on Intellectual Property in Respect of Integrated Circuits.

276   Hector MacQueen and others, *Contemporary Intellectual Property* 7; Michael
      Dizon, "The symbiotic relationship between global contracts and the interna-
      tional IP regime" 559.
277   WIPO, *WIPO Intellectual Property Handbook* 3.
278   See James Boyle, *The Public Domain* 11; Lawrence Lessig, *Code: version 2.0* 185.
279   Lawrence Lessig, *Code: version 2.0* 184; see also James Boyle, *The Public Domain* 4.
280   WIPO International Bureau, "The advantages of adherence to the WIPO Cop-
      yright Treaty (WCT) and the WIPO Performances and Phonograms Treaty
      (WPPT)" 7.
281   Jane Ginsburg, "Copyright and control over new technologies of dissemina-
      tion"1613; James Boyle, *The Public Domain* 1.
282   Niva Elkin-Koren, "Copyright policy and the limits of freedom of contract"
      97 and 100; Pamela Samuelson "Challenges for the world intellectual property
      organisation and the Trade-related aspects of intellectual property rights council
      in regulating intellectual property rights in the information age" 539 and 541;
      see WIPO Standing Committee on the Law of Patents, "Exclusions from patent-
      able subject matter and exceptions and limitations to the rights" 3 and 19.
283   Agreement on Trade-Related Aspects of Intellectual Property Rights, art 7.
284   Michael Dizon, "The symbiotic relationship between global contracts and the
      international IP regime" 565; see also Daniel Gervais, "A principled approach to
      copyright exceptions and limitations" 39.
285   Lawrence Lessig, *Code: version 2.0* 184; see also Directive 2001/29/EC on the
      harmonisation of certain aspects of copyright and related rights in the informa-
      tion society, recital 31.
286   Lawrence Lessig, *Code: Version 2.0* 185.
287   WIPO Standing Committee on Copyright and Related Rights, "WIPO study on
      limitations and exceptions of copyright and related rights in the digital environ-
      ment" 26.
288   Niva Elkin-Koren, "Copyright policy and the limits of freedom of contract"
      100; Jane Ginsburg, "Copyright and control over new technologies of dissemi-
      nation" 1613.
289   Niva Elkin-Koren, "Copyright policy and the limits of freedom of contract"
      100, 102 and 109; see also Michael Dizon, "The symbiotic relationship between
      global contracts and the international IP regime"; Standing Committee on Cop-
      yright and Related Rights, "WIPO Study on limitations and exceptions of copy-
      right and related rights in the digital environment" 25 and 26.
290   Lawrence Lessig, *Code: version 2.0* 185.
291   James Boyle, *The Public Domain* 46, 49 and 50; see also Peter Drahos and John
      Braithwaite, *Information Feudalism* 4–5;
292   WIPO International Bureau, "The WIPO Copyright Treaty (WCT) and the
      WIPO Performances and Phonograms Treaty (WPPT)" 2; see also Michael
      Dizon, "Does technology trump intellectual property?" 129–130.
293   See Pamela Samuelson, "Freedom to tinker" 10; see also Agreement on Trade-
      Related Aspects of Intellectual Property Rights, art 10(1).
294   *Diamond v. Diehr* 450 US 175 (1981); WIPO Copyright Treaty, art 4; Directive
      2009/24/EC on the legal protection of computer programs, art 1; European
      Patent Office, "Patents for software? European law and practice"; see also Robin
      Widdison, "Software patents pending?".
295   See Agreement on Trade-Related Aspects of Intellectual Property Rights; see
      WIPO Copyright Treaty and the WIPO Performances and Phonograms Treaty
      (known as the WIPO Internet Treaties); Directive 2001/29/EC on the har-
      monisation of certain aspects of copyright and related rights in the information

society; see Standing Committee on Copyright and Related Rights, "WIPO study on limitations and exceptions of copyright and related rights in the digital environment" 2; see WIPO International Bureau, "The WIPO Copyright Treaty (WCT) and the WIPO Performances and Phonograms Treaty (WPPT)" 3; see WIPO International Bureau, "The advantages of adherence to the WIPO Copyright Treaty (WCT) and the WIPO Performances and Phonograms Treaty (WPPT)" 5; see WIPO Standing Committee on Copyright and Related Rights, "Updated report on the questionnaire on limitation and exceptions" SCCR/21/7 51.

296 WIPO Copyright Treaty WCT, art 1(4); Directive 2001/29/EC on the harmonisation of certain aspects of copyright and related rights in the information society; WIPO, Agreed Statements concerning the WIPO Copyright Treaty; see also WIPO Standing Committee on Copyright and Related Rights, "WIPO study on limitations and exceptions of copyright and related rights in the digital environment" 56, 78 and 79; see also WIPO International Bureau, "The WIPO Copyright Treaty (WCT) and the WIPO Performances and Phonograms Treaty (WPPT)" 5; see also WIPO International Bureau, "The advantages of adherence to the WIPO Copyright Treaty (WCT) and the WIPO Performances and Phonograms Treaty (WPPT)" 3.

297 See James Boyle, *The Public Domain*; see Peter Drahos and John Braithwaite, *Information Feudalism*; Lawrence Lessig, *Free Culture*; see Lawrence Lessig, *The Future of Ideas*; see Jessica Litman, *Digital Copyright*; see Hal Abelson, Ken Ledeen and Harry Lewis, *Blown to Bits*; see Keith Aoki, James Boyle and Jennifer Jenkins, *Bound by Law*; see Kathy Bowrey, *Law and Internet Cultures*; see James Boyle, *Shamans, Software, and Spleens*.

298 Jane Ginsburg, "Copyright and control over new technologies of dissemination" 1614; see also James Boyle, "A manifesto on WIPO and the future of intellectual property" 2; Peter Drahos, "Bilateralism in intellectual property" 9; see also Declan McCullagh and Milana Homsi, "Leave DRM alone: A survey of legislative proposals relating to digital rights management technology and their problems" 328.

299 Jessica Litman, *Digital Copyright* 18, 54 and 78; see also Daniel Gervais, "A principled approach to copyright exceptions and limitations" 29 and 31; see also Bernt Hugenholtz and Ruth Okediji, "Conceiving an international instrument on limitations and exceptions to copyright" 22, 23, 28; see also Standing Committee on Copyright and Related Rights, "WIPO study on limitations and exceptions of copyright and related rights in the digital environment" 4.

300 Berne Convention for the Protection of Literary and Artistic Works, arts 8, 9, 11, 11*bis*, 11*ter*, 12 and 14; Agreement on Trade-Related Aspects of Intellectual Property Rights, art 11; Directive 2001/29/EC on the harmonisation of certain aspects of copyright and related rights in the information society, arts 2, 3 and 4; see Dutch Copyright Act, arts 12 and 13.

301 Agreement on Trade-Related Aspects of Intellectual Property Rights, art 28(1) (a) and art 28(2); see also WIPO Standing Committee on the Law of Patents, "Exclusions from patentable subject matter and exceptions and limitations to the rights" 18.

302 Agreement on Trade-Related Aspects of Intellectual Property Rights, art 28(1)(b).

303 See Lawrence Lessig, *Code: version 2.0* 192–193; Urs Gasser and Silke Ernst, "A quick look at copyright and user creativity in the digital age" 3, 11 and 13.

304 See Lawrence Lessig, *Code: version 2.0* 192–193.

305 Lawrence Lessig, *Code: version 2.0* 193.

306 See Llewellyn Joseph Gibbons, "Social enforcement or social contracting for governance in cyberspace" 485; see Michael Dizon, "Participatory democracy and information and communications technology" 1.
307 Lawrence Lessig, *Free Culture* 184, 185, 188, 192; see also Keith Aoki, James Boyle and Jennifer Jenkins, *Bound by Law*.
308 Lawrence Lessig, *Code: version 2.0* 196.
309 Daniel Gervais, "A principled approach to copyright exceptions and limitations" 5–6.
310 Standing Committee on Copyright and Related Rights, "WIPO study on limitations and exceptions of copyright and related rights in the digital environment" 3 and 75.
311 Standing Committee on Copyright and Related Rights, "WIPO study on limitations and exceptions of copyright and related rights in the digital environment" 42, 43 and 75; see also Daniel Gervais, "A principled approach to copyright exceptions and limitations" 8–9.
312 Standing Committee on Copyright and Related Rights, "WIPO study on limitations and exceptions of copyright and related rights in the digital environment" 25.
313 Standing Committee on Copyright and Related Rights, "WIPO study on limitations and exceptions of copyright and related rights in the digital environment" 25; see also Daniel Gervais, "A principled approach to copyright exceptions and limitations" 20.
314 See Standing Committee on Copyright and Related Rights, "WIPO study on limitations and exceptions of copyright and related rights in the digital environment" 3, 4, 10, 42 and 43.
315 See Pamela Samuelson, "Freedom to tinker" 3.
316 Directive 2009/24/EC on the legal protection of computer programs, arts 1(1), 5 and 6 and recital (6); see also Council Directive of 1 May 1991 on the legal protection of computer programs (which Directive 2009/24/EC amended and codified); see also Michael Dizon, "Decompiling the Software Directive, the Microsoft CFI case and the I2010 strategy" 213.
317 Michael Dizon, "Decompiling the software directive, the Microsoft CFI case and the I2010 strategy" 214; see also Thomas Vinje, "Compliance with Article 85 in software licensing" 171; see also Erik Kroker, "The computer directive and the balance of rights" 248; see also Case C-406/10 *SAS Institute Inc. v World Programming Ltd* [2012], paras 32, 40 and 46.
318 John Soma, Gus Winfield and Letty Friesen, "Software interoperability and reverse engineering" 195; Michael Dizon, "Decompiling the software directive, the microsoft CFI case and the I2010 strategy" 214.
319 Directive 2009/24/EC on the legal protection of computer programs, art 5(3); see also Dutch Copyright Act, art 45*l*; see also Case C-406/10 *SAS Institute Inc. v World Programming Ltd* [2012], para 62; see also WIPO Standing Committee on Copyright and Related Rights, "Updated report on the questionnaire on limitation and exceptions" SCCR/21/7 48.
320 Directive 2009/24/EC on the legal protection of computer programs, art 5(3); see also *Krause v Titleserv, Inc.*, 402 F.3d 119 (2005) (for US perspective); see also Daniel Gervais, "A principled approach to copyright exceptions and limitations" 23.
321 Michael Dizon, "Decompiling the software directive, the microsoft CFI case and the I2010 strategy" 214; see Erik Kroker, "The computer directive and the balance of rights" 248.
322 Michael Dizon, "Decompiling the software directive, the Microsoft CFI case and the I2010 strategy" 214; see also Thomas Vinje, "Compliance with Article 85 in software licensing" 172.

323 Directive 2009/24/EC on the legal protection of computer programs, art 6(1); see also Dutch Copyright Act, art 45 *m*(1).

324 Directive 2009/24/EC on the legal protection of computer programs, art 6(1) (a), (b) and (c); see also Dutch Copyright Act, art 45 *m*(1)(a-c); Michael Dizon, "Decompiling the Software Directive, the Microsoft CFI case and the I2010 strategy" 214.

325 Directive 2009/24/EC on the legal protection of computer programs, art 6(2) (a), (b) and (c); see also Dutch Copyright Act, art 45 *m*(2)(a-c).

326 Directive 2009/24/EC on the legal protection of computer programs, art 6(3); see also Michael Dizon, "Decompiling the software directive, the microsoft CFI case and the I2010 strategy" 214.

327 Directive 2009/24/EC on the legal protection of computer programs, art 8 and recital (16); Michael Dizon, "Decompiling the software directive, the microsoft CFI case and the I2010 strategy" 218.

328 Case C-406/10 *SAS Institute Inc. v World Programming Ltd* [2012], paras 51, 53 and 59.

329 See Pamela Samuelson, "Freedom to tinker" 14.

330 Directive 2009/24/EC on the legal protection of computer programs, art 5(1) and recital (14); see also Dutch Copyright Act, art 45*j*; see also Case C-406/10 *SAS Institute Inc. v World Programming Ltd* [2012], paras 56 and 58.

331 *Chamberlain Group v Skylink Technologies* 381 F. 3d 1178 (2004), 1202.

332 Directive 2009/24/EC on the legal protection of computer programs, art 5(1) and (2) and recitals 13 and 16; see also Dutch Copyright Act, arts 45*j* and 45*k*.

333 See Michael Dizon, "Decompiling the software directive, the microsoft CFI case and the I2010 strategy" 214; see Robert Hart, "Interoperability information and the microsoft decision" 116.

334 See Robert Hart, "Interfaces, interoperability and maintenance" 111; see Thomas Vinje, "Compliance with Article 85 in software licensing" 165; see Michael Dizon, "Decompiling the software directive, the Microsoft CFI case and the I2010 strategy" 214.

335 Directive 2009/24/EC on the legal protection of computer programs, recital 10.

336 See Michael Dizon, "Decompiling the software directive, the microsoft CFI case and the I2010 strategy" 215–216 (for more on interoperability).

337 See Michael Dizon, "Decompiling the software directive, the microsoft CFI case and the I2010 strategy" 214.

338 See Report on application of Directive 2001/29/EC SEC(2007) 1554, 4; see WIPO Standing Committee on Copyright and Related Rights, "Updated report on the questionnaire on limitation and exceptions" SCCR/21/7 14.

339 Directive 2001/29/EC on the harmonisation of certain aspects of copyright and related rights in the information society, art 5(1); Dutch Copyright Act, art 13a.

340 Directive 2001/29/EC on the harmonisation of certain aspects of copyright and related rights in the information society, art 5(1)(a-b).

341 Directive 2001/29/EC on the harmonisation of certain aspects of copyright and related rights in the information society, art 5(1); Dutch Copyright Act, art 13a.

342 Directive 2001/29/EC on the harmonisation of certain aspects of copyright and related rights in the information society, recital 33.

343 WIPO Standing Committee on Copyright and Related Rights, "WIPO study on limitations and exceptions of copyright and related rights in the digital environment" 79–80.

344 European Commission, "Report on the application of the Directive 2001/29/EC" SEC(2007) 1556, 3; see also Directive 2001/29/EC on the harmonisation of certain aspects of copyright and related rights in the information society, recital 33; see also Bradley J. Nicholson, "The ghost in the machine: *MAI Systems Corp. v. Peak Computer, Inc.*, and the Problem of Copying in RAM".

345 Directive 2001/29/EC on the harmonisation of certain aspects of copyright and related rights in the information society, recital 33; WIPO "Exception and Limits to Copyright and Neighboring Rights" 32 ("logic of a 'necessary act'"); see Bradley J. Nicholson, "The ghost in the machine: *MAI Systems Corp. v. Peak Computer, Inc.*, and the Problem of Copying in RAM"; see Pamela Samuelson, "Hacking intellectual property law" 66 and 67; see WIPO Standing Committee on Copyright and Related Rights, "WIPO study on limitations and exceptions of copyright and related rights in the digital environment" 80.

346 European Commission, "Report on the application of the Directive 2001/29/EC" SEC(2007) 1556, 4; see also WIPO Standing Committee on Copyright and Related Rights, "WIPO study on limitations and exceptions of copyright and related rights in the digital environment" 42–43.

347 WIPO "Exception and limits to copyright and neighboring rights" 12; see also WIPO Standing Committee on Copyright and Related Rights, "Updated report on the questionnaire on limitation and exceptions" SCCR/21/7 10.

348 Directive 2001/29/EC on the harmonisation of certain aspects of copyright and related rights in the information society, art 5(2)(b); see also WIPO Standing Committee on Copyright and Related Rights, "WIPO study on limitations and exceptions of copyright and related rights in the digital environment" 74.

349 Dutch Copyright Act, art 16c(1); see also Dutch Copyright Act, art 16b(1); see also Martin Senftleben, "The wmerging EC fair use doctrine" 531.

350 WIPO Standing Committee on Copyright and Related Rights, "WIPO study on limitations and wxceptions of copyright and related rights in the digital environment" 44.

351 WIPO Standing Committee on Copyright and Related Rights, "WIPO study on limitations and exceptions of copyright and related eights in the digital environment" 75.

352 Directive 2001/29/EC on the harmonisation of certain aspects of copyright and related rights in the information society, art 5(2)(b); see also WIPO Standing Committee on Copyright and Related Rights, "WIPO study on limitations and exceptions of copyright and related rights in the digital environment" 74.

353 Dutch Copyright Act, art 45*n*; Directive 2009/24/EC on the legal protection of computer programs, arts 4–6; see also Directive 2001/29/EC on the harmonisation of certain aspects of copyright and related rights in the information society, recital 50.

354 WIPO Standing Committee on the Law of Patents, "Exclusions from patentable subject matter and exceptions and limitations to the rights" 26.

355 WIPO Standing Committee on the Law of Patents, "Exclusions from patentable subject matter and exceptions and limitations to the rights" 26.

356 WIPO Standing Committee on the Law of Patents, "Exclusions from patentable subject matter and exceptions and limitations to the rights" 26.

357 Dutch Patent Act, art 53(1)(a) and (b); see also WIPO Standing Committee on the Law of Patents, "Report on the international patent system" SCP/12/3 Rev.2, Revised Annex II.

358 Directive 2001/29/EC on the harmonisation of certain aspects of copyright and related rights in the information society, art 5(3)(a); Dutch Copyright Act, art 16.

359 Daniel Gervais, "A principled approach to copyright exceptions and limitations" 32.

360 Directive 2001/29/EC on the harmonisation of certain aspects of copyright and related rights in the information society, recital 42.

361 But see Daniel Gervais, "A principled approach to copyright exceptions and 'limitations" 32.

362 WIPO Standing Committee on Copyright and Related Rights, "WIPO study on limitations and exceptions of copyright and related rights in the digital environment" 15 and 45; Directive 2001/29/EC on the harmonisation of certain aspects of copyright and related rights in the information society, recital 42; Hector MacQueen and others, *Contemporary Intellectual Property: Law and Policy* 181.

363 See WIPO Standing Committee on the Law of Patents, "Exclusions from patentable subject matter and exceptions and limitations to the rights" 27; WIPO Standing Committee on the Law of Patents, "Report on the international patent system" SCP/12/3 Rev.2, Revised Annex II; see also Derek Bambauer and Oliver Day, "The hacker's aegis" 19.

364 Dutch Patent Act, art 53(3).

365 WIPO Standing Committee on the Law of Patents, "Exclusions from patentable subject matter and exceptions and limitations to the rights" 27.

366 WIPO Standing Committee on the Law of Patents, "Exclusions from patentable subject matter and exceptions and limitations to the rights" 27.

367 *Canada – Patent Protection of Pharmaceutical Products*, WT/DS114/R (17March 2000) para 7.69; see also WIPO Standing Committee on the Law of Patents, "Exclusions from patentable subject matter and exceptions and limitations to the rights" 27.

368 WIPO Standing Committee on the Law of Patents, "Exclusions from patentable subject matter and exceptions and limitations to the rights" 29.

369 But see Derek Bambauer and Oliver Day, "The hacker's aegis" 19 and 21 (on limitations on sharing such as commercial use).

370 Directive 2001/29/EC on the harmonisation of certain aspects of copyright and related rights in the information society, art 5(3)(l).

371 See Pamela Samuelson, "Freedom to tinker" 22 (citing *Wilson v Simpson*, 50 US (9 How.) 109 and *Bureau of Nat'l Literature v Sells*, 211 F. 379 (W.D. Wash. 1914).

372 Pamela Samuelson, "Freedom to tinker" 22.

373 See Platform21, "Repair manifesto"; see iFixit, "Self-repair manifesto".

374 See Daniel Gervais, "A principled approach to copyright exceptions and limitations" 38.

375 See Jonathan Band and Jonathan Gerafi, "The fair use/fair dealing handbook" 1; see also Christophe Geiger, Daniel Gervais and Martin Senftleben, "The three-step test revisited" 623–624.

376 WIPO Standing Committee on Copyright and Related Rights, "WIPO study on limitations and exceptions of copyright and related rights in the digital environment" 67; Martin Senftleben, "Bridging the differences between copyright legal traditions – the emerging EC fair use doctrine"; Jonathan Band and Jonathan Gerafi, "The fair use/fair dealing handbook" 1; Martin Senftleben, "Fair use in The Netherlands – a renaissance?" 1.

377 Hector MacQueen and others, *Contemporary Intellectual Property* 179; Berne Convention, arts 10(1) and 10(2); Jonathan Band and Jonathan Gerafi, "The fair use/fair dealing handbook" 1.

378 UK Intellectual Property Office, "Exceptions to copyright: An overview"; *British Academy of Songwriters, Composers and Authors Musicians' Union v Secretary of State for Business, Innovation and Skills* [2015] EWHC 2041 (Admin) (17 July 2015) (in the case of the United Kingdom, while an amendment to the law was passed, it was subsequently struck down by the courts).

379 WIPO Standing Committee on Copyright and Related Rights, "WIPO study on limitations and exceptions of copyright and related rights in the digital

environment" 67; see also Martin Senftleben, "The emerging EC fair use doctrine" 548.

380 US Copyright Act 1976, section 107; see also *Folsom v Marsh* (1841); see also Daniel Gervais, "A principled approach to copyright exceptions and limitations" 38.

381 Martin Senftleben, "The emerging EC fair use doctrine" 527 and 529; Daniel Gervais, "A principled approach to copyright exceptions and limitations" 36.

382 WIPO Standing Committee on Copyright and Related Rights, "WIPO study on limitations and exceptions of copyright and related rights in the digital environment" 68; see also Martin Senftleben, "The emerging EC fair use doctrine" 527.

383 Martin Senftleben, "The emerging EC fair use doctrine" 527.

384 Jane Ginsburg, "Copyright and control over new technologies of dissemination" 1616.

385 *Sony v. Universal* 464 US 417 (1984); *Recording Industry Association of America v. Diamond Multimedia Systems* 180 F.3d 1072 (1999); *Field v. Google* 412 F.Supp.2d 1106 (2006); *Authors Guild v. Hathitrust* 755 F.3d 87 (2014); see also Lawrence Lessig, *Code: version 2.0* 184 and 187; see also Pamela Samuelson, "Hacking intellectual property law" 67.

386 See Martin Senftleben, "The emerging EC fair use doctrine" 522 and 528.

387 Directive 2001/29/EC on the harmonisation of certain aspects of copyright and related rights in the information society, art 5 and recital 32.

388 WIPO Standing Committee on Copyright and Related Rights, "WIPO study on limitations and exceptions of copyright and related rights in the digital environment" 72–73.

389 Directive 2001/29/EC on the harmonisation of certain aspects of copyright and related rights in the information society, art 5(5); Berne Convention, art 9(2); see also Daniel Gervais, "A principled approach to copyright exceptions and limitations" 34–35.

390 Berne Convention, art 9(2); see also Standing Committee on Copyright and Related Rights, "WIPO study on limitations and exceptions of copyright and related rights in the digital environment" 21; WIPO Standing Committee on Copyright and Related Rights, "Updated report on the questionnaire on limitation and exceptions" SCCR/21/7 8.

391 Berne Convention, art 9(2).

392 Berne Convention, art 9(2); see also Standing Committee on Copyright and Related Rights, "WIPO study on limitations and exceptions of copyright and related rights in the digital environment" 21; see also Daniel Gervais, "A principled approach to copyright exceptions and limitations" 4.

393 Standing Committee on Copyright and Related Rights, "WIPO study on limitations and exceptions of copyright and related rights in the digital environment" 72; see also Daniel Gervais, "A principled approach to copyright exceptions and limitations" 23 and 34.

394 Daniel Gervais, "A principled approach to copyright exceptions and limitations" 31.

395 Christophe Geiger, Daniel Gervais and Martin Senftleben, "The three-step test revisited" 582.

396 Standing Committee on Copyright and Related Rights, "WIPO study on limitations and exceptions of copyright and related rights in the digital environment" 3, 20, 22 and 65.

397 Berne Convention, art 9(2); see Martin Senftleben, "The international three-step test: A model provision for EC fair use legislation"; see Daniel Gervais, "A principled approach to copyright exceptions and limitations" 35 and 39; see Christophe Geiger, Daniel Gervais and Martin Senftleben, "The three-step

test revisited" 582; see Standing Committee on Copyright and Related Rights, "WIPO study on limitations and exceptions of copyright and related rights in the digital environment" 23.

398 Agreement on Trade-Related Aspects of Intellectual Property Rights, arts 26 (industrial designs) and 30 (patents); Directive 2009/24/EC on the legal protection of computer programs, recital 15 and art 6(3) (computer programs); Directive 96/9/EC on the legal protection of databases, arts 6(3) and art 7(5) (databases); see also Daniel Gervais, "A principled approach to copyright exceptions and limitations" 35 and 38.

399 Standing Committee on Copyright and Related Rights, "WIPO study on limitations and exceptions of copyright and related rights in the digital environment" 65; Agreement on Trade-Related Aspects of Intellectual Property Rights, arts 13 and 30; WIPO Copyright Treaty, art 10; WIPO Performances and Phonograms Treaty, art 16; see also Martin Senftleben, "The emerging EC fair use doctrine" 544.

400 Daniel Gervais, "A principled approach to copyright exceptions and limitations" 38.

401 Standing Committee on Copyright and Related Rights, "WIPO study on limitations and exceptions of copyright and related rights in the digital environment" 20 (the three-step test "has now come to enjoy something of the status of holy writ"); see also Christophe Geiger, Daniel Gervais and Martin Senftleben, "The three-step test revisited" 586 and 625.

402 See Daniel Gervais, "A principled approach to copyright exceptions and limitations" 38.

403 Niva Elkin-Koren, "Copyright policy and the limits of freedom of contract" 107–108.

404 Raymond Nimmer, "Breaking barriers: The relations between contract and intellectual property law" 878; see Kurt Opsahl and Pamela Samuelson, "Licensing information in the global information market: Freedom of contract meets public policy"; see Jacques De Werra, "Moving beyond the conflict between freedom of contract and copyright policies".

405 Lawrence Lessig, *Code: Version 2.0* 187.

406 Michael Dizon, "The symbiotic relationship between global contracts and the international IP regime" 560; Jacques De Werra, "Moving beyond the conflict between freedom of contract and copyright policies"; Lawrence Lessig, *Code: Version 2.0* 187.

407 Raymond Nimmer, "Breaking barriers: The relations between contract and intellectual property law" 832; Michael Dizon, "The symbiotic relationship between global contracts and the international IP regime" 561.

408 Jacques De Werra, "Moving beyond the conflict between freedom of contract and copyright policies" 246–247; see also Daniel Gervais, "A principled approach to copyright exceptions and limitations" 16.

409 Michael Dizon, "The symbiotic relationship between global contracts and the international IP regime" 559 and 560; see also Michael Madison, "Legal-ware: Contract and copyright in the digital age" 1032.

410 Nicola Lucchi, "The supremacy of techno-governance" 214.

411 Niva Elkin-Koren, "Copyright policy and the limits of freedom of contract" 108–109.

412 Llewellyn Joseph Gibbons, "Social enforcement or social contracting for governance of cyberspace" 531; see Jerome H. Reichman and Jonathan Franklin, "Privately legislated intellectual property rights".

413 See Ronald Leenes, "Framing techno-regulation: An exploration of state and non-state regulation by technology" 165.

414 Lawrence Lessig, *Code: Version 2.0* 187.
415 See WIPO Standing Committee on Copyright and Related Rights, "Updated report on the questionnaire on limitation and exceptions" SCCR/21/7 11.
416 Michael Dizon, "The symbiotic relationship between global contracts and the international IP regime" 560; see also Niva Elkin-Koren, "Copyright policy and the limits of freedom of contract" 105.
417 Michael Dizon, "The symbiotic relationship between global contracts and the international IP regime" 560; Jacques De Werra, "Moving beyond the conflict between freedom of contract and copyright policies" 322; James Maxeiner, "Standard-terms contracting in the global electronic age" 134–141.
418 Lawrence Lessig, *Code: Version 2.0* 187.
419 Pamela Samuelson, "Freedom to tinker" 10.
420 Michael Dizon, "The symbiotic relationship between global contracts and the international IP regime" 562; see also Derek Bambauer and Oliver Day, "The hacker's aegis" 25.
421 Michael Dizon, "The symbiotic relationship between global contracts and the international IP regime" 560; see also J.H. Reichman and Jonathan Franklin, "Privately legislated intellectual property rights" 878; see also Kurt Opsahl and Pamela Samuelson, "Licensing information in the global information market: freedom of contract meets public policy" 390; see also Lawrence Lessig, *Code: Version 2.0* (on the "race to privatize copyright law through contract").
422 See Michael Dizon, "The symbiotic relationship between global contracts and the international IP regime" 561–563; see Beth Noveck, " 'Peer to patent': Collective intelligence, open review, and patent reform"; see Jason Schultz and Jennifer Urban, "The defensive patent license as new approach to patent threats"; see Open Invention Network, "Defensive publications"; see Andrew Katz, "Towards a functional licence for open hardware"; see Open Source Hardware Association, "Open Source Hardware (OSHW) statement of principles 1.0".
423 Electronic Frontier Foundation, "Submission to the European Parliament on the draft directive on attacks against computer systems" 3; see also Christine Galbraith, "Access denied" 338 and 365; see also Cassandra Kirsch, "The grey hat hacker" 399.
424 Marcia Hofman and Rainey Reitman, "Rebooting computer crime law Part 1"; see also Christine Galbraith, "Access denied" 323.
425 Christine Galbraith, "Access denied" 338.
426 Parker Higgins, "Critical fixes for the computer fraud and abuse act"; Orin Kerr, "Interpreting 'access' and 'authorization' in Computer Misuse Statutes" 1598; Electronic Frontier Foundation, "Submission to the European Parliament on the draft directive on attacks against computer systems" 3–4.
427 Electronic Frontier Foundation, "Submission to the European Parliament on the draft directive on attacks against computer systems" 3.
428 Electronic Frontier Foundation, "Submission to the European Parliament on the draft directive on attacks against computer systems" 3–4.
429 Orin Kerr, "Interpreting 'access' and 'authorization' in computer misuse statutes" 1601.
430 Parker Higgins, "Critical fixes for the computer fraud and abuse act"; Electronic Frontier Foundation, "Submission to the European Parliament on the draft directive on attacks against computer systems" 3.
431 Electronic Frontier Foundation, "Submission to the European Parliament on the draft directive on attacks against computer systems" 3–4; see Orin Kerr, "Interpreting 'access' and 'authorization' in computer misuse statutes".

432 See Bert-Jaap Koops, "Cybercrime legislation in The Netherlands" 3 (on the Dutch public prosecutor's "prosecutorial discretion" to decide what acts are "worthy of criminal prosecution").
433 See Orin Kerr, "Vagueness challenges to the computer fraud and abuse act" 1562, 1578, 1579; see Cyrus Chung, "The computer fraud and abuse act" 233–234; see Cindy Cohn, Hanni Fakhoury and Marcia Hofman, "Rebooting computer crime law Part 3".
434 Joseph Olivenbaum, "Rethinking federal computer crime legislation" 605.
435 *United States v Gilberto Valle*, No. 14-2710-cr and No. 14-4396-cr (3 December 2015).
436 Marcia Hofman and Rainey Reitman, "Rebooting computer crime law Part 1"; Electronic Frontier Foundation, "Submission to the European Parliament on the draft directive on attacks against computer systems" 2, 3 and 5; Orin Kerr, "Interpreting 'access' and 'authorization' in computer misuse statutes" 1640.
437 Electronic Frontier Foundation, "Submission to the European Parliament on the draft directive on attacks against computer systems" 3; see also Orin Kerr, "Interpreting 'access' and 'authorization' in computer misuse statutes" 1650 and 1651.
438 Allan Farnsworth, "Legal remedies for breach of contract" 1145–1146; William McBryde, "Remedies for breach of contract" 75; Avery Katz, "Remedies for breach of contract under the CISG" 378–379; see also William Bishop, "The choice of remedy for breach of contract".
439 Marcia Hofman and Rainey Reitman, "Rebooting computer crime law Part 1"; see also Electronic Frontier Foundation, "Submission to the European Parliament on the draft directive on attacks against computer systems" 3; see also Parker Higgins, "Critical fixes for the computer fraud and abuse act".
440 Marcia Hofman and Rainey Reitman, "Rebooting computer crime law Part 1"; Orin Kerr, "Interpreting 'access' and 'authorization' in computer misuse statutes" 1599.
441 Council Directive 2013/40/EU on attacks against information systems, recital 17.
442 See Daniel Gervais, "A principled approach to copyright exceptions and limitations" 34.
443 Declan McCullagh and Milana Homsi, "Leave DRM alone: A survey of legislative proposals relating to digital rights management technology and their problems" 318; see also Michael Dizon, "Participatory democracy and information and communications technology" 14.
444 WIPO International Bureau, "The advantages of adherence to the WIPO Copyright Treaty (WCT) and the WIPO Performances and Phonograms Treaty (WPPT)" 2.
445 WIPO Copyright Treaty, art 11; WIPO Performances and Phonograms Treaty, art 18.
446 WIPO Standing Committee on Copyright and Related Rights, "WIPO study on limitations and exceptions of copyright and related rights in the digital environment" 81.
447 WIPO Copyright Treaty, art 12(1); WIPO Performances and Phonograms Treaty, art 19(1).
448 WIPO Copyright Treaty, art 12(1)(i) and (ii); WIPO Performances and Phonograms Treaty, art 19(1)(i) and (ii).
449 WIPO Copyright Treaty, art 12(2); WIPO Performances and Phonograms Treaty, art 19(2); see also Directive 2001/29/EC on the harmonisation of certain aspects of copyright and related rights in the information society, art 7(2).

450   Directive 2001/29/EC on the harmonisation of certain aspects of copyright
and related rights in the information society, arts 6(1) and 7(1); see also Dutch
Copyright Act, art 29a(2); see also WIPO International Bureau, "The advantages of adherence to the WIPO Copyright Treaty (WCT) and the WIPO Performances and Phonograms Treaty (WPPT)" 9.

451   Directive 2001/29/EC on the harmonisation of certain aspects of copyright
and related rights in the information society, art 6(2).

452   Directive 2001/29/EC on the harmonisation of certain aspects of copyright
and related rights in the information society, art 6(2)(a), (b) and (c).

453   Directive 2001/29/EC on the harmonisation of certain aspects of copyright
and related rights in the information society, art 6(3); see also Dutch Copyright
Act, art 29a(1); see also European Commission, "Report on the application of
the Directive 2001/29/EC" SEC(2007) 1556, 8 (on a Finish court's interpretation of effective); see also Michael Dizon, "Participatory democracy and
information and communications technology" 14; see also Declan McCullagh
and Milana Homsi, "Leave DRM Alone: A survey of legislative proposals relating to digital rights management technology and their problems" 318.

454   Directive 2001/29/EC on the harmonisation of certain aspects of copyright
and related rights in the information society, art 7(1).

455   Directive 2001/29/EC on the harmonisation of certain aspects of copyright
and related rights in the information society, art 7(1).

456   Dutch Copyright Act, art 29a.

457   Directive 2001/29/EC on the harmonisation of certain aspects of copyright
and related rights in the information society, arts 6(1)-(2) and 7(1); see also
Michael Dizon, "Participatory democracy and information and communications
technology" 15; see also WIPO Standing Committee on Copyright and Related
Rights, "WIPO Study on Limitations and Exceptions of Copyright and Related
Rights in the Digital Environment" 82; see also WIPO International Bureau,
"The Advantages of Adherence to the WIPO Copyright Treaty (WCT) and
the WIPO Performances and Phonograms Treaty (WPPT)" 3; see also Michael
Dizon, "Does technology trump intellectual property?" 131.

458   Directive 2001/29/EC on the harmonisation of certain aspects of copyright
and related rights in the information society, recital 50; see also Dutch Copyright Act, art 32a; see also Pamela Samuelson, "Anticircumvention rules: Threat
to science" 2028.

459   Directive 2001/29/EC on the harmonisation of certain aspects of copyright
and related rights in the information society, recital 50.

460   Directive 2001/29/EC on the harmonisation of certain aspects of copyright
and related rights in the information society, recital 50; Directive 2009/24/EC
on the legal protection of computer programs, arts 5(3), 6 and 8.

461   See Phillip Torrone, "Sony's War on makers, hackers, and innovators" (the case
of George Hotz breaking the security of the Playstation 3 to run his own games
and software on the device); see Kristin Eschenfelder, Robert Howard and Anuj
Desai, "A content analysis of web sites posting DVD circumvention software"
1408 (Jon Johansen defeating the copy-protection on DVDs so he could watch
movies on his Linux computer); see also Electronic Frontier Foundation, "Unintended consequences: Fifteen years under the DMCA".

462   Pamela Samuelson, "Freedom to tinker" 3.

463   WIPO International Bureau, "The advantages of adherence to the WIPO Copyright Treaty (WCT) and the WIPO Performances and Phonograms Treaty
(WPPT)" 2 and 3; see also Directive 2001/29/EC on the harmonisation of certain aspects of copyright and related rights in the information society, recital 4;

see also WIPO International Bureau, "The WIPO Copyright Treaty (WCT) and the WIPO Performances and Phonograms Treaty (WPPT)" 4; see also Jane Ginsburg, "Copyright and control over new technologies of dissemination" 1618; see WIPO Standing Committee on Copyright and Related Rights, "Updated report on the questionnaire on limitation and exceptions" SCCR/21/7 11–12.
464 WIPO International Bureau, "The advantages of adherence to the WIPO Copyright Treaty (WCT) and the WIPO Performances and Phonograms Treaty (WPPT)" 2.
465 WIPO International Bureau, "The advantages of adherence to the WIPO Copyright Treaty (WCT) and the WIPO Performances and Phonograms Treaty (WPPT)" 5; see also Directive 2001/29/EC on the harmonisation of certain aspects of copyright and related rights in the information society, recital 9 and 10.
466 WIPO International Bureau, "The WIPO Copyright Treaty (WCT) and the WIPO Performances and Phonograms Treaty (WPPT)" 7.
467 WIPO International Bureau, "The WIPO Copyright Treaty (WCT) and the WIPO Performances and Phonograms Treaty (WPPT)" 7; see also WIPO International Bureau, "The Advantages of Adherence to the WIPO Copyright Treaty (WCT) and the WIPO Performances and Phonograms Treaty (WPPT)" 3.
468 Standing Committee on Copyright and Related Rights, "WIPO Study on Limitations and Exceptions of Copyright and Related Rights in the Digital Environment" 78; Jane Ginsburg, "Copyright and Control Over New Technologies of Dissemination" 1618.
469 Standing Committee on Copyright and Related Rights, "WIPO study on limitations and exceptions of copyright and related rights in the digital environment" 78.
470 WIPO International Bureau, "The advantages of adherence to the WIPO Copyright Treaty (WCT) and the WIPO Performances and Phonograms Treaty (WPPT)" 4; see also Directive 2001/29/EC on the harmonisation of certain aspects of copyright and related rights in the information society, recital 2.
471 Standing Committee on Copyright and Related Rights, "WIPO study on limitations and exceptions of copyright and related rights in the digital environment" 78; see also Directive 2001/29/EC on the harmonisation of certain aspects of copyright and related rights in the information society, recitals 3 and 31.
472 See WIPO International Bureau, "The advantages of adherence to the WIPO Copyright Treaty (WCT) and the WIPO Performances and Phonograms Treaty (WPPT)" 8.
473 Pamela Samuelson, "Freedom to tinker" 16.
474 WIPO International Bureau, "The advantages of adherence to the WIPO Copyright Treaty (WCT) and the WIPO Performances and Phonograms Treaty (WPPT)" 2 and 6; Michael Dizon, "Does technology trump intellectual property?" 131.
475 Michael Dizon, "Participatory democracy and information and communications technology" 16; see also Ian Brown, "The evolution of anti-circumvention law" 240–242.
476 Ian Brown, "The evolution of anti-circumvention law" 255; Declan McCullagh and Milana Homsi, "Leave DRM alone: A survey of legislative proposals relating to digital rights management technology and their problems" 326.
477 WIPO International Bureau, "The advantages of adherence to the WIPO Copyright Treaty (WCT) and the WIPO Performances and Phonograms Treaty (WPPT)" 10.
478 Michael Dizon, "Participatory democracy and information and communications technology" 15; Declan McCullagh and Milana Homsi, "Leave DRM alone: A survey of legislative proposals relating to digital rights management

technology and their problems" 319; Jessica Litman, *Digital Copyright* 27; Jane Ginsburg, "Copyright and control over new technologies of dissemination" 1619; Lawrence Lessig, *Code: Version 2.0* 186.

479 Lawrence Lessig, *Code: version 2.0* 179; see also Jane Ginsburg, "Copyright and control over new technologies of dissemination" 1631–1632.

480 WIPO, Agreed Statements concerning the WIPO Copyright Treaty 1996; see Directive 2001/29/EC on the harmonisation of certain aspects of copyright and related rights in the information society, recital 48 and art 5(2)(b); see Pamela Samuelson, "Anticircumvention ules: Threat to science" 2029.

481 WIPO Standing Committee on Copyright and Related Rights, "Updated report on the questionnaire on limitation and exceptions" SCCR/21/7 12, 13 and 15; Directive 2001/29/EC on the harmonisation of certain aspects of copyright and related rights in the information society, recital 51 and art 6(4); European Commission, "Report on the application of the Directive 2001/29/EC" SEC(2007) 1556, 9; Ian Brown, "The evolution of anti-circumvention law" 249; P. Akester and R. Akester, "Digital rights management in the 21st century" 161 and 165; see also Alvise Maria Casellati, "The evolution of article 6.4 of the European information society copyright directive" 397 (vagueness of limitations and exceptions); but see European Commission, "Report on the application of the Directive 2001/29/EC" SEC(2007) 1556, 7.

482 Directive 2001/29/EC on the harmonisation of certain aspects of copyright and related rights in the information society, art 6(4); Dutch Copyright Act, art 29*a*(4); see also Severine Dusollier, "Exceptions and technological measures in the European copyright directive of 2001 – an empty promise" 71–72; see also Lucie Guibault, Guido Westkamp and Thomas Rieber-Mohn, "Study on the implementation and effect in member states' Laws on Directive 2001/29/EC" 112.

483 Electronic Frontier Foundation, "Unintended consequences: Fifteen years under the DMCA"; see also Ian Kerr, Alana Maurushat, Christian Tacit, "Technical protection measures: Tilting at copyright's windmill" 68–75; see also Pamela Samuelson, "Anticircumvention rules: Threat to science" 2028; see also Michael Dizon, "Participatory democracy and information and communications technology" 14–15.

484 Ian Brown, "The evolution of Anti-Circumvention Law" 240; see also Kristin Eschenfelder and Anuj Desai, "Software as protest: The unexpected resiliency of U.S.-based DeCSS posting and linking" 102; Pamela Samuelson, "Anticircumvention rules: Threat to science" 2028.

485 *Chamberlain Group v Skylink Technologies* 381 F. 3d 1178 (2004), 1202; see also Lucie Guibault, Guido Westkamp and Thomas Rieber-Mohn, "Study on the implementation and Effect in Member States' Laws on Directive 2001/29/EC" 155.

486 Declan McCullagh and Milana Homsi, "Leave DRM alone: A survey of legislative proposals relating to digital rights management technology and their problems" 319; see also Ronald Leenes, "Framing techno-regulation: An exploration of state and non-state regulation by technology" 163–164.

487 See Directive 2001/29/EC on the harmonisation of certain aspects of copyright and related rights in the information society, recital 52 and art 6(4).

488 See WIPO International Bureau, "The advantages of adherence to the WIPO Copyright Treaty (WCT) and the WIPO Performances and Phonograms Treaty (WPPT)" 8; Michael Dizon, "Does Technology Trump Intellectual Property?" 132.

489 *TracFone Wireless, Inc. v. Dixon*, 475 F. Supp. 2d 1236 (2007); see also Pamela Samuelson, "Freedom to tinker" 20.

490 *MDY Industries, LLC. v. Blizzard Ent., Inc.*, 616 F. Supp. 2d 958 (2009).
491 *Storage Technology v. Custom Hardware Engineering*, 421 F.3d 1307 (2005); *Lexmark v. Static Control Components*, 387 F.3d 522 (2004).
492 Pamela Samuelson, "Freedom to tinker" 18–19; Electronic Frontier Foundation, "Unintended consequences: Fifteen years under the DMCA"; see also Derek Bambauer and Oliver Day, "The hacker's aegis" 28; see for example the OV-chipcard hack.
493 Martin Senftleben, "The emerging EC fair use doctrine" 533–534 (the *Mulholland Drive* case).
494 Pamela Samuelson, "Freedom to tinker" 15 and 20.
495 Pamela Samuelson, "Freedom to tinker" 21.
496 Michael Dizon, "Participatory democracy and information and communications technology" 15; see also Christophe Geiger, "The answer to the machine should not be the machine: Safeguarding the private copy exception in the digital environment" 123; see also Lawrence Lessig, *Code: Version 2.0* 175; Daniel Gervais, "A principled approach to copyright exceptions and limitations" 16.
497 Michael Dizon, "Participatory democracy and information and communications technology" 16; see also Directive 2001/29/EC on the harmonisation of certain aspects of copyright and related rights in the information society, arts 5(b) and 6(4) (but the exception is subject to "the absence of voluntary measures taken by rightsholders").
498 Jane Ginsburg, "Copyright and control over new technologies of dissemination" 1634.
499 Lawrence Lessig, *Code: Version 2.0* 191–192; see also Julie Cohen, "A right to read anonymously" 999–1000.
500 Christopher Soghoian, "Caveat venditor: Technologically protected subsidized goods and the customers who hack them"; Graham Longford, "Pedagogies of digital citizenship and the politics of code" 83; Michael Dizon, "Participatory democracy and information and communications technology" 17–18; Lawrence Lessig, *Code: Version 2.0* 179; Michael Dizon, "Does technology trump intellectual property?" 131–132.
501 See Electronic Frontier Foundation, "Unintended consequences: Fifteen years under the DMCA".
502 The Onion Router (Tor), (a system that allows users to use and access the internet anonymously).
503 See Michael Dizon, "Participatory democracy and information and communications technology" 18; see Christopher Kelty, "Geeks, social imaginaries, and recursive publics" 185; see Josh Lerner and Jean Tirole, "The economics of technology sharing: Open source and beyond" 101.

Chapter 5

Hacking's interactions with law

Perceptions and attitudes of hackers toward law and authority

As seen in the preceding chapter, due to the conflicts as well as correspondences between hacker norms and values and the goals and priorities of technology laws and policies, the views and reactions of hackers to law and public authorities are not only complex but also quite fraught.

Problem with authority

According to Levy, one of the tenets of hacker culture is to "mistrust authority".[1] And as with other types of hackers, there is a strong distrust and even disdain of public authorities among makers and hacktivists. Hackers tend to have a rebellious spirit or anti-establishment attitude, and they generally dislike hierarchies and other forms of centralized control or power. Hacktivist D observes, "hackers [mostly] don't assume authority themselves or even reject authority".[2] This animosity towards authority pervades hackerspaces as well. As Maker C points out, "to me, a hackerspace . . . always has this anti-establishment type of feel. And that's the difference for me. It has a kind of, there's this rebelliousness".[3] Maker E also notes that it is possible to view hackerspaces and the maker movement as "being more like a movement against suppression".[4] Hackers' aversion to authority can be reasonably traced to non-conformity, which is a constitutive part of hacking and hacker culture. As Maker I reflects, this is all "part of the non-conformist culture that is . . . a part of hacking".[5]

Makers and hacktivists have varying ideological positions and political leanings. Some refer to themselves as anarchists or communists, others embrace libertarian ideals, many may be called liberals and quite a number can be labeled as apolitical. However, because of the strong connection of the origin and development of the Dutch hacker scene with the squatter movement, their general orientation seems to veer or fall towards the left of the political spectrum. Hacktivist F confirms, "I would call it left. Radical, I don't really like the word. Left, sort of the Dutch squatter scene".[6] While some hackers agree with libertarianism, they seem to approach it critically. As Hacktivist B says, "I can empathize with the libertarian ideology there, although I think as good as libertarianism is in general, it neglects the social aspect of any exchange of goods".[7] Despite the melding of the anti-establishment spirit and the strong communitarian ethos in the hacker community, not many describe themselves as radicals, anarchists or communists, possibly due to the unwanted baggage that accompany these labels. Even a hacktivist who self-defines as an anarchist or communist says, "This new reality we should call it anarcho-communist. It sounds like something that is quite radical but it is totally common sense . . . a kind of framework that is anarcho sort of communist without being dogmatic about it".[8]

The acrimony that hackers, especially hacktivists, feel about public authority is not based solely on ideological or political grounds but also their actual knowledge of and experiences dealing with government. Hacktivist D states, "The problem with authority is that they, [more] often than not, place themselves above the law".[9] On top of that, many hackers believe that the government is technically incapable of tackling important issues relating to the governance of the networked information society. For instance, Hacktivist B cites, "the blatant incompetence [in the way] the state interacts in online affairs".[10] From personal experience, Ethical Hacker A explains, "[when] you're working [with] the government . . . people are avoiding all kinds of risks, all kinds of responsibilities. They're just not interested in improving the system".[11] While the notion that states or governments "are dead"[12] is not shared widely among hackers, many are of the view that hacking and authority are antithetical to each other. As Ethical Hacker A laconically explains, this is so because, when working in or with government, there is "no creativity, no innovation, no curiosity", which are the main motivations and goals of hacking.[13]

As much as possible makers and hacktivists want to have nothing to do with centralized authorities. Hacktivist C says, "I'm not going talk to a politician to try to explain . . . what's going on because it's a waste of time . . . a dead end".[14] During my time with the hacker community, the underlying animosity and tense relationship between hackers and public authorities was quite palpable. Ethical Hacker A points out, "I don't like the government guys [and] the government guys also don't like me".[15] Hacktivist F is more direct, "From a moral perspective, they [the government] should just mind their own business".[16] For Hacktivist D, "I don't really deal very often with the government. They don't get in my way [that's] for sure".[17] The conflict between hackers and public authorities can be attributed to a clash of cultures. According to Hacktivist C, there is "no point in talking to politicians, there's no point . . . because of all these politicians are there because of a mindset that is totally alien to what I'm going to tell them".[18] In general, hackers do not want to deal with the government, much less work for them. "No, I'm explicitly not working for a government organization at all", exclaims Ethical Hacker A.[19] Hackers expressly avoid working in or for government "because governments tend to be soul-crushing operations and are not terribly fit and receptive to" hackers.[20] Ethical Hacker A recounts, "In general, in my experience, they're not interested in improving. And if they're not interested in improving, I'm not interested in that kind of job since it will be the same all over again".[21]

Trouble with the law[22]

Hackers' acrimony toward public authorities also seems to be partly based on their perception that the authorities use the law to attempt to control and restrict their hacking projects and activities. Hackers consider laws and their restrictive applications as having negative effects and adverse impacts on their practices, norms and values. In relation to the perceived lack of fairness in the treatment and response of the law to hacking, makers and hacktivists hold the position that computer crime laws impose "disproportional penalty for" their activities.[23] According to a hacker, there are currently "lots of punishment for [and] measures [against] hackers".[24] And this is made even worse by the government's attempt to impose stricter and harsher laws on hacking. A hacker relates how, "I'm really worried about the proposal that's now in place for" the revision of Dutch computer crime law.[25] Hackers are anxious because "the current proposals, which are . . . a harshening of rules for the computer crime law".[26] Many believe that "the moves are made to worsen . . . [an] already bad situation".[27] They are concerned that "becoming a suspect is very easy" under the proposed legislations.[28] Part of the proposed amendments is the grant of powers to the government to force people to disclose their encryption keys.[29] According to a hacker, the "mandatory giving of your crypto passwords, that really affects us" since encryption is necessary to preserve the security and privacy of people and their systems.[30] "Having to hand over your decryption keys" is extremely problematic for hackers.[31] For example, "because our servers run on encrypted hard disks and we want to be able to maintain the position where we can't be forced into giving [up] other people's data".[32] It should be noted though that the proposed update to the Dutch computer crime laws on decryption orders is limited to the two specific cases of terrorism and child pornography.[33] It is worth noting that the Dutch Public Prosecution Service even "published a questionnaire on hacking and to ask the public how they should punish hacking".[34] This did not go over well with the hacker community and they published an open letter contesting the categorization of hackers as criminals and hacking as a criminal activity.[35]

For hackers, computer crime laws have also impeded computer security, which is not the exclusive domain of security researchers and ethical hackers, but is of paramount concern for all types of hackers. A hacker observes that the law is "affecting security research more and more".[36] According to the same hacker, while admittedly "the amount of, let's say, the number of real prosecution of researchers is still in the low end of the scale", the negative impact on security research is very real.[37] Bambauer and Day note that "[l]egal threats unquestionably influence researchers' actions, as they learn from prior controversies".[38] As the law currently stands, there are "quite a few loopholes that this hacker or other person has to jump through to not get prosecuted. It's still [a] fairly [gray] area".[39] A hacker relays how the law can inhibit the exploration and testing of computer systems: "If you're a web pen tester . . . if you want to . . . make sure some government or company's site is secure then you have way more issues".[40] The hacker continues, "I do think about [it]. Well, is this worth the risk? So if you crawl a website and the system overloads then they might try to get you convicted for a denial-of-service attack or something like that".[41] For another hacker, "I can think of several projects or ideas that I never engaged in because the risks were simply too high and I couldn't be bothered".[42] As a result, when testing and securing systems or disclosing security vulnerabilities, "this is typically something that . . . people try [and] they either get lost or get such a hostile reception".[43] Makers and hacktivists cite examples of security researchers being investigated, sued or criminally prosecuted.[44] A hacker relays how "things like the prosecution of Jeremy Hammond or Weevil", US hackers who were criminally prosecuted for engaging in acts of hacktivism and disclosing security vulnerabilities, "could have happened here" in the Netherlands.[45] A hacker cautions that

> at some point, people must realize that if you make . . . security research impossible, you get into the argument [that] if you outlaw guns only the criminals will have guns. But that is basically what we're slowly moving to actually.[46]

Hackers believe that intellectual property laws also have a detrimental impact on hacking. A hacker explains how the restrictions imposed by copyright affect one's ability to innovate: "I cannot continue doing what I like doing . . . [it has] a negative [impact on] the whole creation process".[47] Another hacker concurs that intellectual property laws "most definitely influences what I do".[48] Hackers dislike the restrictive uses of intellectual property rights and laws. As one hacker states, "I think that many things show that [intellectual property is] a hindrance because there's . . . a psychological effect".[49] Quite a number of hackers stopped working on their projects because of intellectual property concerns or issues.[50] For instance, some desisted in incorporating advanced features in 3D printers because a commercial company owned the patents to the underlying technologies and they did not want to get sued. As one hacker contends,

> I think in the end it's very damaging for society as a whole if only . . . a small group of people in a top-down way decides what technology is built, when it's built, at what price it's sold, and how we're all going to use it.[51]

A hacker similarly believes that "the system that creates those laws is so far outside our democratic system [and how] it's supposed to work because it's basically now entirely privatized and 100 percent non-democratic".[52] Many consider copyright laws to be outdated or "antiquated" and need "a big update".[53] A hacker remarks, "I think . . . intellectual property, especially the way that intellectual property law is being used right now, that needs to change. I mean the hacking ethic is completely at odds" with it.[54]

Difficulties with intellectual property laws are particularly acute among makers. On the one hand, there is the constant fear or threat of being sued for copyright or patent infringement.[55] As one hacker advises, "if you would make a machine you have to check" whether the core technologies are patented and "you want to be very careful about [not] infringing" them.[56] Based on experience, a hacker explains how "the particular technology that I am using, it's still covered by quite a few [patents], so you basically run into hot water".[57] The hacker further states: "The company that developed the technology did such a good job of patenting such a broad range, so you can't really get close [and develop your own technology] without [them] being quite similar" and thus infringe the patent.[58] Many believe the "patent system is kind of broken".[59] A hacker laments the possibility that, "if we're only allowed to create 3D printers that are fairly limited because someone has patented some mechanism, that really limits the powers of hackers".[60] Another hacker is likewise concerned,

> I definitely do not agree with the fact that right now a lot of companies are essentially getting extorted. 'Hey look, we're going to sue. That's going to cost you $20M. Yeah, pay up.' I think that's an abuse of the system.[61]

As a matter of principle, makers do not wish to apply for patents over their creations because this goes against their sharing ethos and the norms and values of openness and freedom of access.[62] But the fact remains that commercial companies file and obtain patents. "Especially in 3D printing, you are seeing now some proliferation of new patenting", explains one hacker, "Stratasys gets patents, now MakerBot also is getting patents".[63] There is a great apprehension among makers that it

> starts becoming something where a lot of people are investing in patents which will not go away for 20 or more years. So we're getting ourselves into a very hairy mess, I would say, if we don't do anything against it.[64]

All in all, restrictive laws and policies tend to have a chilling effect on hacking and increase the levels of concern and anxiety among hackers.[65] Hackers agree that the law "definitely" and "very much so" influences what they do.[66] They are constrained by "computer crime laws" because "you can interpret them very broadly. Anything becomes a crime if you look at it from a certain point" of view.[67] Some are "scared that you could do something that is not allowed or might not be allowed".[68] Others feel that "you lose all transparency because transparency means getting called up" by the police.[69] And a few are "worried about . . . what happens in the shadows".[70] A hacker discloses how, "I try to fight not to get too paranoid, you know, about that".[71] Otherwise, "it institutes paranoia".[72]

Legal and extra-legal means[73]

It was quite surprising to learn from some of hackers that the commencement of formal criminal prosecutions or the filing of court cases is not the usual or preferred way by which public and private actors deal with what they consider problematic hacking technologies or activities. In truth, "a lot more happens via legal intimidation . . . than via actual prosecution".[74] According to another hacker, the police "will first try extra-legal methods" from calling them up and informal warnings to veiled threats and intimidations.[75] The hacker continues, "I've seen [this with] many activist sites. A lot of the legal trouble [they] get into doesn't actually follow [the] law or legal procedures".[76] A hacker also recounts,

> By far, the most censorship I've seen has all been completely extra-judiciary, extra-legal. Simply informal requests of the police . . . or parties like that towards ISPs directly like, 'Hey, can you take that down?' 'Oh sure, we'll take that down'.[77]

A hacker explains how they "sometimes get cease and desist letters or phone calls" regarding websites or services that host potentially copyright-infringing or controversial content.[78] These informal requests to takedown websites "in my experience" happen "a lot more than the official channels through which these [should be] done".[79] Hackers who receive a letter or "lawyer gram" from the government or a private company "tend to stop".[80]

In addition, hackers are subjected to actual or veiled threats, intimidation or harassment from public authorities and private companies. "When I [write] about politicians, I always have to be [careful] that I don't make them angry",[81] explains a hacker. There can be "threats sometimes because in politics people get angry. . . . [They might] say [that] they want to hit you or something".[82] In relation to a court-mandated nationwide block by Dutch internet service providers of the peer-to-peer file sharing website, The Pirate Bay, some hackers sought to provide proxies and other technical means to circumvent the block, but the private companies involved sued "one person and they threatened a whole bunch of others".[83] Most threats of legal action "never actually came to court" since many hackers desisted.[84] However, a hacker explains, "There's one [person] who didn't [take down his proxy] and he's still in a legal mess. They really [went] after him. Like he had his bank account closed, his Paypal account closed off. It's nasty".[85]

In relation to Wikileaks and whistleblowers, the response of many governments has been quite extreme. A hacker relates how

> Everyone who's been seriously involved [in] Wikileaks has actually been physically threatened basically by, not just the US government. There are other organizations and individuals. So we have a Canadian cabinet level adviser who says, on television, "Oh, I think we should just bomb all these guys".[86]

"The most powerful military alliances on the planet are seriously considering extra-judicially killing people and you know they have the means to do it. And you know they have the willingness to do it", the hacker continues,

> And so they're actually considering doing that. So that's also when several people got out of Wikileaks and said, 'Look, you know, this is all fun and well, and you know, I'm not against a little risqué activism, but this is a little bit too much'.[87]

According to the same hacker,

> even worse, they might just extra-judicially kill you. The fact that [it] is even a serious part of a discussion [in relation to] people who have done nothing else than just to report . . . [on] war crimes done by the very same government, by the way . . . you have a fair idea of how messed up we are as a society.[88]

Some makers and hacktivists also point to the Dutch government's animosity towards and harassment of well-known journalist Brenno de Winter who hackers consider to be a member of their community and who sometimes acts as an intermediary between them and the government.[89] After he published how he was able travel for free using a cracked OV-chipcard, de Winter was questioned as a suspect for four hours and investigated by the public prosecutor for months.[90] A hacker notes how the government only investigated de Winter despite the fact that there "were a lot of other people of the big news agencies . . . who [also] did it . . . and they didn't get the police on their door".[91] While the public prosecutor ultimately decided not to file a case against de Winter on the ground of journalistic interest, de Winter still had to go through an arduous process and hire counsel during the period of investigation.[92] It is interesting to note how the hacker and internet communities raised €7,500 for de Winter's legal defense.[93] But even after the investigation against him was dropped, hackers believe that de Winter continues to be scrutinized and hounded by the government. According to some hackers, de Winter is under surveillance by the government and that "he was followed" and the police have "a big dossier about" him.[94] Furthermore, it appears that "all police forces in the Netherlands have been notified of Brenno being a shady person that might be trying to enter government buildings with false or forged identity papers. His picture hangs in certain" places.[95] A hacker relates how de Winter "was visiting a certain ministry in The Hague and there were actually specific protocols to deal with him . . . when [entering] the building".[96]

Many hackers feel that the actions taken by public authorities against them are unfair and disproportionate. For instance, a hacker recounts how "I heard . . . some [teenage] hackers who hacked [their] school website. The High-Tech Crime [Unit] busts into their homes. Six [officers] and some of them [in] complete gear with bullet-proof vests busts into the home of a [16 or 17 year-old] school kid".[97] With respect to the blocking of websites, a hacker is of the opinion that "[if the government decides] that this website is illegal and [they] start blocking access to it and [they] censor it, that is a disproportionate move".[98] Most hackers also balk at the attempts of public authorities to intrude or insinuate themselves into hacker events. For instance, "the Dutch High-Tech Crime Unit . . . wanted to have a presence at OHM", an outdoor hacker conference.[99] A hacker relays how "We had . . . a long discussion about what we [were] going to do. We were violently [opposed to] the participation of the police [at] OHM, which they later withdrew luckily".[100]

Presence rather than the absence of law

Despite their problems with law and authorities, the subject of law is generally not top of mind or a priority concern among makers and hacktivists. Hackers do not usually spend their time thinking about or discussing the meanings, intricacies and nuances of law.[101] They primarily focus on technical and social issues, and legal matters are not normally raised or discussed unless these become a significant concern or have a direct impact on the technical and the social dimensions of hacking. For instance, while there are talks on legal topics and issues at hacker camps, they are meager compared to the overwhelming number of technical presentations and workshops.[102] This is expected given that, echoing the view of many hackers, "Personally, my perspective of the world is not a legal one".[103] Hacktivist F captures how most hackers view the law: "My natural inclination to solve problems is not a legal solution. To me, it's always, if you need a lawyer something [probably went] wrong somewhere or at some point".[104] Maker D goes even further and says that the goal is "to only . . . know the law superficially" since "I just do the bigger picture" and other people like lawyers can take care of the specific legal issues.[105]

Hackers' general attitude towards law can be characterized as a mix of ambivalence and indifference. As discussed in greater detail below on how hackers respond to law, makers and hacktivists prefer to ignore and avoid laws and legal issues, but, as a practical matter, they also see the law as the basis or source of fundamental rights and freedoms and they are willing to directly engage with laws and public authorities to achieve a social goal or to improve the law. Maker J speaks about the relationship between hacking and law: "I mean they're not completely at odds but I see that there is conflict".[106] Maker E adds, "in certain aspects we want to have laws and regulations, and in others we go like, 'Hey don't limit me, I want to be free'".[107] This ambivalence towards law is further exacerbated by a common belief among hackers that law is slow-moving and outpaced by technological change: "If you look at law, [it has] always trailed behind innovation".[108] Maker E continues, "since the industrial revolution innovation is going so much faster . . . the gap between innovation and lawmaking grows every year too".[109]

Despite their initial indifference and ambivalence toward law, hackers still see the importance of having laws and the necessity of dealing with legal and policies issues that affect hacking. Even though most hackers bear a strong animosity against public authorities, their outlook and approach to law in contrast is less antagonistic and can even be described as positive and constructive. So, while many makers and hacktivists can imagine or strive for a world without hierarchies and centralized authorities, they have no wish to achieve a state of "anomie" since they recognize the need to have laws and other rules of behaviors to govern individual and social conduct.[110] They consider law to be an integral part of society. As Maker H explains, "I consider law [to be] part of the social complex that [we] are in".[111] For Maker J, there is no reason for getting rid of law altogether since "I think we have to have something".[112] Asked about their opinions about law, Maker J states, "I mean it has room for improvement, but I think it's good that it's there".[113] Discussing the possibility of having less or more laws that apply to hacking, Maker J says, "The things we have right now is not so bad that I would say that we're better off without them".[114] Maker L believes that "there should be less laws. I think there should be basic laws".[115] Hacktivist B concurs, "I say less probably . . . less would mean a lot less".[116] Others hold the view that "especially for a lot of these cases where we're talking about hacking, there's not really [any] law about it".[117] But Hacktivist D believes, "Law is not like water [that] you can have more or less [of it]. . . . Better, you know, *not more or less but better*. Better laws so they're more broadly defined or something".[118] Hacktivist D continues, "I don't need less of that. I need more of those kind of good laws".[119]

Know the law more

Hackers' knowledge of law varies greatly among individuals and groups. Their legal understanding can range from nil, basic or general to even substantial and specialized. Like many hackers, Maker G is quick to point out that "I'm not really a legal expert".[120] Maker A confesses, "I really don't know a lot about [law]",[121] while Maker E admits that in their hackerspace, "the knowledge about [law] is very little. . . . To be honest, I don't know much about those legal rules for pen testing" and computer crime laws.[122] In relation to intellectual property law, Maker K says, "a lot of young kids don't even know what a patent is and what it really means".[123] Maker H observes that hackers' knowledge of law "varies from person to person. By and large their idea of what [one] can or can't do is not entirely based in reality".[124] This is compounded by the fact that some hackers do not know where to find legal information. "I think there's also very little to be found on [law]", relates Maker E, "I wouldn't know where to find any of that, if it already exists".[125]

But, like the FOSS developers who have become quite well versed in the substance and intricacies of intellectual property and licensing issues,[126] there are some makers and hacktivists who are familiar with specific or specialized areas of law. For instance, Maker J states, "I'm very aware of the law in these fields . . . both in privacy law and security law".[127] Unlike other hackerspaces, Maker L says, a "lot of people in the space . . . know about computer laws, know quite a lot about [it] or know how to find it".[128] Maker C also says that intellectual property "is something everyone is cognizant about" in their hackerspace.[129] Based on my dealings with makers and hacktivists, while there are indeed hackers who are well informed about specific areas of law such as copyright and data protection, their legal knowledge is close to but still not on the same level as a general law practitioner.

Whether they know a little or a lot about the law, hackers are fairly open and willing to learn more about the rules and regulations that affected them. Maker L says, "most of the time I have general information that I read about. But if it really affects me . . . yeah I look up a law book and read about it".[130] For most hackers, the path to legal knowledge is mainly through self-study and a bit of learning and guidance from others. According to Maker D, "I read [the law] by myself. . . . I always do the research by myself ".[131] For Maker L as well, "Yeah, I read the law sometimes, on certain parts, how things work. I find [the law] interesting".[132] Maker J explains the process further, "once I get some kind of grasp of [a legal] area . . . I try to read [and] learn more" about it.[133] For Hacktivist E, "I read the actual laws, related parliamentary papers. I used the website of the Dutch Data Protection Authority, bought books, visited seminars, talked to various lawyers and legal academics".[134] While some hackers actually read pertinent laws and court decisions,[135] others try to keep abreast of legal developments from online sources. For example, Maker L reads the blog of an IT lawyer who "posts about law issues related to IT, computer, web shops and those kinds of things, privacy. . . . [he] gives a lot of information".[136] To learn about cybercrime laws, Hacktivist E reads the blogs of IT law scholars.[137]

Studying the law on one's own is not without difficulty. Some laws like freedom of information regulations are "very hard to read, understand and grasp".[138] While some found that "it was pretty hard"[139] to understand the law, others felt that "most of the law is also pretty straightforward. I don't find it hard to read".[140] "Sometimes I just get the law book on the internet and read the law . . . how does it work, and it's readable", narrates Maker L, "Yeah sometimes it's hard to understand, but sometimes you get the information . . . [on] how [the law] works".[141] Hacktivist D explains how, for ordinary people, law should be easier to understand compared to computer programming since the "law as far as I'm concerned is in my language. Computer language is a different language that I still have to learn".[142] This is one of the reasons why hackers consider it their social responsibility to make technology more open, available and transparent for the general public, because, unlike normal people, they are much more comfortable and adept in the language of computers than the language of law.

Despite their ambivalence towards law, makers and hacktivists still grasp the advantages of knowing more about the law. In the same way they approach technology, hackers view the law as basically a system of rules and processes that they can understand and then use, subvert or remake (in other words hack). According to Maker H, some hackers consider the law to be like any "another system that has its own loopholes and unforeseen consequences".[143] For many hackers, learning about the law is both a practical and a tactical exercise. From a political or ideological point of view, Maker E argues, "you need to know what the law is in order to rebel against it".[144] According to Hacktivist B, it makes sense "to know when you are or aren't breaking the law".[145] As Maker E also explains, "you need to know what is acceptable [or not] in the eyes of [the] people [who] are controlling you whether it's government, [the] police force or [the] military".[146] Maker D recognizes the importance of the fact that "when I am politically active . . . I also have to understand the law".[147] In their day-to-day lives, knowing the law is also a practical necessity.[148] As Ethical Hacker A says, "I'm interested in why [law] works, the way it works. From the professional point of view, for myself . . . it's really, really important, critically important" to know the law.[149] Similarly, Maker L recounts how for "my work, some things [that I do for] my job, I do look up the law book for that. What the rules [are] and how the policy works so [I] know what [I'm] doing".[150] "So for me . . . it's just very important . . . to make sure that I'm on the right side of the line", Ethical Hacker A explains, "I need to be prepared as well for those kind of circumstances" where the law is involved.[151]

Greater access to law and legal assistance

What is really surprising about makers and hacktivists is that, while they show a general ambivalence or indifference to law, they still recognize the value of knowing their rights under the law (especially fundamental rights such as freedom of expression, liberty and privacy) and having access to legal assistance, aid or advice in order to protect or uphold these rights. Hackers agree that they need more help from lawyers since they often do not know what the limits of the law are. Maker E remarks, "It would be nice to at least be able to find out what the law . . . is, or if there are even laws [that] cover" a particular issue or subject.[152] According to Hacktivist B, lawyers can "at least raise awareness [about] what your rights are".[153] Hackers mainly get informal legal advice from acquaintances or friends who are lawyers or legal professionals. For instance, "being friends with [people with a legal background] helps in getting an understanding [of law]".[154] Maker K agrees, "Yeah I've been lucky. I've met quite a few good people along the way" who know the law.[155] When dealing with potential legal issues, "I got my IP lawyer to check it out. . . . He's a friend who's a patent lawyer. That's handy".[156]

Only a few hackers though have this kind or level of access to law and legal assistance. As with most hackers who do not have convenient or immediate access to a lawyer, Maker L relates "But no, [I] don't have my own lawyer".[157] Hacktivist B further explains that while there are a few lawyers who can make themselves available to hackers, they are mostly "not pro bono".[158] Furthermore, digital rights organizations in the Netherlands do not "really provide that kind of support in the way, say the EFF does, [in] assisting with court cases".[159] The current situation severely restricts the ability of makers and hacktivists to receive sufficient legal protection or to properly enforce their rights. Maker D believes that "not having people that help you with the law" is a significant issue.[160] "That's a major problem I think as well", states Hacktivist B on the general lack of access of the hacker community to lawyers or legal assistance. As a result, many makers and hacktivists end up undertaking hacking projects and activities that push the boundaries of technology and law with "no legal advisement of lawyers".[161] Many hackers believe that having access to lawyers would be extremely helpful for them.[162]

Even though makers and hacktivists see the benefits of having access to a lawyer and there are a handful of legal professionals who are active in or have close ties to the Dutch hacker community, Maker H opines, "I would not consider the lack of lawyers to be the most pressing diversity issue in that scene".[163] Despite the common desire to have more legal assistance, Maker H cautions that, "I wouldn't say you should go to a hackerspace if you are an IT lawyer or a lawyer in general" unless one is interested as well in working hands-on with technical projects.[164] In addition, hackers can be quite critical of lawyers specifically with regard to their lack of technical knowledge or understanding. Ethical Hacker A relates how discussions with "legal folks" are "completely out of this world. [They talk] about possible risks, commas, punctuations and that kind of stuff", which are not relevant to technical issues.[165] A hacker recounts similarly disappointing experiences with lawyers when making a security report or disclosure: "Because it goes to the law firm and [the lawyers don't] even . . . know what it's about. They just say, OK we start looking at, you know, similar cases. Oh, [there's a case about] someone who actually broke into a bank, maybe [that's] comparable".[166] The hacker further recounts how legal departments in large companies do not understand the technology and "make . . . stupid comments and [other] annoying stuff".[167] So, while hackers prefer to have better access to law and legal professionals, they are still very much averse to having to deal with government or company lawyers in adversarial proceedings or contentious contexts.

Hackers' responses to law

In light of the above, members of the Dutch hacker community seem to perceive and approach the law in two distinct and opposing ways: first, as restrictive, unjust or outdated prescriptions made by centralized authorities that must be opposed or contested; and, second, as the basis or source of fundamental rights and freedoms that need to be protected or upheld. This dual outlook frames and informs how they respond to technology laws and policies. As Maker G remarks, it "depends per law what [their] action should be".[168] Hackers' general responses to law are: to ignore and avoid it; if it becomes impossible to keep the law away, to change or resist it; and, if it benefits the hacker community and society as a whole, to possibly work with, use or adapt the law. It is worth noting that hackers are rarely inclined to obey or conform to laws of the restrictive kind that they believe to be undemocratic or unjust.

Ignore and avoid

The natural tendency and default response of makers and hacktivists is to ignore or avoid the law, especially those laws that they view as unduly restricting or controlling their rights and freedoms. This response springs directly from hacker norms and values like individual autonomy and liberty and their general indifference and ambivalence to law. "I'm not a big fan [of the law] to put it mildly", explains Hacktivist B, "I generally don't really concern myself that much with law".[169] Likewise, Hacktivist C says, "Basically in terms of law, to me, yeah it's always been a piece of paper. . . . To me it's never been a tool that I even considered as being relevant".[170] For some hackers, the reasons for ignoring or avoiding the law can be ideological or political. Hacktivist C believes that

> law has always been on the side of the people who wrote laws. . . . This sort of code of conduct, the code of law or this codex or set of principles is easily swept aside by those in power when they deem it necessary.[171]

For Hacktivist B, "[laws are] a nuisance and I have to know [how] deal with them".[172]

For others, ignoring or avoiding the law and public authorities is necessary to protect or promote the norms and values of curiosity and creativity and innovation. As Maker A says, "I really don't want to think about [law] when I'm creating something. . . . [I] just don't think about it because that just stops the creative process".[173] Hacktivist C concurs, "To me the very notion of the law [is that it] is part of a system that always . . . [shuts out] these types of innovation".[174] Maker E recounts how it is publicly funded organizations and projects "that are really worried about lawmaking. [They] think . . . and talk about it. It's not the ones who are innovative that [think] about law".[175] Some hackers view the law as a distraction. Maker H relates how some hackers believe "you can only waste your time with [laws] and [they] should best be ignored".[176] Maker E says that in their hackerspace, "most people think that legalese and financial stuff is boring".[177] "We're not really putting a lot of time and effort on [legal issues or concerns] here", explains Maker E.[178] Maker A affirms, "Do I want to know more about it [law]? No, I don't think so".[179]

Makers and hacktivists are aware that ignoring or avoiding the law can lead to breaking the law. But, on the whole, that does not stop them from engaging in hacking projects and activities. For example, the existence of patents over certain 3D printing technologies should normally prevent or stop people from hacking or building on these patented technologies without the inventor's permission. But despite these patents, a hacker argues that, "For individuals and for groups, for social groups, I think it makes sense that people hack regardless of a patent or possibly even because of a patent".[180] The hacker further explains, "doing something that might be patented, it's also, I would say, part of the non-conformist culture that is also a part of hacking".[181] For others, ignoring and breaking the law has a political or moral dimension. Hacktivist A explains,

> For me, copyright law now is a zone of law where the law is so broken and the system that makes the law is so broken that actually the morally right thing to do as a citizen of a democratic country is to essentially ignore it and make your own judgments.[182]

Maker I reflects on the connection between hacking and breaking the law: "There's a paradox there. Hacking is doing something that is not as intended. Then breaking the law and hacking are also to some extent . . . kicking the boundaries. For example, changing something which voids the warranty".[183] "We're often, of course, skating along the edges of the law with so many things that we get up to", points out Hacktivist A, but "that doesn't mean that I break everything all the time".[184] Hacktivist A continues,

> But it does mean that I am now making my own moral judgments. Whereas in many other cases in my life, I defer to the law. I say, 'Look, you know, we agreed that we're going do this. You know, we agreed in this country that we're going to drive in a fashion, no more than 120'.[185]

For Hacktivist B, there's a tactical motive behind ignoring and avoiding the law: it's "not so much because you shouldn't break the law but at least have yourself covered and don't get caught".[186] Maker E adds, while they want to avoid the law, "you need to know what's going on".[187] But skirting rules and voiding warranties are things hackers are not generally worried about. Maker A remarks, "I know that if you open it up you void your warranty. Yeah, but I'm not really someone that brings something back that I broke".[188] "As a consumer, I just open it and I don't claim warranty", says Maker G.[189]

Change and resist

Legal change through hacking

There are many cases and contexts where it is not possible for makers and hacktivists to simply ignore or avoid the law. Whenever it becomes unfeasible or impractical to steer clear or to "route around" laws and other restrictions,[190] hackers' customary reactions are to resist or to change them. These forms of responses are expected given the rebellious, anti-establishment and non-conformist attitudes that run in the hacker community. Furthermore, makers and hacktivists regard these restrictive laws as threats to their hacking practices, norms and values that must be contested and opposed. As Maker G says, "If you don't like a law you should, I guess, strategically try to fix" it.[191] "We need to fight many battles on many different fronts at the same time", relates Hacktivist F, "You need to fight technical battles, legal battles. You need to make sure encryption is still allowed in the future".[192]

There are a number of technological, legal or social ways by which makers and hacktivists change or resist laws, but their seemingly preferred method is quite understandably technical – to change the law through hacking. This is clearly evident in the cases of the campaign against electronic voting computers, Leak-tober and the OV-chipcard hacks, which are discussed in the succeeding sections. Hacktivist D explains how hacking can be useful with regard to changing restrictive or problematic laws: "Sometimes you just [have] to piss people off, you know. It shows where the problems, where the cracks lie".[193] Hacking therefore becomes a way to raise awareness about and directly engage with legal issues and problems. "You get that kind of discussions. And the only way to prove that you are right [to show] that it's actually hackable or you can compromise or . . . manipulate it", claims Ethical Hacker A.[194]

Some hackers are neither hesitant about resisting the law nor deterred by the threat of public sanctions. While makers are generally more concerned about the possibility of being sued for their hacking projects, hacktivists are not as fretful. "There's no reason to be afraid of anything", says Hacktivist C, "one thing [that] they have is jail, [which] you . . . have to sit [in] for a year, so what".[195] A hacker explains how "when I was a teenager, I wasn't repelled by computer crime laws".[196] Other hackers view their resistance to law as a legitimate form of civil disobedience. "For some laws there can be civil disobedience", states Maker G.[197] For Maker L as well, "Civil disobedience . . . [is] a nice way of showing people . . . you can show me what you want but bad luck" since we will it oppose anyway.[198] For instance, after the Snowden revelations, the response of members of the Dutch hacker community was to resist and counteract mass government surveillance by developing, using and promoting the use of encryption and other privacy-enhancing software like Tor, OTR and Tails.[199] While the aim of these actions is not to directly change the law, they seek to counter or neutralize the negative effects of mass surveillance and thus render such government policy ineffectual or irrelevant. A hacker recounts the fallout from the Snowden revelations: "People [reacted by] trying to build new tools and forming new alliances. People getting to know each other and having more politically motivated discussions. [These] might be threatening to the interests of the state".[200] Maker B believes that it's good "to be extreme sometimes to make people aware of things".[201] Similarly, for Hacktivist, F, "you need to do things that are a bit more . . . radical or campaign-like for people to get a feeling that you're working on it" and making a difference.[202] Hacktivist A similarly reflects,

> I actually now consider it a very good metric of [how] effective activism is if you feel the pressure. So if you're not feeling anything, you know, if there's no [pressure], then actually there's no indication that you're achieving anything as an activist, right? Because if nobody's pushing back, then maybe they didn't even notice you yet. And if they didn't notice you as an activist, then obviously you need to try harder, right? Then you didn't do your job.[203]

Hackers believe that hacking can produce legal change when needed.[204] In response to the question of whether hacking can change the law, Hacktivist B sardonically remarks, "It obviously does because we wouldn't have computer crime law".[205]

Hacking electronic voting computers

One of the most well-known and much discussed cases in the Netherlands of hackers resisting and changing the law through hacking involves the campaign against electronic voting. In 2006, a few months before the general elections, a non-profit group that called itself "We don't trust voting computers" launched a campaign to challenge the use of electronic voting machines in the country.[206] The group included and was led by hackers, including Rop Gonggrijp, a prominent member of the Dutch hacker scene.[207] The group was able to get their hands on a few voting machines to study and analyze by way of a loan and purchases from two municipalities.[208]

In order to understand how the voting machines work and to test their security, the group thoroughly hacked the machines. They systematically took apart and analyzed the machines' physical hardware and components.[209] They reverse-engineered the software and reprogrammed the machines to play chess and to purposely miscount votes.[210] The group easily discovered that the password to access the critical software "maintenance mode" was "'GEHEIM', the Dutch word for 'SECRET'".[211] They also showed that the mechanical locks on all of the voting machines could be opened with the same physical master key, and spare keys could be ordered online by anyone "without any problem" for two Euros each.[212] In addition, the locks were trivial to pick.[213] Finally, the group demonstrated how the displays of the machines produced radio emissions that could be captured and reproduced by people outside of the polling place to reveal how a person voted.[214] It was this last vulnerability that proved to be the main undoing of the voting machines since it affected the secrecy of the ballot, which is an essential requirement of free elections.[215] Despite repeated attempts, the machines' vulnerability to the so-called "Tempest attack" (also known as "Van Eck phreaking" which is named after a Dutch security researcher) that compromised voting secrecy could not be adequately fixed.[216]

As a result of the hacking of the voting machines by the group, coupled with their active campaigning, freedom of information requests, and threatening and taking legal action, the Dutch government ultimately changed the law on electronic voting, withdrew the regulation for certifying electronic voting machines, and suspended the use of electronic voting in the country.[217] Jacobs and Pieters, who are academic security researchers, reflect on the triumph of the campaign:

> [it] reached its goals in a remarkably short time. It relied on a clear vision, technical skills, bravery, effective use of freedom of information rights, professional communication via their own newsletter and a very informative

webpage, frequent and convincing media appearances, and, in the end, threats of legal actions.[218]

"There was a large group of people . . . who were helping them and advising them and . . . writing blog posts and talking to journalists and all that stuff", narrates Hacktivist A.[219] Maker B also recounts, "there was public awareness, and the media started to talk about it, and then [the government] could not do anything [to] stop it".[220] A hacker believes that

> the most important aspect of [the campaign] was to get the media's attention. Because if you cannot physically demonstrate a fault then there's no story, and you need a story. Otherwise nothing happens in the Netherlands politically, right? If it's not on television, it didn't happen.[221]

Thus, by 2008, "the Netherlands returned to paper voting, with manual counting of the ballots".[222] According to Hacktivist F, the campaign against voting computers "basically killed the whole electronic voting in the Netherlands. Up until now we still vote with pencil" and paper.[223]

Makers and hacktivists fully subscribe to the aims and methods of the campaign against electronic voting and they deem it a great success and a fine example of how hacking influences the law.[224] They unanimously "agree with those involved in hacking electronic voting computers".[225] Maker G considers it "a nice strategic achievement",[226] while Hacktivist B describes it as "a nice campaign".[227] Maker L statement reveals the sense of pride and elation that hackers feel about the campaign: "I think it was great thing. I was a bit younger then and didn't know much about it. . . . I would like to have been in the middle of it".[228]

Aside from being able to change the law, the other reasons why the campaign is such a touchstone for Dutch hackers is that it required technical mastery to carry out, it involved the common acts of hacking (most especially *break*, *learn* and *secure*), and it directly related to the norm and value of security. Maker L explains, "Yeah that was great. That was a great way to show people what was wrong with voting computers, and let people understand why they are a bad thing".[229] Maker D adds, "It was good to see how it could be faked. It was good to see how the government had a romantic view of ICT and it wasn't reality".[230] Hackers are particularly fond of how hacking itself played a key role in the campaign. "I like the hacking part", explains Ethical Hacker A, "since in many cases, and this was a very good one in my opinion, it's the only way to show that it's really a problem in the real world".[231] According to Ethical Hacker B, "I mean it's good to look at it because there was a lot wrong with it".[232] Through hacking, the campaigners were able to show the real risks and threats posed by the use of electronic voting machines and why the process that people used to exercise their right to vote had to change.

Hackers emphasize the technical aspects of the campaign and the wide disparity between the technological knowledge and skills possessed by the campaigners versus those in government. "Almost everybody involved in computer science thinks that [electronic voting] is a bad idea. I feel that it's a very bad idea", explains Maker J, "It's so unbelievable that the people who are very knowledgeable about the security of and how these kinds of voting computers work . . . are so against it".[233] According to Hacktivist D, "you should be very cautious when basically the people who know most about computers in our society are saying [electronic voting] is a bad idea".[234] Maker E describes how the campaigners were like "scientists [who] basically told government, 'Hey we're playing with very dangerous toys here, and you need to change your policies'".[235] While it is easy to be enamored with technology, the voting computers campaign illustrates the importance of having a critical view or stance in relation to technology. As Hacktivist E points out, "We need to apply critical thinking everywhere we introduce computers".[236] Maker J explains further,

> This is also something that I see very often. They think . . . we can improve this process by using computers. But I think, well, I know about these things and then, often you start thinking about the implicit things that are there in the analog [voting] process

that actually make it better and more secure.[237] According to Maker D, hackers "helped to change [the voting process by showing] that [the government's] view wasn't realistic. It's [also] good to [show] the danger of technology".[238]

Hackers also tend to have a commonsensical approach to the subject of voting and elections. Maker H argues that, "there are no good objective reasons why pencil and paper won't suffice".[239] Maker J explains the problems with electronic voting: "You have to balance the costs to the improvement. I don't see that there is such a big improvement in the process. It's just a very high cost to implement [electronic voting] in a very secure way, and the risks they are just so great".[240] From a practical standpoint, Maker J continues, "There's no way, there's no easy way to make a secure voting process in the same way we have right now. . . . The anonymity of it is too hard to implement".[241] Hackers are aware of some of the advantages of electronic voting: "the modern character and administrative efficiency and advantages of these machines: easy, push-button voting, reduction of the number of polling stations, fast delivery of results".[242] However, they believe that the attendant risks of electronic voting far outweigh its benefits. Ethical Hacker A remarks, "If some kind of politician decides that democracy is, I don't know, too expensive and we need voting computers. We vote once in four years but we cannot wait for an extra hour" for the election results to be announced.[243] Hacktivist D concurs, "you're [talking] four hours [of] quicker results. You don't really think about the [social and democratic] costs at all".[244]

The security of elections is considered a serious matter for hackers since it concerns the validity and legitimacy of democratic rule and governance. According to the members of the campaign against voting computers: "Any vulnerabilities discussed herein affect the very foundations of our democracy. . . . In the case of a voting system, it is obvious that any lack of security has the potential to directly affect all of society".[245] Hacktivist F agrees, "you need to be sure" about "the integrity of the voting system . . . in a democracy".[246] As a hacker acerbically puts it: it is never a good idea "to fuck around with voting and elections".[247] Hackers and politicians alike are keenly aware that "once trust in the voting system declines, it is hard to win this back. Without this support, the legitimacy of the chosen legislator will diminish" and so too the democratic foundations of government and society.[248]

Leaktober

Aside from the electronic voting computers campaign, Leaktober (in Dutch *lektober*) is another noteworthy case of hackers resisting or changing the law through hacking. Leaktober, a portmanteau of the words leak and October, illustrates how hacking can influence technology laws and policies. As the term suggests, the aim of this campaign was to make public a computer security leak or vulnerability of a government or company website or IT system every day in October 2011.[249] Leaktober was principally carried out by Brenno de Winter, a well-known "hacker-journalist", together with the IT news website *Webwereld*.[250] The impetus for Leaktober was their frustration with receiving daily reports about security vulnerabilities and leaks that could have been easily prevented or fixed.[251] The goal of the campaign was to bring greater public attention to these vulnerabilities and to force government and companies to take action and improve the security of their systems.[252] In order to disclose the security vulnerabilities responsibly, de Winter and *Webwereld* informed the affected party before they published any information.[253] In addition, they did not copy or publicly release any personal data or information that they were able to gain access to through their security testing.[254] The primary targets of Leaktober were government websites, particularly those of municipalities and cities.[255] As Maker D explains, de Winter "called the city . . . each day, each week, saying your security is broken. . . . But he published it also online so the whole world could see the city . . . had a data leak that day".[256] The aim of disclosing a security leak per day was easily met since many government websites and online services were vulnerable to easily exploitable weaknesses.[257] Leaktober quickly achieved its objective because, once informed of the breaches, the affected organizations including the Association of Dutch Municipalities immediately took down their websites and services and sought to fix them.[258]

Leaktober is of great import to the hackers because, not only did it actually raise awareness about computer leaks and make the government and companies take action, but it promoted the norms and values of security and privacy. Some consider it an act of hacktivism because "people became more aware [about computer security]. It was more of a campaign, a strategic hacking for raising awareness [and] making those sites more secure".[259] Many hackers support the objectives and tactics of Leaktober and think very highly of de Winter and what he was able to accomplish. According to Maker D, "Brenno de Winter did good things for society. By proving that we have a lot of ICT problems and he brings them [out] in the open".[260] Maker B adds, "He found leaks, holes in the security, and then he told this to the cities. And he made a public fuss about it. . . . He was proving [to the] cities that their computer systems, websites were not secure".[261] The hacking activities that were carried out as part of Leaktober ultimately helped improved the security of many IT systems. "Yeah, it was successful because [local government officials] still talk about it, and they are more aware of it", continues Maker B.[262]

The affected organizations, including local governments, were not too pleased with being the subject of public naming and shaming. As Maker B relates, "In the media, in the public, they were of course not so happy but they were admitting that it was important and they would work on it. . . . But behind the doors, of course, they were not so polite".[263] But, in the end, the municipal governments accepted the fact that they needed to prioritize security and makes changes. According to Maker D, "the city . . . said well you're welcome, because it's only testing our ICT and it's very good".[264] Despite its success in changing government policy and forcing government action to improve computer security, Leaktober also produced unexpected results for hackers. One of the unintended effects of Leaktober was that, by raising awareness of security issues, some hackers believe that it also made the general public more afraid and fearful of hackers and hacking. As Maker G explains, "It might have made people aware and also . . . afraid, is my web shop going to be the next one".[265] Furthermore, in the wake of Leaktober, both the public and the mainstream press were no longer interested in the issue of security leaks "because of *lektober*, it wasn't newsworthy" anymore.[266] It appears that, after Leaktober, it is harder for hackers to receive the same level of media coverage and public attention for publicizing security vulnerabilities and to get the government or the public to take action.

Hacking the OV-chipcard

Among the hackers I spoke to, the positive outcomes of the voting computers campaign and Leaktober are often contrasted with their inability to prevent the introduction and use of the Dutch national public transport card (the OV-chipcard or *OV-chipkaart* in Dutch)[267] despite the numerous objections and hacks against it. The OV-chipcard is "a common means of payment for all forms of public transport in The Netherlands" and has a "contactless chipcard, which can be loaded with a balance in Euros and specific travel products".[268] The roll out and use of this "smart card based e-ticketing system for all forms of public transport: bus, train, metro, etc." within the Netherlands has been and continues to be a hotly debated and highly contested topic ever since security issues with the card gained widespread public and media attention in 2007.[269] "The stakes are high" with respect to the OV-chipcard, writes Jacobs, "the invested economical and political interests and the prestige at risk are high".[270] In addition, the

OV-chipcard involves many public and private stakeholders and their concerns and interests around:

> fair division of revenues and/or subsidies and improvement of service via detailed travel logs, public safety via restricted access (via electronic gates), fraud reduction, cost reduction (fewer inspectors needed), convenience for travelers, behavioural targeting and direct marketing via personal travel profiles, and simply the desire to look modern and high-tech.[271]

Ethical Hacker B explains, "that was really a hot item because it cost like a billion Euros. It was funded by public money. Nobody really wanted it, but it was still pushed".[272] Hacktivist A adds, "None of the citizens actually asked for this system. Many of them protested against the privacy violations. The government ignored it".[273]

Between May 2007 and March 2008, the security of the various underlying technologies of the OV-chipcard was compromised on four separate occasions by three different groups of security researchers and students connected with universities in the Netherlands, Germany and the United States.[274] Basically, the researchers found that the security of the card, which relied on "a proprietary authentication protocol and stream cipher using [encryption] keys", could be broken or circumvented with the right tools or techniques.[275] This meant that once the security of a card was compromised, an attacker could, among other things, gain access to and steal a cardholder's personal data and travel information that are stored on the card, fraudulently top-up the value on the card, or create cloned or fake cards.[276] In all four cases, the findings and security reports of the students and researchers were disclosed to the general public as well as the entities responsible for rolling out the OV-chipcard.[277] Hacktivist A recalls,

> A bunch of experts in this area – these students and professors – wrote a letter to the Ministry saying, 'Look, this is not a good plan. This is going to be hacked six ways to Sunday on day one of implementation. So either pick a new technology or start over'. And that letter was ignored. Then they sent follow-up letters. And the follow-up letters, they were also all ignored.[278]

However, the company that produced the chips for the cards, NXP Semiconductors, sought a court injunction to stop the security researchers at Radboud University Nijmegen from releasing their results.[279] The Dutch court ruled against NXP Semiconductors and held that the research could be published on the grounds that the

> the chance of damage must be attributed largely to the production and entry into service of a chip with intrinsic defects, which is the responsibility of NXP and not of Radboud University Nijmegen who only laid bare [such defects] by research.[280]

The court also held that the finding and disclosure of security vulnerabilities "is to some extent something that in an open democratic society should be accepted".[281]

A few years later, the OV-chipcard was once again in the news when journalist Brenno de Winter wrote about how he was able to travel for three weeks using a cracked OV-chipcard.[282] A hacker explains how cracked cards are used:

> You can take a cash, pre-paid *OV-chipkaart* and you can just charge it up with whatever you want. Or you can check yourself in at a station and then you get on a train, and you go to the other side of the country and when the conductor comes, your card says that you are checked in.[283]

Doing it for journalistic purposes and to show the relative ease of breaking the OV-chipcard,[284] de Winter even got Members of Parliament to travel using cracked or fake cards. Maker H recounts how de Winter "had several Members of Parliament travel for a few weeks with fake OV-chipkaarts . . . using their parliamentary immunity".[285]

Despite the many attempts by hackers and security researchers to stop the implementation and use of the OV-chipcard through hacking and exposing its security vulnerabilities, on the whole, these hacks have not produced the desired effect. The hacks have had "little direct impact on the actual roll-out of the OV-chipkaart" aside from "some additional delays, and in the development of a migration plan".[286] According to Jacobs, "After a phase of denying, dismissing and trivialising these findings the main players started accepting them and began working on a replacement plan towards a new card. In the meantime the actual roll-out went ahead".[287] So, while disclosing security issues resulted in "a lot of pressure from Parliament" and "delayed the introduction of" the OV-chipcard,[288] hackers admit that "the situation itself didn't change".[289] At most, the hacks raised awareness about the card's security issues and forced technical improvements specifically in relation to fraud prevention.[290] As Jacob writes, "In the Netherlands politicians and industrials have become aware of the fact that large ICT-projects can be made or broken by security issues".[291] Maker H notes that the companies who were responsible for the OV-chipcard "were receptive, responsive to that, and replaced the old vulnerable card to much more modern cards which . . . undoubtedly also have their weaknesses".[292] Maker L adds, "they took some action . . . to make [the cards] better. But yeah, I hoped it would have more effect. I hoped".[293] As Maker J points out though, "the end result was that [it] improved the security a little bit, but the fundamental problems . . . are not solved".[294]

For hackers, the fundamental problems of the OV-chipcard concern both security and privacy. They do not trust the OV-chipcard to protect their privacy because it is not secure. "The system is fundamentally broken. It is ridiculously easy to hack. It doesn't take a lot of effort", points out Hacktivist A.[295] Moreover, they believe that the card infringes on their privacy because copious amounts of data are collected about them and they can be profiled and their movements monitored. Despite the disclosures of security vulnerabilities, members of the hacker community admittedly were not able to control the debate and change public opinion. Rather than focusing on privacy issues, public discussions centered mainly on how the security issues could lead to fraud through the creation and use of fake or cracked cards.[296] As Ethical Hacker B notes, the companies who were behind the OV-chipcard, "one of the main things they used as propaganda was . . . we move to this because then we don't [want] people traveling without paying".[297] But as Maker H points out, "The fundamental issue with the *OV-chipkaart* is not fraud".[298] Maker G agrees, "my objection with the *OV-chipkaart* is not that you can fake, you can cheat. But it's more that. It's [the] electronic registration of your movements".[299] Maker H claims that

> The fundamental issues with the *OV-chipkaart* are not necessarily . . . affected by the vulnerabilities in the card itself. It didn't really affect the fundamental question, at least one of the fundamental questions of the *OV-chipkaart*. I would say [the] almost unprecedented collection [of the] . . . physical movement of people.[300]

The privacy concerns over the OV-chipcard stem from the fact that, as explained by Jacobs, "the OV-chip smart card based e-ticketing system involves a centralised architecture giving the travel companies unprecedented access to individual travel behaviour".[301] Jacobs explains the specifics of how the OV-chipcard system works:

> each entry or exit into the public transport system, in a bus or at a train station, generates an entry in the back-office of the travel companies, involving among others the identity of the entry/exit point (often connected to a fixed location), time-of-day, and identity and balance of the card.[302]

Hacktivist B points out, "Then you get to the more fundamental problem of the *OV-chipkaart*".[303] Hacktivist B continues:

> One of the major failures with the whole thing about the *OV-chipkaart* was that in publicizing how the chip was hackable . . . the only thing they disclosed was a very private problem for the company exploiting this card that they were susceptible to a means of fraud. . . . They didn't expose any form of critique on the data gathering or anything. It was just we can travel for free. Why is this a problem?[304]

Hacktivist A concurs, "The privacy implications of that are just horrendous. Think, a central database run by a private company that is not on a democratic oversight, that now stores, and God knows what they do with the data. They might be reselling it. They might not be securing it properly".[305] According to

Maker G, "unless people really see [this as] a threat. . . . I don't know if this can change".306

Some hackers believe that there's no point in hacking the OV-chipcard any further: "Yeah, hacking it again doesn't prove a point anymore".307 However, others believe that there could have been better tactics that would have placed the issue of privacy squarely on center stage. For example, a hacker imagines how "it would have been way more interesting if someone were to hack the database and just dump that online and [say], here you go fuckers".308 While mindful of the ethical, social and legal consequences, the hacker contends, "Then you immediately get the question of if it's not OK to . . . dump this online, why is it OK if the NS [national railway company] keeps track of this and sells this data to other private companies?".309

Work with, use and adapt

While it may not be their preferred approach, hackers are also open to pursuing legal means, which may include working with, using or adapting the law tactically to achieve their goals. The two examples discussed below do not technically involve hacking since they are primarily concerned with changing and using laws and policies rather than technology *per se*. These cases also required working within the legal system and according to established legal procedures and rules. Nevertheless, the actions and activities that hackers carried out in relation to these cases were still very much grounded on and impelled by hacker culture and in furtherance of their norms and values. In addition, the targets of these cases were not simply general laws but specific technology laws and policies that are germane to hacking.

Net neutrality rules

The hacker community played a key role in the enactment of net neutrality legislation in the Netherlands as they lobbied and worked with Members of Parliament to get the law passed. The campaign to introduce a formal net neutrality law was mainly led by Bits of Freedom, a digital rights organization that has relatively strong ties with hackers. In fact, some hackers consider Bits of Freedom to be a part of the hacker community since the organization was re-launched during the quadrennial Dutch outdoor hacker conference in 2009310 and it was very active during the same hacker conference in 2013, particularly at the more political NoisySquare village.311 Moreover, the organization counts a number of hackers as its volunteers or members. Maker L confirms that, "Bits of Freedom comes from the hacker community".312

Bits of Freedom began its net neutrality campaign in 2009 when it published a position paper encouraging the adoption of net neutrality principles and rules.313 However, it was only in April 2011 when a controversy broke out about the use of deep packet inspection (DPI) by the dominant Dutch telecommunications provider KPN to monitor the internet activities of its customers and the applications and services that they used that the campaign finally gained traction and widespread attention of legislators and the public.[314] The spark came when an executive at KPN mentioned during a meeting with the company's investors that it had DPI technology that could be used to monitor the internet traffic of its customers and potentially charge them tariffs for using messaging services like WhatsApp in order to offset the company's declining voice and SMS revenues.[315] A lawyer from Bits of Freedom, Janneke Slöetjes, explains,

> KPN was proud to announce that they used DPI to determine which kind of websites customers visited and then to offer specialized packages. It wasn't the case that they were necessarily doing it, but it was enough evidence for us.[316]

Maker L narrates, "It was a great fight when they found the part of the interview with some shareholders [and] the KPN [official] who said they want to do DPI to get people to pay for WhatsApp".[317] The significance of the controversy over DPI was that "people saw the negative outcomes that would be possible if you don't have net neutrality law. People were warning about that for a long time".[318]

Bits of Freedom, together with hackers and the wider internet community,[319] seized the opportunity to fan the public outcry over KPN's use of DPI to demand the inclusion of net neutrality rules in the Telecommunications Act, which was coincidentally being revised by Parliament at the time.[320] Maker L explains, "a lot of people in the hacker community worked together with Bits of Freedom and [they were] very vocal about" the issues.[321] According to Bits of Freedom, "The use of DPI gained much attention when KPN admitted that it analysed the traffic of its users to gather information on the use of certain apps".[322] Slöetjes further recounts:

> DPI is a violation of communications confidentiality. We told people to report crimes to the police, and they did. We had a draft law ready. It was short. The government was reviewing telecommunications law at the time, and there was room to add extra provisions.[323]

According to a person knowledgeable about the campaign,

> We had a very lucky break because the spokesperson from KPN . . . in a different context boasted about their ability to do deep packet inspection. Which then led to sort of a big media downfall and then allowed the law to pass very quickly.[324]

In a little over a year, the net neutrality campaigners were able to use the media attention and the public outrage (especially online) generated by the DPI controversy to effectively lobby the major political parties to adopt net neutrality provisions as part of the revision of the telecommunications law.[325] The net neutrality law had the support of the majority of the Dutch Parliament,[326] and was adopted by Parliament in May 2012 and took effect on 1 January 2013.[327] The Netherlands thus became one of the first countries to have "specific net neutrality standards in place. It was the first country to do so in the European Union".[328] According to Ot van Daalen, the Director of Bits of Freedom at the time, "The net neutrality law prohibits internet providers from interfering with the traffic of their users".[329] He further explains, "the law includes an anti-wiretapping provision, restricting internet providers from using invasive wiretapping technologies, such as deep packet inspection".[330]

Bits of Freedom, other non-governmental organizations and members of the hacker community were all instrumental in the adoption of the net neutrality law.[331] A person who had intimate knowledge about the campaign relates how Bits of Freedom "wrote the key net neutrality provision".[332] The person continues, "People were working on that. We were actively trying to find a political majority to pass an amendment [to] the Telecoms Act that we've basically written".[333] Higgins notes how the Dutch net neutrality rules came "after vigorous campaigning by civil society groups including influential digital rights group, Bits of Freedom".[334] Van Eijk confirms, "A lot of reactions were the result, advocating a more material, more concrete approach to net neutrality. These reactions were partly caused by a call from Bits of Freedom, a very active NGO, to react".[335] Maker L explains how "a lot of people talked to . . . parliament people and protested right way on Twitter and other [ways] . . . to get it done".[336]

Hackers supported and were actively involved in the campaign because they saw the net neutrality rules as playing a critical part in preserving freedom on the internet, which they consider essential for fostering greater techno-social creativity and innovation. One of the main goals of net neutrality is "to safeguard an open and secure internet in The Netherlands" because "Internet access is very important for functioning in an information society".[337] According to the explanatory memorandum on the net neutrality provisions:

> This restriction on the behavior of providers of Internet services is necessary to ensure open and unrestricted access to the Internet for (online) service providers, citizens and business. It should be prevented that Internet access service providers block or restrict specific information or services.[338]

Echoing the sentiment of many hackers, the Dutch deputy prime minister, Maxime Verhagen, told the press that:

> The blocking of services or the imposition of a levy is a brake on innovation. . . . That's not good for the economy. This measure guarantees a completely free Internet which both citizens and the providers of the online services can then rely on.[339]

Furthermore, the net neutrality rules concern the all-important hacker norms and values of freedom of access, individual autonomy and liberty, and privacy (to use the internet without being monitored). These norms and values are recognized in the explanatory memorandum as well. For instance, it states that, "End-users should be able to decide what content they want to send and receive, and which services, applications, hardware and software they want to use for such purposes".[340] The explanatory memorandum further highlights the need to preserve or "to maximise choice and freedom of expression on the Internet for end users".[341] According to Bruno Braakhuis, the Member of Parliament who originally sponsored the net neutrality rules, "For us, this is really a basic right. . . . We consider network neutrality to be as important as freedom of the press, freedom of speech".[342]

A number of hackers were part of net neutrality campaign and they are quite proud of their achievement.[343] As Maker L proclaims, "one thing that was a big success in the Netherlands is the net neutrality law. . . . I think we hacked us a nice law [and got] the politics right to get that law enacted".[344] Some hackers consider it "probably our biggest [and] most impactful success" in terms of changing technology law and policy.[345] They proudly claim that the Dutch net neutrality law has become "the model inside the EU for the people who support true net neutrality [and want] to get [this] enacted over there as well".[346] Many hackers admittedly share Maker J's sentiment that, "it was sort of a surprise in how well it was actually implemented".[347] They concede though that the net neutrality campaign "was a very legal approach to the problem rather than" hacking and "the majority of it was advocacy and policy work done by legal people" and not hackers.[348] While some hackers consider this a deficiency, on the contrary, I believe this perfectly illustrates how hackers, lawyers and government officials can work together to develop and improve technology laws and policies. This position is borne out by the adoption of responsible disclosure rules and the development of open data hackathons, which are discussed in Chapter 6.

Open source projects

As explained in Chapter 2, hackers use copyleft and FOSS licenses not merely to subvert intellectual property laws but also to constructively change and adapt these legal rules to serve and support various hacker norms and values. For instance, the development of open source projects and the use of FOSS licenses help promote openness and freedom of access, which enable fellow hackers and members of the public to freely use, build on and *share* their creations and innovations. According of Maker I, "If a project I'm working [on is] not a closed source project, [it's] an open source project or a free software project, people who want to participate are able to participate. So it's not a closed group".[349] Open source projects can also advance the norms and values of efficiency and creativity and innovation. Hacktivist B underscores the ability of open source to create "products comparable and even better quality-wise to those produced within the capitalist framework, but completely volunteer-based".[350] Hacktivist D likewise says, "We have people who would say I like open source because it allows me to build . . . my own project. . . . I just think it's cool to have all of this free code which I can use and hack".[351] Maker I explains the essential role open source plays in supporting community development and social development: "Yes, I think open source is really important. I look at it at two ways. I think, in itself, open source is a process which is a good thing. For society, it's important [and] has a good effect".[352] Maker I continues, "the benefits definitely include . . . access to a lot of knowledge and enthusiasm and also, I would say, social capital".[353] Open source is undeniably a core practice and ethos among hackers. Hacktivist B recounts how the use of open source "was really one of the core values" when they established their hackerspace.[354] Maker I adds, "There's a lot of open source values and culture in, for example, all of the entrepreneurs who come from the RepRap community".[355]

The use of free and open source technologies and licenses remains strong among makers and hacktivists, and many Dutch hackers consciously or by default choose to use and work on open source projects, particularly in relation to open source hardware. There is a very active RepRap community in the Netherlands that continues to build and develop this open source 3D printer.[356] The Ultimaker 3D printer, which is based on RepRap and is developed by Dutch makers, is often cited as the poster child of open source hardware since, unlike MakerBot, the hardware and software of Ultimaker remain completely open source and everybody is free to work and build on it.[357] Maker G explains that, when working on projects, "I try to just make it open source. . . . I use open source software myself".[358] According to Maker K, "I know most people who develop stuff just [release them] under the Creative Commons license".[359] Similarly, Ethical Hacker B relates how "I made all [of my software] open source. I just pushed it [to] the community. Everybody can start playing with it".[360]

Open source technologies and practices have admittedly become prevalent and influential both within and outside the hacker community. Maker D narrates how "we don't try to lobby as hard for open source as before because the industry of open source is now very good and very self-[sustaining]. It's not the highest priority".[361] Maker D continues, "Open source [is] really important, but [it] has matured. The market has matured".[362] Some hackers though remain frustrated by the absence of a formal government policy on open source. Since the early 2000s, hackers have been lobbying the Dutch government to enact policies on the adoption and use of open source software.[363] "They were talking about implementing it. It was all, it was all mostly still talking. Which was good, which is always where everything begins", recounts Hacktivist A.[364] While the discussions were initially promising, "certainly, by the summer of 2010, it was dead in the water. . . . That's been completely killed" possibly due to pressure from powerful political and economic interests.[365] Nevertheless, open source has proven to be very resilient in relation to particular legal issues. "Intellectual property law does affect [the open hardware movement] and likewise . . . software development in general", Maker

H explains, "But thanks to all of the work done in the open source [and] free software movement, that is much less of an issue nowadays than it used to be".[366] In fact, open source has also been used as a tactic or defense against legal actions and restrictions. A hacker explains how "a lot of guys are . . . doing whatever the hell they want and then kind of use . . . open source as an inoculation against" potential legal liability.[367] "No big company wants to sue an open source company", continues the hacker, "it's a defense, a PR defense and people actively use it".[368] Using open source as a kind of incantation to dispel legal issues, "you can inoculate yourself against it by saying, 'Hey we're open source man'. . . . You cannot go on the record in today's tech community and do anything anti-open source".[369]

Despite its influence and creative uses, open source is far from being immune to all legal problems and conflicts. For example, patents remain a critical issue for open source projects. Within the "open source community, it seems like we also have to get patents to be able to sustain ourselves", explains Maker I, "We feel that [it's] a problem if we get patents because we are at least on some level against that" because patents can restrict openness and freedom of access.[370] Nonetheless, Maker I notes how openness can also be employed to defeat the restrictions of patents: "I don't think there's a lot of protection [for open source]. There's at least one protection that I know of, by publishing, you create prior art".[371] So, by publicly releasing and sharing their inventions and technological creations online, makers can prevent others from patenting and closing off an invention and exercising exclusive rights over it. "That's one thing, one reason, to be open sourcing something and making a project out of it", explains Maker I.[372]

Complex relations and reactions

As evinced by the above perceptions, attitudes and responses of hackers to law, the relationship between hacking and the law can be characterized as multifaceted, complicated and ostensibly paradoxical. Do hackers consider laws to be irrelevant? Would hackers prefer a world without laws? Do hackers loathe public authorities? Are laws and public authorities antithetical to hacking? As this chapter has shown, such questions cannot be satisfied with simple yes or no answers since they demand more nuance and contextualization. As seen in the campaign against electronic voting machines, hackers can strive to change technology laws and policies that they disagree with through technical means. But, they can also utilize or work within the legal system to change and improve laws, as demonstrated by the adoption of the net neutrality legislation in the Netherlands and the continued development and use of open source projects and licenses to counteract the restrictions and restrictive uses of intellectual property laws and rights. So, while the relations between hacking and the law may be far from cordial, they are not completely adversarial. In certain cases, hackers are willing to work with the public authorities if they believe that such projects or activities will have a social impact and redound to the benefit of their community and the wider public. Hackers generally prefer to focus on developing their technologies and communities, but, as a practical matter and as a means to an end, they are ready to engage with law and public authorities to resolve critical issues that affect hacker norms and values and impact society as a whole.

Makers and hacktivists value their individual autonomy and liberty, yet they are also socially conscious and they recognize the importance of using their rights to protect the freedoms of others and to advance community and social development. Furthermore, even though hackers may have problems with law and authority due to their non-conformist and anti-establishment attitudes, they are surprisingly open to knowing more about the law, receiving greater legal protection for their fundamental rights and freedoms, and even ensuring the integrity of a system that elects public officials. This apparent incongruity can be explained by the fact that hackers perceive and approach the law and authority in two distinct ways: restrictive or unjust laws and governments must be opposed, while laws and systems that uphold basic human rights and promote democratic freedoms and processes should be supported. It is true that many hackers are not fond of politics or politicians, but they view hacking as a political act and they, for the most part, subscribe to the ideals and values of democracy.

Understanding the complex and competing relationship and interactions between hackers and law is paramount and a necessary prerequisite in order to reasonably determine and properly prescribe optimal approaches to the regulation and governance of hacking projects and activities. The next chapter discusses the normative implications and legal recommendations concerning hacking.

Notes

1 Steven Levy, *Hackers* 29.
2 Interview with Hacktivist D.
3 Interview with Maker C.
4 Interview with Maker E.
5 Interview with Maker I.
6 Interview with Hacktivist F.
7 Interview with Hacktivist B.
8 Interview.
9 Interview with Hacktivist D.
10 Interview with Hacktivist B.
11 Interview with Ethical Hacker A.
12 Interview with Hacktivist C.
13 Interview with Ethical Hacker A.
14 Interview with Hacktivist C.
15 Interview with Ethical Hacker A.
16 Interview with Hacktivist F.
17 Interview with Hacktivist D.
18 Interview with Hacktivist C.
19 Interview with Ethical Hacker A.
20 Interview with Maker H.
21 Interview with Ethical Hacker A.

22 Note that, due to the sensitive nature of the topics and information contained in this section, the references to my interviews and conversations with hackers are completely anonymized so as not to reveal their identities or make them identifiable.
23 Interview.
24 Interview.
25 Interview.
26 Interview.
27 Interview.
28 Interview.
29 Interview.
30 Interview.
31 Interview.
32 Interview.
33 F.W.J. van Geelkerken, "Proposal for the dutch computercrime act III; A critique" 2.
34 Interview.
35 "Open brief aan OM: Hacken"; "Open brief aan OM: Hacken".
36 Interview.
37 Interview.
38 Derek Bambauer and Oliver Day, "The hacker's aegis" 34.
39 Interview.
40 Interview.
41 Interview.
42 Interview.
43 Interview.
44 Interviews.
45 Interview; see also Cassandra Kirsch, "The grey hat hacker" 386–387; see also Janet Reitman, "The rise and fall of Jeremy Hammond: Enemy of the state"; see also Hanni Fakhoury, "The US crackdown on hackers is our new war on drugs".
46 Interview.
47 Interview.
48 Interview.
49 Interview.
50 Interviews.
51 Interview.
52 Interview.
53 Interviews.
54 Interview.
55 Interviews.
56 Interview.
57 Interview.
58 Interview.
59 Interviews.
60 Interview.
61 Interview.
62 Interview.
63 Interview.
64 Interview.
65 Interviews.
66 Interviews.
67 Interview.
68 Interview.
69 Interview.

70 Interview.
71 Interview.
72 Interview.
73 Note that the references to my interviews and conversations with hackers are completely anonymized so as not to reveal their identities or make them identifiable.
74 Interview.
75 Interview.
76 Interview.
77 Interview.
78 Interview.
79 Interview.
80 Interview.
81 Interview.
82 Interview.
83 Interview.
84 Interview.
85 Interview.
86 Interview.
87 Interview.
88 Interview.
89 Interviews.
90 Sander van der Meijs, "OM vervolgt Brenno de Winter niet om hack OV-chipkaart".
91 Interview.
92 Sander van der Meijs, "OM vervolgt Brenno de Winter niet om hack OV-chipkaart".
93 Sander van der Meijs, "OM vervolgt Brenno de Winter niet om hack OV-chipkaart".
94 Interviews.
95 Interview.
96 Interview.
97 Interview.
98 Interview.
99 Interview.
100 Interview.
101 Interview with Hacktivist B.
102 See OHM2013, "Call for participation"; see OHM2013, "Program".
103 Interview with Hacktivist F.
104 Interview with Hacktivist F.
105 Interview with Maker D.
106 Interview with Maker J.
107 Interview with Maker E.
108 Interview with Maker E.
109 Interview with Maker E.
110 See Bruce Dohrenwend, "Egoism, altruism, anomie, and fatalism: A conceptual analysis of durkheim's types"
111 Interview with Maker H.
112 Interview with Maker J.
113 Interview with Maker J.
114 Interview with Maker J.
115 Interview with Maker L.
116 Interview with Hacktivist B.
117 Interview with Maker J.
118 Interview with Hacktivist D (emphasis added).
119 Interview with Hacktivist D.
120 Interview with Maker G.

121 Interview with Maker A.
122 Interview with Maker E.
123 Interview with Maker K.
124 Interview with Maker H.
125 Interview with Maker E.
126 Gabriella Coleman, "Code is speech" 425–426.
127 Interview with Maker J.
128 Interview with Maker L.
129 Interview with Maker C.
130 Interview with Maker L.
131 Interview with Maker D.
132 Interview with Maker L.
133 Interview with Maker J.
134 Interview with Hacktivist E.
135 Interview with Hacktivist D.
136 Interview with Maker L.
137 Interview with Hacktivist E.
138 Interview.
139 Interview.
140 Interview.
141 Interview with Maker L.
142 Interview with Hacktivist D.
143 Interview with Maker H.
144 Interview with Maker E.
145 Interview with Hacktivist B.
146 Interview with Maker E.
147 Interview with Maker D.
148 Interview with Ethical Hacker A.
149 Interview with Ethical Hacker A.
150 Interview with Maker L.
151 Interview with Ethical Hacker A.
152 Interview with Maker E.
153 Interview with Hacktivist B.
154 Interview with Hacktivist B.
155 Interview with Maker K.
156 Interview with Maker K.
157 Interview with Maker L.
158 Interview with Hacktivist B.
159 Interview with Hacktivist B.
160 Interview with Maker D.
161 Interview with Ethical Hacker A.
162 Interviews.
163 Interview with Maker H.
164 Interview with Maker H.
165 Interview with Ethical Hacker A.
166 Interview.
167 Interview.
168 Interview with Maker G.
169 Interview with Hacktivist B.
170 Interview with Hacktivist C.
171 Interview with Hacktivist C.
172 Interview with Hacktivist B.

173 Interview with Maker A.
174 Interview with Hacktivist C.
175 Interview with Maker E.
176 Interview with Maker H.
177 Interview with Maker E.
178 Interview with Maker E.
179 Interview with Maker A.
180 Interview.
181 Interview.
182 Interview with Hacktivist A.
183 Interview with Maker I.
184 Interview with Hacktivist A.
185 Interview with Hacktivist A.
186 Interview with Hacktivist B.
187 Interview with Maker E.
188 Interview with Maker A.
189 Interview with Maker G.
190 See Jack Balkin, "Digital speech and democratic culture" 12.
191 Interview with Maker G.
192 Interview with Hacktivist F.
193 Interview with Hacktivist D.
194 Interview with Ethical Hacker A.
195 Interview with Hacktivist C.
196 Interview.
197 Interview with Maker G.
198 Interview with Maker L.
199 Tor Project; Off-the-Record Messaging; Tails.
200 Interview.
201 Interview with Maker B.
202 Interview with Hacktivist F.
203 Interview with Hacktivist A.
204 Interview with Maker H.
205 Interview with Hacktivist B.
206 Rop Gonggrijp and Willem-Jan Hengeveld, "Studying the Nedap/Groenendaal
     ES3B voting computer" 2; see also "We don't trust voting computers"; see also
     Bart Jacobs and Wolter Pieters, "Electronic voting in The Netherlands" 11; see
     also Leontine Loeber, "E-voting in The Netherlands" 24.
207 Bart Jacobs and Wolter Pieters, "Electronic voting in The Netherlands" 11;
     see also Rop Gonggrijp and Willem-Jan Hengeveld, "Studying the Nedap/
     Groenendaal ES3B voting computer" 16; see also Leontine Loeber, "E-voting
     in The Netherlands" 24.
208 Rop Gonggrijp and Willem-Jan Hengeveld, "Studying the Nedap/Groenendaal
     ES3B voting computer" 2 and 16; see also see also Leontine Loeber, "E-voting
     in the Netherlands" 24; see also Bart Jacobs and Wolter Pieters, "Electronic vot-
     ing in The Netherlands" 11.
209 Rop Gonggrijp and Willem-Jan Hengeveld, "Studying the Nedap/Groenendaal
     ES3B voting computer" 4–6; see also Bart Jacobs and Wolter Pieters, "Elec-
     tronic voting in The Netherlands" 11.
210 Rop Gonggrijp and Willem-Jan Hengeveld, "Studying the Nedap/Groenendaal
     ES3B voting computer" 6–8; Bart Jacobs and Wolter Pieters, "Electronic vot-
     ing in The Netherlands" 5; see also see also Leontine Loeber, "E-voting in The
     Netherlands" 24.

211 Rop Gonggrijp and Willem-Jan Hengeveld, "Studying the Nedap/Groenendaal ES3B voting computer" 4.
212 Rop Gonggrijp and Willem-Jan Hengeveld, "Studying the Nedap/Groenendaal ES3B voting computer" 3.
213 Rop Gonggrijp and Willem-Jan Hengeveld, "Studying the Nedap/Groenendaal ES3B voting computer" 3.
214 Rop Gonggrijp and Willem-Jan Hengeveld, "Studying the Nedap/Groenendaal ES3B voting computer" 10–12; see also Bart Jacobs and Wolter Pieters, "Electronic voting in the Netherlands" 5, 11 and 12.
215 Bart Jacobs and Wolter Pieters, "Electronic voting in the Netherlands" 12; see also Leontine Loeber, "E-voting in The Netherlands" 24.
216 Bart Jacobs and Wolter Pieters, "Electronic voting in The Netherlands" 11 and 12.
217 Bart Jacobs and Wolter Pieters, "Electronic voting in the Netherlands" 11, 12 and 13; see also Leontine Loeber, "E-voting in The Netherlands" 24, 25 and 26.
218 Bart Jacobs and Wolter Pieters, "Electronic voting in The Netherlands" 14.
219 Interview with Hacktivist A.
220 Interview with Maker B.
221 Interview.
222 Bart Jacobs and Wolter Pieters, "Electronic voting in The Netherlands" 2 and 14; see also Leontine Loeber, "E-voting in The Netherlands" 26.
223 Interview with Hacktivist F.
224 Interview with Maker B; Interview with Maker I; Interview with Hacktivist F; Interview with Ethical Hacker A.
225 Interview with Hacktivist E.
226 Interview with Maker G.
227 Interview with Hacktivist B.
228 Interview with Maker L.
229 Interview with Maker L.
230 Interview with Maker D.
231 Interview with Ethical Hacker A.
232 Interview with Ethical Hacker B.
233 Interview with Maker J.
234 Interview with Hacktivist D.
235 Interview with Maker E.
236 Interview with Hacktivist E.
237 Interview with Maker J.
238 Interview with Maker D.
239 Interview with Maker H.
240 Interview with Maker J.
241 Interview with Maker J.
242 Bart Jacobs and Wolter Pieters, "Electronic voting in The Netherlands" 3.
243 Interview with Ethical Hacker A.
244 Interview with Hacktivist D.
245 Rop Gonggrijp and Willem-Jan Hengeveld, "Studying the Nedap/Groenendaal ES3B voting computer" 2.
246 Interview with Hacktivist F.
247 Interview.
248 Leontine Loeber, "E-voting in The Netherlands" 29.
249 Nicole van der Meulen and Arno Lodder, "Cybersecurity".
250 Sander van der Meijs, "Lektober: iedere dag een privacylek"; see also Interview with Maker B (who uses the term "hacker-journalist" to describe Brenno de Winter); see also Nico van Eijk, "Datalekken: een reality check" 30.

251 Sander van der Meijs, "Lektober: iedere dag een privacylek".
252 Sander van der Meijs, "Lektober: iedere dag een privacylek".
253 Sander van der Meijs, "Lektober: iedere dag een privacylek".
254 Sander van der Meijs, "Lektober: iedere dag een privacylek".
255 Nicole van der Meulen and Arno Lodder, "Cybersecurity".
256 Interview with Maker D.
257 Brenno de Winter, "Lektober superknaller: Megalek treft 50 gemeenten"; see also Nicole van der Meulen and Arno Lodder, "Cybersecurity".
258 Brenno de Winter, "Lektober superknaller: Megalek treft 50 gemeenten"; see also Nicole van der Meulen and Arno Lodder, "Cybersecurity".
259 Interview with Maker B.
260 Interview with Maker D.
261 Interview with Maker B.
262 Interview with Maker B.
263 Interview with Maker B.
264 Interview with Maker D.
265 Interview with Maker G.
266 Interview with Maker G.
267 Bart Jacobs, "Security and privacy issues in transport and beyond" 291; see also "OV-chip".
268 TNO, "Security analysis of the Dutch OV-ChipKaart" 3.
269 Bart Jacobs, "Security and privacy issues in transport and beyond" 291–292; see also "OV-chip"; see also Leontine Loeber, "E-voting in The Netherlands" 29.
270 Bart Jacobs, "Security and privacy issues in transport and beyond" 294.
271 Bart Jacobs, "Security and privacy issues in transport and beyond" 292.
272 Interview with Ethical Hacker B.
273 Interview with Hacktivist A.
274 "OV-chip"; see also TNO, "Security analysis of the Dutch OV-ChipKaart" 3.
275 Bart Jacobs, "Security and privacy issues in transport and beyond" 292; see also Adrian Cho, "University hackers test the right to expose security concerns" 1322–1323.
276 Bart Jacobs, "Security and privacy issues in transport and beyond" 292–294; see also TNO, "Security analysis of the Dutch OV-Chipkaart" 5, 6, 11 and 12.
277 "OV-chip"; see also Bart Jacobs, "Security and privacy issues in transport and beyond" 292.
278 Interview with Hacktivist A.
279 Adrian Cho, "University hackers test the right to expose security concerns" 1322; see also Elinor Mills, "Dutch chipmaker sues to silence security researchers".
280 NXP Semiconductors vs Radboud Universiteit Nijmegen, Arnhem Court Case Number 171900 (18 July 2008) 4.20 and 4.23; see also Elinor Mills, "Dutch court allows publication of Mifare security hole research"; see also Adrian Cho, "University hackers test the right to expose security concerns" 1322.
281 NXP Semiconductors vs Radboud Universiteit Nijmegen, Arnhem Court Case Number 171900 (18 July 2008) 4.20 and 4.23.
282 Sander van der Meijs, "OM vervolgt Brenno de Winter niet om hack OV-chipkaart".
283 Interview.
284 Sander van der Meijs, "OM vervolgt Brenno de Winter niet om hack OV-chipkaart".
285 Interview with Maker H.
286 Bart Jacobs, "Security and privacy issues in transport and beyond" 295.
287 Bart Jacobs, "Security and privacy issues in transport and beyond" 292.
288 Interview with Maker L.

289 Interview with Maker J.
290 TNO, "Security analysis of the Dutch OV-ChipKaart" 11–12; interview with Hacktivist E.
291 Bart Jacobs, "Security and privacy issues in transport and beyond" 295.
292 Interview with Maker H; see also TNO, "Security Analysis of the Dutch OV-ChipKaart" 12.
293 Interview with Maker L.
294 Interview with Maker J.
295 Interview with Hacktivist A.
296 See TNO, "Security analysis of the Dutch OV-ChipKaart" 11–12.
297 Interview with Ethical Hacker B.
298 Interview with Maker H.
299 Interview with Maker G.
300 Interview with Maker H.
301 Bart Jacobs, "Security and privacy issues in transport and beyond" 294.
302 Bart Jacobs, "Security and privacy issues in transport and beyond" 293.
303 Interview with Hacktivist B.
304 Interview with Hacktivist B.
305 Interview with Hacktivist A.
306 Interview with Maker G.
307 Interview with Maker L.
308 Interview.
309 Interview.
310 Joris van Hoboken, "Relaunch bits of freedom!"; see also see also Bits of Freedom "Nieuwsbrief Nr. 6.15".
311 OHM2013, "Village: Noisy square".
312 Interview with Maker L.
313 Bits of Freedom, "Position paper netwerkneutraliteit"; see also Roslyn Layton, "Net neutrality in the Netherlands: Dutch solution or Dutch disease?" Florence, Italy, 20–23 October 2013, 9.
314 Andreas Udo de Haes, "KPN luistert abonnees af met Deep packet inspection"; see also Bits of Freedom, "Onze Successen"; see also Parker Higgins, "The Netherlands passes net neutrality legislation"; see also Roslyn Layton, "Net neutrality in The Netherlands: Dutch solution or Dutch disease?" Florence, Italy, 20–23 October 2013, 9; see also Kevin O'Brien, "Dutch Lawmakers adopt net neutrality law".
315 Roslyn Layton, "Net neutrality in the Netherlands: Dutch solution or Dutch disease?" Florence, Italy, 20–23 October 2013, 5 and 9; see also Nico van Eijk, "Net neutrality in practice, the Dutch example"; see also Archibald Preuschat, "KPN admits to using deep packet inspection"; see also Kevin O'Brien, "Dutch Lawmakers adopt net neutrality law".
316 Roslyn Layton, "Net neutrality in the Netherlands: Dutch solution or Dutch disease?" Florence, Italy, 20–23 October 2013, 33; see also Archibald Preuschat, "KPN admits to using deep packet inspection".
317 Interview with Maker L.
318 Interview with Hacktivist F.
319 Interview with Maker J.
320 Bits of Freedom, "Onze Successen"; see also Roslyn Layton, "Net neutrality in the Netherlands: Dutch solution or Dutch disease?" Florence, Italy, 20–23 October 2013, 10 and 11.
321 Interview with Maker L.
322 Ot van Daalen, "Netherlands First Country in Europe with Net Neutrality".

323 Roslyn Layton, "Net neutrality in the Netherlands: Dutch solution or Dutch disease?" Florence, Italy, 20–23 October 2013, 5 and 34.
324 Interview.
325 Roslyn Layton, "Net neutrality in the Netherlands: Dutch solution or Dutch disease?" Florence, Italy, 20–23 October 2013, 9 and 10; see also Nico van Eijk, "Net neutrality in practice, the Dutch example" 10; see also Parker Higgins, "The Netherlands passes net neutrality legislation"; see also Kevin O'Brien, "Dutch lawmakers adopt net neutrality law".
326 Kevin O'Brien, "Dutch lawmakers adopt net neutrality law".
327 Nico van Eijk, "Net neutrality in practice, the Dutch example" 11; see also Ot van Daalen, "Netherlands first country in Europe with net neutrality"; see also Roslyn Layton, "Net neutrality in The Netherlands: Dutch solution or Dutch disease?" Florence, Italy, 20–23 October 2013, 11.
328 Nico van Eijk, "Net neutrality in practice, the Dutch example" 7; see also Ot van Daalen, "Netherlands first country in Europe with net neutrality"; see also Kevin O'Brien, "Dutch lawmakers adopt net neutrality law"; see also interview with Maker L.
329 Ot van Daalen, "Netherlands first country in Europe with net neutrality"
330 Ot van Daalen, "Netherlands first country in Europe with net neutrality".
331 Roslyn Layton, "Net neutrality in the Netherlands: Dutch solution or Dutch disease?" Florence, Italy, 20–23 October 2013, 4; see also Ot van Daalen, "Netherlands first country in Europe with net neutrality".
332 Interview.
333 Interview.
334 Parker Higgins, "The Netherlands passes net neutrality legislation".
335 Nico van Eijk, "Net neutrality in practice, the Dutch example" 9–10; see also Parker Higgins, "The Netherlands passes net neutrality legislation".
336 Interview with Maker L.
337 Ot van Daalen, "Netherlands first country in Europe with net neutrality".
338 Bits of Freedom, "Translations of key dutch internet freedom provisions".
339 Kevin O'Brien, "Dutch lawmakers adopt net neutrality law".
340 Bits of Freedom, "Translations of key Dutch internet freedom provisions".
341 Bits of Freedom, "Translations of key Dutch internet freedom provisions".
342 Kevin O'Brien, "Dutch lawmakers adopt net neutrality law".
343 Interview with Maker J; interview with Maker L.
344 Interview with Maker L.
345 Interview with Hacktivist F.
346 Interview with Hacktivist F; see also Ot van Daalen, "Netherlands first country in Europe with net neutrality".
347 Interview with Maker J.
348 Interview with Hacktivist F.
349 Interview with Maker L.
350 Interview with Hacktivist B.
351 Interview with Hacktivist D.
352 Interview with Maker I.
353 Interview with Maker I.
354 Interview with Hacktivist B.
355 Interview with Maker I.
356 Interview with Hacktivist C.
357 Anna Kaziunas France, "Shiny! new! ultimaker 2!"; see also 3D Hubs Blog, "Open source 3D printers stand up to giants stratasys and 3D systems".
358 Interview with Maker G.

359 Interview with Maker K.
360 Interview with Ethical Hacker B.
361 Interview with Maker D.
362 Interview with Maker D.
363 Interview with Hacktivist A.
364 Interview with Hacktivist A.
365 Interview with Hacktivist A.
366 Interview with Maker H.
367 Interview.
368 Interview.
369 Interview.
370 Interview with Maker I.
371 Interview with Maker I.
372 Interview with Maker I.

Chapter 6

Normative conclusions and areas of law reform

Normative implications

Hackers as technical, social and legal actors

As borne out in the preceding chapters, hackers are highly technical yet socially aware individuals and communities. Technology lies at the heart of their culture and all of their practices and activities involve or revolve around it. Hackers are exceedingly passionate about technology and they desire to understand how it works in order to improve their personal knowledge and skills and also to produce something new, innovative or surprising from it. Makers and hacktivists hack and build all sorts of technologies from 3D printers and other digital fabrication tools to encryption and security software. While they can admittedly be playful and cause some disruption with their hacking projects and activities, they are not motivated by malice and they do not willfully or intentionally cause damage. They are simply curious about technology and what interesting things they can do with it. Despite their seemingly inordinate focus and possibly even obsession with technical matters, makers and hacktivists are very socially conscious and responsible. They are quite sociable, have a strong sense of community and care much about the impact of technology on society. Even though they cherish the personal values of creativity and innovation, curiosity and individual autonomy and liberty, in practice, these always go hand-in-hand with the more communitarian goals of community development and social development. For example, makers may get personal gratification from building a laser cutter or CNC machine from scratch but they are not completely satisfied with their work unless they are able to share what they learned with others and their creations have a positive impact on society. Similarly, hacktivists do their utmost to protect not only their own security and privacy but also those of others.

Makers and hacktivists are not only internally and community focused, but also outwardly and socially oriented. While they may have issues with public authorities and certain hacking-related laws, they are willing to engage with and change technology laws and policies so as to uphold and protect fundamental rights and freedoms and democratic values. As seen in Chapter 5, hacktivists hacked the electronic voting machines to protect the right to vote and the secrecy of the ballot and preserve the validity of the electoral system. In the cases of Leaktober and the hacking of the OV-chipcard, hackers sought to highlight and safeguard the important values of security and privacy in public and private information systems. Furthermore, through the net neutrality campaign and the development and use of open source projects, hackers worked within the legal system to achieve the goals of greater openness, transparency and freedom of access to technology. These examples illustrate how hackers, as non-state actors, can have a significant influence on the substance and implementation of laws and play an important role in the governance of the networked information society.

Resolving conflicts by building on commonalities

While the relations and interactions between hacking and law are complex and often tense, given that they essentially share some of the same social goals, it may be possible to lessen or resolve the conflicts between them by building on the values they hold in common. Public authorities have worked with and supported different types of hackers before. The hacking projects and activities of the original computer hackers at MIT were encouraged and funded by the US government, and a number of countries are promoting the adoption and use of FOSS.[1] As illustrated in the enactment of net neutrality legislation in the Netherlands, hackers and public authorities can align their priorities and goals and work to preserve open and equal access to the internet.

Of course, the ability of hackers and public authorities to resolve some of their differences and work for a common purpose is heavily dependent on their level of trust, understanding and willingness to work with the other. A key consideration in this regard is their general animosity to each other. As explained in Chapter 5, the aversion of hackers to public authorities is founded on their anti-establishment spirit and their overall dislike of centralized authorities, hierarchies and bureaucracies. It may be possible though to narrow the gap and bring hackers and public authorities closer together if both sides develop a more tolerant or empathetic view of each other.

With regard to hackers, while it is true that they mistrust public authorities,[2] they are not completely against the latter. The campaign against electronic voting machines is particularly noteworthy and can shed light on this issue. I was initially perplexed by the apparent contradiction: why were hackers so concerned about the dangers of electronic voting and the importance of preserving the security and integrity of the electoral process, when it ultimately resulted in the election of public officials? If hackers really despised public authority (as most of them claim), would it not have served their purposes better to allow the continued use of the voting machines and then subsequently show the problems with the voting process, and thus call into question the authority of elected public officials? I believe that, in the same manner that hackers understand law in two different senses (i.e., as restrictive or unjust prescriptions of centralized authorities but also as the foundation or source of fundamental rights and freedom), hackers similarly conceive of public authorities in two distinct ways. Hackers mainly see public authorities as embodiments of centralized power and control, but they also consider authorities to be representatives or agents of the demos. While hackers may oppose the former conception of public authorities, they are willing to support the latter notion. By de-emphasizing their concerns about the risks and threats of centralized control and power and seeing authorities as public servants who equally strive to achieve liberal democratic goals, hackers can have a fairer and more nuanced view of public authorities. With this change of perspective, makers and hacktivists would be more willing to constructively engage with state actors if they see themselves not so much as *working for or under* a centralized authority, but *working in common* with them to protect or advance democratic systems and values. With regard to public authorities, the following sections explain how, due in part to their better understanding and appreciation of hacker culture, they have started to adopt and implement policies that support hacking.

Support and reach out to hackers

Given the above findings and the fact that hackers hold and share principally the same liberal democratic principles and goals that governments seek to protect and promote and they do not engage in malicious activities or intend to cause damage, it would be more productive if the law and public authorities viewed and treated hackers as co-participants, collaborators or equal partners in the development of technology laws and policies, especially with regard to those laws that particularly affect hacking. Responsible disclosure and open data are two of the most noteworthy examples of hackers and public authorities in the Netherlands constructively working together. These two cases demonstrate how supporting and reaching out to hackers is a more practical and useful alternative to dealing with hacking than criminal prosecution.

Responsible disclosure

Responsible disclosure rules

Recognizing the difficult and complex nature of computer security, public authorities are beginning to adopt policies that acknowledge and support the crucial roles that hackers play in protecting and improving the security and safety of public and private information networks and systems.[3] In the Netherlands, the Ministry of Security and Justice through the National Cyber Security Centre (NCSC) issued a "Policy for arriving at a practice for Responsible Disclosure" in early 2013.[4] The central goal of the responsible disclosure guideline is to establish a policy framework that clarifies the roles and responsibilities of hackers and owners of computer systems and encourages them to adhere to practices and processes for the expedient and efficient discovery, disclosure and rectification of security vulnerabilities.[5] The responsible disclosure guideline seeks to accomplish these goals by setting out the basic principles and actions that both the discloser and the system owner must follow or perform.[6] The guideline, for instance, provides that the system owner is primarily responsible for its security.[7]

Pursuant to the guideline, a discloser of a security vulnerability (who is usually an ethical hacker or security researcher) should report the vulnerability first and "as quickly as is reasonably possible" to the system owner or administrator.[8] In reporting the vulnerability, the discloser must do so "in a manner that safeguards the confidentiality of the report".[9] With regard to the discovery of the vulnerability, the discloser's actions "must not be disproportionate".[10] The guideline lists a number of acts that are considered disproportionate or improper, including the discloser "using social engineering", "building his or her own backdoor", "using brute force attack to gain access to the system", or "copying, modifying or deleting data on the system".[11] Under the guideline, rather than copying data to prove that he or she was able to gain access, the discloser should simply make "a directory listing of the system".[12]

On their part, system owners and administrators are encouraged to draft and implement their own responsible disclosure policies and make them publicly available and accessible so that hackers and security researchers are aware of what systems and data they can access and test, what techniques they can use and what procedures they should follow.[13] Pursuant to the guideline, a system owner's responsible disclosure policy should also explicitly state whether it would decline "to take legal action where the discloser acts in accordance with the policy".[14] In addition, when they receive a vulnerability report, system owners should have an "adequate response" and this may entail contacting the discloser to discuss the vulnerability, entering into a contract or agreement with the discloser that sets out how the vulnerability and its disclosure will be handled, and keeping the discloser informed about the progress of the rectification process.[15] Furthermore, in consultation with the discloser, the system owner or administrator must decide if or when the vulnerability is disclosed to the wider security community and the public at large.[16] Under the guideline, the standard term for fixing software vulnerabilities is 60 days, while for hardware it is six months.[17] The system owner is also urged to give "the discloser credit for the report, if the discloser so desires" or even "some form of remuneration/recognition" for discovering and disclosing the security vulnerability.[18]

The responsible disclosure guideline is compatible with the developing practice of bug bounty programs. Through bug bounty programs, companies actively solicit hackers and security researchers to find and report computer bugs and security vulnerabilities in their systems, software and services by publicly offering rewards for such reports and disclosures.[19] The rationale behind bug bounties is founded on a well-known hacker principle dubbed Linus's Law (named after Linus Torvalds, the creator of Linux), which states that "Given enough eyeballs, all bugs are shallow".[20] Within the information security industry, it is acknowledged that one "can't rely on automated approaches or occasional consultants. You need a big group with a diverse set of skills constantly probing your system for weakness".[21] With bug bounty programs, companies can "tap into the supply of global hackers" and "they are cheaper than hiring full-time security research-ers".[22] Within a short period of time, bug bounty programs have become a widely accepted practice in the information technology industry, and major companies like Google, Microsoft and PayPal now offer gifts, recognition and even sig-nificant sums of money to hackers who discover and disclose bugs pursuant to prescribed procedures,[23] which hew closely to the extant responsible disclosure practices of ethical hackers and security researchers.[24] Offering bug bounties for security vulnerabilities is also spreading to other industries.[25]

From a legal and policy perspective, the responsible disclosure guideline is quite noteworthy for a number of reasons. First, it expressly acknowledges that there are ethical hackers and security researchers who are not interested in maliciously accessing or damaging computers but are motivated to "improving the safety of ICT systems by probing vulnerabilities and risks".[26] Their aims are "exposing vulnerabilities in public and government systems to improve system and network security, while promoting advances in technology and consumer protection".[27] Second, the guideline was a result of and based on consultations and open dis-cussions with a number of public and private stakeholders including members of the hacker and computer security communities.[28] Third, it emphasizes the importance of a cooperative and collaborative approach that brings together hackers, private organizations and the government to work together as partners on "the common goal of increasing the security of information systems".[29] It is particularly noteworthy how the NCSC has played a pivotal role in serving as an intermediary between hackers and private organizations.[30] In one case, when a vulnerability was reported to a company, the company "didn't act initially" so the discloser "had to ask the NCSC and then they pressured them into a response and then finally they did something about it".[31] "In the end, it did help that the NCSC worked with" the discloser "to tell them that this was actually very serious and that they had to do something about it. That helps".[32] Finally, the principles and rules contained in the responsible disclosure guideline are based on and may be considered a codification of the actual and existing customs, practices and pro-cesses of security researchers and other hackers involved in computer security.[33]

The responsible disclosure guideline manifests a changing attitude of public authorities towards hackers, and is an example of a pragmatic and nuanced regu-lation that constructively responds to and takes into account some of the tech-nical and social benefits of hacking. But certain issues and limitations remain. The guideline is best characterized as a form of soft law for government actors, organizations and hackers to voluntarily follow. This means that, while the guide-line is highly persuasive, it is not in itself legally binding or enforceable.[34] Further, it does not create a legal exemption from liability for hackers since even if a system owner's policy expressly provides that

no police report will be filed if the reporter has acted in accordance with the agreements. The independent power of the Public Prosecutor to proceed with the prosecution if the suspicion exists that a crime has been committed will continue to exist.[35]

As confirmed by the Dutch Board of Procurators General, after and in response to the issuance of the NCSC's guideline,

> If, in revealing the vulnerability, the person making the report has committed a punishable act, the responsible reporting of the vulnerability does not in any way safeguard him against the police . . . a criminal investigation, and/ or that legal proceedings may ensue.[36]

So, even if a system owner has a responsible disclosure policy in place and a discloser has complied with both the general guideline and the specific policy in disclosing the security vulnerability, the Public Prosecution Service may still pursue the matter further as "it may be necessary first to instigate a criminal investigation and to regard the hacker as a suspect" to be able "to discover whether a reporting by a hacker was necessary and proportional under the given circumstances".[37] Of course, if it is determined that a discloser acted properly pursuant to the responsible disclosure rules, the investigation should not lead to prosecution.[38]

Hackers' reactions

As can be expected, members of the Dutch hacker community have mixed feelings about the responsible disclosure rules. According to Maker G, "I know people who are in favor of the current rules, I know people who are against them".[39] Some hackers believe that the guideline is part of an attempt by public authorities to co-opt or recruit hackers to work for government.[40] "I think part of the reason is the NCSC is a governmental agency and they started promoting the responsible disclosure procedure", explains Maker J, "I know that this is something that is felt among some of the hackers".[41] In addition to their general distrust of things produced by a centralized authority, hackers' negative opinions about responsible disclosure guideline mostly center on the fact that it does not provide a legal exemption from criminal prosecution. As Hacktivist B says, "I think it's is a complete façade. Because, in the end, whether or not you're prosecuted is still up to the public prosecutor".[42] Maker L recounts, "the Justice Department said, even if you follow those rules, we may still want to, we think it's good to prosecute you. We are still allowed to prosecute you".[43] Ethical Hacker A further elaborates on their dissatisfaction,

> That's why I don't fully agree with the content. It says, well if you're the researcher, you should do this and this and this and this and this and that. And if you do that, we cannot guarantee anything. Yah, ok, so why should I do it in the first place?[44]

On top of that, "even if the company says, 'Great job, no problem that you did it', the government still can prosecute you without any claim from the company itself".[45] The perennial threat of prosecution is thus a clear disincentive to complying with the guideline or making a disclosure at all. Reporting security vulnerabilities is very risky because "you are making yourself very vulnerable because you're saying, yes, I hacked your organization and I found this problem".[46] Another issue with the responsible disclosure guideline is that, for the rules to actually apply, system owners must put the rules into effect by creating their own responsible disclosure policies. Maker H explains,

> So if you don't have any procedures in your organization and someone comes along and says 'I have this', they would adhere to the strictest responsible disclosure that are applied elsewhere but nonetheless are not [free from liability]. And then it says, by and large, even when you have followed these rules we still may be able to prosecute you.[47]

Aside from the lack of an express legal exemption from prosecution in the responsible disclosure rules, several hackers also took issue with the very use of the term "responsible disclosure". Maker J states that the term is "a bit ill-chosen . . . because responsible disclosure puts the act with the hacker, with the discloser, saying that it is his responsibility to act responsibly".[48] Hacktivist D agrees, "As far as I know, now the rules are a little bit lopsided. They do protect the companies quite a bit, not so much the person exposing the vulnerability".[49] And to make matters worse, "the biggest problem is there's been a bad track record with companies not dealing . . . well with people saying what they are doing wrong" and who expose security vulnerabilities.[50] "I think it's not really clear how [or] who takes responsibility for" the security issues that were discovered, says Ethical Hacker B.[51] Moreover, Hacktivists B believes, "I think it trivializes responsible disclosure" because "what is and what isn't responsible isn't in every case an individual ethical dilemma, which cannot be formalized in like a rule or one policy".[52] In Hacktivists F's view, "To me this is about the individual's responsible disclosure".[53] Hacktivist E also has concerns about how public authorities may interpret the meaning of responsible:

> I do find the name "responsible disclosure" a bit troublesome: it seems to imply that any disclosure that does not comply with it is irresponsible. Probably disclosures have occurred that NCSC would consider to be irresponsible . . . that I would consider to be acceptable [or] reasonable.[54]

Maker J prefers the term "coordinated disclosure" because "it's actually more of a coordinated process, where they both have to" work together to resolve the security issue.[55]

Despite these issues and concerns, a number of hackers have a relatively positive opinion of the responsible disclosure rules.[56] Maker J thinks the guideline is "very good",[57] and Maker D says, "I like it. It's good. It's change".[58] Maker H is critical yet pragmatic about the rules, "I would say that I'm not happy with the responsible disclosure rules as they are. However in practice they seem to be working reasonably well".[59] Ethical Hacker A holds a similar view, "I do not fully agree with the content but I'm really happy with the process. . . . The content can be better but the process of addressing the issue is ok".[60] Like other hackers, Hacktivist D generally considers the guideline to be a step in the right direction because "in principle, of course, it's good to protect people who try to do good by exposing vulnerabilities".[61] For Hacktivist E, "I consider the guideline to be a good development because it may trigger organizations into establishing a some-what hacker-friendly disclosure policy".[62] Hacktivist E further explains how the guideline "helps clarify communications between organizations and those who want to report vulnerabilities. Hopefully, organizations will embrace unsolicited vulnerability reports rather than fear or fight them. Then we're all be better off in the end".[63] Hacktivist F points out though that aside from being "long overdue", the adoption of the guideline is "simple . . . not rocket science".[64] "I have a hard time thinking of how if you're a sane and sensible person you would come to any-where else than sort of a responsible disclosure measure", explains Hacktivist F.[65]

Changing attitudes, changing laws

For all of its above benefits and shortcomings, what is truly remarkable about the responsible disclosure guideline is that it codifies or formalizes existing customs and practices of hackers and security researchers. Rather than being determined or imposed from the top-down, the responsible disclosure rules were developed from the bottom-up and are based on the social norms and values of the relevant community or society – in this case, hackers.[66] Ethical Hacker B confirms, "to be fair, before the law was there, we did it in this way. The law actually describes exactly what we do".[67] "We always did that. . . . They [the NCSC] kind of basi-cally wrote down what we were already doing for years. So yeah, I'm totally happy with" this development.[68] The procedures and processes prescribed by the guideline are not new to hackers. Ethical Hacker A recounts, "we had the discussions, if you were interested at the time. This type of discussions started in the '90s with Microsoft, for example. With the bugs, and what should you do, should you do full disclosure or not. And that was a 1990s discussion".[69] "Most people . . . I know they respect at least the part of informing the target system or the company that runs the target system first. Wait for their response and do something", explains Ethical Hacker A, "As long as the process of informing someone, giving them a reasonable amount of time to fix it and then disclosing. As long as that process is followed I'm comfortable with that".[70]

What also makes the responsible disclosure rules exceptional is that they exhibit a changing response of the law to hacking. Instead of attempting to restrict or control, public authorities and private companies are trying to constructively sup-port and reach out to hackers. The benefit of having a formal responsible disclo-sure guideline is that "you can show" system owners that "on a government level they're also working on it. And if they're already working on it on a government level, well then it's well accepted".[71] Maker H notes how "by and large, people in the industries affected feel, yes we should deal with that, not bring out the full brunt of the law and try to find a middle ground".[72] The change of attitude is taking place among public authorities as well. Maker J relates, "I've had discussions and I think we're seeing now that judges are looking at these kind of things. . . . If you follow the responsible disclosure guidelines they will take you seriously and they see this as you acting responsibly".[73] Even the Board of Procurators General expresses the opinion that Dutch law

> does not provide a specific defense for a hacker who is acting out of ideological or ethical motives. Although the law does not provide for it, this does not mean that 'ethical' motives cannot play any role in assessing the criminality of the perpetrator's actions.[74]

The responsible disclosure rules are indeed a significant step in the right direction and other countries should adopt similar rules. However, as Ethical Hacker B remarks, "I do like that it is changing, but I think we're not there" yet.[75] It is my position that the responsible disclosure rules can still be improved by either: including an express legal exemption for security research in computer crime or other relevant laws;[76] or getting a court or another adjudicatory body to render a ruling and establish a precedent or jurisprudence that no crime is committed and no liability should attach when activities are done pursuant to the responsible disclosure rules. With regard to the first proposal, I am convinced that this legislative change of granting a legal exemption for security research, while useful from the perspective of the expressive function of law,[77] will take a lot of time and effort to implement and may not even be necessary. It should be recalled that "without right" is an essential requisite of each of the first four types of computer security crimes discussed in Chapter 4. It is my view that if system owners have responsible disclosure policies that explicitly solicit or permit the public (including hackers) to test their systems (e.g., through bug bounty programs),[78] then this amounts to their express consent or authorization to hackers to explore and hack their systems.[79] Since such access and use are with right or permission, an essential element of the crime is lacking and there would be no legal ground for any criminal prosecution. Furthermore, it behooves Dutch public prosecutors, especially in light of their prosecutorial discretion,[80] to refrain from commencing or pursuing any investigation against a discloser or hacker who has complied with the responsible disclosure rules because, absent a complaint from the system owner or other evidence that such consent was subsequently withdrawn, no crime has *prima facie* been committed since such access and use are presumptively lawful based on the express consent or authorization given by the system owners in their responsible disclosure policies.[81] The second proposal can be promptly realized if a relevant court or judicial body agrees with the above legal reasoning and interpretation and formally enters a judgment stating that no legal liability attaches if a person has complied with the responsible disclosure rules. A more expedient solution would be to include in a Guideline or Directive

of the Public Prosecutor a principle or rule that no criminal investigation or prosecution should be undertaken if a discloser has complied with the system owner's
responsible disclosure policy since such access is authorized.

Open data

Policies and initiatives

Open data policies and initiatives are another notable example of the law and
public authorities productively reaching out to and embracing hacker culture.
An open data policy is normally enacted through a legislative or policy measure,
initiative or program of a national, regional or local state body.[82] The European
Commission, for instance, amended the PSI Directive[83] to encourage the re-use
of public data and make laws and policies across Europe more amendable to public access and innovative uses of such data in light of new and emerging technologies.[84] The Commission even adopted a Decision on the Re-use of Commission
Information covering its own data and how to make it as widely accessible and
reusable as possible.[85] There are a number of countries that have open data policies.[86] The United States and the United Kingdom have publicized their open
data strategies.[87] In Europe, the Netherlands, France and Italy have established
online portals for public data.[88] As Maker B recounts, "The notion of open data is
very old, but it started to get public awareness when Tim Berners-Lee had a TED
talk about it" and "had a plea for opening up data from governments".[89] Maker
B continues, "in the Netherlands . . . people started to work with it" as well.[90]

The idea of making existing public data freely available to ordinary citizens
and users to re-use and build on has captured the interest of many state actors
because of the potential political, social and economic benefits.[91] Policy makers
wish to support open data because it may produce economic growth, improve
social welfare, and lead to scientific and technical advancements.[92] Governments
are further motivated to promote open data because, by being or appearing
to be more inclusive and transparent, it may improve their own administrative
operations and their relationships with their citizens.[93] As the European Commission explains, "Beyond fuelling the innovation and creativity that stimulate
economic growth, open public data also empowers citizens, thereby enhancing
participatory democracy and promoting transparent, accountable and more efficient government".[94] Open data policies are generally embodied in or carried out
through four types of measures, namely: "(a) education and training, (b) voluntary approaches, (c) economic instruments and (d) legislation and control".[95]
As Huijboom and Van den Broek explain, education and training programs can
involve knowledge exchange platforms, guidelines, and conferences, sessions and
workshops.[96] Voluntary approaches may consist of overall strategies and programs, general recommendations, and public voluntary schemes; while economic
instruments include competitions, app contests and camps (e.g., hackathons),
and financing of open data portals.[97] Finally, open data legislation or regulation

can take the form of public sector information laws, freedom of information acts, and technical standards and monitoring.[98]

While public authorities visibly champion open data, the main "drivers lie predominantly outside government. . . . Important drivers for open data policy are for instance citizen pressure, market initiatives, emerging technologies and the ideas of thought leaders".[99] In contrast, the primary obstacles to open data can be found within governments themselves such as "the closed culture, limited quality of data, lack of standardization and existing charging models".[100] These general observations are evident as well in the Dutch experience of open data. "On the top, the Dutch government, and the city council, and the mayor . . . everybody is happy with open data. They say, 'Yes, we have to do it'," narrates Maker B, "But then there's this middle layer in organizations. They are trained to keep data away from people, to close it in dossiers".[101] Maker L relays the experience of getting access to public data: the data is sort of available "but it's not like they have a big website. Here is our open data, here's an API, get it out of there, and those kinds of things".[102] And, "if you want to have some more [data], you can ask them".[103] So, while public data is technically available, it is not easily accessible by the public. As Maker L says, "There is a lot of open data, but it needs to be used. The people need to be able to find it, and I don't think they promoted it enough to let people use it".[104] It appears then that, for open data to really succeed, public authorities themselves need to be more open, transparent and willing to collaborate with others. "To get really good open data it requires a change in practice . . . of a lot of people" in government, argues Maker B.[105] The impediments then to open data are primarily "cultural because the technical . . . can be solved".[106] Of course, the systems for accessing and using such public data must themselves promote the principles of openness, transparency, and freedom of access. As Maker L says, "others have nice sites where they published everything . . . you could download, easy to use".[107] Maker L continues, "I think if they really want to have open data then they should make it more a priority and promote it".[108]

Hackathons

Among the many types of open data projects and initiatives, open data hackathons are especially noteworthy because, aside from their growing popularity, they recognize and manifest the importance of free and open access to and use of information as a matter of public policy. A hackathon, which is portmanteau of the words "hacking" and "marathon", is defined as a "periodic event where programmers get together at some venue to collaboratively create a new application or software system within a few hours or a few days".[109] Companies like Facebook regularly organize hackathons among its employees to spur the development of new technologies and applications.[110] Open data hackathons are a type of hackathon where public sector information (PSI) (i.e., "information produced, collected or paid for by public organisations") is re-used to produce new products and services for commercial and non-commercial use.[111] These hackathons are conducted under the auspices of governments' open data policies that encourage the organization of "events to award innovative service creation based on public data".[112] The main goal of hackathons is the creation of new applications and technical innovations that produce "innovation, growth and transparency" in society, the economy and government, respectively.[113] As Maker D explains, a hackathon is a convenient "way of getting a lot of people together doing technological activities. It's very good".[114] According to Maker B, hackers "are totally happy with the idea of open data. They want to do things with it".[115] Maker B continues, "the power of real open data is that you make applications and networks . . . with it" such as "social related apps and also smart embedded electronics".[116]

Open data hackathons are taking place all over the world and they are among the most visible and well-publicized activities concerning open data.[117] They generate much interest and attention from both the public and private sectors because the applications and technologies developed at these events can have significant socio-economic impacts. Examples of successful software and services that were developed during hackathons include Taarifa (an open source web platform for finding working water points in Africa),[118] GroupMe (a group text messaging app that was acquired by Skype for US$80M),[119] Appetas (a website builder for restaurants that was purchased by Google),[120] and Easy Taxi (a taxi hailing mobile app).[121] In the Netherlands, open data hackathons have been held in various cities with the support of local governments and private individuals and groups.[122] During the nationwide activities of the *Open Innovatie Festival 2012* (Open Innovation Festival 2012) in the Netherlands, I participated in a hackathon in Leeuwarden.[123] Quite interestingly, the national theme for that year was "mutiny" and, quoting Steve Jobs, their motto was "It's more fun to be a pirate than to join the Navy".[124] Dubbed "Kickstart058", the hackathon was jointly organized by the municipal council and the local hackerspace Frack.[125] The 24-hour "hack the government" event was aimed at finding "new ways of working together . . . between government, knowledge institutions, citizens and entrepreneurs".[126] While the organizers of the hackathon sought the development of apps that produced "social and economic value", greater emphasis and preference seem to have been placed on innovations with commercial application or economic impact.[127] The organizers specifically sought to stimulate "new business opportunities" through the creation of new applications and services based on public data provided by the municipality of Leeuwarden and the province of Friesland.[128] It is quite notable that one of the stated criteria for selecting the winner of the hackathon was that "the application can be made profitable. This would require a business model that is clear and an idea that is viable".[129] Participants could access and re-use data sources such as, among others, population figures, social services information, housing income, migration statistics, economic figures, unemployment numbers, spatial plans and city maps.[130] It is worth noting that while the municipality was very open to giving access to its data and had technical people on hand to help assist participants, the teams had some difficulties fully working with or using the data since the latter were saved in file formats or stored in databases that were not as easily accessible, interoperable or extractable.

As with most hackathons, there was no fee to enter the event and it was open to the public.[131] "Officials, entrepreneurs, artists, students and professionals" were especially encouraged to participate.[132] Even people with no technical expertise or background were enjoined to take part since the conceptualization, marketing and distribution of a new application or product would require non-technical skills as well.[133] During the hackathon, government employees, hackers, students and designers formed and worked in teams on various projects such as an augmented reality mobile app that showed cultural and historical information as the user walked around the municipality, a web-based crowd funding service for community projects, and a housing website. During the 24 hours that the teams worked on their projects, the atmosphere was convivial, although some hackers felt that some of their team members, particularly those who worked for the municipality, were too critical and not open to suggestions. In the end, the augmented reality app that was originally proposed and developed by local design students was awarded the prize, which included the allocation of development time for the app from a local technology company.

Despite the numerous hackathons being held throughout the Netherlands, it is true that they have yet to produce a truly novel "killer application" that can produce significant or far-reaching socio-economic effects that are much sought after. Maker B admits that "there's no big breakthrough, I think, resulting from the open data movement" in the Netherlands.[134] Maker D agrees, "Yeah, there are a lot of people who are still inspired, still doing good stuff, but [no] really killer app".[135] Of course, the applications and technologies developed during open data hackathons are nonetheless quite useful for their intended audiences and offer much value in their own right. Nevertheless, the lack of a killer app and the difficulties of inculcating the values of freedom of access, openness and transparency in government have led to a perceived decline in the interest in open data. Among makers, there is a sentiment that the hype around open data has already peaked and the government's support for open data has started to wane. "I think there was a momentum at one point but the momentum went away a bit", relates Maker L, "In the end, [it] slowed down and died a bit".[136] For makers, taking part in hackathons "was very interesting. We learned a lot about it. We had a nice amount of fun . . . but there was not a lot of follow up" from government.[137] Maker B observes that "there's a lot of progress in different directions and different fields but it is crawling and it's spread . . . it's not one big breakthrough".[138]

Notwithstanding these problems and setbacks, open data policies and hackathons attest to a shift in technology law and policy whereby public authorities seek not only to promote greater availability of and access to public data, but also to openly support innovative and creative uses of that data. This change of policy and attitude towards hackers is all the more significant given that the public visibility of hackathons provides hacking with a sense of acceptance and legitimacy. Furthermore, open data hackathons illustrate how public authorities, hackers and ordinary citizens can come together to produce techno-social change and innovation.[139]

Change and improve the law

Responsible disclosure rules and open data hackathons are indicators of a discernable change in direction and orientation of technology laws and policies whereby public authorities have begun to see the benefits and desirability of welcoming and even embracing hacker culture and constructively collaborating with hackers. However, in order to genuinely and meaningfully improve the laws concerning hacking and to encourage hacking's creativity and innovation, existing computer crime, intellectual property and other relevant laws must be changed bearing in mind the attendant practices, norms and values of hackers. As set out below, the proposed legal reforms can be achieved through legislative amendments, judicial rulings, and/or executive interpretations and implementations.

Computer crime laws

Hacking as a legitimate and common activity

Improving the treatment of hackers under the law requires a change in how hacking is viewed and dealt with by public authorities. As previously mentioned in Chapter 4, computer crime laws provide that "legitimate and common activities inherent in the design of networks, or legitimate and common operating or commercial practices should not be criminalised".[140] This means that social norms and customary practices in the field of information and communications technology should be taken into account when determining whether an activity is legitimate and common.

From the early computer hackers at MIT to present-day makers and hacktivists,[141] it is evident that hacking, which is basically the creative and innovative use of technology, has always been present and is an integral part of the creation and development of computers and information technologies and networks. There are compelling grounds to argue that hacking is the quintessential activity or practice in the fields of computing and information technology. Verily, is there any other activity or practice that is as singular and inherent in the design and use of computers and information networks as hacking? While this claim may sound radical at first, it is borne out by the symbiotic histories of hacking and technological advances. Hackers and hacking have been the driving force behind the invention or subsequent innovation of many world-changing technologies such as personal computers, open source and commercial software, computer gaming, the internet, the World Wide Web, encryption, peer-to-peer file sharing, social networking sites and personal 3D printers, to name a few.[142] When it comes to information technology, hacking is neither aberrant nor illicit because, in actuality, it embodies the very essence of technical creativity and innovation. Hacking is a creative rather than a criminal activity since it is normally carried out for useful purposes and without any malice or intent to cause damage. For a practice that has produced so much socio-technical breakthroughs, how can it be viewed as anything but a legitimate and common activity? The creative and unexpected uses of technology, which hacking epitomizes, are socially accepted and expected not just among hackers but also the growing number of users who desire to have greater freedom and control over their technologies. Hacking definitely resides at the very heart of technological innovation and is in itself an unmistakably legitimate and common practice.

It should be remembered that, like any element or aspect of culture, technical practices and usages in the field of information and communications technology are never static and they are constantly developing, changing and evolving. It may be said that given the premium that both hackers and the information technology industry place on continually producing innovation and furthering technical advances, technological activities and practices intrinsically demand the pushing of boundaries (whether they be technical, legal or social) in order to create something new, different or surprising. Being innovative necessitates the freedom to use technology in unusual, unexpected and creative ways, which is what hacking is all about. Hacking and the creative-destructive dynamic that it engenders are therefore, not only legitimate and common, but also essential for technological and social progress. Hacking projects and activities that are carried out without malice or intent to cause damage should be supported rather than proscribed by technology law and policy.

Essential requirement of criminal intent

Beyond the shadow of a doubt, the most consequential improvement to hacking-related laws would be the reform of computer crime laws, particularly in relation to illegal access and other computer security crimes. As discussed at length in Chapter 4, computer security crimes are overly broad and vague and the law over-criminalizes hacking. The law fails to properly distinguish between malicious attacks and attackers and the innovative albeit disruptive activities of hackers. The most sensible approach to improve computer crime laws is to include the subjective criteria of malice, dishonest intent or intent to cause damage as essential elements of the crimes of illegal access, illegal interception and possibly even other computer security crimes. Including these additional requisites for the commission of computer security crimes would not require a dramatic change in the law because the Convention on Cybercrime already allows state parties to "require that the offence be committed by infringing security measures, with the intent of obtaining computer data or *other dishonest intent*" for illegal access and, likewise, "require that the offence be committed with *dishonest intent*" with respect to illegal interception.[143] Signatory countries to the Convention can thus simply incorporate the requirement of malicious, dishonest or criminal intent into their domestic computer crime laws.[144] A few states have already included such additional qualifying circumstances for the crime of illegal access in their national laws. For example, the Slovakian Criminal Code provides that unauthorized access to a computer system must be committed "with the *intent to cause damage or any other prejudice* to another, or to *obtain undue advantage* for himself or for another",[145] while the Brazilian Criminal Code criminalizes "[t]respassing a third party's computing device . . . by undue breach of the security mechanism, *to obtain, tamper with or destroy data or information* without express or tacit consent from the owner of the device or install vulnerabilities *to obtain illicit advantage*".[146] Under the New Zealand Crimes Act, illegal access is committed when a person "directly or indirectly, accesses any computer system and thereby, *dishonestly or by deception*, and without claim of right".[147]

It is worth pointing out that the inclusion of additional qualifying circumstances to computer security crimes is not unheard of. In fact, the amended Cybercrime Directive has made "infringing a security measure" a mandatory requirement for the commission of illegal access in Europe.[148] While this legislative reform is commendable, it may be said that it does not go far enough in resolving the over-criminalization of hacking and the lack of nuance in the application of the illegal access provision to hackers. It is true that the overt acts of placing security measures by the system owner and the infringement of such measures by an attacker makes it quite clear for both sides whether a line has been crossed. A person who defeats or breaches a security measure to gain access to a system cannot claim that the entry or access was unintentional. However, as explained in Chapter 4, owners and rights holders often protect their information and technologies with security measures and anti-circumvention technologies that prevent ordinary users and hackers from engaging in legitimate forms of access and use such as scientific research, security testing or protecting their privacy.[149] So, ethical hackers who endeavor to audit and improve the security of a system will still be held liable under the amended Directive (unless they have permission from the computer owner for the testing) since infringing a security measure is often a necessary part of good security testing. By not having a subjective criterion like malicious or dishonest intent, the law fails to distinguish between legitimate activities like security research versus malicious cyber attacks. While the amended illegal access provision in the Cybercrime Directive makes it easier to determine the intentionality of an act (i.e., whether the act of access was intentional or not),[150] it stops short of ascertaining the substance and context of the act – whether the actual intention was malicious or benign.[151] The law's deficiency then lies in the fact that it invites "prosecutorial attention to technology rather than to the culpability of conduct",[152] and it does not reasonably account "for intent".[153] Malicious intent and the effects of an act should be the ultimate bases on which to judge whether a particular use or access to information or technology is criminal or not. Otherwise, hacking remains overly criminalized since any infringement of a security measure, regardless of actual intent, is prohibited and penalized.

The introduction of a *mens rea* requirement or similar subjective criteria is extremely important because it makes computer crime laws more precise and equitable in their application. The problem with the current formulation of computer security crimes is that by not requiring "malicious intent or *mens rea*" (which is "often required in criminal law"), the law "turns general behaviors" like mere entry or access "into strict liability crimes".[154] Principles of fairness and justice dictate that the lawfulness or legitimacy of an act should be judged based on the person's intent (as evidenced or borne out by his or her overt acts) rather than the mere presence or absence of the system owner's authorization. Requiring the element of "*mens rea* or criminal intent" would ensure that the law "does not criminalize the legitimate activities and use of tools needed for independent security research, academic study, and other good-faith activities that serve the public interest and ultimately make the public more safe".[155] Establishing this higher threshold of culpability for illegal access and other computer security crimes is in line with the goals and rationale of computer crime laws. It bears stressing that the Cybercrime Directive unequivocally states that: "This Directive does not impose criminal liability where the objective criteria of the offense laid down in this Directive are met but the acts are committed *without criminal intent*".[156] It is quite clear from this recital, which has a controlling effect on the implementation and interpretation of national computer crime laws in Europe, that mere entry, access to or use of a computer without malicious or criminal intent is not a punishable offense.

As a matter of public policy then, it make sense to argue that no crime is or should be deemed committed unless the act of trespass, access or use of a computer or information system is attended with malice, dishonest intent or intent to cause damage. The illegal access provision of the Cybercrime Directive can be amended as follow:

> Member States shall take the necessary measures to ensure that, when committed intentionally *and with malice, dishonest intent, or intent to cause damage*, the access without right, to the whole or to any part of an information system, is punishable as a criminal offence where committed by infringing a security measure, at least for cases which are not minor.[157]

Amending the illegal access provision (and potentially the other computer security crimes) in this way would have a positive impact on hacking. As shown in the previous chapters, the hackers are not interested in causing damage to computers and data since they generally view malicious activities as having nothing to do with the essence of hacking, which involves the creative, masterful and communitarian uses of technology.[158] With these proposed amendments, makers and hacktivists would be able to finally raise a formidable legal argument against possible criminal prosecution – that their hacking activities were carried out without malicious, dishonest or criminal intent. Certain quarters may argue that including a *mens rea* requirement would weaken the effectiveness of the computer crime laws since "criminal hackers would simply claim in their defence they were carrying out research".[159] In practice though, "bona fide research" can be proved or disproved in various ways, including the use of basic police investigation and computer forensics.[160] The fact that it might become less convenient for police and law enforcement agencies to gather evidence and prosecute persons for computer security crimes should not be a ground for failing to improve the law.

Intellectual property laws

Three-step test as akin to fair use

As discussed at length in Chapter 4, many countries in Europe and around the world adhere to a closed list approach to limitations and exceptions to intellectual property rights. This means that, unless a particular access or use of a protected work or invention falls within a specific, statutorily granted limitation or exception (e.g., private and non-commercial use), such access or use is not permitted under intellectual property laws. Because the limitations and exceptions are contained in a static and exclusive list, the closed list approach does not afford the much needed room for makers and other hackers to push the boundaries, develop new technologies, and discover surprising and innovative uses of creative works. Many hackers relayed how they refrained from exploring technologies or systems or undertaking projects because their activities were not strictly authorized under the law.[161] In contrast, an open-ended approach such as the fair use doctrine followed in the United States and a few other countries,[162] allows intellectual property laws to flexibly adjust and dynamically carve out new limitations and exceptions on a case-by-case basis in light of new socio-technical advances and practices.[163] The closed list approach can be dramatically improved to support the innate creativity and innovativeness of hacking by incorporating or adopting into a state's national law or jurisprudence an open-ended standard (akin to the fair use doctrine) that is founded on the three-step test.

The three-step test provides that limitations and exceptions to intellectual property rights should: (1) apply only "in certain special cases"; (2) "not conflict with a normal exploitation of the work"; and (3) "not unreasonably prejudice the legitimate interests of the author".[164] Using the three-step test as an open-ended criteria akin to the fair use doctrine can be readily accomplished especially by European countries since, not only are they signatories to international intellectual property conventions like the Berne Convention and the TRIPS Agreement that already provide for the three-step test,[165] but the test is already part of European law having been included in the Copyright Directive as well as other Directives.[166] As explained by Senftleben, "Given the appearance of the three-step test in several EC Directives, the provision can moreover be regarded as part of the established legal principles of EC law".[167] Using the three-step test as an operative principle or guideline for determining the legitimacy of new technologies and social practices vis-à-vis intellectual property makes sense because judicial, legislative and other regulatory bodies that have to decide whether a reproduction or use of a protected work or invention is permitted or excepted would inevitably need to refer to or apply the three-step test and consider the "potential, as well as current and actual, uses or modes of extracting value from a work".[168] As confirmed by the WIPO Standing Committee on Copyright and Related Rights, the three-step test "is consciously framed as an omnibus or umbrella provision that is prospectively applicable to all exceptions to the reproduction right" and other rights as well.[169] As such, it can and should be used to expand the limitations and exceptions to intellectual property rights or create new ones.[170]

There have been a number of national courts that have applied the three-step test, not as a restrictive check on the validity of a statutory limitation and exception to copyright,[171] but as "flexible, open-ended criteria" for assessing and determining the extent and scope of intellectual property protection in the context of technological developments and innovative uses and activities.[172] In the Netherlands, while "the three-step test has little impact on the Dutch catalogue of statutory exceptions . . . the Directive inspired a line of decisions that use the three-step test to override the closed Dutch system of precisely-defined user privileges".[173] For instance, a Dutch court resorted to the three-step test rather than the statutory exceptions to resolve a case on the legitimacy of press reviews.[174] What is noteworthy about this decision is that the court's "discussion of non-compliance with the three-step test resembles a US fair use analysis rather than a close inspection of a continental-European statutory limitation".[175] Similarly in Switzerland, the Supreme Court applied the three-step test to create an exception for a commercial service that provided summaries of news articles.[176] Outside Europe, the Colombian Supreme Court also used the three-step test to create an exception for format-shifting of content for private and non-commercial purposes.[177] These courts notably applied the three-step in an "enabling sense"[178] so as to broaden or add to the existing limitations and exceptions to intellectual property rights.[179] Cases such as these illustrate how national courts can simply and effectively adopt or use the three-step test to modify or even establish new limitations and exceptions beyond those explicitly provided in national statutes.[180] These examples bear evidence to the fact that the three-step test "can be used to enable limitations and enhance flexibility in copyright" and other intellectual property laws.[181]

Besides courts and judges, it makes perfect sense for national lawmakers and regulators to "take full advantage of the flexibility inherent in the three-step test that has already become a cornerstone of EC legislation in the field of copyright limitations" and globally as well.[182] Quite interestingly, several countries have incorporated the actual text of the three-step test into their national laws. In Europe, the three-step test is expressly provided for in the laws of Croatia, France, Greece, Portugal and Spain.[183] By having the three-step test embodied in national law, it can be used as a legal basis to further enhance or refine the scope of limitations and exceptions to intellectual property rights.[184] With the three-step test acting akin to the fair use doctrine, national legislators and courts can "use the three-step test either to make specific lists of exceptions or to create open-ended exceptions".[185] Moreover, having the test as part of domestic law would permit local "courts to identify new use privileges on the basis of the test's abstract criteria".[186] This dynamic interpretation and approach to the three-step test is in accord with international law: "The WIPO Internet Treaties confirmed that the three-step test allows the extension of traditional copyright [limitations and exceptions] into the digital environment and the development of appropriate new [limitations and exceptions]".[187] Furthermore, "the Agreed Statement concerning Article 10 of WCT confirms that the test is intended to serve as a basis for the further development of existing and the creation of new [limitations and exceptions] in the digital environment".[188] Quite interestingly, the practice of directly applying the three-step as part of national law is gaining ground.[189] While some countries have adopted an open-ended approach to limitations and exceptions by incorporating the fair use doctrine into their national laws,[190] Australia is quite unique in the way it used the elements of the three-step test to craft a fair use-like provision into its copyright law.[191] According to the Australian lawmakers, the "proposed section 200AB seeks to provide an open-ended exception in line with the US model, and allows courts to determine if other uses should be permitted as exceptions to copyright".[192] It is worth noting that

> The three-step test was not only incorporated in the Australian provision . . . it was a central consideration in preparing this Bill. In addition to being addressed directly to courts in section 200AB, the three-step test was used to justify limitations in the formulation of exceptions.[193]

Regardless of which approach a country ultimately chooses, whether through judicial interpretation, legislative enactment or both, what is essential is the adoption of a dynamic and open-ended standard for the establishment and development of more reasonable and fair limitations and exceptions to intellectual property rights. Having such a standard in place is necessary in order to permit intellectual property laws and policies to quickly and adequately respond to new technological developments and innovative uses of intellectual creations that are being produced as such a heightened pace today.[194] This is especially true since "public policy considerations are hardly ever static: they change over time, reflecting the needs and realities of the various countries".[195] The three-step test is a robust and compelling legal basis for making the system of limitations and exceptions more responsive to techno-social advances because its provides "a flexible framework, within which national legislators enjoy the freedom of safeguarding national limitations and satisfying domestic social, cultural and economic needs".[196] As Senftleben declares, "the time is ripe to . . . open up the current restrictive system, [and] offer sufficient breathing space for social, cultural and economic needs, and enable [laws] to keep pace with the rapid development of the Internet" and other technologies.[197] By interpreting and applying the three-step test in this manner, intellectual property laws would be able to improve and adapt to changing technologies and social practices and support rather than impede technical and cultural innovation.

Three-step test plus

The three-step test is certainly an excellent foundation on which to build an open-ended, fair use-like standard in countries that follow a closed list approach to limitations and exceptions to intellectual property rights. I would further argue though that to promote the creative and innovative spirit of hacking and to maintain and preserve the intellectual property balance between the rights of creators vis-à-vis the rights of users, the test can still be enhanced by adding another criterion and make it effectively a three-step test *plus*.[198] The proposed additional requirement to the three-step test is far from being fanciful and is firmly based on developments in international intellectual property law. Article 30 of the TRIPS Agreement provides for the three-step test in relation to patents:

> Members may provide limited exceptions to the exclusive rights conferred by a patent, provided that such exceptions do not unreasonably conflict with a normal exploitation of the patent and do not unreasonably prejudice the legitimate interests of the patent owner, *taking account of the legitimate interests of third parties*.[199]

Article 26(2) of the TRIPS Agreement on industrial designs contains the same additional wording.[200] What is curious about these legal provisions is that, aside from the usual requirements of the three-step test, they include an extra requirement in the third test that it must take into account "the legitimate interests of third parties".[201] It should be noted that the three-step test as originally worded in the Berne Convention does not contain this last phrase.[202] According to the WIPO Standing Committee on the Law of Patents, "the term 'legitimate interest' must be 'defined in the way that it is often used in legal discourse – as a normative claim calling for protection of interests that are 'justifiable' in the sense that they are supported by relevant public policies or other social norms'".[203]

For hackers and the general public, a three-step test plus provision can be vital because, not only does it promote the intellectual property balance, but, for the first time, the rights and interests of users and the public (including hackers) who make up the other side of the balance are expressly acknowledged in the letter of the law. As originally worded, the three-step test is arguably oriented or leans towards the side of authors and creators. It may be said that the test favors authors and creators because their rights and interests are the bases on which to determine whether an access or use by others is permitted or excepted under the law. The three-step test plus provision is of great consequence and import because, by including the additional requirement, the test is finally properly balanced since it must consider the interests of all the parties involved: not just authors, creators and rights holders, but also users, consumers, technology developers and the general public. The three-step test plus provision is all the more significant because it expresses and embodies the principle of the intellectual property balance in a legally actionable form. Policy statements about the intellectual property balance and the need to preserve the public's right to access and use intellectual creations are normally found in the preamble of the law or its explanatory memoranda and they do not make it to the operative text or body of the law. By including an express statement recognizing the rights of users and third parties in the three-step test plus provision, public access and use of intellectual property is no longer just an abstract or nebulous policy recommendation to guide legislators, regulators and courts in interpreting or implementing the law, but it has become a substantive legal requirement that must be employed to evaluate and judge the legitimacy or propriety of various forms of access to and uses of intellectual property.

The three-step test plus provision is meant to promote greater creativity and innovation for both authors and creators and society as whole. The WIPO Standing Committee on the Law of Patents explains the rationale for the additional wording: "the scope of the enforceable exclusive rights is carefully designed under national patent laws in order to strike the right balance between the legitimate interests of the right holders and the legitimate interests of third parties".[204] Affirming the desirability of preserving the intellectual property balance, the Committee states:

> the exclusive rights conferred by a patent and the exceptions and limitations to such rights are two sides of the same coin seeking to balance the legitimate interests of the patent owner and the legitimate interests of third parties with a view to promote innovation, disseminate technical knowledge and encourage transfer of technology.[205]

With the inordinate focus on broadening and strengthening the exclusive rights granted to creators and inventors in past decades, the public interest goals and social objectives of intellectual property laws have been neglected. The three-step test plus provision reaffirms and reasserts that intellectual property has "the ultimate goal of promoting innovation and enhancing public welfare".[206] The grant of intellectual property rights is therefore meant "to promote innovation and to improve the social benefits resulting from that innovation".[207] As a consequence, the "underlying consideration is that the public interest justifies, under certain circumstances, denying the enforcement of the exclusive rights granted to patentees" as well as other creators for the benefit of the public.[208]

While the three-step test plus is already contained in the TRIPS Agreement, it is such a monumental provision that it should be incorporated as well into other international, regional and national laws and applied to other forms of intellectual property and not just patents and industrial designs. Since the principle of the intellectual property balance applies to all intellectual property rights and the three-step test plus provision superbly encapsulates and upholds this balance, it seems logical to similarly apply the three-step test plus to copyright and other forms of intellectual property. This would require either updating the wording of the three-step test in these laws to include the phrase "taking account of the legitimate interests of third parties", or, more simply, national courts or adjudicatory bodies could read the phrase into the law or render judgment that it is applicable in their jurisdictions. While this is a seemingly minor amendment to the law, it has far-reaching consequences that can benefit hackers and society as a whole. Patents are particularly problematic for makers because the grant of rights to patent holders is so extensive that it effectively bars them from publicly and openly developing and distributing a project (e.g., a 3D printer) that involves a protected invention (e.g., an essential technology for 3D printing) even though the project is non-commercial and open source. With a three-step test plus provision in place, a judge or court would also have to take into account the legitimate interests of makers, the hacker community and those of the general public in arriving at the decision. This is much better than the original wording of the three-step test where only the interests of the owners and creators are considered. Given that the great majority of hacker projects and activities (especially those of makers) are undertaken for personal and non-commercial purposes and with a view to producing new technologies or innovative uses for the benefit of their communities and the wider society, these acts of hacking will most likely be deemed permissible or excepted under the proposed three-step test plus provision.

Anti-circumvention and contract laws

More limitations and exceptions to anti-circumvention

Anti-circumvention rules as currently worded and applied seriously hinder the ability of makers, hacktivists and ordinary users from accessing information and creatively using their technologies. Since it is highly unlikely and it would not be reasonable to expect or demand the complete abolition of anti-circumvention rules given the well-entrenched regime of international, regional and national laws that support them, the sensible option then is to work within the legal framework and introduce and develop more limitations and exceptions in the law. Many countries in Europe have not formally adopted specific limitations and exceptions to the anti-circumvention prohibitions despite an express provision in the Copyright Directive allowing them to do.[209] Therefore, the first step in improving anti-circumvention laws would be for states to explicitly provide in their national laws specific limitations and exceptions to the prohibitions against circumvention such as for teaching and scientific research and for private and non-commercial use as stated in the Copyright Directive.[210] Furthermore, European countries would do well to further clarify and enhance the list of limitations and exceptions to anti-circumvention that are contained in the Copyright Directive particularly in relation to temporary acts of reproduction, repair, and even the three-step test (or fair use if applicable). Countries may also draw inspiration from the United States whose anti-circumvention legislation lays down specific limitations and exceptions for activities such as encryption research, security testing and protecting personally identifying information.[211] Another possible model is the triennial review procedure adopted in the United States where the US Librarian of Congress reviews the anti-circumvention rules every three years with the aim of establishing new limitations and exceptions based on current technologies and practices.[212] It should be noted that the Copyright Directive does state that the "legal protection" of technological protection measures "should respect proportionality and should not prohibit those devices or activities which have a commercially significant purpose or use other than to circumvent the technical protection. In particular, this protection should not hinder research into cryptography".[213] These exemptions would prove quite valuable to makers and hacktivists since many of their hacking projects and activities concern information security and privacy protection.

In light of the values and goals sought to be protected and promoted by copyright laws vis-à-vis anti-circumvention laws, it can justifiably be argued that all activities that fall within any of the statutory limitations and exceptions to copyright and related rights should be automatically or presumptively *prima facie* exempted from the application of anti-circumvention rules since such acts are legitimate or permitted under the law.[214] While this interpretation is implied in the legislative context and purposes of anti-circumvention laws, so as to avoid any doubt and promote legal certainty, there should be an explicit legal provision (or alternatively, a judicial or policy confirmation) that anti-circumvention rules do not or should not apply or interfere with existing and future limitations and exceptions to copyright and related rights. US anti-circumvention rules contain such a provision, which incontrovertibly states: "*Nothing in this section shall affect* rights, remedies, *limitations, or defenses to copyright infringement, including fair use*, under this title".[215] A similar statutory provision or policy statement can be adopted in the laws of countries where no such an express doctrine exists.

Necessary nexus between circumvention and copyright infringement

Aside from the need to have additional and more explicit limitations and exceptions to anti-circumvention rules, many of the problems and issues hounding technological protection measures can be remedied by reiterating, as a matter of public policy, that these rules should only apply in cases where the act or technology of circumvention is reasonably connected to actual or potential copyright infringement. This proposal seems self-evident but, as described in Chapter 4, anti-circumvention laws have been applied or sought to be enforced in situations that have absolutely nothing to do with copyright piracy. This goes against the intent of both copyright laws and anti-circumvention rules. As the European Commission clearly states:

> According to the Directive, the protection of TPM [technological protection measures] complements the protection of copyright. The Directive only requires Member States to protect TPM in respect of works or any subject-matter covered by 'copyright or any right related to copyright as provided by the law or the sui generis right in databases'. TPM applied to protect other subject matter or works in the public domain are thus not protected under the Directive.[216]

The European Commission further clarifies that, "Article 6(3) [of the Copyright Directive] requires that TPM are applied to restrict acts which are not author-ised by the rightholders of the protected subject matter. . . . This implies that Article 6(3) only protects technological measures that restrict acts which come within the scope of the exclusive rights".[217] The Commission's interpretation is based on the text of the WIPO Copyright Treaty, which states that the protected technological measures are those used "in connection with the exercise of their [authors'] rights under this Treaty or the Berne Convention" (i.e., copyright and related rights).[218] Article 12 of the WIPO Copyright Treaty also provides that circumvention of rights management information is unlawful if "it will induce, enable, facilitate or conceal an infringement of any right covered by this Treaty or the Berne Convention".[219] Anti-circumvention rules are "therefore aimed at pre-venting an act which would amount to an infringement of copyright".[220] For this reason, absent this indispensable connection between circumvention and copy-right infringement,[221] the anti-circumvention rules should not apply. This was the conclusion as well in the landmark US case of *Chamberlain Group v Skylink Technologies* where the Court of Appeals held that:

> The DMCA [Digital Millennium Copyright Act] does not create a new property right for copyright owners. Nor, for that matter, does it divest the public of the property rights that the Copyright Act has long granted to the public. The anti-circumvention and antitrafficking provisions of the DMCA create new grounds of liability. . . . A copyright owner seeking to impose liability on an accused trafficker must demonstrate that the trafficker's device *enables either copyright infringement or a prohibited circumvention. . . . This connection is critical to sustaining a cause of action under the DMCA.*"[222]

Thus, lacking "the *critical nexus between access and protection*" no claim can be filed and no liability should attach under anti-circumvention laws.[223] According to the Court, "the broad policy implications of considering 'access' in a vacuum devoid of 'protection' are both absurd and disastrous".[224] The Court explained that, "This distinction between property and liability is critical. Whereas copyrights, like patents, are property, liability protection from unauthorized circumvention merely creates a new cause of action under which a defendant may be liable".[225] Examining the legislative histories of both the WIPO Copyright Treaty and the US Digital Millennium Copyright Act (DMCA), the Court ruled, "circumvention is not a new form of infringement but rather a new violation prohibiting actions or products that facilitate infringement".[226] The Court ultimately concluded that DMCA "prohibits only forms of access *that bear a reasonable relationship* to the protections that the Copyright Act otherwise affords copyright owners".[227]

In light of the crucial requirement that there must be a nexus between circumvention and copyright infringement for anti-circumvention rules to apply, most makers and hacktivists would not run afoul of the law since their circumvention activities do not usually involve infringing copyrighted materials and they largely fall within existing limitations and exceptions or widely recognized normal or customary uses of intellectual property such as reverse engineering, decompilation for purposes of interoperability, scientific research, personal and non-commercial use, and time, place and format shifting of content.[228] Following this recommended interpretation of anti-circumvention rules, which can be judicially confirmed by the relevant court, hackers should be able to lawfully hack technological protection measures and have reasonably free and open access to the information and technologies that they legitimately own, possess, create or remake.

No contractual waivers of limitations and exceptions

As shown in the preceding chapters, freedom of contract when applied in combination with intellectual property laws can be a double-edged sword. Contracts can impair the rights of users through restrictive terms of service and licensing agreements, but they can also allow members of the public (including hackers) to freely use and openly access information and technologies through the use of copyleft and other free and open source licenses. In any event, contract law can still be improved in order to advance rather than impede cultural change and technical innovation. For one, the rules that prohibit any contractual waiver, diminution or bargaining away of the rights to reverse engineer, decompile, correct errors and make back-up copies of computer programs should be applied as well to other fundamental limitations and exceptions to intellectual property rights.[229] According to Samuelson, "[c]ourts and legislatures should be willing to affirm the ownership interests of purchasers of digital content that should not be overridden by mass-market license restrictions".[230] Since undertaking legislative reform will take much time and effort, it would be quicker and simpler for the relevant national courts to render judgment or set a precedent that the prohibition against contractual waivers should likewise cover other limitations and exceptions such as private and non-commercial copying and use, scientific research and teaching, repair, and the three-step test or fair use. Limitations and exceptions are extremely valuable to hackers because these serve as the legal bases for them to explore and study, creatively hack and satisfy their curiosity about technologies or creative works.

Extending the bar against contractual waivers to include other limitations and exceptions to intellectual property rights is imperative because, not only are they few and far between, but they are also the primary mechanisms by which the all-important intellectual property balance is preserved. Surely, the legal principles and public interest rationales that underlie the intellectual property regime, which aim to maintain a careful balance between the rights of creators vis-à-vis the rights of the public, should not be defeated or nullified through the mere expedient of resorting to contractual stipulations to the contrary. Laws and matters of public policy should not be so easily set aside. Members of the hacker community, most especially makers, would benefit from a legal prohibition against contractual waivers of limitations and exceptions as this would ensure that those permitted or excepted uses granted to them under the law (e.g., private and non-commercial use) would be preserved. In this way, what hackers and users can or cannot do with a creative work or invention is set out and determined by laws and jurisprudence and not the one-sided contractual terms imposed by intellectual property owners.

Rights of users

Another way to improve the laws on hacking is for public authorities to recognize and respect the rights of users. This requires making the crucial distinction between *commercial versus non-commercial*[231] and *malicious versus benign*[232] users and uses of information and technologies. Existing laws and policies generally tend to lump together ordinary users with commercial infringers in relation to intellectual property and contracts, and to conflate hackers with malicious attackers in matters concerning computer crime and anti-circumvention.[233] The problem with the overly broad, restrictive and punitive application of these laws is that, while their purported aims are to arrest, punish or deter acts that are threatening, harmful or cause damage, they inevitably end up interfering with or penalizing normal, *de minimis* or even innovative activities and practices of ordinary users and hackers. More can be done to make technology laws and policies more precise and nuanced in their application and impact. In the context of computer crime laws, introducing the element of criminal intent can help public authorities more fairly and effectively distinguish between permissible acts of hacking as opposed to unlawful cyber attacks. With respect to intellectual property laws, recognizing the difference between non-commercial uses versus those that are commercially infringing or damaging can be done by examining the specific user and uses of a protected work in a particular case, and interpreting or applying an existing limitation and exception or the proposed three-step test plus provision strictly against commercial infringers but favorably when it comes to ordinary users.[234] Differentiating between commercial and non-commercial uses is admittedly not an easy or straightforward task but the distinction can and has to be made otherwise ordinary users (including hackers) may be penalized for undertaking common, benign or creative activities. This is not to say that ordinary users are free from liability for copyright infringement (e.g., in the case of peer-to-peer file sharing). However, the law and the courts should distinguish between ordinary users and commercial infringers and only impose reasonable restrictions on and appropriate penalties for the respective groups.[235]

In order to properly distinguish creative and common users and uses from those that are malicious and infringing, it is essential for the law and public authorities to affirm or recognize people's *right to hack* the information and technologies that they lawfully own or possess. As discussed throughout this book, this right to hack includes the ability to *explore, break, learn, create, share* and *secure* technologies and intellectual creations. It is about the "freedom to understand, discuss, repair, and modify the technological devices you own" and creatively use the content or information that one has.[236] As Samuelson explains,

> [p]eople tinker with technologies . . . for a variety of reasons: to have fun . . . to learn how things work, to discern their flaws or vulnerabilities, to build their skills . . . to repair or make improvements . . . to adapt them to new purposes, and occasionally, to be destructive.[237]

The freedom to hack or tinker is the crux or cornerstone that underpins many user rights in the information age. The significance of hacking and tinkering is that they enable "freedom of thought, study, inquiry, self-expression, diffusion of knowledge, and building a community of highly skilled tinkerers. In addition, freedom to tinker fosters privacy, autonomy, human flourishing, and skills building interests".[238] Whether one calls it a right to hack or freedom to tinker, according to Samuelson, it necessarily involves or requires the following rights and freedoms: "intellectual freedom", "intellectual privacy and autonomy", "a right to build one's skills", "liberty to become more actualized as a person through tinkering", a right to learn, "a right to repair", "a right to innovate" and "a right to share".[239] These are basically the same digital rights and technological freedoms that are expressed and demanded by makers, hacktivists and other hackers in their manifestos (see Chapter 3). For example, they have articulated and advocated for the following user rights and freedoms: to create,[240] to repair,[241] to make, share, learn about and change our own devices,[242] to fix and improve,[243] to "open and repair our things without voiding the warranty",[244] "to devices that can be opened",[245] "to repair things in the privacy of our own homes",[246] "to hardware that doesn't require proprietary tools to repair",[247] "to run, copy, distribute, study, change and improve . . . software",[248] to "free and equal access to all publicly-produced information"[249] and to free access to computers and information.[250] Whether for hackers or ordinary users, it is crucial to preserve and promote these freedoms associated with hacking and tinkering because they "generally 'promote the progress of science and useful arts,' as well as other fundamental values".[251]

In sum, while formal legal reform through legislative amendments or judicial rulings are ultimately needed to provide legal certainty and clarity and to fully carry out the preceding legal recommendations, based on the successful outcomes of the responsible disclosure rules and open data hackathons, it appears that a change in technology policy, greater participation of and collaborations with hackers and the public, and other soft law approaches offer more immediate and practical solutions to improving the laws on hacking.

Hacking can be change for good

The legal and normative recommendations proposed in this chapter are fairly straightforward and do not require unreasonable costs and efforts to implement. The suggested improvements to regulatory approaches and policies concerning hacking are based on an extensive and empirically grounded analysis of both the socio-technical practices of hackers and the laws that affect them. However, in spite of the strong empirical and legal bases to support these proposals, I am well aware that undertaking such reforms will still most likely face strong objections from certain sectors (e.g., commercial companies, law enforcement agencies and government departments) and will be politically contentious.[252] This is expected given the lack of progress in reforming computer crime laws even after the much-publicized suicide of hacktivist Aaron Swartz, who at the time of his death was being criminally prosecuted and faced years of imprisonment for trying to make publications in an academic database accessible to the wider public.[253] There were attempts in the United States to amend the law, including one called "Aaron's Law".[254] According to the sponsors of the bill, "Aaron's Law is . . . about refocusing the law away from common computer and Internet activity and toward damaging hacks . . . distinguish the difference between common online activities and harmful attacks"[255] Aaron's Law sought "to bring balance back to" the US Computer Fraud and Abuse Act by including the qualification of infringing a security measure as a requirement for illegal access.[256] However, these efforts to improve computer crime laws "appear to be foundering" and "Aaron's Law would not be passing".[257] According to Maker H, "The Aaron Swartz movement never got any real traction on Capitol Hill as far as my understanding goes".[258] Without a doubt, the revelations of Edward Snowden played a part in hampering the passage of Aaron's Law and other similar reforms. According to Fakhoury, "Before Edward Snowden showed up, 2013 was shaping up as a year of reckoning for the much criticized federal anti-hacking statute, the Computer Fraud and Abuse Act".[259] The current attitude of public authorities to amending computer crime laws can be described in this way:

> But unfortunately, not much has changed; if anything, the growing recognition of the powerful capabilities of modern computing and networking has resulted in a 'cyber panic' in legislatures and prosecutor offices across the country. Instead of reexamination, we've seen aggressive charges and excessive punishment.[260]

So, the reverse is happening – there have been moves to further ratchet up the law. This is, of course, in line with the historic tendency of computer crime laws to become all the more restrictive and punitive.²⁶¹ According to the Electronic Frontier Foundation, "As if the law's current magnitude of punishment isn't overwhelming enough, Congress has been thinking about beefing up" the US Computer Fraud and Abuse Act.²⁶² Rather than making the law less restrictive in order to accommodate benign or productive activities like hacking, because of the Snowden revelations and many high profile security breaches, "many want to see [the Computer Fraud and Abuse Act] punishments made more severe".²⁶³ Even the amended Cybercrime Directive considers it "appropriate to provide for more severe penalties".²⁶⁴ While the imposition of harsher penalties may be appropriate for malicious attackers and cybercriminals, unless a clear distinction is made in the law between destructive cyber attacks and the innocuous activities of hackers, hacking will remain over-criminalized.

It is evident that for the improvements recommended in this book to come to fruition they must be accompanied by cultural change most especially on the part of the law and public authorities. Without this *metanoia*, no genuine or effective legal change can be expected. Nevertheless, even though reforms may appear distant or slow to come, hackers as well as ordinary citizens and users can still aim to reshape the law through their everyday practices and the very technologies that they make and use. While entrenched government culture may impede the improvement of hacking-related laws, socio-cultural change can serve as a starting point or impetus for much needed legal reform. Recall that, in relation to intellectual property laws, FOSS developers were able to fundamentally remake how software is developed, licensed and used, not by political lobbying, but through their individual choices and group actions and the novel use of intellectual property licenses to ensure that computer programs are free and open for everyone to use.

In a similar vein, the collaborative and bottom-up approach of the responsible disclosure rules has helped make the enforcement of computer crime laws more nuanced and can ultimately result in better information security for private and public individuals and entities. Cultural change in the form of developing techno-social practices like bug bounty programs can likewise impact computer crime laws. What is noteworthy about bug bounty programs is how hackers and commercial companies are able to develop legitimate and common practices and rules that are mutually beneficial to them and actually result in improved computer security,²⁶⁵ despite or regardless of computer crime laws. Bug bounty programs can attribute their success to companies being more open to working with hackers and treating them as equal partners or co-participants in information security.²⁶⁶

In this way, even though reforms to hacking-related laws may not be immediately forthcoming, hackers and other actors in the networked information society (including ordinary users and citizens) will continue to carry out and develop their own customs and conduct concerning access to and use of information and technology. As long as these practices and technologies are not incompatible with fundamental rights and democratic values, once they become established and internalized as legitimate and common activities by the relevant community and society as a whole, it would be reasonable for the law to recognize and build on the socio-technical rules that are already in place. This is so because, particularly in relation to technological and cultural innovation, laws should ultimately reflect as well as promote existing and changing norms and values. As with hacking, this can be change for good.

Notes

1 James Andrew Lewis, "Government open source policies"; see also Robert Hahn, "Government policy toward open source software: An overview".
2 Steven Levy, *Hackers* 29.
3 See Arjen Kamphuis, "Dining with assange and spies".
4 Loek Essers, "Dutch government aims to shape ethical hackers' disclosure practices".
5 Ministry of Security and Justice, National Cyber Security Centre, "Policy for arriving at a practice for Responsible Disclosure" 5–6; Ministry of Security and Justice, National Cyber Security Centre, "Policy of public prosecution service on ethical hackers in line with responsible disclosure guidelines".
6 Ministry of Security and Justice, National Cyber Security Centre, "Policy for arriving at a practice for responsible disclosure" 7.
7 Ministry of Security and Justice, National Cyber Security Centre, "Policy for arriving at a practice for responsible disclosure" 7; see also Council Directive 2013/40/EU on attacks against information systems, recital 26.
8 Netherlands Ministry of Security and Justice, "Policy for arriving at a practice for responsible disclosure" 8; see also Derek Bambauer and Oliver Day, "The hacker's aegis" 36.
9 Netherlands Ministry of Security and Justice, "Policy for arriving at a practice for responsible disclosure" 8; see also Derek Bambauer and Oliver Day, "The hacker's aegis" 39.
10 Netherlands Ministry of Security and Justice, "Policy for arriving at a practice for responsible disclosure" 8.
11 Netherlands Ministry of Security and Justice, "Policy for arriving at a practice for responsible disclosure" 8.
12 Netherlands Ministry of Security and Justice, "Policy for arriving at a practice for responsible disclosure" 8.
13 Netherlands Ministry of Security and Justice, "Policy for arriving at a practice for responsible disclosure" 7.
14 Netherlands Ministry of Security and Justice, "Policy for arriving at a practice for responsible disclosure" 7.
15 Netherlands Ministry of Security and Justice, "Policy for arriving at a practice for responsible disclosure" 7.
16 Netherlands Ministry of Security and Justice, "Policy for arriving at a practice for responsible disclosure" 7.
17 Netherlands Ministry of Security and Justice, "Policy for arriving at a practice for responsible disclosure" 7.
18 Netherlands Ministry of Security and Justice, "Policy for arriving at a practice for responsible disclosure" 7.
19 HackerOne, "Vulnerability disclosure guidelines"; Cassandra Kirsch, "The grey hat hacker" 397; Ben Popper, "A new breed of startups is helping hackers make millions – legally".
20 Eric Raymond, *The Cathedral and the Bazaar* 30; see also Derek Bambauer and Oliver Day, "The hacker's aegis" 9.

21 Ben Popper, "A new breed of startups is helping hackers make millions – legally"; see also James Conrad, "Seeking help: The important role of ethical hackers"; see also Chris Evans, "Announcing project zero".

22 Ben Popper, "A new breed of startups is helping hackers make millions – legally"; see also Derek Bambauer and Oliver Day, "The hacker's aegis" 49.

23 Andy Greenberg, "Meet 'Project zero,' Google's secret team of bug-hunting hackers"; Bugcrowd, "The bug bounty list"; Ben Popper, "A new breed of start-ups is helping hackers make millions – legally"; HackerOne, "Vulnerability disclosure guidelines"; Cassandra Kirsch, "The grey hat hacker" 386 and 397.

24 HackerOne, "Vulnerability disclosure guidelines".

25 Ben Popper, "A new breed of startups is helping hackers make millions – legally"; Bugcrowd, "The bug bounty list".

26 Netherlands Ministry of Security and Justice, "Policy for arriving at a practice for Responsible Disclosure" 3 and 5; see also Government of the Netherlands, "Guidelines for responsible disclosure of IT vulnerabilities"; see also Ministry of Security and Justice, National Cyber Security Centre, "Public-private cooperation".

27 Cassandra Kirsch, "The grey hat hacker" 388.

28 Interview with Maker H; Interview with Ethical Hacker A; Netherlands Ministry of Security and Justice, "Policy for arriving at a practice for Responsible Disclosure" 3 and 5; Government of the Netherlands, "Guidelines for responsible disclosure of IT vulnerabilities"; Ministry of Security and Justice, National Cyber Security Centre, "Public-private cooperation".

29 Netherlands Ministry of Security and Justice, "Policy for arriving at a practice for Responsible Disclosure" 3 and 5; see also Government of the Netherlands, "Guidelines for responsible disclosure of IT vulnerabilities"; see also Ministry of Security and Justice, National Cyber Security Centre, "Public-private cooperation".

30 Interview; see also Derek Bambauer and Oliver Day, "The Hacker's Aegis" 5 and 49 (on voluntary intermediaries for security vulnerabilities or vulnerability clearinghouses)

31 Interview; see also Cassandra Kirsch, "The grey hat hacker" 388.

32 Interview.

33 Netherlands Ministry of Security and Justice, "Policy for arriving at a practice for responsible disclosure" 3 and 5; Government of the Netherlands, "Guidelines for responsible disclosure of IT vulnerabilities"; see Ministry of Security and Justice, National Cyber Security Centre, "Public-private cooperation"; see also Derek Bambauer and Oliver Day, "The hacker's aegis" 35–36.

34 Government of the Netherlands, "Guidelines for responsible disclosure of IT vulnerabilities"; Board of Procurators General, "Responsible disclosure (how to deal with 'ethical' hackers?)" (18 March 2013) 2.

35 Government of the Netherlands, "Guidelines for responsible disclosure of IT vulnerabilities"; see also Ministry of Security and Justice, National Cyber Security Centre, "Policy of public prosecution service on ethical hackers in line with responsible disclosure guidelines".

36 Board of Procurators General, "Responsible disclosure (how to deal with 'ethical' hackers?)" (18 March 2013) 1.

37 Board of Procurators General, "Responsible disclosure (how to deal with 'ethical' hackers?)" (18 March 2013) 2.

38 Board of Procurators General, "Responsible disclosure (how to deal with 'ethical' hackers?)" (18 March 2013) 1–2; see also Jurriaan de Haan, "The new Dutch law on euthanasia" 58, 60, 62, 66 (Interestingly, the responsible disclosure rules

for disclosing computer security vulnerabilities bears some similarities with the reporting procedures for euthanasia in the Netherlands. Under Dutch law, a physician who has committed euthanasia will not be prosecuted if, among other requirements, he or she has complied with stated reporting rules. While Dutch law does not deprive the public prosecutor of the right to investigate and prosecute cases of euthanasia (or hacking), as a matter of government policy, it will not do so if the specific reporting rules are observed.).

39 Interview with Maker G.
40 Interviews.
41 Interview with Maker J.
42 Interview with Hacktivist B.
43 Interview with Maker L.
44 Interview with Ethical Hacker A.
45 Interview with Maker L.
46 Interview.
47 Interview with Maker H.
48 Interview with Maker J.
49 Interview with Hacktivist D.
50 Interview with Hacktivist D.
51 Interview with Ethical Hacker B.
52 Interview with Hacktivist B.
53 Interview with Hacktivist F.
54 Interview with Hacktivist E.
55 Interview with Maker J.
56 Interview with, among others, Maker D, Maker L and Ethical Hacker B.
57 Interview with Maker J.
58 Interview with Maker D.
59 Interview with Maker H.
60 Interview with Ethical Hacker A.
61 Interview with Hacktivist D.
62 Interview with Hacktivist E.
63 Interview with Hacktivist E.
64 Interview with Hacktivist F.
65 Interview with Hacktivist F.
66 See Amitai Etzioni, "Social norms: Internalization, Persuasion, and History" 159.
67 Interview with Ethical Hacker B.
68 Interview with Ethical Hacker B.
69 Interview with Ethical Hacker A.
70 Interview with Ethical Hacker A.
71 Interview with Ethical Hacker A.
72 Interview with Maker H.
73 Interview with Maker J.
74 Board of Procurators General, "Responsible disclosure (how to deal with 'ethical' hackers?)" (18 March 2013) 1.
75 Interview with Ethical Hacker B.
76 See Derek Bambauer and Oliver Day, "The hacker's aegis" 5 and 40; see also Convention on Cybercrime, art 6 (2).
77 See Cass Sunstein, "On the expressive function of law".
78 See HackerOne, "Vulnerability disclosure guidelines"; see Ben Popper, "A new breed of startups is helping hackers make millions – legally"; see "The bug bounty list".
79 Cassandra Kirsch, "The grey hat hacker" 398.

80　See Bert-Jaap Koops, "Cybercrime legislation in The Netherlands" 3 (on prosecutorial discretion)

81　See Derek Bambauer and Oliver Day, "The hacker's aegis" 40.

82　Noor Huijboom and Tijs Van den Broek, "Open data: An international comparison of strategies" 10.

83　Directive 2013/37/EU of the European Parliament and of the Council amending Directive 2003/98/EC on the re-use of public sector information; see also Directive 2003/98/EC of the European Parliament and the Council on the re-use of public sector information.

84　Proposal for a Directive on Amending Directive 2003/98/EC on re-use of public sector information; Communication on Open data: An engine for innovation, growth and transparent governance 6–8; see also European Commission, "Guidelines on recommended standard licences, datasets and charging for the reuse of documents" (2014/C 240/01).

85　Commission Decision of 12 December 2011 on the re-use of Commission documents (2011/833/EU).

86　Noor Huijboom and Tijs Van den Broek, "Open data: An international comparison of strategies" 2–3.

87　Data.gov; Data.gov.uk.

88　Data.overheid.nl; Data.gouv.fr; "Open data services"; "Publicdata.eu".

89　Interview with Maker B.

90　Interview with Maker B.

91　Communication on Open data: An engine for innovation, growth and transparent governance 11; Proposal for a Directive on Amending Directive 2003/98/EC on re-use of public sector information 2–3.

92　Communication on Open data: An engine for innovation, growth and transparent governance 3–4.

93　Noor Huijboom and Tijs Van den Broek, "Open data: An international comparison of strategies" 4.

94　Proposal for a Directive on Amending Directive 2003/98/EC on re-use of public sector information 3; Communication on Open data: An engine for innovation, growth and transparent governance 4.

95　Noor Huijboom and Tijs Van den Broek, "Open data: An international comparison of strategies" 5.

96　Noor Huijboom and Tijs Van den Broek, "Open data: An international comparison of strategies" 5–6.

97　Noor Huijboom and Tijs Van den Broek, "Open data: An international comparison of strategies" 5–6.

98　Noor Huijboom and Tijs Van den Broek, "Open data: An international comparison of strategies" 5–6.

99　Noor Huijboom and Tijs Van den Broek, "Open data: An international comparison of strategies" 9.

100　Noor Huijboom and Tijs Van den Broek, "Open data: An international comparison of strategies" 9; see Anneke Zuiderwijk and others, "Socio-technical Impediments of open data"; see European Commission Staff Working Paper Executive Summary of the Impact Assessment accompany the document Proposal for a Directive amending Directive 2003/98/EC on the re-use of public sector information 2–3; see Ton Zijlstra, "The state of open data in Europe – achievements and challenges".

101　Interview with Maker B.

102　Interview with Maker L.

103　Interview with Maker L.

104 Interview with Maker L.
105 Interview with Maker B.
106 Interview with Maker B.
107 Interview with Maker L.
108 Interview with Maker L.
109 Computer Desktop Encyclopedia, "Hackathon".
110 Steven Levy, *Hackers* 475; Mark Zuckerberg, "The hacker way".
111 Communication on Open data: An engine for innovation, growth and transparent governance 2, 8 and 11; see also Proposal for a Directive on Amending Directive 2003/98/EC on re-use of public sector information 3.
112 Noor Huijboom and Tijs Van den Broek, "Open data: An international comparison of strategies" 6.
113 Communication on Open data: An engine for innovation, growth and transparent governance 11; Proposal for a Directive on Amending Directive 2003/98/EC on re-use of public sector information 2–3.
114 Interview with Maker D.
115 Interview with Maker B.
116 Interview with Maker B.
117 See "Open Data Day 2013"; see "Europeana hackathons".
118 Taarifa; see also Taarifa.
119 GroupMe; Spencer Ante, "Skype to acquire start-up groupme".
120 Appetas; see also Vinnie Mancuso, "5 Hackathon success stories".
121 Easy Taxi.
122 Interview with Maker D; see also Open Cultuur Data; see also "Open data NEXT".
123 Open Innovatie Festival 2012.
124 Open Innovatie Festival 2012.
125 "Kickstart leeuwarden"; Frack.
126 "Hackathon 'Kickstart058'".
127 "Hackathon 'Kickstart058'"; "Kickstart Leeuwarden".
128 "Hackathon 'Kickstart058'"; "Kickstart Leeuwarden".
129 "Hackathon 'Kickstart058'"; "Kickstart Leeuwarden".
130 "Kickstart Leeuwarden".
131 "Hackathon 'Kickstart058'".
132 "Hackathon 'Kickstart058'".
133 "Hackathon 'Kickstart058'".
134 Interview with Maker B.
135 Interview with Maker D.
136 Interview with Maker L.
137 Interview.
138 Interview with Maker B.
139 See Publicdata.eu; see MapLight.
140 Explanatory Report to the Convention on Cybercrime, para 38.
141 See Chapter 2 (on the history of hacking and the different types of hackers).
142 Steve Wozniak, creator of the Apple II (see Steven Levy, *Hackers* 249), Richard Stallman, founder of the Free Software Foundation (see Sam Williams, *Free As In Freedom* 8), Linus Torvalds, developer of Linux (see Linus Torvalds and David Diamond, *Just for Fun* 122), Bill Gates, who helped create the software industry (see Robert Cringely, *Accidental Empires* 9), John Carmack, founder of Id Software (see Henry Lowood, "Players as Innovators in the Making of Machinima" 170), Vint Cerf and other internet pioneers (see Katie Hafner and Matthew Lyon, *Where Wizards Stay Up Late* 158, 179 and 190), Tim

Berners-Lee, inventor of the World Wide Web (see Tim Berners-Lee, "Aaron is dead" W3C mailing list), Shawn Fanning, creator of Napster (see Steve O'Hear, "Inside the billion-dollar hacker club"), Bram Cohen, developer of the BitTorrent protocol (see Clive Thompson, "The bittorrent effect"), Mark Zuckerberg, founder of Facebook (Mark Zuckerberg, "The hacker way"), and Adrian Bowyer, inventor of the RepRap open source 3D printer (see RepRap, "About") are considered or view themselves as hackers.

143 Convention on Cybercrime, arts 2 and 3 (emphasis added).
144 See also Recommendation No. R (89) 9 on computer-related crime 53 and 61 (other subjective criteria to consider are "dishonest or harmful intentions" or "malicious acts").
145 Slovakian Criminal Code, section 247 (emphasis added).
146 Brazilian Criminal Code, art 154-A (emphasis added).
147 New Zealand Crimes Act 1961, sec 249 (emphasis added).
148 Council Directive 2013/40/EU on attacks against information systems, art 3.
149 See Electronic Frontier Foundation, "Submission to the European Parliament on the Draft Directive on Attacks against Computer Systems" 5; see Cassandra Kirsch, "The grey hat hacker" 398.
150 See Cyrus Chung, "The computer fraud and abuse act" 237.
151 See Tom Brewster, "US cybercrime law being used to target security researchers".
152 Joseph Olivenbaum, "Rethinking federal computer crime legislation" 605.
153 Tom Brewster, "US cybercrime law being used to target security researchers".
154 Electronic Frontier Foundation, "Submission to the European Parliament on the draft directive on attacks against computer systems" 5; see also Oliver Wendell Holmes, Jr., "Privilege, malice, and intent"; see also Samantha Jensen, "Why broad interpretations of the CFAA Fail" 97; see also Orin Kerr, "Interpreting 'access' and 'authorization' in computer misuse statutes" 1667.
155 Electronic Frontier Foundation, "Submission to the European Parliament on the draft directive on attacks against computer systems" 5.
156 Council Directive 2013/40/EU on attacks against information systems, recital 17 (emphasis added); see also Electronic Frontier Foundation, "Submission to the European Parliament on the draft directive on attacks against computer systems" 5.
157 See Council Directive 2013/40/EU on attacks against information systems, art 2.
158 Paul Taylor, "From hackers to hacktivists" 628; Tim Jordan, *Hacking* 19; Sam Williams, *Free As In Freedom* 178; "Cracker", *The New Hacker's Dictionary*.
159 Tom Brewster, "US cybercrime law being used to target security researchers".
160 See Tom Brewster, "US cybercrime law being used to target security researchers".
161 Interviews.
162 See Jonathan Band and Jonathan Gérafi, "The fair use/fair dealing handbook" 1; see also Christophe Geiger, Daniel Gervais and Martin Senftleben, "The three-step test revisited" 623–624.
163 See WIPO Standing Committee on Copyright and Related Rights, "WIPO study on limitations and exceptions of copyright and related rights in the digital environment" 68; see Martin Senftleben, "The emerging EC fair use doctrine" 527.
164 Berne Convention, art 9(2).
165 Berne Convention, art 9(2); Agreement on Trade-Related Aspects of Intellectual Property Rights, arts 26 and 30.
166 Directive 2001/29/EC on the harmonisation of certain aspects of copyright and related rights in the information society, art 5(5); Directive 2009/24/EC on the legal protection of computer programs, art 6(3); Directive 96/9/EC on the legal protection of databases, arts 6(3) and art 7(5); Martin Senftleben, "The

emerging EC fair use doctrine" 543; see also Martin Senftleben, "The emerging EC fair use doctrine" 531–532.

167 Martin Senftleben, "The emerging EC fair use doctrine" 543.

168 Standing Committee on Copyright and Related Rights, "WIPO study on limitations and exceptions of copyright and related rights in the digital environment" 23 and 35; see also Daniel Gervais, "A principled approach to copyright exceptions and limitations" 32.

169 Standing Committee on Copyright and Related Rights, "WIPO study on limitations and exceptions of copyright and related rights in the digital environment" 25.

170 Martin Senftleben, "The emerging EC fair use doctrine" 551.

171 See Martin Senftleben, "The emerging EC fair use doctrine" 529, 531 and 532.

172 Martin Senftleben, "The emerging EC fair use doctrine" 548; see also Christophe Geiger, Daniel Gervais and Martin Senftleben, "The three-step test revisited" 616 and 618; see also Daniel Gervais, "A principled approach to copyright exceptions and limitations" 35.

173 Martin Senftleben, "The emerging EC fair use doctrine" 530.

174 Martin Senftleben, "The emerging EC fair use doctrine" 530.

175 Martin Senftleben, "The emerging EC fair use doctrine" 531.

176 Christophe Geiger, Daniel Gervais and Martin Senftleben, "The three-step test revisited" 619–620.

177 Christophe Geiger, Daniel Gervais and Martin Senftleben, "The three-step test revisited" 620–621.

178 Martin Senftleben, "The emerging EC fair use doctrine" 545–546; see also Christophe Geiger, Daniel Gervais and Martin Senftleben, "The three-step test revisited" 618.

179 Christophe Geiger, Daniel Gervais and Martin Senftleben, "The three-step test revisited" 621.

180 See Daniel Gervais, "A principled approach to copyright exceptions and limitations" 35 (who argues that this may be the case even "where no such specific exception exists, if permitted under domestic law").

181 Martin Senftleben, "The emerging EC fair use doctrine" 546; see also Christophe Geiger, Daniel Gervais and Martin Senftleben, "The three-step test revisited" 618.

182 Martin Senftleben, "The emerging EC fair use doctrine" 551.

183 Daniel Gervais, "A principled approach to copyright exceptions and limitations" 35.

184 Christophe Geiger, Daniel Gervais and Martin Senftleben, "The three-step test revisited" 582.

185 Christophe Geiger, Daniel Gervais and Martin Senftleben, "The three-step test revisited" 622; see also Martin Senftleben, "The emerging EC fair use doctrine" 542–543.

186 Christophe Geiger, Daniel Gervais and Martin Senftleben, "The three-step test revisited" 582.

187 Christophe Geiger, Daniel Gervais and Martin Senftleben, "The three-step test revisited" 625–626.

188 Christophe Geiger, Daniel Gervais and Martin Senftleben, "The three-step test revisited" 617.

189 Daniel Gervais, "A principled approach to copyright exceptions and limitations" 34.

190 See Jonathan Band and Jonathan Gerafi, "The fair use/fair dealing handbook" 1; see Christophe Geiger, Daniel Gervais and Martin Senftleben, "The three-step test revisited" 623–624.

191 Australian Copyright Amended Act 2006, section 200AB; see also Daniel Gervais, "A principled approach to copyright exceptions and limitations" 35 and 36.
192 Daniel Gervais, "A principled approach to copyright exceptions and limitations" 36.
193 Daniel Gervais, "A principled approach to copyright exceptions and limitations" 36.
194 See Martin Senftleben, "The emerging EC fair use doctrine" 540.
195 WIPO Standing Committee on the Law of Patents, "Exclusions from patentable subject matter and exceptions and limitations to the rights" 2.
196 Martin Senftleben, "The emerging EC fair use doctrine" 550–551.
197 Martin Senftleben, "The emerging EC fair use doctrine" 522 and 539.
198 See Peter Drahos, "Bilateralism in intellectual property"; see Susan Sell, "TRIPS-plus free trade agreements and access to medicines" (This term "three-step test plus" is a play on "TRIPS-plus", which are international or bilateral agreements between states that impose "more extensive protection" for intellectual property that are over and above those provided under the TRIPS Agreement. But in this instance, the plus is used to enable rather than restrict access to and use of intellectual property).
199 Agreement on Trade-Related Aspects of Intellectual Property Rights, art 30 (emphasis added); but see Agreement on Trade-Related Aspects of Intellectual Property Rights, art 13 (for copyright and related rights).
200 Agreement on Trade-Related Aspects of Intellectual Property Rights, art 26(2).
201 Agreement on Trade-Related Aspects of Intellectual Property Rights, art 30; see also Berne Convention, art 9(2); see also WIPO Standing Committee on the Law of Patents, "Exclusions from patentable subject matter and exceptions and limitations to the rights" 21.
202 Berne Convention, art 9(2).
203 WIPO Standing Committee on the Law of Patents, "Exclusions from patentable subject matter and exceptions and limitations to the rights" 22.
204 WIPO Standing Committee on the Law of Patents, "Exclusions from patentable subject matter and exceptions and limitations to the rights" 19; see also Lawrence Lessig, *Code: Version 2.0* 183.
205 WIPO Standing Committee on the Law of Patents, "Exclusions from patentable subject matter and exceptions and limitations to the rights" 25.
206 WIPO Standing Committee on the Law of Patents, "Exclusions from patentable subject matter and exceptions and limitations to the rights" 2, 3 and 19.
207 WIPO Standing Committee on the Law of Patents, "Exclusions from patentable sSubject matter and exceptions and limitations to the rights" 2.
208 WIPO Standing Committee on the Law of Patents, "Exclusions from patentable subject matter and exceptions and limitations to the rights" 19; see also Lawrence Lessig, *Code: Version 2.0* 183.
209 Directive 2001/29/EC on the harmonisation of certain aspects of copyright and related rights in the information society, art 6(4); European Commission, "Report on the application of the Directive 2001/29/EC" SEC(2007) 1556, 9; see also Urs Gasser and Michael Girsberger, "Transposing the Copyright Directive: Legal Protection of Technological Measures in EU-Member States" 22 and 30.
210 Directive 2001/29/EC on the harmonisation of certain aspects of copyright and related rights in the information society, arts 6(4).
211 17 US Code section 1201, arts (g), (i) and (j); see also Derek Bambauer and Oliver Day, "The Hacker's Aegis" 31.
212 17 US Code section 1201, arts (a)(1)(B)-(D); see also Pamela Samuelson, "Freedom to Tinker" 19; see also Derek Bambauer and Oliver Day, "The hacker's aegis" 32.

213 Directive 2001/29/EC on the harmonisation of certain aspects of copyright and related rights in the information society, recital 48.
214 See Daniel Gervais, "A principled approach to copyright exceptions and limitations" 22.
215 17 US Code section 1201, art (c)(1) (emphasis added).
216 European Commission, "Report on the application of the Directive 2001/29/EC" SEC(2007) 1556, 7.
217 European Commission, "Report on the application of the Directive 2001/29/EC" SEC(2007) 1556, 7.
218 WIPO Copyright Treaty, art 11.
219 WIPO Copyright Treaty, art 12.
220 European Commission, "Report on the application of the Directive 2001/29/EC" SEC(2007) 1556, 8.
221 See European Commission, "Report on the application of the Directive 2001/29/EC" SEC(2007) 1556, 7.
222 *Chamberlain Group v Skylink Technologies* 381 F. 3d 1178 (2004), 1204 (emphasis added).
223 *Chamberlain Group v Skylink Technologies* 381 F. 3d 1178 (2004), 1204 (emphasis added); see also Pamela Samuelson, "Freedom to Tinker" 19.
224 *Chamberlain Group v Skylink Technologies* 381 F. 3d 1178 (2004), 1200–1201.
225 *Chamberlain Group v Skylink Technologies* 381 F. 3d 1178 (2004), 1192–1193.
226 *Chamberlain Group v Skylink Technologies* 381 F. 3d 1178 (2004), 1197.
227 *Chamberlain Group v Skylink Technologies* 381 F. 3d 1178 (2004), 1202 (emphasis added); see also Pamela Samuelson, "Freedom to Tinker" 19 and 21; but see *MDY Industries v Blizzard Entertainment,* 629 F. 3d 928 (2010); see also Pamela Samuelson, "Freedom to Tinker" 19 (the *MDY* case "rejecting the nexus to infringement requirement set forth in *Chamberlain*"); see also *Universal City Studios v Reimerdes* 111 F.Supp.2d 294 (2000), *Universal City Studios v Corley,* 273 F.3d 429 (2001).
228 See Pamela Samuelson, "Freedom to tinker" 19 and 23; see Lawrence Lessig, *Code: version 2.0* 191.
229 See Directive 2009/24/EC on the legal protection of computer programs, arts 5 and 6 and recital 13.
230 Pamela Samuelson, "Freedom to tinker" 23.
231 See Barton Beebe, "An empirical study of US copyright fair use opinions, 1978–2005" 597–603; see Creative Commons, "Defining 'noncommercial'.
232 Richard Hollinger and Lonn Lanza-Kaduce, "The process of criminalization: The case of computer crime laws" 104; see also Oliver Wendell Holmes, Jr., "Privilege, malice, and intent".
233 Pamela Samuelson, "Freedom to tinker" 2.
234 Debora Halbert, "Mass culture and the culture of the masses: A manifesto for user-generated rights" 958; see also Urs Gasser and Silke Ernst, "A quick look at copyright and user creativity in the digital age" 10.
235 See Pamela Samuelson, "Freedom to tinker" 23.
236 Pamela Samuelson, "Freedom to tinker" 2 (citing Edward Felten).
237 Pamela Samuelson, "Freedom to tinker" 1–2.
238 Pamela Samuelson, "Freedom to tinker" 21.
239 Pamela Samuelson, "Freedom to tinker" 2.
240 Pekka Himanen, *The Hacker Ethic and the Spirit of the Information Age* 139–141.
241 Platform21, "Repair manifesto".
242 Mark Hatch, *The Maker Movement Manifesto* 1–2.
243 Sugru, "The fixer's manifesto".

244 iFixit, "Self-repair manifesto".
245 iFixit, "Self-repair manifesto".
246 iFixit, "Self-repair manifesto".
247 iFixit, "Self-repair manifesto".
248 "The free software definition".
249 Eben Moglen, "The dotcommunist manifesto".
250 Steven Levy, *Hackers* 28–34.
251 Pamela Samuelson, "Freedom to tinker".
252 See Derek Bambauer and Oliver Day, "The hacker's aegis" 42 and 43.
253 Glenn Greenwald, "The inspiring heroism of Aaron Swartz"; Lothar Determann, "Internet freedom and computer abuse" 429.
254 Sarah Constant, "Computer fraud and abuse act: A prosecutor's dream and a hacker's worst nightmare – the case against Aaron Swartz and the need to reform the CFAA" 244–245; see also Mark Murfin, "Aaron's law: Bringing sensibility to the computer fraud and abuse act" 479.
255 Zoe Lofgren and Ron Wyden, "Introducing Aaron's law".
256 Zoe Lofgren and Ron Wyden, "Introducing Aaron's law".
257 Tom Brewster, "US cybercrime law being used to target security researchers".
258 Interview with Maker H.
259 Hanni Fakhoury, "The US crackdown on hackers is our new war on drugs".
260 Hanni Fakhoury, "The US crackdown on hackers is our new war on drugs".
261 Reid Skibell, "Cybercrimes & misdemeanors" 911.
262 Electronic Frontier Foundation, "Let's fix draconian computer crime law"; see also Sarah Constant, "Computer fraud and abuse act: A Prosecutor's dream and a hacker's worst nightmare – the case against Aaron Swartz and the need to reform the CFAA" 247; see also Mark Murfin, "Aaron's law: Bringing sensibility to the computer fraud and abuse act".
263 Tom Brewster, "US cybercrime law being used to target security researchers".
264 Council Directive 2013/40/EU on attacks against information systems, recital 13.
265 See Cassandra Kirsch, "The grey hat hacker" 385 and 398.
266 See Cassandra Kirsch, "The grey hat hacker" 397.

Research methods

For data collection and analysis, I utilized a mixed approach that combined doctrinal legal research with various types of qualitative research methods. I conducted: semi-structured interviews with hackers in the Netherlands; participant observation at hackerspaces and hacker events in the Netherlands; qualitative content analysis of documents, texts and materials produced by or about hackers; doctrinal legal research on technology laws and policies relating to hacking; and secondary research on literature and materials about hackers.

Interviews and participant observation were the main sources of the empirical data. Data collection and fieldwork were conducted in the Netherlands from October 2012 to April 2015. The interviewees and field sites were selected using non-probability sampling, specifically snowball sampling and purposive sampling.[1] Through snowball sampling, I was able to slowly expand and grow my network of contacts by asking gatekeepers and members of the hacker community to recommend other hackers that I should meet and places and events to which I should go.[2] As a complement to snowball sampling, I also used purposive sampling in selecting persons to interview.[3] Interviewees were chosen based on the following non-cumulative criteria: (1) they were active members of a hackerspace or the hacker community; (2) they were engaged in hacking projects or activities that had legal implications or impact; (3) they were involved in or knowledgeable about cases where hackers challenged or sought to change technology laws and policies in the Netherlands; and/or (4) they had personal experience dealing with the law and public authorities because of their projects or activities.

With regard to interviews, each respondent was provided a copy of the participant information sheet, which explained: the purpose of the study, the benefits and disadvantages of participating, that their identities and personal information would be kept confidential, and what would happen to the collected data. For their respective interviews, respondents were requested to sign a consent form. The semi-structured interviews were conducted using an interview guide. The interview guide contained a list of general topics for discussion, but each interview was customized based on the respondent's specific background and depending on whether he or she was a maker, a hacktivist, or another type of hacker. Regardless of the differences among the respondents, all interviews concentrated on the following main discussion points: the meaning or purpose of hacking for them; the techno-social projects or campaigns they were involved in; the legal problems or difficulties they encountered; their knowledge or awareness of applicable laws; their attitudes or responses to laws and public authorities; and their views and opinions about cases where hackers came into conflict with law. A total of 21 interviews were conducted. Most were face-to-face interviews, three were done through telephone or internet telephony, and one via email. The interview respondents consisted of 12 makers, six hacktivists, two ethical hackers, and one government official. The in-person and telephone interviews, which were approximately an hour long, were audio recorded and then transcribed. I also had many informal conversations with members of the hacker community at hackerspaces and other hacker events.

Empirical data was also collected through participant observation during fieldwork at various hacker events and sites. As it was neither practical nor feasible to request all participants and attendees to sign consent forms in these situations, I informed the organizers or gatekeepers about my purpose and provided them copies of the participant information sheet. In one event, the organizers even announced my presence to the attendees so the latter would be made aware or informed of who I was and what I was doing, and they could approach me to ask questions. In order to ensure the anonymity and confidences of the people that I observed or informally conversed with, I focused on the behaviors and statements of people in general or in aggregate rather than attributing such actions to specific individuals. Thus, people at these events would not be specifically identified or identifiable. If it so happened that a person needed to be singled out because his or her actions were especially significant or unique, I would have asked that person to sign a formal consent form. But this was never the case. In total, I undertook participant observation at 13 places and events (i.e., six hackerspaces, two hacker camps, three hacking and technology-related conferences, one technology fair and one hackathon). My field notes from these events formed part of the empirical data and were analyzed as well.

The collected data was analyzed using thematic analysis. A priori codes[4] based on my research questions and analytical framework were initially used to code and examine the data. As the analysis progressed, inductive codes[5] and in vivo codes[6] were also reflexively developed and applied. Together, these a priori, inductive and in vivo codes comprised the code list or coding system.[7] All of the empirical data was coded and analyzed using the qualitative data analysis software ATLAS.ti.[8]

Notes

1 Maggie Walter, *Social Research Methods* 111.
2 See Mike Crang and Ian Cook, *Doing Ethnographies* 19–20.
3 Alan Bryman, *Social Research Methods* 418.
4 Maggie Walter, *Social Research Methods* 324–325.

5 Maggie Walter, *Social Research Methods* 325.
6 Alan Bryman, *Social Research Methods* 573; see also Susanne Friese, *Qualitative Data Analysis with ATLAS.ti* 92.
7 Maggie Walter, *Social Research Methods* 263; see also Alan Bryman, *Social Research Methods* 298–299.
8 See Susanne Friese, *Qualitative Data Analysis With ATLAS.ti.*

Bibliography

3D Hubs Blog, "Open Source 3D Printers stand up to giants Stratasys and 3D Systems" blog.3dhubs.com/post/66187555251/open-source-3d-printers-stand-up-to-giants-stratasys, accessed 27 November 2013.

Abelson, H., Ledeen, K. and Lewis, H.R., *Blown to Bits: Your Life, Liberty and Happiness After the Digital Explosion* (Boston: Addison-Wesley 2008).

Access to Knowledge, www.cptech.org/a2k/, accessed 12 August 2013.

Akester, P. and Akester, R., "Digital rights management in the 21st century" *European Intellectual Property Review* 28 (2006), 159.

Alleyne, B., " 'We are all hackers now': Critical sociological reflections on the hacking phenomenon" Goldsmiths Research Online, http://eprints.gold.ac.uk/6305/, accessed 2 October 2012.

Altman, M., "Hacking at the crossroad: US military funding of hackerspaces" *Journal of Peer Production* Issue #2 (2012).

Alvarez, N. and Stephenson, J., "A manifesto for manifestos" *Canadian Theatre Review* 3 (2012), 150.

Anderson, C., *Makers: The New Industrial Revolution* (London: Random House Business Books 2012).

Anderson, C., "The new makerBot replicator might just change your world" wired.com/design/2012/09/how-makerbots-replicator2-will-launch-era-of-desktop-manufacturing/all/, accessed 24 September 2012.

Anonymous, "An anonymous manifesto", anonnews.org/press/item/199/, accessed 17 July 2013.

Ante, S.E., "Skype to acquire start-up groupme", www.wsj.com/articles/SB10001424053111903327904576522964260277734, accessed 15 January 2016.

Aoki, K., Boyle, J. and Jenkins, J., *Bound by Law? Tales From the Public Domain* (Durham: Duke University Press 2006).

Appetas, www.appetas.com/, accessed 15 January 2016.

Arduino, "Frequently asked questions", arduino.cc/en/Main/FAQ, accessed 30 August 2013.

Arduino, "What is Arduino?" www.arduino.cc/en/Guide/Introduction, accessed 12 February 2016.

Arduino, www.arduino.cc/, accessed 30 August 2013.

Artisan's Asylum, "Make a makerspace", artisansasylum.com/?page_id=2555, accessed 9 February 2013.

Assange, J. and others, *Cypherpunks: Freedom and the Future of the Internet* (New York: OR Books 2012).

Baichtal, J., "Brazilian 3D printer company weighs in on the makerbot controversy", http://makezine.com/2012/10/02/brazilian-3d-printer-company-weighs-in-on-the-makerbot-controversy/, accessed 11 February 2016.

Balkin, J.M., "Digital speech and democratic culture: A theory of freedom of expression for the information society" *New York University Law Review* 79 (2004), 1

Bambauer, D.E. and Day, O., "The hacker's aegis" *Emory Law Journal* 60 (2010), 1051.

Band, J. and Gerafi, J., *The Fair Use/Fair Dealing Handbook* (Washington DC: Policybandwidth 2013).

Banzi, M., "Fighting for arduino", http://makezine.com/2015/03/19/massimo-banzi-fighting-for-arduino/, accessed 5 February 2016.

Bardzell, J. and others, "Virtual worlds and fraud: Approaching cybersecurity in massively multiplayer online games", Digital Games Research Association (DiGRA) 2007 Conference.

Baurmann, M. and others, *Norms and Values: The Role of Social Norms as Instruments of Value Realisation* (Baden-Baden: Nomos 2010).

Bazzichelli, T., *Networking: The Net as Artwork* (Aarhus: Digital Aesthetics Research Centre 2009).

Beall, R., "Developing a coherent approach to the regulation of computer bulletin boards" *Computer/Law Journal* 7 (1986), 499.

Beebe, B., "An empirical study of U.S. copyright fair use opinions, 1978–2005" *University of Pennsylvania Law Review* 156 (2008), 549.

Belfiore, M.P., *The Department of Mad Scientists: How DARPA Is Remaking Our World, From the Internet to Artificial Limbs* (New York: Harper Collins 2010).

Berners-Lee, T., "Aaron is dead", W3C mailing list, https://lists.w3.org/Archives/Public/www-tag/2013Jan/0017.html, accessed 15 February 2016.

Berry, D.M., "The contestation of code: A preliminary investigation into the discourse of the free/libre and open Source Movements" *Critical Discourse Studies* 1 (2004), 65.

Best, K., "The hacker's challenge: Active access to information, visceral democracy and discursive practice" *Social Semiotics* 13 (2003), 263.

Best, K., "Visceral hacking or packet wanking? The ethics of digital code" *Culture, Theory & Critique* 47 (2006), 213.

Bhattacharjee, S. and others, "Impact of legal threats on online music sharing activity: An analysis of music industry legal actions" *Journal of Law and Economics* 49 (2006), 91.

Bijker, W.E., Hughes, T.P. and Pinch, T.J. (eds), *The Social Construction of Technological Systems: New Directions in the Sociology and History of Technology* (Cambridge: The MIT Press 1987).

Bishop, W., "The choice of remedy for breach of contract" *The Journal of Legal Studies* 14 (1985), 299.

Bits of Freedom, "Internet-freedom toolbox", www.bof.nl/ons-werk/internetvrijheid-toolbox/, accessed 29 July 2015.

Bits of Freedom, "Nieuwsbrief Nr. 6.15", www.bof.nl/live/wp-content/uploads/nieuwsbrief160810.txt, accessed 24 August 2015.

Bits of Freedom, "Onze successen", www.bof.nl/over-ons/onze-successen/, accessed 18 June 2015.

Bits of Freedom, "Position paper netwerkneutraliteit", www.bof.nl/live/wp-content/uploads/Position-Paper-netneutraliteit.pdf, accessed 24 June 2015.

Bits of Freedom, "Translations of key Dutch Internet freedom provisions", www.bof.nl/2011/06/27/translations-of-key-dutch-internet-freedom-provisions/, accessed 18 June 2015.

BloomBecker, J., "Computer crime update: The view as we exit 1984" *Western New England Law Review* 7 (1984), 627.

Board of Procurators General, "Responsible disclosure (how to deal with 'ethical' hackers?)", accessed 18 March 2013.

Bonnici, J.P.M., *Self-Regulation in Cyberspace* (The Hague: TMC Asser Press 2007).

Borland, J., "'Hacker space' movement sought for U.S.", www.wired.com/threatlevel/2007/08/us-hackers-moun/, accessed 3 July 2013.

Bowrey, K., *Law and Internet Cultures* (New York: Cambridge University Press 2005).

Boyle, J., "A manifesto on WIPO and the future of intellectual property" *Duke Law & Technology Review* 9 (2004), 2.

Boyle, J., *The Public Domain: Enclosing the Commons of the Mind* (New Haven: Yale University Press 2008).

Boyle, J., *Shamans, Software, and Spleens: Law and the Construction of the Information Society* (Cambridge: Harvard University Press 1996).

Bradshaw, S., Bowyer, A. and Haufe, P., "The intellectual property implications of low-cost 3D printing" *SCRIPTed* 7 (2010), 5.

Brand, S., *The Media Lab: Inventing the Future at MIT* (New York: Penguin Books 1988).

Brand, S., "SPACEWAR: Fanatic life and symbolic death among the computer bums" *Rolling Stone*, 7 December 1972.

Brewster, T., "US cybercrime law being used to target security researchers", www.theguardian.com/technology/2014/may/29/us-cybercrime-laws-security-researchers, accessed 9 June 2014.

Brown, I., "The evolution of anti-circumvention law" *International Review of Law, Computers & Technology* 20 (2006), 239.

Bryman, A., *Social Research Methods* (Oxford: Oxford University Press 2012).

Bugcrowd, "The bug bounty list", https://bugcrowd.com/list-of-bug-bounty-programs/, accessed 13 August 2015.

Cangialosi, C., "The electronic underground: Computer piracy and electronic bulletin boards" *Rutgers Computer & Technology Law Journal* 15 (1989), 265.

Casellati, A.M., "The evolution of article 6.4 of the European information society copyright directive" *Columbia-VLA Journal of Law & the Arts* 24 (2000), 369.

Castells, M., *The Internet Galaxy: Reflections on the Internet, Business, and Society* (Oxford: Oxford University Press 2001).

Cavalcanti, G., "Is it a hackerspace, makerspace, techShop or fablab?" http://makezine.com/2013/05/22/the-difference-between-hackerspaces-makerspaces-techshops-and-fablabs/, accessed 11 February 2016.

Caws, M.A. (ed), *Manifesto: A Century of isms* (Lincoln: University of Nebraska Press 2001).

Chadwick, A., *Internet Politics: States, Citizens, and New Communication Technologies* (Oxford: Oxford University Press 2006).

Chandler, J.A., "Security in cyberspace: Combatting distributed denial of service attacks" *University of Ottawa Law & Technology Journal* 1 (2004), 231.

Chaos Computer Club, "Hacker ethics", www.ccc.de/hackerethics, accessed 17 July 2013.

Cho, A., "University hackers test the right to expose security concerns" *Science* 322 (2008), 1322.

Chung, C.Y., "The computer fraud and abuse act: How computer science can help with the problem of overbreadth" *Harvard Journal of Law & Technology* 24 (2010), 233.

Cohen, J.E., *Configuring the Networked Self: Law, Code, and the Play of Everyday Practice* (New Haven: Yale University Press 2012).

Cohen, J.E., "A right to read anonymously: A closer look at 'copyright management' in Cyberspace" *Connecticut Law Review* 28 (1995), 981.

Cohn, C. and Hoffman, M., "Rebooting computer law part 2: Protect tinkerers, security researchers, innovators, and privacy seekers", www.eff.org/deeplinks/2013/02/rebooting-computer-crime-law-part-2-protect-tinkerers-security-researchers, accessed 11 February 2016.

Cohn, C. and Fakhoury, H. and Hoffman, M., "Rebooting computer law part 3: The punishment should fit the crime", www.eff.org/deeplinks/2013/02/rebooting-computer-crime-part-3-punishment-should-fit-crime, accessed 11 February 2016.

Coleman, E.G., "Anonymous: From the lulz to collective action", mediacommons.futureofthebook.org/tne/pieces/anonymous-lulz-collective-action, accessed 22 August 2013.

Coleman, E.G., "Code is speech: Legal tinkering, expertise, and protest among free and open source software developers" *Cultural Anthropology* 24 (2009), 420.

Coleman, E.G., *Coding Freedom: The Ethics and Aesthetics of Hacking* (Princeton: Princeton University Press 2013).

Coleman, E.G., "The hacker conference: A ritual condensation and celebration of a lifeworld" *Anthropological Quarterly* 83 (2010), 47.

Coleman, E.G., "Hacker politics and publics" *Public Culture* 23 (2011), 511.

Coleman, E.G. and Golub, A., "Hacker practice: Moral genres and the cultural articulation of liberalism" *Anthropological Theory* 8 (2008), 255.

Computer Desktop Encyclopedia, http://lookup.computerlanguage.com/host_app/search?cid=C999999&def=6861636b6174686f6e.htm, accessed 20 August 2013.

Computer History Museum, "PDP-1 restoration project", www.computerhistory.org/pdp-1/, accessed 12 February 2016.

Conrad, J., "Seeking help: The important role of ethical hackers" *Network Security* 8 (2012), 5.

Constant, S.A., "Computer fraud and abuse act: A prosecutor's dream and a hacker's worst nightmare – the case against Aaron Swartz and the need to reform the CFAA" *Tulane Journal of Technology and Intellectual Property* 16 (2013), 231.

Crang, M. and Cook, I., *Doing Ethnographies* (London: Sage 2007).

Creative Commons, https://creativecommons.org/, accessed 12 June 2017.

Creative Commons Corporation, "Defining 'noncommercial': A study of how the online population understands 'noncommercial use' " (2009).

Cringely, R.X., *Accidental Empires: How the Boys of Silicon Valley Make Their Millions, Battle Foreign Competition, and Still Can't Get a Date* (London: Penguin Books 1993).

Critical Art Ensemble, *Electronic Civil Disobedience and Other Unpopular Ideas* (New York: Autonomedia and Critical Art Ensemble 1996).

Data.gov, www.data.gov/, accessed 21 August 2013.

Data.gouv.fr, www.data.gouv.fr/, accessed 21 August 2013.

Data.gov.uk, http://data.gov.uk/about-us, accessed 21 August 2013.

Data.overheid.nl, https://data.overheid.nl/, accessed 21 August 2013.

de Haan, J., "The new Dutch law on Euthanasia" *Medical Law Review* 10 (2002), 57.

de Haes, A.U., "KPN luistert abonnees af met deep packet inspection", http://webwereld.nl/beveiliging/53691-kpn-luistert-abonnees-af-met-deep-packet-inspection, accessed 18 June 2015.

De Werra, J., "Moving beyond the conflict between freedom of contract and copyright policies: In search of a new global policy for online information licensing transactions – a comparative analysis between US law and European law" *Columbia Journal of Law & the Arts* 25 (2003), 239.

de Winter, B., "Lektober superknaller: Megalek treft 50 gemeenten", http://webwereld.nl/beveiliging/54950-lektober-superknaller-megalek-treft-50-gemeenten, accessed 16 June 2015.

Denison, D.C., "Reactions to the makerbot-stratasys deal", http://makezine.com/2013/06/20/reactions-to-the-makerbot-stratasys-deal/, accessed 11 February 2016.

Denmead, K., "MakerBot origins: The revolution will be squirted", http://makezine.com/2013/06/20/makerbot-origins-the-revolution-will-be-squirted/, accessed 11 February 2016.

Denmead, K. "Why the maker movement is here to stay", http://makezine.com/2013/06/03/why-the-maker-movement-is-here-to-stay/, accessed 11 February 2016.

Determann, L., "Internet freedom and computer abuse" *Hastings Communications & Entertainment Law Journal* 35 (2012), 429.

Dizon, M.A.C., "Decompiling the software directive, the Microsoft CFI case and the I2010 strategy: How to reverse engineer an international interoperability regime" *Computer and Telecommunications Law Review* 14 (2008), 213.

Dizon, M.A.C., "Does technology trump intellectual property? Re-framing the debate about regulating new technologies" *SCRIPTed* 8 (2011), 124.

Dizon, M.A.C., "Participatory democracy and information and communications technology: A legal pluralist perspective" *European Journal of Law and Technology* 1(3) (2010), 1.

Dizon, M.A.C., "Rules of a Networked society: Here, there and everywhere" in R. Leenes and E. Kosta (eds), *Bridging Distances in Technology and Regulation* (Oisterwijk: Wolf Legal Publishers 2013).

Dizon, M.A.C., "The symbiotic relationship between global contracts and the international IP regime" *Journal of Intellectual Property Law & Practice* 4 (2009), 559.

Doctorow, C., "Lockdown: The coming war on general-purpose computing" *Boing Boing*, boingboing.net/2012/01/10/lockdown.html, accessed 24 June 2013.

Dohrenwend, B.P., "Egoism, altruism, anomie, and fatalism: A conceptual analysis of Durkheim's types" *American Sociological Review* 24 (1959), 466.

Dougherty, D., "From hackers to makers", http://summit.oshwa.org/files/2012/07/From-Hackers-to-Makers.pdf, accessed 19 October 2012.

Doyle, C., *Cybercrime: An Overview of the Federal Computer Fraud and Abuse Statute and Related Federal Criminal Laws* (Congressional Research Service 2010).

Drahos, P., *Bilateralism in Intellectual Property* (London: Oxfam 2001).

Drahos, P. and Braithwaite, J., *Information Feudalism* (London: Earthscan Publications 2002).

Dusollier, S., "Exceptions and technological measures in the European copyright directive of 2001 – an empty promise" *International Review of Intellectual Property and Competition Law* 34 (2003), 62.

Dyson, G., *Turing's Cathedral: The Origins of the Digital Universe* (New York: Random House Audio 2012).

Easy Taxi, www.easytaxi.com/, accessed 15 January 2016.

Ebert, T.L., "Manifesto as theory and theory as material force: Toward a red polemic" *JAC* 23 (2003), 553.

Edwards, K., "Epistemic communities, situated learning and open source software development", http://orbit.dtu.dk/fedora/objects/orbit:51813/datastreams/file_2976336/content, accessed 8 November 2012.

Electronic Frontier Foundation, "In the wake of Aaron Swartz's death, let's fix draconian computer crime law", www.eff.org/deeplinks/2013/01/aaron-swartz-fix-draconian-computer-crime-law, accessed 12 February 2016.

Electronic Frontier Foundation, "Submission to the European parliament on the draft directive on attacks against computer systems" (February 2011).

Electronic Frontier Foundation, "Surveillance self-defense", https://ssd.eff.org/en, accessed 29 July 2015.

Electronic Frontier Foundation, "Unintended consequences: Fifteen years under the DMCA" (March 2013), www.eff.org/pages/unintended-consequences-fifteen-years-under-dmca, accessed 12 February 2016.

Elkin-Koren, N., "Copyright policy and the limits of freedom of contract" *Berkeley Technology Law Journal* 12 (1997), 93.

Elkin-Koren, N., "Exploring creative commons" in P.B. Hugenholtz and L. Guibault (eds), *The Future of the Public Domain* (Alphen aan den Rijn: Kluwer Law International 2006).

Elliot, M.S. and Scacchi, W., "Mobilization of software developers: the free software movement" *Information Technology & People* 21 (2008), 4.

Eschenfelder, K.R. and Desai, A.C., "Software as protest: The unexpected resiliency of U.S.-based DeCSS posting and linking" *The Information Society* 20 (2004), 101.

Eschenfelder, K.R., Howard, R.G. and Desai, A.C., "Who posts DeCSS and why?: A content analysis of web sites posting DVD circumvention software" *Journal of the American Society for Information Science and Technology* 56 (2005), 1405.

Essers, L., "Dutch government aims to shape ethical hackers' disclosure practices", www.pcworld.idg.com.au/article/445591/dutch_government_aims_shape_ethical_hackers_disclosure_practices/, accessed 11 February 2016.

Etzioni, A., "Social norms: Internalization, persuasion, and history" *Law & Society Review* 34 (2000), 157.

European Commission, "Communication on open data: An engine for innovation, growth and transparent governance".

European Commission, "Guidelines on recommended standard licences, datasets and charging for the reuse of documents" (2014/C 240/01).

European Commission, "Questions and answers: Directive on attacks against information systems" MEMO/13/661, accessed 4 July 2013.

European Commission, "Report based on article 12 of the council framework decision of 24 February 2005 on attacks against information system" COM (2008) 444, 14 July 2008.

European Commission, "Report on the application of the Directive 2001/29/EC" SEC (2007), 1556.

European Commission, "Staff working paper executive summary of the impact assessment accompanying the document proposal for a directive amending Directive 2003/98/EC on the re-use of public sector information".

European Patent Office, "Patents for software? European law and practice", www.epo.org/news-issues/issues/software.html, accessed 24 July 2015.

Europeana, "Hackathons", http://pro.europeana.eu/web/guest/hackathon-proto types, accessed 21 August 2013.

Evans, C., "Announcing project zero", http://googleprojectzero.blogspot.nl/2014/07/announcing-project-zero.html, accessed 16 July 2014.

"The Fab Charter", fab.cba.mit.edu/about/charter/, accessed 15 August 2013.

Fakhoury, H., "The U.S. crackdown on hackers is our new war on drugs", www.wired.com/opinion/2014/01/using-computer-drug-war-decade-dangerous-excessive-punishment-consequences/, accessed 24 January 2014.

Farnsworth, E.A., "Legal remedies for breach of contract" Columbia Law Review 70 (1970), 1145.

Farr, N., "Respect the past, examine the present, build the future", blog.hackerspaces.org/2009/08/25/respect-the-past-examine-the-present-build-the-future/, accessed 3 July 2013.

Farr, N., "The rights and obligations of hackerspace members", blog.hackerspaces.org/2009/08/19/rights-and-obligations-of-hackerspace-members/, accessed 15 August 2013.

Fauteux, B., " 'New noise' versus the old sound: Manifestos and the shape of punk to come" Popular Music and Society 35 (2012), 465.

Feenberg, A., "Democratizing technology: Interest, codes, rights" The Journal of Ethics 5 (2001), 177.

Feenberg, A., "Escaping the iron cage, or, subversive rationalization and democratic theory" in R. Schomberg (ed), Democratising Technology: Theory and Practice of Deliberative Technology Policy (Hengelo: International Centre for Human and Public Affairs 1999).

Fine, G., "Enacting norms: Mushrooming and the culture of expectations and explanations" in M. Hechter and K.D. Opp (eds), Social Norms (New York: The Russel Sage Foundation 2001).

Flichy, P., Understanding Technological Innovation: A Socio-Technical Approach (Cheltenham: Edward Elgar 2007).

Frack, http://frack.nl/, accessed 21 August 2013.

France, A.K., "In the shed: Shiny! new! ultimaker 2!" http://makezine.com/2013/12/06/in-the-shed-shiny-new-ultimaker-2/, accessed 11 February 2016.

Free Software Foundation, "The free software definition", www.gnu.org/philoso phy/free-sw.html, accessed 2 July 2013.

Free Software Foundation, "What is copyleft?" www.gnu.org/licenses/copyleft. en.html, accessed 12 June 2017.

Free Software Foundation, "What is free software", www.gnu.org/philosophy/free-sw.html, accessed 7 November 2012.

Freitas, P.M.F. and Gonçalves, N., "Illegal access to information systems and the Directive 2013/40/EU" *International Review of Law, Computers & Technology* 29 (2015), 50.

Friese, S., *Qualitative Data Analysis With ATLAS.ti* (London: Sage 2014).

Galbraith, C.D., "Access denied: Improper use of the computer fraud and abuse act to control information on publicly accessible Internet Websites" *Maryland Law Review* 63 (2004), 320.

Gates, B., "Open letter to hobbyists", https://upload.wikimedia.org/wikipedia/ commons/1/14/Bill_Gates_Letter_to_Hobbyists.jpg, accessed 7 February 2013.

Gasser, U. and Ernst, S., "From Shakespeare to DJ danger mouse: A quick look at copyright and user creativity in the digital age", Berkman Center for Internet & Society Research Publication No. 2006–05.

Gasser, U. and Girsberger, M., "Transposing the copyright directive: Legal protec-tion of technological measures in EU-member states – A genie stuck in the bottle?" Berkman Center for Internet & Society Research Publication No. 2004–10.

Gehling, R., Ashley, C.R. and Griffin, T., "Electronic emissions security: Danger in the air" *Information Systems Management* 24 (2007), 305.

Geiger, C., "The answer to the machine should not be the machine: Safeguarding the private copy exception in the digital Environment" *European Intellectual Property Review* 30 (2008), 121.

Geiger, C., Gervais, D. and Senftleben, M., "The three-step test revisited: How to use the test's flexibility in national copyright law" *American University International Law Review* 29 (2013), 581.

Gerschenfeld, N., "How to make almost anything: The digital fabrication revolution" *Foreign Affairs* 91 (2012), 43.

Gervais, D.J., "Making copyright whole: A principled approach to copyright excep-tions and limitations" *University of Ottawa Law & Technology Journal* 5 (2008), 1.

Gibbons, L.J., "No regulation, government regulation, or self-regulation: Social enforcement or social contracting for governance in cyberspace" *Cornell Journal of Law and Public Policy* 6 (1997), 475.

Gibbs, J.P., *Norms, Deviance, and Social Control: Conceptual Matters* (New York: Elsevier 1981).

Gibbs, J.P., "Norms: The problem of definition and classification" *American Journal of Sociology* 70 (1965), 586.

Giddens, A., *Sociology* (Cambridge: Polity Press 2009).

Gillen, M., "Human versus inalienable rights: is there still a future for online pro-test in the anonymous world?" *European Journal of Law and Technology* 3(1) (2012), 1.

Ginsburg, J.C., "Copyright and control over new technologies of dissemination" *Columbia Law Review* 101 (2001), 1613.

Giseburt, R., "Is one of our open source heroes going closed source?" blog.makezine.com/2012/09/19/is-one-of-our-open-source-heroes-going-closed-source/, accessed 24 September 2012.

Giseburt, R., "MakerBot's mixed messages about open source, their future", http://makezine.com/2012/09/22/makerbots-mixed-messages-about-open-source-their-future/, accessed 11 February 2016.

GNU Emacs General Public License, www.free-soft.org/gpl_history/emacs_gpl.html, accessed 8 August 2013.

GNU General Public License version 1, www.gnu.org/licenses/gpl-1.0-standalone.html, accessed 25 April 2012.

Gonggrijp, R. and Hengeveld, W., "Studying the Nedap/Groenendaal ES3B voting computer", http://wijvertrouwenstemcomputersniet.nl/images/9/91/Es3b-en.pdf, accessed 11 February 2016.

Good, T., "What is 'making'?" http://makezine.com/2013/01/28/what-is-making/, accessed 15 February 2016.

Google, "Crawling & indexing", www.google.com/intl/en/insidesearch/howsearchworks/crawling-indexing.html, accessed 21 August 2014.

Gordon, D., "Forty years of movie hacking: Considering the potential implications of the popular media representation of computer hackers from 1968 to 2008" *International Journal of Internet Technology and Secured Transactions* 2 (2010), 59.

Government of the Netherlands, "Guidelines for responsible disclosure of IT vulnerabilities", www.government.nl/news/2013/01/03/guideline-for-responsible-disclosure-of-it-vulnerabilities.html, accessed 21 August 2013.

Graham, P., *Hackers & Painters: Big Ideas From the Computer Age* (Sebastopol: O'Reilly Media 2004).

Greenberg, A., "Meet 'project zero,' Google's secret team of bug-hunting hackers", www.wired.com/2014/07/google-project-zero/, accessed 16 July 2014.

Greenwald, G., "The inspiring heroism of Aaron Swartz", www.theguardian.com/commentisfree/2013/jan/12/aaron-swartz-heroism-suicide1/print, accessed 26 August 2013.

Grenzfurthner, J. and Schneider, F.A., "Rewriting hacking the spaces", hackerspaces.org/wiki/rewriting_Hacking_the_Spaces, accessed 3 July 2013.

GroupMe, https://groupme.com/, accessed 15 January 2016.

Guadamuz, A., "The software patent debate" *Journal of Intellectual Property Law & Practice* 1 (2006), 196.

Guibault, L., Westkamp, G. and Rieber-Mohn, T., "Study on the implementation and effect in member states' laws on directive 2001/29/EC on the harmonisation of certain aspects of copyright and related rights in the information society", Amsterdam Law School Legal Studies Research Paper No. 2012–28.

Gunkel, D.J., "Editorial: introduction to hacking and hacktivism" *New Media & Society* 7 (2005), 595.

"GURPS Cyberpunk", www.sjgames.com/gurps/books/cyberpunk/, accessed 28 April 2014.

HackerOne, "Vulnerability disclosure guidelines", https://hackerone.com/disclosure-guidelines, accessed 13 August 2015.

Hackerspace Open Day, https://revspace.nl/HackerspaceDagEn2012, accessed 27 March 2013.

Hackerspaces – The beginning, http://archive.org/details/hackerspaces-the-begin ning, 2011, accessed 2 October 2012.

Hackerspaces.nl, http://hackers.nl, accessed on 12 November 2015.

Hackerspaces.org, http://hackerspaces.org/wiki/, accessed on 15 August 2013.

Hafner, K. and Lyon, M., *Where Wizards Stay Up Late: The Origins of the Internet* (New York: Simon & Schuster 1996).

Hahn, R., "Government policy toward open source software: An overview", www. brookings.edu/press/books/chapter_1/governmentpolicytowardopensourcesoft ware.pdf, accessed 11 February 2016.

Halbert, D., "Discourses of danger and the computer hacker" *The Information Society* 13 (1997), 361.

Halbert, D., "Mass culture and the culture of the masses: A manifesto for user-generated rights" *Vanderbilt Journal of Entertainment & Technology Law* 11 (2009), 921.

Hampson, N.C.N., "Hacktivism: A new breed of protest in a networked world" *Boston College International and Comparative Law Review* 35 (2012), 511.

Hart, R.J., "Interfaces, interoperability and maintenance" *European Intellectual Property Review* 13 (1991), 111.

Hart, R.J., "Interoperability information and the Microsoft decision" *European Intellectual Property Review* 28 (2006), 361.

Hatch, M., *The Maker Movement Manifesto: Rules for Innovation in the New World of Crafters, Hackers, and Tinkerers* (New York: McGraw Hill Professional 2013).

Higgins, P., "Critical fixes for the computer fraud and abuse act", www.eff.org/deep links/2013/01/these-are-critical-fixes-computer-fraud-and-abuse-act, accessed 11 February 2016.

Higgins, P., "The Netherlands passes net neutrality legislation", www.eff.org/deep links/2012/05/netherlands-passes-net-neutrality-legislation, accessed 18 June 2015.

Himanen, P., "A brief history of computer hackerism" in P Himanen (ed) *The Hacker Ethic and the Spirit of the Information Age* (London: Secker & Warburg 2001).

Himanen, P., *The Hacker Ethic and the Spirit of the Information Age* (London: Secker & Warburg 2001).

Himma, K.E., "Hacking as politically motivated digital civil disobedience: Is hacktivism morally justified?" http://dx.doi.org/10.2139/ssrn.799545, accessed 11 February 2016.

Hitlin, S. and Piliavin, J.A., "Values: Reviving a dormant concept" *Annual Review of Sociology* 30 (2004), 359.

Hofman, M. and Reitman, R., "Rebooting computer crime law part 1: No prison time for violating terms of service", www.eff.org/deeplinks/2013/01/reboot ing-computer-crime-law-part-1-no-prison-time-for-violating-terms-of-service, accessed 11 February 2016.

Hollinger, R.C., "Computer crime", http://users.clas.ufl.edu/rhollin/Computer_ Crime.pdf, accessed 15 February 2016.

Hollinger, R.C., "Hackers: Computer heroes or electronic highwaymen?" *Computers & Society* 21 (1991), 6.

Hollinger, R.C. and Lanza-Kaduce, L., "The process of criminalization: The case of computer crime laws" *Criminology* 26 (1988), 101.

Holmes, O.W. Jr., "Privilege, malice, and intent" *Harvard Law Review* 8 (1894), 1.

Horne, C., "Sociological perspectives on the emergence of social norms" in M. Hechter and K.D. Opp (eds), *Social Norms* (New York: The Russell Sage Foundation 2001).

Hugenholtz, P.B. and Okediji R., "Conceiving an international instrument on limitations and exceptions to copyright", Amsterdam Law School Research Paper No. 2012–43.

Hughes, E., "A cypherpunk's manifesto", w2.eff.org/Privacy/Crypto/Crypto_misc/cypherpunk.manifesto, accessed 17 July 2013.

Huijboom, N. and Van den Broek, T., "Open data: an international comparison of strategies" *European Journal of ePractice* 12 (2011), 1.

Hutchby, I., "Technologies, texts and affordances" *Sociology* 35 (2001), 441.

iFixit, "Self-Repair manifesto", www.ifixit.com/Manifesto, accessed 27 May 2014.

IKEA hackers, www.ikeahackers.net/, accessed 16 August 2013.

Instructables, "Arduino projects", www.instructables.com/id/Arduino-Projects/, accessed 12 February 2016.

Instructables, www.instructables.com/, accessed 12 June 2017.

Interference, "Calling for papers", http://interference.io/cfp.php, accessed 6 May 2014.

Internet Society, "Brief history of the Internet", www.internetsociety.org/internet/what-internet/history-internet/brief-history-internet, accessed 20 November 2012.

Iwahashi, R., "How to circumvent technology protection measures without violating the DMCA: An examination of technological protection measures under current legal standards" *Berkeley Technology Law Journal* 26 (2011), 491.

Jacobs, B., "Architecture is politics: Security and privacy issues in transport and beyond" in S. Gutwirth and others (eds), *Data Protection in a Profiled World* (Dordrecht: Springer 2010).

Jacobs, B. and Pieters, W., "Electronic voting in the Netherlands: From early adoption to early abolishment" in A. Aldini, G. Barthes and R. Gorrieri (eds), *Foundations of Security Analysis and Design V* (Berlin: Springer 2009).

Jasanoff, S., "Beyond epistemology: Relativism and engagement in the politics of science" *Social Studies of Science* 26 (1996), 393.

Jensen, E.C., "An electronic soapbox: Computer bulletin boards and the first amendment" *Federal Communications Law Journal* 39 (1987), 217.

Jensen, S., "Abusing the computer fraud and abuse act: Why broad interpretations of the CFAA fail" *Hamline Law Review* 36 (2013), 81.

Jordan T., *Activism! Direct Action, Hacktivism and the Future of Society* (London: Reaktion books 2002).

Jordan, T, *Hacking: Digital Media and Technological Determinism* (Cambridge: Polity Press 2008)

Jordan, T. and Taylor, P., "A sociology of hackers" *The Sociological Review* 46 (1998), 757.

Kamphuis, A., "Dining with assange and spies", www.huffingtonpost.co.uk/arjen-kamphuis/dining-with-julian-assange_b_2565962.html?view=print&comm_ref=false, accessed 26 August 2013.

Karanasiou, A.P., "The changing face of protests in the digital age: On occupying cyberspace and Distributed-Denial-of-Service (DDoS) attacks" *International Review of Law, Computers & Technology* 28 (2014), 98.

Katz, A.W., "Remedies for breach of contract under the CISG" *International Review of Law and Economics* 25 (2006), 378.

Katz, A.W., "Towards a functional licence for open hardware" *International Free and Open Source Software Law Review* 4(1) (2012), 41.

Kelty, C.M., "Culture's open sources: Software, copyright, and cultural critique" *Anthropological Quarterly* 77 (2004), 499.

Kelty, C.M., "Geeks, social imaginaries, and recursive publics" *Cultural Anthropology* 20 (2005), 185.

Kelty, C.M., *Two Bits: The Cultural Significance of Free Software* (Durham: Duke University Press 2008).

Kera, D., "Hackerspaces and DIYbio in Asia: Connecting science and community with open data, kits and protocols" *Journal of Peer Production* Issue #2 (2012).

Kerr, I.R., Maurushat, A. and Tacit, C.S., "Technical protection measures: Tilting at copyright's windmill" *Ottawa Law Review* 32 (2002–2003), 7.

Kerr, O.S., "Cybercrime's scope: Interpreting 'access' and 'authorization' in computer misuse statutes" *New York University Law Review* 78 (2003), 1596.

Kerr, O.S., "Vagueness challenges to the computer fraud and abuse act" *Minnesota Law Review* 94 (2010), 1561.

"Kickstart Leeuwarden", http://frack.nl/wiki/Kickstart_Leeuwarden, accessed 19 November 2012.

"Kickstart058 Hackathon", http://oif058.fikket.com/event/hackathon-kickstart 058, accessed 19 November 2012.

Kirsch, C., "The Grey hat hacker: Reconciling cyberspace reality and the law" *Northern Kentucky Law Review* 41 (2014), 383.

Klang, M., "Civil disobedience online" *Journal of Information, Communication and Ethics in Society* 2 (2004), 75.

Kluckhohn, C. and others, "Values and value-orientations in the theory of action" in T. Parsons and E.A. Shils (eds), *Toward a General Theory of Action* (New York: Harper Torchbooks 1951).

Koops, B., "Cybercrime legislation in the Netherlands", International Congress on Comparative Law 2010.

Kreimer, S.F., "Technologies of protest: Insurgent social movements and the first amendment in the era of the Internet" *University of Pennsylvania Law Review* 150 (2001), 119.

Kroker, E.R., "The computer directive and the balance of rights" *European Intellectual Property Review* 19 (1997), 247.

Kurutz, S., "One big workbench" *The New York Times*, www.nytimes.com/2013/05/02/garden/the-rise-of-the-hacker-space.html?pagewanted=all&_r=1&&pagewanted=print, accessed 17 May 2013.

Langman, L., "From virtual public spheres to global justice: A critical theory of Inter-networked social movements" *Sociological Theory* 23 (2005), 42.

Lapsely, P., "The definitive story of Steve Wozniak, Steve Jobs, and phone phreaking" *The Atlantic*, 20 February 2013.

Lapsley, P., *Exploding the Phone: The Untold Story of the Teenagers and Outlaws Who Hacked Ma Bell* (London: Audible 2013).

Layton, R., "Net neutrality in the Netherlands: Dutch solution or Dutch disease?" 24th European Regional Conference of the International Telecommunication Society 2013.

Lee, G.K. and Cole, R.E., "From a firm-based to a community-based model of knowledge creation: The case of the Linux Kernel development" *Organizational Science* 14 (2003), 633.

Leenes, R., "Framing techno-regulation: An exploration of state and non-state regulation by technology" *Legisprudence* 5 (2011), 143.

Lerner, J. and Tirole, J., "The economics of technology sharing: Open source and beyond" *The Journal of Economic Perspectives* 19 (2005), 99.

Lessig, L., *Code: Version 2.0* (New York: Basic Books 2006).

Lessig, L., *Free Culture: How Big Media Uses Technology and the Law to Lock Down Culture and Control Creativity* (New York: Penguin 2004).

Lessig, L., *The Future of Ideas: The Fate of the Commons in a Connected World* (New York: Vintage Books 2002).

Levy, S., *Hackers: Heroes of the Computer Revolution* (Sebastopol: O'Reilly Media, Inc. 2010).

Lewis, J.A., "Government open source policies", https://csis.org/publication/gov ernment-open-source-policies-0, accessed 5 February 2016.

Li, X., "Hacktivism and the first amendment: Drawing the line between cyber protests and crime" *Harvard Journal of Law & Technology* 27 (2013), 301.

Lindup, K., "The cyberpunk age" *Computers & Security* 13 (1994), 637.

Lindsay, C., "From the shadows: Users as designers, producers, marketers, distributors, and technical support" in N. Oudshoorn and T. Pinch (eds), *How Users Matter: The Co-Construction of Users and Technologies* (Cambridge: The MIT Press 2003).

Litman, J., *Digital Copyright* (New York: Prometheus books 2001).

Lloyd, I.J., *Information Technology Law* (Oxford: Oxford University Press 2008).

Lloyd, I.J. and Simpson, M., "Computer crime" in C. Reed (ed), *Computer Law* (London: Blackstone Press Limited 1996).

Loeber, L., "E-voting in the Netherlands: From general acceptance to general doubt in two years" in R. Krimmer and R. Grimm (eds), *Proceedings of 3rd International Conference on Electronic Voting 2008* (Bonn: Gesellschaft für Informatik 2008).

Lofgren, Z. and Wyden, R., "Introducing Aaron's Law, a desperately needed reform of the computer fraud and abuse act", www.wired.com/opinion/2013/06/aar ons-law-is-finally-here/, accessed 2 July 2013.

Longford, G., "Pedagogies of digital citizenship and the politics of code" *Techne* 9 (2005), 68.

Lowood, H., "Found technology: Players as innovators in the making of machinima" in T. McPherson (ed), *Digital Youth, Innovation, and the Unexpected* (Cambridge: The MIT Press 2008).

Lucchi, N., "The supremacy of techno-governance: Privatization of digital content and consumer protection in the globalized information society" *International Journal of Law and Information Technology* 15 (2007), 192.

Ludlow, P., "Wikileaks and hacktivist culture" *The Nation*, New York, 4 October 2010.

Lunden, I., "The megabreach is back: Hacktivists To blame for 58 percent of stolen data in 2011, says Verizon study", techcrunch.com/2012/03/22/the-megab reach-is-back-hacktivists-to-blame-for-58-percent-of-stolen-data-in-2011-says-ver izon-study/, accessed 10 February 2013.

MacQueen, H. and others, *Contemporary Intellectual Property: Law and Policy* (Oxford: Oxford University Press 2011).

Madison, M.J., "Legal-ware: Contract and Copyright in the Digital Age" *Fordham Law Review* 67 (1998), 1025.

Maggie, W. (ed), *Social Research Methods* (Australia: Oxford University Press 2013).

Maker Faire Africa, "This is the maker manifesto", makerfaireafrica.com/maker-man ifesto/, accessed 17 July 2013.

Mancuso, V., "5 Hackathon success stories", https://finance.yahoo.com/news/5-hackathon-success-stories-131311777.html, accessed 15 January 2016.

MapLight, http://maplight.org/about, accessed 21 August 2013.

Markoff, J., *What the Dormouse Said: How the Sixties Counterculture Shaped the Personal Computer Industry* (New York: Viking 2005).

Maxeiner, J.R., "Standard-terms contracting in the global electronic age: European alternatives" *Yale Journal of International Law* 28 (2003), 109.

Maxigas, "Hacklabs and hackerspaces" *Journal of Peer Production* Issue #2 (2012).

McBryde, W.W., "Remedies for breach of contract" *Edinburgh Law Review* 1 (1996), 43.

McCarthy, R., "Our lawyer explains the thingiverse terms of service", www.makerbot.com/blog/2012/09/26/our-lawyer-explains-the-thingiverse-terms-of-service/, accessed 5 October 2012.

McCullagh, D. and Homsi, M., "Leave DRM alone: A survey of legislative proposals relating to digital rights management technology and their problems" *Michigan State Law Review* 2005 (2005), 317.

McLaurin, J., "Making cyberspace safe for democracy: The challenge posed by Denial-of-service attacks" *Yale Law & Policy Review* 30 (2011), 211.

The Mentor, "The conscience of a hacker" *Phrack*, http://phrack.org/issues/7/3.html, accessed 17 July 2013.

Michael, G. "The PDP-1", www.computerhistory.org/pdp-1/, accessed 11 February 2016.

Milan, S. and Hintz, A., "Dynamics of cyberactivism: Organisations, action repertoires, and the policy Arena" ECPR Conference 2011.

Mills, E., "Dutch chipmaker sues to silence security researchers", www.cnet.com/news/dutch-chipmaker-sues-to-silence-security-researchers/, accessed 11 February 2016.

Mills, E., "Dutch court allows publication of Mifare security hole research", www.cnet.com/news/dutch-court-allows-publication-of-mifare-security-hole-research/, accessed 11 February 2016.

Mims, III F.M., "The tenth anniversary of the Altair 8800" *Computers & Electronics*, January 1985.

"MIT TX-0 computer 1953", www.computermuseum.li/Testpage/MIT-TX0-Computer.htm, accessed 12 February 2016.

Moglen, E. "The dotcommunist manifesto", http://emoglen.law.columbia.edu/my_pubs/dcm.html, accessed 23 February 2014.

Morris, R.T., "A typology of norms" *American Sociological Review* 21 (1956), 610.

Murfin, M., "Aaron's law: Bringing sensibility to the computer fraud and abuse act" *Southern Illinois University Law Journal* 38 (2014), 469.

Murray, A.D., *The Regulation of Cyberspace: Control in the Online Environment* (Oxford: Routledge-Cavendish 2007).

Naughton, J., *A Brief History of the Future: The Origins of the Internet* (London: Phoenix 1999).

Netherlands Ministry of Security and Justice, National Cyber Security Centre, "Policy of public prosecution service on ethical hackers in line with responsible disclosure guidelines", www.ncsc.nl/english/current-topics/news/policy-of-public-prosecution-service-on-ethical-hackers-in-line-with-responsible-disclosure-guidelines.html, accessed 21 August 2013.

Netherlands Ministry of Security and Justice, National Cyber Security Centre, "Public-private cooperation", www.ncsc.nl/english/organisation/partners/public-private. html, accessed 21 August 2013.

The New Hacker's Dictionary, www.outpost9.com/reference/jargon/jargon_toc. html, accessed 12 February 2016.

Nicholson, B.J., "The ghost in the machine: *MAI Systems Corp. v. Peak Computer, Inc.*, and the problem of copying in RAM" *Berkeley Technology Law Journal* 10 (1995), 147.

Nimmer, R.T., "Breaking barriers: The relations between contract and intellectual property law" *Berkeley Technology Law Journal* 13 (1998), 827.

Nissenbaum, H., "Hackers and the contested ontology of cyberspace" *New Media & Society* 6 (2004), 195.

Noveck, B.S., "'Peer to patent': Collective intelligence, open review, and patent reform" *Harvard Journal of Law & Technology* 20 (2006), 123.

O'Brien, K., "Dutch lawmakers adopt net neutrality law", www.nytimes.com/2011/ 06/23/technology/23neutral.html?_r=5&pagewanted=all&, accessed 24 June 2015.

O'Carroll, L., "Scientist banned from revealing codes used to start luxury cars", www. theguardian.com/technology/2013/jul/26/scientist-banned-revealing-codes-cars, accessed 2 March 2015.

O'Hear, S., "Inside the billion-dollar hacker club", http://techcrunch.com/2014/ 03/02/w00w00/, accessed 10 October 2015.

O'Mahony, S. and Ferraro, F., "The emergence of governance in an open source community" Technology, Innovation and Institutions Working Paper Series TII-3.

Off-the-Record Messaging, https://otr.cypherpunks.ca/, accessed 1 December 2015.

Ohlig, J. and Weiler, L., "Building a hacker space" 24th Chaos Communication Congress 2007.

OHM2013, "Call for participation", https://ohm2013.org/site/call-for-participa tion/, accessed 28 November 2012.

OHM2013, "FAQ", https://ohm2013.org/wiki/FAQ, accessed 23 July 2013.

OHM2013, "Guidelines", https://ohm2013.org/site/about/578-2/, accessed 23 July 2013.

OHM2013, "Hack", https://ohm2013.org/site/2013/02/16/hack/, accessed 25 February 2013.

OHM2013, "Make", https://ohm2013.org/site/2013/02/22/make/, accessed 25 February 2013.

OHM2013, "Observe", https://ohm2013.org/site/2013/02/08/observe/, accessed 25 February 2013.

OHM2013, "Press release", https://ohm2013.org/site/press-releases/press-release/, accessed 23 July 2013.

OHM2013, "Program", https://program.ohm2013.org, accessed 5 August 2013.

OHM2013, "Village: Noisy square", https://ohm2013.org/wiki/Village:Noisy_ Squarem, accessed 24 June 2015.

OHM2013, https://ohm2013.org, accessed 28 November 2012.

Olivenbaum, J.M., "<CTRL> <ALT> <DEL>: Rethinking federal computer crime legislation" *Seton Hall Law Review* 27 (1997), 574.

Olson, P., *We Are Anonymous* (New York: Little, Brown and Company 2012).

The Onion Router (Tor), www.torproject.org/, accessed 28 July 2015.

"Open brief aan OM: Hacken", http://computervrede.nl/2014-08-26-Open baarMinisterie/, accessed 30 August 2014.

"Open brief aan OM: Hacken", www.randomdata.nl/blogs/node/85, accessed 30 August 2014.

Open Cultuur Data, www.opencultuurdata.nl/, accessed 21 August 2013.

Open Data Commons, http://opendatacommons.org/, accessed 12 August 2013.

Open Data Day 2013, http://wiki.opendataday.org/2013/City_Events, accessed 21 August 2013.

Open data NEXT, https://data.overheid.nl/english, accessed 21 August 2013.

Open Data Services, www.dati.piemonte.it/, accessed 21 August 2013.

"Open Data Sites", www.data.gov/opendatasites, accessed 12 August 2013.

Open Government Initiative, www.whitehouse.gov/open, accessed 12 August 2013.

Open Innovatie Festival 2012, www.oif2012.nl/ and www.oif2012.nl/oif058/, accessed 21 August 2013.

Open Invention Network, "Defensive publications", www.defensivepublications. org/, accessed 9 December 2014.

Open Source Hardware Association, "Open Source Hardware (OSHW) statement of principles 1.0", www.oshwa.org/definition/, accessed 9 December 2014.

Open Source Initiative, "The open source definition", https://opensource.org/osd, accessed 12 February 2016.

Open Technology Fund, "Projects", www.opentechfund.org/projects, accessed 12 February 2016.

OpenScience Project, www.openscience.org/blog/, accessed 12 August 2013.

Opsahl, K. and Samuelson, P., "Licensing information in the global information market: Freedom of contract meets public policy", http://people.ischool.berkeley. edu/~pam/papers/2bEIPR.pdf, accessed 15 February 2016.

"OV-chip", https://ovchip.cs.ru.nl/Main_Page, accessed 18 February 2015.

Oxblood Ruffin, "Hacktivismo", http://w3.cultdeadcow.com/cms/2000/07/ hacktivismo.html, accessed 12 February 2016.

Praetox Technologies, "LOIC", http://sourceforge.net/projects/loic/, accessed 18 September 2014

Pertierra, R., *The Anthropology of New Media in the Philippines* (Quezon City: Institute of Philippine Culture 2010).

Pettis, B., "Fixing misinformation with information", www.makerbot.com/blog/ 2012/09/20/fixing-misinformation-with-information/, accessed 24 September 2012.

Pettis, B., "Let's try that again", www.makerbot.com/blog/2012/09/24/lets-try-that-again/, accessed 5 October 2012.

Pettis, B., "Open source ethics and dead end derivatives", www.makerbot.com/ blog/2010/03/25/open-source-ethics-and-dead-end-derivatives/, accessed 5 October 2012.

Pettis, B., "Thingiverse updates terms of use and license options", blog.thingiverse. com/2012/02/10/thingiverse-updates-terms-of-use-and-license-options/, accessed 24 September 2012.

Picotti, L. and Salvadori, I., "National legislation implementing the convention on cybercrime – comparative analysis and good practices" (Directorate General of Human Rights and Legal Affairs Council of Europe 2008).

Platform21, "Repair manifesto", www.platform21.nl/download/4375, accessed 28 November 2012.

Pool, R., "A history of the personal computer" in M.D. Ermann and M.S. Shauf (eds), *Computers, Ethics, and Society* (Oxford: Oxford University Press 2002).

Popper, B., "A new breed of startups is helping hackers make millions – legally", www.theverge.com/2015/3/4/8140919/get-paid-for-hacking-bug-bounty-hackerone-synack, accessed 22 June 2015.

Posner, R.A., "Social norms and the law: An economic approach" *The American Economic Review* 87 (1997), 365.

Press, L., "Before the Altair: The history of personal computing" *Communications of the ACM* 36 (1993), 27.

Preston-Werner, T., "Open source (almost) everything", tom.preston-werner.com/2011/11/22/open-source-everything.html, accessed 5 October 2012.

Preuschat, A., "KPN admits to using deep packet inspection", http://blogs.wsj.com/tech-europe/2011/05/12/kpn-admits-to-using-deep-packet-inspection, accessed 24 June 2015.

Principe, L., "Renaissance natural magic" in L. Principe (ed), *History of Science: Antiquity to 1700* (Chantilly: Teaching Company 2002).

Prusa, J., "Occupy thingiverse test cube", www.thingiverse.com/thing:30808, accessed 2 September 2013.

Publicdata.eu, http://publicdata.eu/, accessed 21 August 2013.

Puchner, M., "Manifesto = theatre" *Theatre Journal* 54 (2002), 449.

Raether, R. Jr., "Data security and ethical hacking" *Business Law Today* 18 (2008), 55.

Raulerson, J., "Cyberpunk politics: Hacking and bricolage" in M. Leaning and B. Pretzsch (eds), *Visions of the Human in Science Fiction & Cyberpunk* (Oxford: Inter-Disciplinary Press 2010).

Raymond, E.S., "A brief history of hackerdom" in E. Raymond (ed), *The Cathedral and the Bazaar: Musings on Linux and Open Source by an Accidental Revolutionary* (Sebastopol: O'Reilly Media 2001).

Raymond, E.S., *The Cathedral and the Bazaar: Musings on Linux and Open Source by an Accidental Revolutionary* (Sebastopol: O'Reilly Media 2001).

Reichman, J.H. and Franklin, J.A., "Privately legislated intellectual property rights: Reconciling Freedom of Contract with Public Good Uses of Information" *University of Pennsylvania Law Review* 147 (1999), 875.

Reitman, J., "The rise and fall of Jeremy Hammond: Enemy of the state", www.rollingstone.com/culture/news/the-rise-and-fall-of-jeremy-hammond-enemy-of-the-state-20121207, accessed 9 December 2012.

RepRap, "About", http://reprap.org/wiki/About, accessed 2 October 2015.

RepRap Project, reprap.org/wiki/Main_Page, accessed 30 August 2013.

Riseup, https://help.riseup.net/, accessed 29 July 2015.

Roberts, E.H. and Yates, W., "ALTAIR 8000: The most powerful minicomputer project ever presented – can be built for under $400" *Popular Electronics*, January 1975.

Rokeach, M., *The Nature of Human Values* (New York: The Free Press 1973).

Rosenbaum, R., "Secrets of the Little Blue Box" *Esquire,* October 1971.

Rosenberg, N., "Technological Change in the Machine Tool Industry, 1840–1910" *The Journal of Economic History* 23 (1963), 414.

Rumbles, W., "Reflections of hackers in legal and popular discourse" in W. Rumbles (ed), *Cultural Cyborgs* (Oxford: Inter-Disciplinary Press 2011).

Samuelson, P., "Anticircumvention rules: Threat to science" *Science* 293 (2001), 2028.

Samuelson, P., "Challenges for the world intellectual property organisation and the trade-related aspects of intellectual property rights council in regulating intellectual property rights in the information age" *European Intellectual Property Review* 21 (1999), 578.

Samuelson, P., "Freedom to tinker", http://papers.ssrn.com/sol3/papers.cfm?abstr act_id=2605195, accessed 12 February 2016.

Samuelson, P., "Hacking intellectual property law" *Communications of the ACM* 51 (2008), 65.

Sather, J.F., *Understanding the Apple II E* (California: Quality Software 1985).

Schellekens, M.H.M., "Robot.txt: Balancing interests of content producers and content users" in R. Leenes and E. Kosta (eds), *Bridging Distances in Technology and Regulation* (Oisterwijk: Wolf Legal Publishers 2013).

Schrock, A., "What keeps hacker and maker spaces going?" www.transfabric.org/collectives-in-hacker-and-maker-spaces/, accessed 16 April 2013.

Schultz, J. and Urban, J.M., "Protecting open innovation: The defensive patent license as new approach to patent threats, transactions costs, and tactical disarmament" *Harvard Journal of Law & Technology* 26 (2012), 1.

Sell, S.K., "TRIPS-plus free trade agreements and access to medicines" *Liverpool Law Review* 28 (2007), 41.

Senftleben, M., "Bridging the differences between copyright legal traditions – the emerging EC fair use doctrine" *Journal Copyright Society of the U.S.A.* 57 (2009–2010), 521.

Senftleben, M., "Fair use in The Netherlands – a renaissance?" *Tijdschrift voor auteurs, media en informatierecht (AMI)* 33 (2009), 1

Senftleben, M., "The international three-step test: A model provision for EC fair use legislation" *Journal of Intellectual Property, Information Technology and Electronic Commerce Law* 1 (2010), 67.

Shmeck, "25 years of summercon" *Phrack*, www.phrack.org/issues.html?issue=68&id=18&mode=txt, accessed 24 July 2013.

"A short history of the CCC" in *Hackerspaces – The Beginning*, 2011, http://archive.org/details/hackerspaces-the-beginning, accessed 2 October 2012.

Skibell, R., "Cybercrimes & misdemeanors: A reevaluation of the computer fraud and abuse act" *Berkeley Technology Law Journal* 18 (2003), 909.

Skibell, R., "The myth of the computer hacker" *Information, Communication & Society* 5 (2002), 336.

Slatalla, M. and Quittner, J., *Masters of Deception: The Gang that Ruled Cyberspace* (New York: HarperCollins 1995).

Soghoian, C., "Caveat venditor: Technologically protected subsidized goods and the customers who hack them" *Northwestern Journal of Technology and Intellectual Property* 6 (2007), 46.

Soma, J.T. and others, "Legal analysis of electronic bulletin board activities" *Western New England Law Review* 7 (1985), 571.

Soma, J.T., Winfield, G. and Friesen, L., "Software interoperability and reverse engineering" *Rutgers Computer and Technology Law Journal* 20 (1994), 189.

Spates, J.L., "The sociology of values" *Annual Review of Sociology* 9 (1983), 27.

Stallman, R., "The GNU manifesto", www.gnu.org/gnu/manifesto.html, accessed 22 May 2014.

Stallman, R., "The GNU project", www.gnu.org/gnu/thegnuproject.en.html, accessed 15 February 2016.

Stallman, R., "Initial announcement", www.gnu.org/gnu/initial-announcement.html, accessed 7 August 2013.

Stallman, R., "Why open source misses the point of free software", www.gnu.org/philosophy/open-source-misses-the-point.en.html, accessed 15 February 2016.

Sterling, B., *The Hacker Crackdown* (Virginia: IndyPublish.com 2002).

Stratasys, "Stratasys to acquire makerBot, merging two global 3D printing industry leaders", www.businesswire.com/news/home/20130619006431/en/Stratasys-Acquire-MakerBot-Merging-Global-3D-Printing, accessed 21 June 2013.

Sugru, "The fixer's manifesto", https://raw.github.com/sugru/manifesto/master/manifesto.pdf, accessed 20 April 2016.

Sunstein, C. "On the expressive function of law" *University of Pennsylvania Law Review* 144 (1996), 2012.

Taarifa, http://taarifa.org/, accessed 15 January 2016.

Taarifa, https://taarifa.wordpress.com/, accessed 15 January 2016.

Tails, https://tails.boum.org/, accessed 1 December 2015.

Tactical Technology Collective, "Security in-a-box", https://tacticaltech.org/projects/security-box, accessed 29 July 2015.

Taylor, P.A., "Editorial: Hacktivism" *The Semiotic Review of Books* 12 (2001), 1.

Taylor, P.A., "From hackers to hacktivists: Speed bumps on the global superhighway" *New Media & Society* 7 (2005), 625.

Taylor, P.A., *Hackers: Crime in the Digital Sublime* (London: Routledge 1999).

Therborn, G., "Back to norms! On the scope and dynamics of norms and normative action" *Current Sociology* 50 (2002), 863.

Thingiverse, "Things tagged with 'arduino'", www.thingiverse.com/tag:arduino, accessed 12 February 2016.

Thingiverse, www.thingiverse.com/, accessed 12 February 2016.

Thomas, D., *Hacker Culture* (Minneapolis: University of Minnesota Press 2002).

Thompson, C., "The bittorrent effect", www.wired.com/2005/01/bittorrent-2/, accessed 15 February 2016.

Tigoe, "In defense of open source innovation and polite disagreement", www.tigoe.net/blog/category/open-innovation/408/, accessed 5 October 2012.

TNO, "Security analysis of the Dutch OV-ChipKaart" TNO Report 34643.

Tocchetti, S., "DIY biologists as 'makers' of personal biologies: How MAKE Magazine and Maker Faires contribute in constituting biology as a personal technology" *Journal of Peer Production* Issue #2 (2012).

Torrone, P., "Life, $10M in funding, and beyond", http://makezine.com/2011/10/06/makes-exclusive-interview-with-bre-pettis-of-makerbot-life-10m-in-funding-and-beyond/, accessed 12 February 2016.

Torrone, P., "Sony's war on makers, hackers, and innovators", http://makezine.com/2011/02/24/sonys-war-on-makers-hackers-and-innovators/, accessed 12 February 2016.

Torrone, P., "The {Unspoken} rules of open source hardware", blog.makezine.com/2012/02/14/soapbox-the-unspoken-rules-of-open-source-hardware/, accessed 5 October 2012.

Torvalds, L. and Diamond, D., *Just for Fun: The Story of an Accidental Revolutionary* (New York: TEXERE Publishing 2001).

Troxler, P., "Libraries of the peer production era", http://opendesignnow.org/index.php/article/libraries-of-the-peer-production-era-peter-troxler/, accessed 2 April 2013.

Turkle, S., *Alone Together: Why We Expect More From Technology and Less From Each Other* (New York: Basic Books 2012).

Turkle, S., *The Second Self: Computers and the Human Spirit* (Cambridge: The MIT Press 2005).

Tweney, D., "DIY freaks flock to 'hacker spaces' worldwide", www.wired.com/gad getlab/2009/03/hackerspaces, accessed 3 July 2013.

"TX-0 computer", http://museum.mit.edu/150/23, accessed 12 February 2016.

UK Intellectual Property Office, "Exceptions to copyright: An overview", October 2014.

van Daalen, O., "Netherlands first country in Europe with net neutrality", www.bof.nl/2012/05/08/netherlands-first-country-in-europe-with-net-neutrality/, accessed 18 June 2015.

van der Meijs, S., "Lektober: iedere dag een privacylek", http://webwereld.nl/beveiliging/54847-lektober-iedere-dag-een-privacylek-op-webwereld, accessed 16 June 2015.

van der Meijs, S., "OM vervolgt Brenno de Winter niet om hack OV-chipkaart", http://webwereld.nl/overheid/54678-om-vervolgt-brenno-de-winter-niet-om-hack-ov-chipkaart, accessed 16 June 2015.

van der Meulen, N.S. and Lodder, A.R., "Cybersecurity" http://dare.ubvu.vu.nl/bitstream/handle/1871/49680/rc2014%20H13%20Van%20der%20Meulen%20Lodder_Cybersecurity_final.pdf?sequence=1, accessed 12 February 2016.

van Eck, W., "Electromagnetic radiation from video display units: An eavesdropping risk?" *Computers & Security* 4 (1985), 269.

van Eijk, N., "Datalekken: Een reality check", http://dare.uva.nl/document/2/122176, accessed 12 February 2016.

van Eijk, N., "Net neutrality in practice, the Dutch example", http://ssrn.com/abstract=2417933, accessed 24 June 2015.

van Geelkerken, F.W.J., "Proposal for the Dutch computercrime act III: A critique", www.kau.se/sites/default/files/Dokument/subpage/2011/02/computer_crime_a_critique_pdf_14472.pdf, accessed 12 February 2016.

van Hoboken, J., "Relaunch bits of freedom!", www.jorisvanhoboken.nl/?p=300, accessed 24 August 2015.

Vance, A., "Bre pettis: 3D printing's first celebrity", www.businessweek.com/articles/2012-05-09/bre-pettis-3d-printings-first-celebrity 2/16, accessed 5 October 2012.

Verizon, "2012 data breach investigations report".

Vinje, T.C., "Compliance with Article 85 in software licensing" *European Competition Law Review* 13 (1992), 165.

von Hippel, E., "Democratizing innovation: The evolving phenomenon of user innovation" *International Journal of Innovation Science* 1 (2009), 29.

Waalboer, J. and others, "Open brief aan OM: Hacken", http://computervrede.nl/2014-08-26-OpenbaarMinisterie/, accessed 30 August 2014.

Wall, D.S., *Cybercrime: The Transformation of Crime in the Information Age* (Cambridge: Polity Press 2007).

Walter, "The Makerbot/Thingiverse move to the Dark Side", blog.hackerspaces.org/2012/09/23/the-makerbotthingiverse-move-to-the-dark-side/, accessed 24 September 2012.

"We don't trust voting computers", http://wijvertrouwenstemcomputersniet.nl/ English, accessed 12 June 2015.

Widdison, R., "Software patents pending" *The Journal of Information, Law and Technology* (2000), http://elj.warwick.ac.uk/jilt/00-3/widdison.html

Williams, S., *Free as in Freedom: Richard Stallman's Crusade for Free Software* (Sebastopol: O'Reilly Media 2011).

WIPO International Bureau, "The advantages of adherence to the WIPO Copyright Treaty (WCT) and the WIPO Performances and Phonograms Treaty (WPPT)".

WIPO International Bureau, "The WIPO Copyright Treaty (WCT) and the WIPO Performances and Phonograms Treaty (WPPT)".

WIPO Intellectual Property Handbook (Geneva: WIPO 2004).

WIPO Standing Committee on Copyright and Related Rights, "Updated report on the questionnaire on limitation and exceptions" SCCR/21/7 (2010).

WIPO Standing Committee on Copyright and Related Rights, "WIPO study on limitations and exceptions of copyright and related rights in the digital environment" SCCR/9/7 (2003).

WIPO Standing Committee on the Law of Patents, "Exclusions from patentable subject matter and exceptions and limitations to the rights" SCP/13/3 (2009).

WIPO Standing Committee on the Law of Patents, "Report on the international patent system" SCP/12/3 Rev.2, Revised Annex II.

Wiseman, L., "Beyond the photocopier: Copyright and publishing in Australia" *Media & Arts Law Review* 7 (2002), 299.

Wozniak, S., "Foreword" in J. Sather (ed), *Understanding the Apple II E* (California: Quality Software 1985).

Wu, T., "Does a company like Apple need a genius like Steve Jobs", www.newyorker. com/news/news-desk/does-a-company-like-apple-need-a-genius-like-steve-jobs, accessed 4 March 2013.

Wu, T., *The Master Switch: The Rise and Fall of Information Empires* (New York: Vintage 2011).

Wuermeling, U., "New dimensions of computer-crime – hacking for the KGB – a report" *The Computer Law and Security Report* 4 (1989–1990), 20.

Yanoshevsky, G., "Three decades of writing on manifesto: The making of a genre" *Poetics Today* 30 (2009), 257.

Yiull, S., "All problems of notation will be solved by the masses: Free open form performance, free/libre open source software, and distributive practice" *International Journal of Cultural Policy* 10 (2004), 64.

Ziccardi, G., *Resistance, Liberation Technology and Human Rights in the Digital Age* (Dordrecht: Springer Science+Business Media 2012).

Zijlstra, T., "The state of open data in Europe – achievements and challenges", www. zylstra.org/blog/2013/02/the-state-of-open-data-in-europe-achievements-and-challenges/, accessed 21 August 2013.

Zittrain, J., *The Future of the Internet – and How to Stop It* (New Haven: Yale University Press 2008).

Zuckerberg, M., "The hacker way", www.wired.com/business/2012/02/zuck-letter/, accessed 19 August 2013.

Zuiderwijk, A. and others, "Socio-technical impediments of open data" *Electronic Journal of e-Government* 10 (2012), 156.

Treaties, statutes and legislation

Agreement on Trade-Related Aspects of Intellectual Property Rights
Australian Copyright Amended Act 2006
Berne Convention for the Protection of Literary and Artistic Works
Brazilian Criminal Code
Commission Decision of 12 December 2011 on the reuse of Commission documents (2011/833/EU)
Convention on Cybercrime
Convention on the Grant of European Patents (European Patent Convention)
Council Directive of 1 May 1991 on the legal protection of computer programs (as amended and codified by Directive 2009/24/EC)
Council Directive 2013/40/EU of 12 August 2013 on attacks against information systems and replacing Council Framework Decision 2005/222/JHA [2013] OJ L218/8
Council Framework Decision 2005/222/JHA of 24 February 2005 on attacks against information systems [2005] OJ L069
Directive 96/9/EC on the legal protection of databases
Directive 2001/29/EC on the harmonisation of certain aspects of copyright and related rights in the information society
Directive 2003/98/EC of the European Parliament and the Council on the re-use of public sector information
Directive 2009/24/EC on the legal protection of computer programs
Directive 2013/37/EU of the European Parliament and of the Council amending Directive 2003/98/EC on the re-use of public sector information
Dutch Copyright Act
Dutch Criminal Code
Dutch Patent Act
European Commission, "Proposal for a directive on attacks against information systems" COM(2010), 517.
European Commission, "Proposal for a directive of the European Parliament and of the Council on attacks against information systems and repealing Council Framework Decision 2005/222/JHA" COM(2010), 517.
European Commission, "Proposal for a directive on Amending Directive 2003/98/EC on re-use of public sector information".
European Commission, "Proposal for a directive of the European Parliament and of the Council on attacks against information systems and repealing Council Framework Decision 2005/222/JHA" COM(2010), 517.
Explanatory Report to the Convention on Cybercrime
Netherlands Ministry of Security and Justice, National Cyber Security Centre, "Policy for arriving at a practice for Responsible Disclosure"
New Zealand Crimes Act
Paris Convention for the Protection of Industrial Property
Recommendation No. R (89) 9 on computer-related crime and final report of the European Committee on Crime Problems (1990)
Report on application of Directive 2001/29/EC SEC(2007) 1554
Slovakian Criminal Code

Treaty on Intellectual Property in Respect of Integrated Circuits
US Copyright Act 1976
US Computer Fraud and Abuse Act
US Digital Millennium Copyright Act (17 U.S. Code section 1201)
WIPO, Agreed Statements concerning the WIPO Copyright Treaty 1996
WIPO Copyright Treaty
WIPO Performances and Phonograms Treaty

Cases

Authors Guild v. Hathitrust 755 F.3d 87 (2014)
British Academy of Songwriters, Composers and Authors Musicians' Union v Secretary of State for Business, Innovation and Skills [2015] EWHC 2041 (Admin) (17 July 2015)
Canada – Patent Protection of Pharmaceutical Products, WT/DS114/R (17 March 2000)
Case C-406/10 *SAS Institute Inc. v World Programming Ltd* [2012]
Chamberlain Group v Skylink Technologies 381 F. 3d 1178 (2004)
Diamond v. Diehr 450 U.S. 175 (1981)
Field v. Google 412 F.Supp.2d 1106 (2006)
Folsom v Marsh (1841)
Krause v Titleserv, Inc., 402 F.3d 119 (2005)
Lexmark v. Static Control Components, 387 F.3d 522 (2004)
MDY Industries, LLC. v. Blizzard Ent., Inc., 616 F. Supp. 2d 958 (2009)
MDY Industries v Blizzard Entertainment, 629 F. 3d 928 (2010)
NXP Semiconductors vs Radboud Universiteit Nijmegen, Arnhem Court Case Number 171900 (18 July 2008)
Recording Industry Association of America v. Diamond Multimedia Systems 180 F.3d 1072 (1999)
SCO Group v. IBM WL 318784 (2005)
Sony v. Universal 464 U.S. 417 (1984)
Storage Technology v. Custom Hardware Engineering, 421 F.3d 1307 (2005)
TracFone Wireless, Inc. v. Dixon, 475 F. Supp. 2d 1236 (2007)
United States v Gilberto Valle, No. 14-2710-cr and No. 14-4396-cr (3 December 2015)
Universal City Studios v Reimerdes 111 F.Supp.2d 294 (2000)
Universal City Studios v Corley, 273 F.3d 429 (2001)

Index

Printed in the United States
By Bookmasters